MW00475252

Bobby Hoppe behind the defense table at his murder trial in 1988

A
Matter of
Conscience

Redemption of a hometown hero,
Bobby Hoppe

Sherry Lee Hoppe
with Dennie B. Burke

Wakestone Press

Nashville, Tennessee

A Matter of Conscience:
Redemption of a hometown hero, Bobby Hoppe.

Copyright © 2010 by Sherry Lee Hoppe with Dennie B. Burke
All rights reserved.
Published in the United States by Wakestone Press, LLC.

ISBN   978-1-60956-001-0   Hardcover
        978-1-60956-002-7   Trade paperback
        978-1-60956-003-4   E-book

Library of Congress Control Number: 2010935383

For additional material, hearing transcript summaries and photos:
http://www.wakestonepress.com/amatterofconscience/

*Lovingly dedicated to the memory of my
husband Bobby Hoppe,
whose conscience has been set free,
whose search for peace has ended*

Sherry Lee

Auburn running back Bobby Hoppe posing for his Tiger football program photograph in 1957.

A Matter of Conscience

CONTENTS

A Matter of Conscience

AUTHORS' NOTES

This is the story of Bobby Hoppe, based primarily on court transcripts, newspaper articles, and interviews. In general, it is a work of non-fiction. Lawyers, witnesses, the judge, and others depicted are real people, and there are no composite characters. All names, with the exception of jurors, are actual people who were a part of Bobby's life or trial. When possible, the spoken word has been quoted verbatim. However, when that is not possible, conversations and scenes have been reconstructed as closely as possible to reality, based on notes and recollections of those who were present during the trial or other phases of Bobby's life. The description of specific personalities, actions, scenes, thoughts, feelings, conversations, and motivations outside those parameters were created as the authors imagine they would be if the characters acted in a manner consistent with testimonies or the time period.

Because this is Bobby's biography, his successes at Chattanooga Central and Auburn, as recorded in various newspapers and other sources, have been highlighted. Bobby would take issue with that focus, because he was quick to say he was just part of great teams at those institutions. Readers who want to learn more about other outstanding players on Central's three state championship teams in the early '50s and Auburn's national championship team in 1957 are encouraged to consult some of the sources at the end of the book.

FOREWORD

My husband Bobby shot a man, and he died. I wish it were not so, but it is. It happened in 1957, and Bobby hid the terrible truth for 31 years.

Within three weeks of the shooting, a coroner's inquest concluded with no findings. Nine years later, long before I met Bobby, a grand jury found insufficient evidence to proceed to trial. Although some people suspected Bobby pulled the trigger that killed Don Hudson, few wanted to believe it. Even law enforcement officials turned their heads. A hometown hero, Bobby had earned respect far and wide.

People like Stan Farmer, one of Bobby's high school football coaches, refused to accept that the fun-loving, compassionate young man could kill anyone. Even at Bobby's trial in 1988 after he publicly proclaimed his guilt, some friends—including former Auburn teammate Sentell Harper—suspected he was covering for someone. But Bobby never stopped believing he had taken another man's life, and his certainty convinced me—despite any doubts.

For 31 years, guilt hung over Bobby like a dark cloud. Even after the grand jury's verdict, remorse shadowed the next twenty years of his life. Bobby's conscience had been colored so deeply he could never fully accept the goodness of his life.

I did not write this book to revise history or whitewash the ugliness of what occurred. But for reasons unveiled in this book, I decided it's time for the full tale to be told. Obviously, there's no way I can be totally objective when it comes to Bobby's story, but I've endeavored, through extensive research and interviews, to be as factual as possible. In retrospect, I'm able to acknowledge the agony of the victim's family and understand their relentless pursuit of justice.

On the night Bobby shot Don Hudson, the universe shifted forever for two families. If I bring any bias to the book, I ask the reader's forgiveness. In my heart I know I've tried my best to tell the truth, though I sometimes viewed it through a prism of pain.

A Matter of Conscience

PROLOGUE

Whoever survives the test, whatever it may be, must tell the story.
That is his duty.
–Elie Wiesel

On what would become the worst day of my life, weak sunlight was spilling into the valleys of east Tennessee, illuminating the redbuds and forsythia bravely splashing color along the winter-raw hillsides.

Harbingers of spring in the Appalachian mountains, the redbuds and forsythia meant it was time for Bobby and me to prepare our yard for planting flowers, flowers that would last until the first frost—longer than our remaining time together.

At the time, I did not know that.

I did seem to know we'd lingered too long in our Chattanooga home, waiting for Bobby's sheepdog, Sugarplum, to die—her death from cancer, inevitable. But death chose the wrong victim, forever erasing Bobby's dream of retiring to our oceanfront condo where he always found peace. There he could sit for hours on our 19th floor balcony watching a storm build over the ocean—gray cumulus clouds, shot through with surreal streaks of pink and gold. In the evenings, he allowed himself the luxury of gazing at a line of shrimp boats, their nets hoisted for the day, crawling along the red rim of the horizon.

But in April 2008, like all but 15 days since I retired eight months previously, we sat suspended in time, bound to the city by his dog's impending death. On that seemingly innocuous day, after running errands, Bobby and I had stopped at Five Guys restaurant. Afterward, I was ready to shop for flowers, but Bobby insisted on returning home to give Sugarplum her cancer medicine.

After taking Bobby home, I headed out to select the flowers we would enjoy in the days ahead. Over his shoulder, Bobby said, "Be careful. I love you"—his usual parting words to me. At the door, I glanced back and saw him preparing Sugarplum's medicine with a pharmacist's precision. I knew he'd soon stretch out on the sofa with his huge dog snuggled beside him.

I smiled to myself as I drove away. All around me, the first buds of spring seemed to reflect our new beginning—a time to enjoy each other, content with life.

1

Prologue

After 20 years, the nightmare from which Bobby could never fully escape had receded into a rarely visited nook of his mind. A few weeks earlier, discerning he was increasingly at peace with his past, I had begun secretly writing his story. Amazingly, when I read him the initial pages, he seemed open to the idea. In fact, he agreed to assist me—with one caveat: "Sherry Lee, even if I let you write my story, I may never let you have it published."

Bobby's tenuous agreement to let me tell his story might have been an omen, but I didn't catch it. Until then he had steadfastly rejected any mention of writing a book about his 1988 trial. After the trial, book agents and media representatives eager to pay for his story had approached him, but he refused, never wanting to make money from the tragedy.

As we discussed writing about Bobby's life, he said emphatically that before anyone could understand the man he had become—the man accused of murder—the story must begin with his childhood. So we agreed that's where we would start. It was where I would begin to unwrap the layers of this complex man who was sometimes witty, even roguish; at other times, reserved and somber. Whose emotions were often as fragile as butterfly wings, and sometimes as hard as steel from a blast furnace; a man who cared deeply about old friends, but isolated himself from their love.

Although I knew much of Bobby's biography, I looked forward to hearing more about his family, his youthful escapades, and his illustrious sports career—well aware I would have to pull from him anything about his football feats. Unlike many sports heroes, Bobby always shunned the spotlight, acutely uncomfortable in its glare.

During his glory days on the turf of powerful Central High School, where he ran so fast the media tagged him "Hippety Hoppe," Bobby developed into the first All-American to come out of Chattanooga. After signing with Auburn University, he was riding high, feeling bullet proof.

Three years into college, Bobby had proven himself to be a talented multi-position player on what would become Auburn's first, and to date, only national championship team. Some say, on Auburn's football field, Bobby ran with unsurpassed agility and speed. Few realized that during the national championship season he was running to escape unseen demons, their breath hot on his heels.

2

A Matter of Conscience

Most people who knew Bobby during his days at Central and Auburn agreed that, until the early morning of July 21, 1957, he could outrun his own shadow. After the tragic event, his football fame interested him less and less. Following a brief foray into the National Football League, Bobby returned home, ready to begin what would become a rewarding coaching career.

On the surface, everything seemed fine. But Bobby could not rid himself of the dark curtain that hung heavy over his mind and soul; sheltering a secret he shared with no one—not even me. Some days the old Bobby resurfaced—the man with a rowdy sense of humor who kept family and friends laughing. At other times, he withdrew into a shell, wanting only his dogs for company. Bobby was never quite sure if folks were whispering behind his back, so he chose his friends carefully. They became the trusted few that got to enjoy his wry wit and incredible knowledge of the world.

That April afternoon, I returned home, my arms full of larkspurs and snapdragons and my heart filled with excitement about our days ahead, days as promising as the new season bursting to life around me.

Instead of walking into the warmth of Bobby's arms, I found him sprawled on his back on the kitchen floor; his eyes wide open. I somehow called 911 and then began trying to resuscitate him—but I knew it was too late. That realization was more horrific than I could ever imagine.

Since finding Bobby on the floor that day, I am haunted by his eyes. I see them in their myriad hues. Twinkling bright blue, like sunlight on water, when he was laughing. Steel blue when he was upset or sad. For me, their color was a gauge of his emotions. When Bobby appears in my dreams—day or night—what I see first are his eyes. I hope that never changes.

Several weeks after his death, with a heavy heart I returned to the story we had begun. To my surprise, writing about Bobby helped me grieve. But it's difficult, even today, to realize how much richer the book would be if Bobby had lived to tell his story.

So, although I wrote this book, it is Bobby Hoppe's story—the story of a sports legend who shielded those he loved from his dark secret for 31 years, and, as the lyrics of our favorite song said, who loved me as I loved him—"until the Twelfth of Never."

I wrote this for you, Bobby, because I wanted your story to be told. I wanted others to hear what really happened that night—not just to Don

Prologue

Hudson, but also to you. And I want to share why I have come to believe that, in Pliny the Elder's words, "In these matters the only certainty is that nothing is certain." I've shared a bit more about your football stardom than you would have allowed, but otherwise, I hope you are pleased.

Until the Twelfth of Never,
Sherry

CHAPTER ONE

Valley of the Shadow of Death

The day goes by like a shadow o'er the heart, with sorrow, where all was delight.
--Stephen Foster

In the language of the Creek Indians, Chattanooga means "rock coming to a point," a reference to Lookout Mountain, which begins in Chattanooga and runs 88 miles into Alabama and Georgia.

During the American Civil War, President Abraham Lincoln declared, "Whoever controls Chattanooga will win the war." If northern troops seized the city, they would be able to march, almost unimpeded, into Atlanta and the heart of the Confederacy. Thus, the hills and valleys around Chattanooga became massive battlefields.

On Sept. 21, 1863, Chickamauga Creek, located 20 miles south of Chattanooga in north Georgia, ran red with blood as Confederate soldiers surprised the Union troops and pushed them northward. Considered a Confederate victory for halting the Union advance, the Battle of Chickamauga claimed almost 35,000 lives.

The retreating Union troops took possession of Chattanooga. Only the relief forces of Gen. Ulysses S. Grant and William T. Sherman could break Confederate Gen. Braxton Bragg's grip on the city during the Battle of Chattanooga in November 1863.

History would prove this bloody battle to be pivotal to the outcome of the Civil War.

* * *

July 20-22, 1957. Almost a century later, a different civil war was being waged in and around Chattanooga as moonshiners defended their territory and what they believed was their right to transport and sell untaxed, illegal liquor in "dry" counties. In such skirmishes, moonshine-runners sometimes shot and killed law-enforcement officers and competing runners.

Like other southern cities that were founded in the 1800s to take advantage of the deep rivers to trade and transport goods, Chattanooga sprang from a tiny river town into a bustling industrial city and, later, a

5

thriving tourist attraction. By the mid-1900s, Chattanooga had begun to crowd both sides of the wide Tennessee River, which winds through the city like a fat brown snake.

After leaving downtown, the river sweeps around a bend, creating a dramatic backdrop for the homes of Chattanooga's prominent citizens. Just across Barton Avenue in North Chattanooga, a large park separates those less fortunate from their prosperous neighbors.

Being brazen, young boys often slipped through the park onto the riverside Chattanooga Golf and Country Club course before returning home to play street ball. For a few golden moments, the boys walked in the land of the haves before crossing the road, back to the homes of the have-nots.

During summer's cloying heat and humidity, house windows, propped open with broken broom-handles, were unspoken prayers for a breeze to sweep down the hilltops into North Chattanooga, carrying cool mountain air and the sweet smell of honeysuckle.

At 11 p.m. on July 19, 1957, most folks were sprawled on sweat-damp sheets, fast asleep. Inside stifling homes, the only light was the flash of fireflies captured by children at dusk. Tiny lights briefly flickering in mason jars with hole-punched lids.

A few cars glided toward North Market Street, young men hustling to get their dates home by curfew. Beneath the neon sign at Nikki's Drive-In, the jukebox was hushed, the party crowd having drifted away.

In the crevices between the Appalachian Mountains, darkness fell quickly and stillness spread over the valleys like a blanket. Even the songs of tree frogs or an owl's hoot on a nearby hill were muffled.

As the clock ticked into the wee hours of July 21, the city seemed asleep. But at 1 a.m. two young men, both near their homes, began a fateful drive down Bell Avenue.

At 1:07 a.m., a sudden flash of light and an echoing shotgun blast shattered the peaceful night. A car sped away, tires squealing. Another explosion ripped the air as a second car plowed into a power pole and stonewall, knocking an eight-inch gap between the sidewalk curb and wall.

Don Hudson, 24, slumped sideways onto the passenger seat of the 1948 Desoto sedan—shot at close range in the right side of his face.

A Matter of Conscience

* * *

At Georgia and Roy Hudson's home at 204 W. Manning Street, Don's older brother, Roy Jr., heard the crash and rushed to the scene, then back to tell the family Don had been in a wreck.

In disbelief, Ken Hudson, 14, insisted on going back to the wreck with his brother, Roy.

Thirty-one years later, Ken recalled first seeing his brother's favorite trigger-top shoes, red with blood, lying on the floorboard of the wrecked car.

"I remember it all," Ken said. "I remember sticking my head in the window of that car. I smelled that smell of death. His brains, smashed on the windshield."

Witnesses said Don's right eye had been blown from its socket. Blood pooled on the floorboard and ran onto the sidewalk.

When the first police officers arrived, they treated the scene as an automobile accident. Hudson, taken by ambulance to the emergency room at nearby Erlanger Hospital, died 30 minutes later, never regaining consciousness.

A headline in the July 21, 1957, edition of the *Chattanooga News-Free Press* proclaimed, "Young Reputed Liquor Runner Slain Gangland Style in N. Chattanooga."

Given Hudson's past reputation as a rough and reckless moonshine runner with a police record, it was a logical supposition. Confirming there were no reported clues at the scene, the article said, "A 24-year-old reputed whisky runner, Teddy Donald (Don) Hudson, was killed in North Chattanooga early this morning in what police said was a gangland-style shooting."

* * *

Considered a real badass, Don Hudson was feared by folks who knew him, detested by other moonshine runners, and notorious among law-enforcement officials.

Hudson grew up in North Chattanooga in a family with too many children and too little money, like most of their neighbors. Don realized, early on, if he wanted spending money, it was up to him.

Rather than channeling his youthful energy into neighborhood games, Don Hudson became a surly young man—swarthy complexion,

7

dark hair, full lips, wide-set eyes. His photo in the local paper showed a solemn man looking straight ahead, unsmiling. Eyes, flat. Emotionless.

To be so young when he was killed, Hudson already had quite a rap sheet, as well as an official FBI record. If police or revenuers weren't after him, other liquor-runners were. He didn't give a damn. In fact, he seemed to relish his growing reputation as a reckless rebel.

By 1957, young Hudson was already an experienced moonshine-runner—a "career" that, though exciting and lucrative, was extremely dangerous. The threat of getting caught by the law or, even worse, by another whisky-runner, was an adrenalin rush for Hudson.

By then, the business of transporting illegal liquor was common in the hills of Appalachia. Some folks even believed it was their Constitutional right to make "white lightning" and sell it without Uncle Sam sticking his long, boney finger into the pie.

Bootlegging, with its long and wildly storied history, was born at the end of the era of Prohibition when, in 1933, a huge tax was imposed on whisky. Some Southern planters, failing to make a profit on their corn crops, began to turn them into corn whisky. Sheltered from prying eyes in the tree-covered foothills of Appalachia, they sold it under the table in neighboring cities.

Developing this new business venture required someone to transport the product down tortuously winding, narrow roads without guardrails. Miss a curve and the car took flight, rudely ending up hundreds of feet below in a ravine.

To avoid catching the eye of the law, a moonshine car was made to look as common, or "stock," as possible, so it blended in with the other rattletraps traveling the circuitous roads.

But there was a big difference—under the hood.

A tell-tale sign a car had been outfitted to carry moonshine in special tanks, each of which held more than 150 gallons, was that the car's back end sat lower to the ground than the front. So, besides souping up their cars for speed, liquor-runners installed heavy shocks and springs to prevent the cars from sagging under the load of liquid gold.

Entrepreneurial moonshiners needed skilled drivers willing to push their cars for maneuverability and maximum speed—often the difference between freedom and jail.

The word "bootlegger" came from "bootleg"—a speed-spin in which the driver, without hitting his brakes, spun the car around, totally changing directions. Due to his daring and willingness to push the limits of the car, a good bootlegger was almost impossible to catch.

In the 1940s and '50s, all bootleggers wanted to be known as the top runner. When not transporting illegal liquor, they often tested their skills against each other, racing their souped-up cars along the curving roads, often side by side.

Long after the transportation of illegal liquor diminished, the races continued and, according to history, NASCAR was born. In the 1950s, NASCAR racing was just beginning—but bootlegging was illegal, dangerous and profitable—all of which suited Don Hudson just fine.

The young man was fearless and violent—a volatile combination.

* * *

On Christmas Eve 1951, the FBI wasn't watching for Santa.

On that cold night, the FBI arrested Hudson and charged him with violating internal revenue laws. In 1952, the FBI placed him on probation. But the boy could not stay out of trouble, so in September 1953, his parole was revoked, and he spent 18 months in a federal reformatory.

Almost as soon as he left the reformatory, Hudson and a friend were arrested for kidnapping and bludgeoning a black man, leaving him beside the road for dead. All three were "known whisky men," according to the police report. Hudson was bound over to the grand jury, but charges were dropped May 3. It was a chance to start afresh.

But on January 7, 1957, while riding around with two buddies, a shot was fired from a passing car, the bullet going through Hudson's hand and costing him the use of several fingers. The shooter, moonshine runner Marlin Sims, was arrested for felony assault.

But Hudson would be damned if he'd let a lost finger or two stop him. As soon as he could steer with his good hand and shift with his bad, he was flying down roads that twisted back and forth, dizzyingly, like thin snakes wriggling through thick woods.

The week before he was shot, Hudson was fleeing police when he collided with another car. When Hudson's car flipped, catching fire, he took off on foot. In his car, officers found illegal whisky. The next day, he was arrested for transporting unstamped whisky, reckless driving, and hit-and-run. Amazingly, he was set free on bond.

Valley of the Shadow of Death

On July 21, 1957, just four days after he was released from jail, Don Hudson was shot and killed. When folks heard, they just assumed it involved a "corn-liquor feud."

* * *

In the 1950s, there were few, if any, interstates in the rural South. The road between Chattanooga and Auburn, Ala., was a paved, two-lane highway. After twisting free of the hills of southeast Tennessee and northern Georgia, it cut straight through the red-clay dirt of Alabama.

Fields of cotton and low-growing peanut plants bordered the highway as far as the eye could see. A few pecan trees clustered near white-painted homes with wide porches and near unpainted shanties with no porches at all. The trees provided little shade but offered sweet pecan meat once the fat nuts were shelled.

On a long stretch of road, a couple of barefooted black boys, eight or nine, walked side by side, one pushing an old bike, their shorts wet from a dip in their favorite swimming hole. The one with the bike bumped it off the road, making way for the passing car. Above them, still nailed to a power pole, a sun-faded red, white, and blue "We Like Ike— Eisenhower for President" poster fluttered a bit, stirred by the passing car. It was a pastoral scene.

But on this day, July 22, 1957, one driver was oblivious. He didn't know how long he'd been on the road, racing along in his sister's car, floating on the waves of heat shimmering off the pavement. He recalled hugging his mama, avoiding his dad. Trying to act normal.

Touching his wet cheeks, he wondered how long he'd been crying. In the car, he didn't have to suck it up, so he sobbed.

"Dear God, dear God," he said out loud, words of anguish, a prayer. "Dear God. Help me. Please help me." Tears he'd held in for almost 24 hours broke free like water over a spillway.

He had never felt more alone in his life. No one to turn to—no one. Then a thought struck him: "Mama always said God cares. And that's what the preachers preach. God cares—and God forgives our sins. Oh, God! I need your forgiveness. Right now."

The road stretched ahead of him. Somehow he drove. He didn't stop. What was that Bible verse? The road to hell is paved with good intentions. Or was that just an old saying? The road to hell...I'm on the road to hell—and I can't get off. He almost laughed. Sick joke. For a second, he forgot the horror of yesterday.

Two days before, skimming over the road toward home, he had been a different person. Now, he was...he didn't know who he was. Driving up from Auburn, he had been happy—anticipating his date Saturday night and time to hang out with old high school buddies at Nikki's and the Riverside Pharmacy, a chance to talk with Mama about the next season and the games she would attend.

What are you going to do now, big man? How do you push past this kind of pain? Many times, he'd played football with broken ribs, sprained ankles, strained muscles...but nothing like this pain. Trainers couldn't wrap this in layers of tape so it could heal. This would never heal.

So much that had happened seemed like a dream, but one thing he knew for sure—there would be no happy ending to this nightmare. He'd killed a man. Regardless of the circumstances, he'd taken another's life. He said it out loud, to make it real. "I shot a man, shot him in the face.

"Can't call that play back, boy.

Somehow, he found himself on the outskirts of Auburn, heading to campus. The thought of facing teammates made him nauseous. Swallowing back the bile filling his throat, he looked in the rearview mirror—a pale face with red-rimmed eyes looked back. He didn't know this man.

Entering a school zone, he automatically slowed to 15 mph. He became aware of the quiet in the car. The only sound was his heart beating inside his ears. He always tuned in the radio as soon as he got in his car—but he'd driven for hours and never turned it on. Music soothed the soul. Soothed the savage beast.

A refrain from childhood, from a hymn he sang at church, played in his head: "Just as I am, and waiting not to rid my soul of one dark blot, To Thee whose blood can cleanse each spot, O Lamb of God, I come, I come..."

A soundless sob slipped past the lump in his throat. He made a quick turn and headed toward Auburn's First Baptist Church—the last church he had attended. It had been the past spring, after football season. He reached into the glove box, pulled out sunglasses to hide his red eyes and walked into the church office.

11

"I need to talk to the pastor," he said loudly, startling the woman at the desk. He learned the minister was out of town at a meeting. "If you want to talk with someone, we had a guest preacher here yesterday— Joseph Godwin. That's his name," she said, trying to be helpful. "He's taking classes at Auburn this summer, working on a graduate degree in psychology, I believe."

Bobby rushed to his car, turned the key in the ignition and, without meaning to, scratched off, eager to find this Preacher Godwin, to unburden his heart, to ask God for forgiveness.

Silently, he recited a Bible verse he recalled from Sunday school: "Yea, though I walk through the valley of the shadow of death, I shall fear no evil, for Thou art with me. Thy rod and thy staff, they comfort me...."

He needed that comfort. He needed it bad, real bad.

CHAPTER TWO

The Child Is Father to the Man

The deepest definition of youth is life as yet untouched by tragedy.
--Alfred North Whitehead (1861-1947)

Throughout America in the early 1940s, mothers hugged their sons and husbands and sent them off to war. Then, crying quietly in bed at night, they begged God for their safe return.

In small towns like Chattanooga, far from the power-center of Washington, D.C., folks talked about little but the war. Foreign-sounding places became part of their vocabulary: Battle of the Bulge, White Cliffs of Dover, Hiroshima.

Although they chatted with the swagger of those who had seen those sites, most got what they knew from the radio and news reels shown in theaters before the main attraction—American warships launching explosives into the bellies of enemy planes, bearing the sign of the rising sun or the Nazi swastika. As flaming planes spiraled into the sea, the audience clapped and cheered.

By the 1950s, parades with confetti raining down, given to honor returning conquerors, had become memories. Americans were healing from the loss of hometown boys now resting in family plots just outside town, fresh flowers placed less and less often on their graves.

After the drama of the war ended and the humdrum of life settled back in, small-town folks hungered for new heroes to worship, for weekend excitement that could carry them through long and tedious workdays at the local factory or corner service station.

Then like citizens of ancient Rome who cheered on the gladiators in a fight to the finish, folks in Chattanooga discovered a new diversion in the rough-and-tumble of contact sports. On Friday nights, they once again had heroes to root for, enemies to unite against.

Like most southern states, football was king in Tennessee. Baby boys cut their teeth on football-shaped rattles. In school, recess became a quick quarter in a pick-up football game.

The Child is Father to the Man

Too soon, it seemed to his mother, Bobby Hoppe went from playing kick-the-can on the streets of North Chattanooga to playing football for Central High School.

Central coaches had zeroed in on the tough junior high kid—last name, Hoppe—who played with dedication, and pure heart. They began courting Bobby, recruiting hard—hard enough to pull him across town, away from City High where his neighborhood friends would go.

And it was at Central High, where he left it all on the field for the Purple Pounders, that Hoppe became a living legend.

* * *

Bobby's growing-up years shaped the complex, circumspect man he would become.

The baby of the family, Bobby was doted on and protected from the "ugly" side of life by his mother and three older sisters, Joan, Martha and Doris.

Although the Hoppes were not big on hugs and kisses, Bobby never doubted the love of his mother and sisters. And throughout his life, his beloved mother inculcated into the very fiber of Bobby's being a skewed perspective on the importance of what others thought of him. Her clear expectation was that he would always do the right thing and never bring reproach on the family—it was a heavy load for a young man and one that would forever shape the way he viewed his place in the world.

Unlike his relationship with his mother and sisters, as hard as Bobby tried to please his dad, to make him proud, he hit a wall, never feeling any fatherly love or acceptance. For a boy trying to be tougher than he was, a father's pat on the back would have meant the world. It never happened.

Later, some speculated that's why young Hoppe, even in high school, sought the advice of older men, why he adored his coaches. In all of them, he found pieces of the father he never had.

When he allowed himself to think about it, Bobby tried to understand why his mother, Juanita, even married Robert Hoppe. Surely, he thought, when they were courting, Mama must have seen something lovable in him; she must have glimpsed some part of him that made her believe he'd be a good husband and father.

A Matter of Conscience

Whatever initially drew his parents together no longer existed. They seldom spoke or even touched. And even Bobby, at his young age, realized they no longer slept in the same bed.

The reality was that Juanita's husband—his father—was a bitter man—a bitter man, who became a mean drunk.

Bobby didn't recall when his dad shipped out to serve his country in World War II. And he was only in the first grade when his dad returned—not as a hero, wounded in battle, but as a disabled vet, paralyzed by a stroke. The stroke, it seemed to Bobby, not only froze his dad's frail body, it also turned his heart to ice.

One morning, overhearing that, once again, Daddy had drunk up Uncle Sam's disability check before Mama could buy groceries or pay the rent, Bobby felt rage toward his father.

"Damn him," Bobby said, hitting the kitchen table with his fist, just out of Mama's earshot.

In desperation, Juanita began looking for a job, finally finding one as a housemother at Baroness Erlanger School of Nursing, where she would work for 15 years.

Now it was official: Mama was the breadwinner. While his dad slept it off until noon, snoring in the bedroom with the shades still down, Mama was up before the sun, baking homemade biscuits, washing clothes, and cleaning the house before leaving for her job at 7 a.m.

At day's end, Juanita managed to create special times for her children, often making Bobby his favorite—peanut butter and banana sandwiches with a glass of cold sweet milk.

She carried the picnic supper to Bobby on the back porch, stopping to drop a quick kiss on top of his sweaty little head.

Patting the step beside him, Bobby would say, "Put it right here, Mama."

Again, he'd connived to eat outside, so he could spend a bit more time in the fresh air, slipping bits of food to his dog, watching fireflies, and gazing at the night sky.

From inside the tiny kitchen, Bobby heard his dad's voice, gravelly from the Camel cigarettes always dangling from his lips. "Juanita, goddammit, you're babying that boy."

And she'd gotten a job. "Wearing the pants in the family," he murmured, sorry for himself.

The Child is Father to the Man

Initially he refused to try out the specially equipped, handicap-friendly car provided by the Army—a big, fat kiss-off from Uncle Sam—but soon he started hitting the road. Now, despite his disability, he headed to his favorite bar and spent the days shooting the breeze with drinking buddies, dragging home before dark, stinking of stale cigarette smoke and gin.

Bobby learned to be thankful for his dad's absence. And when his father finally did come home, he would pass out on the couch or on the bed, leaving Bobby alone, so he was free to play in the streets with friends or hang out at Riverview Park, lying in dew-damp grass, looking for the Big Dipper and the Little Dipper. Just dreaming.

One evening, after another day downtown in a bar, Robert Hoppe was making his way home when he saw his son and some other boys playing football in the street.

And they saw him—his car weaving on and off the road. Glancing furtively at their friend Bobby, the boys hustled off the street. But one of them dropped the football and, breathlessly, they watched it wobble back into the street.

Mortified, Bobby saw his dad swerve his car sharply, catching the ball—with a loud thump—under the right front tire, intentionally flattening it against the pavement.

One of the boys playing on the street that day was Doug Meyer, former Chattanooga criminal court judge now retired to Florida. In the summer of 2008, Meyer recalled the incident. "All of us heard Mr. Hoppe laughing as he ran over our ball. I felt awful for Bobby. His daddy was a mean man. A mean man."

Pausing, Meyer said, "You know, Bobby's daddy never saw him play football. Not in high school. Not at Auburn. Never. It must have just killed Bobby inside."

Ironically, after Bobby's football career ended, someone told him his dad reveled in talking with his drinking cronies about his son's football exploits. "He bragged to his buddies," Bobby said. "But he never told me one time he was proud of me."

* * *

It was time to pack up his clothes and favorite collections—two plastic Army tanks, a tiny fire truck, baseball cards he'd traded with friends. Tuck it all into bags from the Piggly-Wiggly.

A Matter of Conscience

Moving was just a way of life for Bobby. He thought it was normal—and, in North Chattanooga during the Great Depression and for years afterward, maybe it was. You couldn't make a house payment so, eventually, the bank foreclosed and you lost your home.

Too young to see parentheses of worry deepening around his mother's mouth and furrows forming between her eyes, Bobby was excited about moving a few streets over to a smaller house. For a little boy, it was an adventure.

But, within six months, they had missed two rent payments, all because Daddy beat Mama to the mailbox and grabbed the disability check first—grabbing it real quick for a disabled man before heading to his old haunts.

So it was moving day again. For a while the family lived in government-subsidized housing. "The projects" is what it was called. And the way people said it Bobby knew there was something not good about living there.

Bobby also realized moving constantly was not what regular families did. "We're poor," he thought, feeling the shame of it, like a hot rash, rising up his neck.

The next time Bobby played football in the streets, he hit harder, ran faster, got hurt. He could take it. Perhaps he realized, even then, that the way out for him was football.

Regardless, he threw himself into it, becoming a force to contend with, becoming the player that bigger opponents dreaded to face across the line of scrimmage.

At Central High, although he wasn't big and brawny, he was fast, he was smart and, thanks to growing up a street-tough kid, he was fearless.

Bobby listened closely to Coach Eugene Boneparte "Red" Etter and Coach Stanley "Boomer" Farmer. What they said was gospel. Twice a day, he ran plays on the football field and, at night, deep in his warm feather bed, he ran them in his head.

He learned the game so well it seemed as if he could read the opposing team's playbook before they took the field. He got in their heads, he shook them up and, what's more, if given a tiny crack in the line, he ran like hell.

They didn't call him Hippity Hoppe for nothing.

17

CHAPTER THREE

Glory Days

Young people are in a condition like a permanent intoxication,
Because youth is sweet and they are growing.
--Aristotle (384–322 BC)
Nicomechean Ethics

Back in the early 1950s, Donnie Allen's favorite number was 33.

While his older brother played in the high school marching band, Donnie sat in the stands with his parents every time the Central High Purple Pounders bounded onto the field.

His mom watched his brother's precision movements, almost oblivious to the other action on the turf. But Donnie's eyes were glued on No. 33—Bobby Hoppe.

Even after his brother graduated, Allen coerced his dad into taking him to all of Central's 1951, '52 and '53 home games. By 1953, Donnie refused to attend any school but Central. He was determined to meet his hero, Bobby Hoppe.

At home, Donnie's bedroom was a shrine to Hoppe. "My room had No. 33 on everything. I thought that guy hung the moon."

In the 1950s, Central High was a huge school—in building size and population. When Donnie registered as a 7th grader, Central's enrollment exceeded 1,800, including more than 350 seniors.

For Donnie, the first weeks were intimidating, even scary. He felt like a baby around the upperclassmen who strolled the halls with easy confidence. "After a couple months trying to find my hero among the hordes of students, I began to think I would never see him," Donnie said. Then one day at lunch, Donnie and a few friends were shooting marbles in an alley near the school. For reasons Donnie cannot recall, a huge 9th grader pummeled him to the ground.

"In my mind, he was 200 pounds and I was maybe 90," Donnie remembered.

"All of a sudden, this big kid was no longer on top of me. Someone literally picked me up and carried me into the school under his arm—like you would carry a large bag of seed—and gently put me down.

"When I looked up, it was Bobby Hoppe. Standing right there beside me was my hero!"

Hoppe asked Donnie if he was OK.

Donnie recalled, "All I could say was—and I actually said this stupid line, not even realizing I had reversed the words—'I am your hero, Bobby, I am your hero.'"

* * *

Bobby didn't consider himself a hero. He didn't commit himself 100 percent to the rigors of football for fame. He played his heart out for one reason: He loved the intensity of the game.

From the top of his head to the tips of his toes, Bobby's nerve-endings fired like automatic machine guns as he skimmed over the ground with the football clutched in his arms, a sleek fox with hounds on his heels. For Bobby, it was an adrenalin rush like no other.

In the football stadium, Bobby was just one of the guys. He relished the camaraderie on and off the field. Being in the team huddle, smelling crushed grass beneath their feet and the salty sweat of men bound together by a common goal, was next to heaven for Bobby.

And it was an escape. Lined up in a T formation, Bobby could focus on only one thing—what would happen when the center snapped the ball. No time to worry about his mother working so hard. No concerns about what friends thought about his drunken dad. No humiliation from his family having to constantly move because of unpaid rent.

Cradling the pigskin like a baby, Hoppe was in another world—a world where, in the midst of personal chaos, he found peace, where what he did mattered. It was a world he loved.

* * *

High school is a time like no other. The globe seems to spin on its axis around you and your friends. Nothing is more important, not wars, not floods, not drought.

High school memories are acute—and lasting. Just four short years, but during those years, girls become women and boys become men. High school is an era of emotional extremes—dizzying highs and seemingly bottomless lows with nothing in between.

In the 1950s in Chattanooga, when the alarm clock went off on most school days, it was still pitch black outside. Students rose from a sleep so soul-deep it belonged only to the young. They rolled out, hearts thumping, knowing the day's happiness or humiliation hung by a thread.

In Central High, an opaque layer of chalk dust was bonded to classroom windowpanes, diffusing the light rays spilling over the windowsills, darkening letters and words carved into the wooden desks—a Braille of youthful dreams and hopes.

As the bell rang between classes, doors up and down the hall were thrown wide. Students flooded the locker-bordered halls. Groups clustered together, talking rapidly, laughing loudly, eyeing couples that walked as one—a boy with his arm across his girl's shoulder, where she proudly wore his letterman's jacket, the gold C bright against the deep-purple fabric.

Through the years, teachers came and went—a wax and wane of personalities. There was the pretty teacher—long blonde hair, an hourglass figure. Her bra was visible through her thin blouse—if the light was just right and you held your breath—every teenage boy's fantasy.

Then there was the old geezer who should have retired long before. When the room grew quiet, he dozed until being jolted awake by the splat of a spitball on his cheek.

Across the hall was the new teacher with eyes in the back of her head—you couldn't get by with a damned thing in her class. She was tough; made you study hard. Decades later, you recalled her and wished you'd said thanks.

And there were teachers like J. Pope Dyer, who brought political science to life with his real anecdotes and his resolve that pupils would come to understand the importance of politics.

Dyer cared about his students, even football players. Many teachers viewed jocks as dumb, but Dyer saw their potential far beyond the playing field.

Although he may have never known, Dyer instilled in Bobby a lifelong love of politics—and geography, which Dyer insisted students must learn to comprehend politics.

Bobby took Dyer's instructions to heart. Over the years, he learned the globe like the back of his hand. He could explain the complexities of Arab/Israeli politics, the changing face of the United States as the world's largest superpower, China's rapid rise in the world economy, and the religious and political intricacies of terrorist countries.

A Matter of Conscience

When world events made news, Bobby could put the pieces together like a jigsaw puzzle.

* * *

In the 1950s, Bobby and Paul Allen Campbell were part of a tightly knit group of athletes who enjoyed playing together on and off the field.

In high school, the group you run with is vital. It marks you for four years, some say, for life. For many reasons, these high school groups tend to migrate to the same cafeteria tables at noon each weekday, like those who sit in the same church pews on Sunday.

At Central, jocks like Bobby staked out prime tables near the cheerleaders and the hot girls. High school lunchtime is less about eating than socializing, goofing off. On one typical day, Bobby started a mashed potato fight. Standing on a rickety cafeteria table, he flipped a forkful of potatoes into another football player's face. Soon, half the first string was on tables with potatoes flying everywhere—a scene reminiscent of the food fight in "Animal House."

Suddenly, Hobart Millsaps walked in. A no-nonsense principal, Millsaps started calling the culprits by name, motioning them to follow him to his office. As they walked toward the door—heads down, giggles stifled—someone noticed Bobby wasn't among the chastised crew.

Looking around, they saw Bobby sitting beside his girlfriend at a table, calmly sipping milk through a straw, an angelic look on his face. It wasn't the first or last time he would start tomfoolery and then disappear just before everyone else got busted.

* * *

In the early 1950s, students at Chattanooga's Northside Junior High went on to City High. But not Bobby Hoppe. Hearing repeatedly about Hoppe's athletic talents, Central coaches came calling. They loved what they saw, so they began recruiting him, showering him with the fatherly attention he craved. He agreed to forego City High to play for Central.

It was a match made in Heaven—one neither Hoppe nor the coaches ever regretted. Over the four years he played for Central, Hoppe developed a close relationship with his coaches, especially head coach "Red" Etter and line coach "Boomer" Farmer.

21

Within his first year at Central, his coaches knew Hoppe would live up to his reputation. He went on to letter all four years, as well as being elected class president three of those years.

But, as a green freshman, Hoppe had a lot to prove, so he got down to it immediately. Early in the 1950 fall season, the team traveled to northeast Tennessee to take on Kingsport. Not intimidated by the massive young men of Kingsport High, most in their fourth year on the varsity, Hoppe grabbed every crack in the line and blew through it like the wind.

Central skunked Kingsport by 53 points, but the game took its toll on Hoppe, who had five teeth knocked out. Tough as a pine knot, he spit out blood and broken teeth and played on.

When the game ended and Etter told line coach Farmer he was amazed at Hoppe's grit, Farmer replied, "He'll either quit or be the best back this town has ever seen."

Farmer spent the night with Hoppe at a dentist's office. Bobby was insistent: he wanted a permanent bridge. He liked the ladies, and he didn't want to look like a damn jack-o-lantern.

Finally, Farmer relented—and Bobby got a permanent bridge.

In the next game, the permanent bridge proved to be not so permanent. In a smash-mouth play, opponents sent it flying onto the turf—along with two more of Hoppe's teeth.

The coaches shook their heads in dismay. What were they going to do with the boy? Bruised and now snaggle-toothed, Hoppe refused to sit it out, playing through the pain.

The coaches had to do something, so Etter designed a plastic mask to protect Hoppe's teeth.

"It was made of hard plastic but was transparent so Bobby could look down and see the ball as the quarterback handed it off to him," Etter's son Gene recalled. "It was 3-4 inches high, about three-fourths of an inch thick and was attached to each side of the helmet. I never saw any other player wear something like that—in high school or college."

The facemask not only protected Hoppe's teeth, it scared the hell out of opponents who lined up across from him. Above the mask, all they could see were Hoppe's blue eyes, burning holes through them, as Central finished the season with eight wins, two losses, and one tie.

A Matter of Conscience

Central opened its 1951 season at Fayetteville. As he did in his freshman year, Hoppe used his speed to go from 0 to 60 in a split second, leading the Purple Pounders to a 20-0 victory.

To be honest, Bobby didn't care for the contact side of the sport as much as some players. Coach Etter said, "The fleet-footed Bobby prefers to grab an opposing player and throw him down on defense rather than hit him. Hoppe doesn't have to run over someone; he's so fast he just runs around them."

Described by *Chattanooga Times* sports writer George Short as a "demon pass-defense halfback," against Fayetteville Hoppe climaxed a 16-play, 85-yard drive to "skirt across on a five-yard knife through the left side on a quick opening play."

The game was a textbook study of strategic moves and outstanding players who understand how to work together. In the fourth quarter, teaming up with Billy Hale and tiny Tommy Tillman on offense, Hoppe added to their 12 yards, taking the ball on fourth down and four to go. Sweeping 24 yards on a right reverse, Hoppe got the ball to Fayetteville's 10.

"From there," Short reported, "he reversed to the left side on the very next play and scored behind a cluster of blockers."

But the next challenger, Chattanooga Baylor, was a tough one. Central fans showed up in droves. The night before the game, a local sports writer called Coach Etter to tell him who had been selected All-City. Bobby Hoppe, now a sophomore, was not on the list.

"What are you going to do when Hoppe runs wild against Baylor tomorrow night?" an irked Etter asked.

And he did—real wild. In a stroke of genius, Etter broke out a rash of new offensive plays, capitalizing on "the heretofore latent ground-gaining ability of sophomore Bobby Hoppe."

According to *Free-Press* sports writer Austin White, Hoppe slashed "relentlessly through Baylor's riddled line on well-executed tackle-trap plays," taking the Purple Pounders to victory.

And so the season went. Central won seven of eight games, allowing opponents only 62 points. The state championship belonged to the Purple Pounders.

Glory Days

* * *

Purple Pounder pride swept Chattanooga. Loyal fans began to follow the team wherever it went. Having tasted the sweetness of a state championship, the city hungered for another.

Again starting the season with Fayetteville in Bobby's junior year, Central returned most of its starters, except for linemen. Jimmy Pack, Central's All-State quarterback, headed a veteran quartet that included All-City Hoppe, Tillman, and Hale, described as a "trio of speedsters." Captain Don Duncan, another All-City returnee, topped the list of lineman.

Lacking other experienced linemen and dealing with two pre-season injuries, Etter wasn't optimistic about the upcoming game—or season. "We don't look like we're ready for anybody."

Disproving their coach's dower prediction, his players handed him a 31-0 victory.

The Purple Pounders were off to a roaring start. The next week they bested Knoxville Young 26-6, with Hoppe as the "star of the night, sparkling both on offense and defense."

Getting so much individual credit bothered Bobby. And when he was named Tennessee's high school football player of the week, Etter added to the praise, crowing, "Bobby is the best all-around back we've had at Central in years. He can do just about everything well on both offense and defense."

With the season's end looming, Central met one of its biggest foes, Chattanooga Baylor, in front of 8,000 screaming fans.

In the early 1950s, teams were beginning to specialize in two platoons, so a player who went all the way on both offense and defense was becoming something of a rarity. One Chattanooga sports writer noted that players going both ways for an entire game were "hailed as iron men."

At Central, Duncan was the only Pounders' lineman playing offensive and defensive tackle. Offensive fullback Hoppe and halfback Hale pulled double duty as defensive halfbacks.

After watching Hoppe go both ways for an entire game, George Short reported, "Central's Purple Pounders, led by a wild-running bull named Bobby Hoppe, defeated Baylor School...."

On the wind-chilled night, Hoppe scored three touchdowns, on 74, 16, and 67-yard runs.

A Matter of Conscience

Humpy Heywood, Baylor's head coach, explained why Hoppe was so difficult to stop. "It is a combination of speed, a desire to win, a desire not to be tackled, plus a surprising amount of determination."

* * *

Just one game left for another state championship.

Over Thanksgiving weekend in 1952, Central's team traveled to Oak Ridge to play.

In 1961, Red Etter, talking with Eddie Baker of the *Chattanooga News-Free Press*, recalled the Oak Ridge game.

"I remember the game, in '52 I believe, against Oak Ridge. They had a good team and we had a good team, but neither one of our kickers could make a point so we tied, 18-18.

"We threw a screen pass to Hoppe, and he ran all the way for a touchdown. But a flag was thrown on the play, and the official said we had an ineligible lineman downfield. So we ran the screen pass again, and it worked again, except another flag went down for the same thing."

Etter was furious. Because the game would decide the state championship, college officials had been hired instead of the regular referees. But the refs had used a college rule to call a high school play illegal.

As soon as Etter got the game film the next day, he drove it straight down to Birmingham to show the head of the officiating association. After reviewing the film, they issued a press release admitting the play should have been a touchdown. So, unofficially, Central won the game, 24-18.

With that settled, Etter called the chairman of the Tennessee Associated Press high school poll to explain the situation. The final poll declared Central the No. 1 team—and state champs.

Years later, after Bobby and I were married, someone told me the story of the now-famous two long runs, so I asked Bobby about it when he came home from a long day of coaching.

"Bobby, is it really true you ran an 80-yard touchdown at a Litton game when the temperature was below zero and, after it was called back, you ran it again on the next play?"

"No, it's not true," he replied. Then, with a twinkle in his eye, he said, "It was at Oak Ridge—and it was 87 yards."

Bobby's running style made such feats possible, Gene Etter surmised. "While running full speed, he would veer slightly, and the combination of his speed and strength would cause would-be tacklers to miss or fall off without slowing him down. On many of his long TD runs, he was in the clear ten yards downfield, and no one was going to catch Bobby Hoppe from behind."

Did Coach Etter teach Bobby this? "No. Dad always said it was a God-given talent."

CHAPTER FOUR

The Trial Begins

Give no decision til both sides thou'st heard.
–Phocylides

Bobby's years at Central High School, all the hours he poured his heart into running, blocking, and bringing home the gold for the Purple Pounders fade like a hazy dream. So long gone, it's difficult to draw a straight line from the happy-go-lucky high school hero to the weary man now fighting for his life in a Chattanooga courtroom.

The hundreds of shots of Hippity Hoppe running with the football tucked under his arm or blocking like a boulder—at Central and Auburn—have been blurred by a tsunami of newspaper photos and television footage of the former star being handcuffed and fingerprinted, followed by daily coverage of the trial. Looking at the 1988 photos of the gaunt-faced, silver-haired Hoppe, it's difficult to find much evidence of the muscular, carefree young football player of the mid-1950s. The guilt he's carried thirty-one years has exacted an immeasurable toll.

We each slowly cede our carefree childhood to age and maturity. But few have the glorious days of youth ripped away so abruptly as Bobby in 1957. Just as his life should have been falling into place, it began to fall apart. A Humpty-Dumpty future, broken beyond repair.

* * *

Although it's only 8:30 in the morning, blinding sunrays bounce off the buildings as we're making the short—but seemingly endless—walk from defense attorney Leroy Phillips' office to the courthouse.

Each step draws us closer to the end. An end we may not want. A possible life sentence we cannot fathom. I fear any time in prison would be a sure death for Bobby.

Marching along like POWs as waves of heat shimmer off the concrete, I try to pray. Shakespeare was right, "My words fly up, my thoughts remain below." My mind races back to the evidentiary hearing two weeks ago where many lies and exaggerations were framed as truth.

27

The Trial Begins

Now, at the defense table a few feet in front of me, Bobby sits quietly, flanked by Phillips and Bobby Lee Cook, the two attorneys to whom we've entrusted his life.

As Bobby leans toward Cook, I glimpse his strong profile, and I will him to look back. He doesn't turn, but I know his blue eyes are steely and focused.

A hush shrouds the courtroom as the judge enters, his black robe, partially unzipped, billowing slightly at his sides.

Watching Judge Joseph DiRisio settle behind the bench, I'm surprised. He doesn't look the way I'd pictured him. Unimposing is the word that comes to mind. Slender. Not tall—5'9" or 5'10". He's about 60, but there's no gray in his hair or in the moustache outlining his upper lip. He scans the packed courtroom, eyes pausing briefly on Bobby, who gazes back with intensity.

DiRisio is hard to read. He's a New Yorker who traveled to the South to attend Vanderbilt University's School of Law, never expecting to stay. But a law-school buddy persuaded DiRisio to join him in practice in Chattanooga.

Twenty years later in 2008, Doug Meyer, a retired criminal court justice who, in 1988, presided over cases in the courtroom adjacent to DiRisio's, said Joe DiRisio was the smartest judge he'd ever known, highly respected among the legal community.

"He was brilliant," Meyer said. "But, to be honest, not very likable."

Although Meyer thought highly of DiRisio, many who went before his bench as defendants left feeling differently. In fact, some believed DiRisio increased their odds of becoming a casualty of the judicial system. In his book, *Beyond Prison Walls,* author Jeris Bragan told of being convicted of first-degree murder in 1977. Before his trial, a Chattanooga attorney friend warned, "Whenever DiRisio presides at a trial, the State has an extra prosecutor."

Bragan says he found truth in his friend's words. It took fifteen years, but a federal judge overturned the verdict handed down by DiRisio, ruling Bragan had been convicted in violation of his constitutional rights. Bragan was released from prison in the early 1990s.

Today in the packed courtroom, the spectators, some seated and some standing, stop talking—all eyes on the judge. Numerous lawyers swell the crowd. Throughout the trial, they come and go, popping in between cases, lining the back wall, eager to see Bobby Lee Cook in action.

As DiRisio starts to address the assembly, he speaks so softly I find myself leaning forward, afraid I'll miss a word.

It's time. The jury has been sworn. The gavel is struck. The trial begins. Finally.

It's June 22, 1988. I glance at Bobby, rigid in his hard chair. After assessing DiRisio, Bobby stares straight ahead. What he's feared for decades is now unfolding.

He remembers his mother's lifelong sermons about the importance of one's good reputation. In his head, he can still hear her voice, telling him she knows he would never do anything to hurt the family name.

Today, embarrassed by this public humiliation, Bobby's face burns like a hot iron. "I'm just glad Mama's not living," he thinks.

He sits up straighter and stifles a sigh, refusing to look away from the judge. This is it. After 31 years of hell, he can no longer shield his family from the knowledge he killed a man.

Making his face blank, Bobby focuses on his strong, sinewy, very sure hands. He stares at them momentarily, before folding them on the table. Abruptly, he hears the rat-a-tat-tat of the court secretary's agile fingers flying over the keyboard as DiRisio begins: "The indictment was read by Assistant District Attorney Tom Evans and a plea of not guilty was entered by Leroy Phillips on behalf of the defendant."

Not guilty. The same words Bobby uttered a few days before at the preliminary hearing, the same words we pray the jury foreman will speak after the 12 in the jury box have sifted through all testimony in the days ahead.

Not guilty. Two tiny words said with dignity tinged with sorrow, his belief in himself softened by years of regret and a hint of resignation for what's to come. But no more silence.

As Bobby Lee Cook's opening statement will reveal, after 31 years, Bobby wants to face his accusers and unburden his soul.

I remember reading about the trial of Dr. John Bodkin Adams, a doctor accused of murder by "easing the passing" of patients. Before Bodkin's trial got underway, writer Sybille Bedford declared the ideal trial "is supposed to start from scratch, with the tale unfolding step by step with no stone left unturned and the jury assuming nothing."

The Trial Begins

She said the jury is to listen, hear the tale corroborated, denied, pulled to pieces and put together again. The jury hears the story backward and forward.

"But," she concluded, "They should never have heard it before. When they first walk into that court, sit down in that box, they are like people before the curtain has gone up."

Her words reflect my concerns as Bobby's trial begins. Since Bobby was first indicted in March 1988, the 31-year-old case has been covered coast to coast by newspapers, magazines, radio, and television. It has also been re-enacted on television.

Without doubt, the curtain on Bobby's case rose long before the jury assembled. We fear jurors have already decided, influenced by the barrage of news about the case.

DiRisio says the jury will not be sequestered. Although the law requires sequestering only in a death-penalty case, I am shocked. Regardless of the law, a judge can sequester jurors if he expects headlines every day, but neither DiRisio nor an attorney mentions isolating the jury.

In each of the days ahead, the judge will admonish the jury to avoid all news concerning the trial; he'll tell the 12 not to discuss the case before deliberations. But it's a farce. We learn later, despite DiRisio's warnings, one juror not only heard the tale in the courtroom, she heard it in other places and discussed it with her husband. She should have been tossed off the jury, but no one stepped up to tell DiRisio.

Trial by jury. With the adoption of the 6th and 7th amendments to our Constitution, trial by jury came to America early in our history. Twelve ordinary citizens are expected to set aside personal prejudices, listen to the evidence and, together, render a verdict. They don't have to know the law. Their education and experiences should not affect their judgment of the accused.

I look at the jurors, willing them to see through the subterfuge, to pick up on discrepancies in testimonies based on faded memories and embellished recall. Trying to separate the wheat from the chaff.

Earlier, on *voir dire*, I tried to detect jurors who might be quick to judge, prone to make a decision without considering evidence and testimonies. I remember Marjorie Simpkins, the juror I wanted to strike. I felt uncomfortable with her, as did Sally Weaver, my friend and an Atlanta attorney, who was here to support me.

But concerned that we would need the last strike later, Cook let her pass. Now she sits in the jury box, a smug smile on her face.

* * *

Silence bounces off the mahogany walls of the courtroom as tension grips the accused and the accuser, the spectator and the participant, when Tom Evans, assistant district attorney assigned to the case by District Attorney Gary Gerbitz, slowly stands.

Evans strides toward the jury, wearing confidence like a cloak. A shock of unruly hair dangles from his high forehead, and large horn-rimmed glasses guard his eyes. Oddly, the giant spectacles on the billboard in *The Great Gatsby* come to mind. Ironically, Bobby thinks of the same book. But in Bobby's mind, Evans' glasses morph into a microscope lens, examining his history, magnifying his every word and action.

Local reporters describe Evans as "a meticulous, tough, tenacious courtroom opponent."

Gerbitz told the reporters, "If I could have 20 prosecutors, I'd take 20 just like him. He meticulously prepares for each trial he is involved in and uses only relevant material."

Saying the Hoppe case will "show two contrasting courtroom styles," Gerbitz paints Evans as an only-the-facts guy and calls Leroy Phillips and Bobby Lee Cook, "more showy."

Downplaying the importance of the case, Evans tells a reporter this is not his biggest case. But, he admits, this one is "different" because it occurred more than 30 years ago and "because he's a football player."

Witnesses, dead... Memories, eroded by time... Evidence, lost... Different.

* * *

Evans approaches the jury slowly, head bent in thought. No creak from the hardwood floor, built solid many years ago.

A line from Carl Sandburg's poem, "Fog," runs through my head. Evans is walking "on little cat feet."

I think of the hundreds of lawyers who have stood here before a jury like this, professing the guilt or innocence of clients.

"Ladies and gentlemen of the jury," Evans says, pausing to gather attention like eggs from a nest. "The Court indicated our comments to you at no time during the course of this trial are to be considered as evidence."

That sounds good, but I know once words are spoken, they stick in jurors' minds like flypaper. Lawyers make comments they know will draw objections. Before the judge sustains the objection, the words leave near-visible question marks above the jurors' heads.

"Hopefully, neither party...I'm sure neither party is intentionally going to mislead you," Evans tells the jury.

Evans pauses before continuing, letting what he has said sink in. "We have charged that Mr. Hoppe, back in 1957, did, in fact, murder Donald Hudson, and we have charged that that murder was done in the first degree, that the killing was malicious, that it was intentional and it was done premeditatedly."

What Evans doesn't, or maybe can't, say is that the only charge the State *can* prosecute is first-degree murder since the statute of limitations has expired on other options, and Bobby has declined to waive his rights. The other charges—second-degree murder and voluntary manslaughter—carry significantly less prison time than first-degree (20 years to life for first-degree compared to 10-20 and 2-10 for the other two, respectively).

As Evans tells the jury Bobby killed Hudson—and that it was premeditated—I recall an intense meeting Bobby and I had with his two attorneys and Sally Weaver a few days ago. It occurred in Phillip's office, around his elongated mahogany conference table.

* * *

Shortly after taking our seats that bright June morning, I noticed Bobby Lee Cook seemed unusually quiet, almost somber, his silence spilling across the softly buffed table. Our chatter subsided, and we turned our eyes on Cook. Something was coming—good or bad, I didn't know.

Cook pushed away from the table and slowly stood, tall and commanding, his broad shoulders slightly stooped with age. Our eyes followed him as he began to pace around the table, sifting through his thoughts.

When he had made a full circuit, he stopped and placed his big hands on the chair he had just vacated, looking at us, one by one. Then he began to speak in a quiet, almost reverent tone.

A Matter of Conscience

To convict Bobby of first-degree murder, Evans must prove that Bobby planned the killing in advance and did it maliciously.

But if Bobby waived his right to other charges, the burden of proof on Evans would be less stringent. To convict Bobby of second-degree murder, Evans would *not* have to prove premeditation; he would just need to convince the jury Bobby's actions showed a lack of concern for human life.

If jurors were given that choice, a second-degree murder charge could be a middle ground, that nebulous area somewhere between first-degree murder and manslaughter. An easy way out.

Voluntary or non-negligent manslaughter is the intentional killing of a person without prior intent, Cook told us. To convict on this charge, the jury must believe Bobby acted in the heat of passion in a situation that would cause a reasonable person to lose self-control. Again, premeditation would not be a factor.

Once more, it could provide a compromise for a jury having difficulty reaching a decision.

Looking down at his client as he towered over the table, Cook saw what I saw in Bobby—a man who would not survive a year in jail.

But as insightful as he was, Cook didn't know something I knew: In one of his coat pockets, Bobby carried a set of earplugs. Should the worst happen, he wanted to shut out the clanging of cell doors, the rowdy banter of prisoners, the rough commands of guards.

In his other coat pocket Bobby had a laminated card on which I had penned scripture verses to help him through the nightmare of waiting for the trial to begin. Now it would help sustain him through the trauma of the trial. And, if he were convicted, the card would go with him to prison. He kept it close always, touching it when stress became overwhelming.

But Bobby simply cannot go to prison, I thought, giving my head a slight shake. I glanced back up at Cook. Looking from one of us to the other around the table, Cook said, "An attorney's job is to lay out the options and let the defendant choose for himself. But in this case, I'm going to do something I've never done before."

Tears standing in his eyes, Cook spoke directly to Bobby, although with his long, lean arms outstretched, he drew us all in.

"Bobby, you cannot give the jury a choice. Don't let them have a chance to compromise on a lesser charge," he said with heartfelt passion. "Force the jurors to make the hard decision."

Cook paused, riding the crest of emotion washing over the room.

* * *

As Bobby's trial proceeded, I came to appreciate Cook's uncanny ability to read people. Whether he's talking to his client or picking jurors, Cook uses his intuition to play an audience like a master violinist with a Stradivarius.

In the March 2009 *American Bar Association Journal*, Mark Curriden wrote about another case in which Cook "used his extraordinary ability to relate to jurors...in defending C.H. Butcher Jr. of Knoxville in what was then one of the largest federal banking-fraud cases in history."

During jury selection, several attorneys advised Cook to use a peremptory strike to remove an 81-year-old woman. "They thought she was too damn old and would fall asleep during the highly complicated financial testimony."

He thanked them for their advice. Then over the top of his half-moon glasses, Cook studied the elderly woman for a moment or two. After offering her a slow smile, he turned to tell the judge he accepted her as a juror.

Later asked why he didn't listen to the other attorneys, Cook laughed. "I never use jury experts because I think they are full of shit. Picking a jury is about common sense and something down deep in your gut. It's not about science."

At the end of the six-week trial, the jury acquitted the defendant on all counts. After the jury was dismissed, the 81-year-old woman caught Cook as he was leaving the courtroom. Smiling up at him, she whispered, "I was with you from the beginning, Bobby Lee."

* * *

The sky outside the large windows shimmered with sunlight—in stark contrast to the dark mood within Leroy's office moments ago. As the imminence of Bobby's trial hovered over us, we turned our faces up to Cook as he spoke, his words like rain on parched earth.

When the lanky lawyer took his seat, everyone around the table—Phillips, Sally Weaver, Bobby, and me—dabbed away tears.

A Matter of Conscience

The magnitude of the decision overwhelmed us. Bobby's choice would no doubt affect the jurors' deliberations and thus their verdict.

Bobby had never shied away from taking chances—on the football field or, in a more modest way, in a casino. But this was not a game of chance—with nothing more at risk than an attempted TD or quarters in a slot machine. This was a game of life—and the result could be prison.

Bobby understood the odds. He comprehended why Cook thought he should not waive the statute of limitations on lesser charges. It was a gamble. It could mean 20 years or more in prison instead of two. When given two paths from which to choose, like Robert Frost says in his poem "The Road Not Taken," Bobby took the one less traveled by. He wouldn't waive his rights. He would not give Evans the opportunity to prove a lesser charge. No compromise for the jury.

The jury would have to convict him of first-degree murder or find him innocent.

The Rubicon has been crossed.

* * *

Not knowing what Bobby's defense will be, Evans must convince the jury Bobby thought about killing Hudson, planned to do it, and followed through, not just willingly but intentionally.

As Bobby listens to Evans say he committed murder, he visibly flinches. The words have sharp corners; they're unforgiving. For 31 years he's tried to forgive himself.

"Nothing Evans can say will make me feel worse than I already do," Bobby thinks, but hearing the words aloud cuts to the quick. For decades, Bobby's breach of his own moral code has left him wounded. This public humiliation only compounds the sickness of his spirit.

Mulling Evans' words of condemnation, Bobby knows he faced the truth about himself long ago. For him, just to exist is to be broken.

But hearing Evans call him a murderer—so much worse than being called a killer—is like being in Flannery O'Connor's allegory, *The Revelation*: When Mary Grace calls Mrs. Turpin a wart hog and tells her to "go to hell," Mrs. Turpin is perplexed. How can she be both a hog and herself? How can she be from hell and also be saved?

In O'Connor's worldview, such extremes are entirely consistent. O'Connor's story is one of redemption, where salvation is possible even though a person may wallow in a pigpen.

Bobby identifies with this story, the tale of a pauper, begging for justice and grace. Ultimately, that is all that is needed. After human virtues burn away, what remains is grace.

The State theorizes Bobby killed Teddy Donald Hudson, an acknowledged moonshine-runner, because Hudson had physically and mentally abused Bobby's sister, Joan.

To Bobby's embarrassment, the torrid affair had been the talk of the town. The couple seemed to hate each other as much as they desired each other. Couldn't live together and couldn't stay apart. And like gasoline tossed on fire, almost without exception, there was an explosion.

Evans pre-empts the defense by admitting "on occasion" Hudson mistreated Joan. And he reminds the Court that Don and Joan's relationship "was looked upon with a great deal more disdain [in 1957] than it would be today." A motive for murder, he declares decisively.

Like a violin virtuoso, Evans plays Bobby's illustrious sports career at Central High and at Auburn and, in a swelling crescendo, says Bobby killed Hudson "because this sports hero, well thought of in the community, had a problem in his family he did not like. He did not like the relationship between Donald Hudson, who [ran] moonshine, and his sister, Joan Hoppe Voiles, who was married to another man."

Evans lets that settle in, then adds, "Ladies and gentlemen, we will show you, beyond a reasonable doubt—where it rests easy in your mind—that at approximately one o'clock in the morning on July 21, 1957, Mr. Hoppe shot Donald Hudson with a shotgun while driving [or] riding alongside him in a car.

"Mr. Hudson was in a car. Mr. Hoppe was in a car. We don't know who else was in a car with Hoppe."

Evans puts credibility on the testimony of his one "eye-witness," Tommy Smith, a high school student at the time of the incident. And he has confidence in Dr. Joseph Godwin, a witness whom he says was "incidentally" a preacher.

Bobby rolls his shoulders forward to relieve the stress, remembering Godwin's words at the preliminary hearing.

Thirty-one years ago, in spiritual agony, Bobby had turned to this minister. Now, in 1988, the preacher fires words wildly, rarely hitting Bobby's tortured utterances long ago in an Auburn dorm room.

Then, with a bit of hesitancy, Evans turns to Odene Neal, who didn't come forward in 1957, who didn't know anything about the case the first two times detectives interviewed her in 1987 and 1988 and then belatedly remembered Bobby threatened to kill Hudson.

Evans tells the jury Mrs. Neal now remembers a night, 31 years ago, better than she recalls what she told police investigators only months ago.

Bobby looks at the jury, hoping to see they realize how ridiculous this is. He sees nothing.

But the bailiff, Larry Kelley, who has stood by countless juries over the years, was present at the hearing and realizes a fiasco is unfolding. His expression says it all.

Evans ends his opening statement with a new take on the passing of time. "I would ask you, in considering the lapse of time that has been referred to, it is part of the State's theory there was one individual who had the key, the key, ladies and gentlemen, to end that lapse of time, day after day after day, and did not choose to use that key."

Confident in his opening presentation, Evans taps the rail of the jury box lightly for emphasis, before yielding the floor to the defense.

* * *

Bobby Lee Cook hails from Summerville, Ga., a small sleepy town about an hour south of Chattanooga. Today, dressed in a charcoal-gray suit carefully tailored just for him, the gangly attorney strides toward the jury.

Like a kindly old southern gentleman, he looks over the top of his gold half-moon spectacles, offering a slight "I'm one-of-you" smile to the jury as he slowly rubs his white goatee. He looks toward the well-worn floor, appearing momentarily lost in thought.

But Cook's appearance can be deceptive. The "everyman" façade hides an eloquent orator who can woo juries like a sweet lover and hold them, breathless, in the palm of his hand.

The kind smile and the sun-weathered face mask a hard-nosed interrogator who can be merciless toward lying witnesses. Describing Cook in the June 22, 1988, *Chattanooga News-Free Press*, the writer says, "He will often hem a witness in, citing inconsistencies in testimony or in sworn statements made on prior occasions, and then pounce with a thundering, *were you lying then, or are you lying now?*"

In his March 2009 *American Bar Association Journal* article, Curriden told of a 1975 case in which Cook represented seven men accused of killing Atlanta pathologists Drs. Warren and Rosina Matthews. Years after Georgia courts had refused to take another look at the case, Cook had one more chance to question Deborah Kidd, the case's key witness—"Hell, the only witness," Cook says.

Kidd, who earlier testified she was with the seven defendants when they killed the victims, had received total immunity for her testimony. At first, Kidd stuck to the same story she had told at trial. Then, slowly but surely, Cook took her testimony apart.

Curriden wrote, "Finally, Cook presented evidence that Kidd and the lead detective had been sleeping together during the trial. Overwhelmed, Kidd broke down and confessed to Cook and the federal judge that she and the police had framed the seven defendants."

The convictions were thrown out, and later, prosecutors admitted the seven were innocent. Discussing the case in the March 2009 *ABA Journal*, Cook declared, "If you can railroad a bad man to prison, you can railroad a good man."

So Bobby and I did not pick Cook's name from the phone book. By the time we needed him, he had a well-earned reputation for defending both moral and immoral clients. On his roster were clients like Nicaraguan strongman Anastasio Somoza, later overthrown by the Sandinistas, and South Korean businessman Tongsun Park, charged with 36 counts of bribing Congress.

Bobby Lee Cook was not new to the dance. Tales of his courtroom antics had become part of Southern folklore. Cook's courtroom style and exploits inspired the hit television show, "Matlock," popular during the late 1980s and 1990s. But, as Robin McDonald noted in *Secrets Never Die*, Cook is "far more shrewd, far more cosmopolitan, and far more eccentric than Griffin's rumpled character." Fine wines, elegant gardens, and old books comprise part of his world, although he says he's just a country lawyer.

Cook has been called a lawyer's lawyer. In a June 1991 magazine article, Atlanta author Tom Chaffin quoted Alan Dershowitz, the Harvard Law School attorney who won the acquittal of Claus von Bulow in his wife's murder, as saying, "If I'm ever in a mess and in front of a jury, I'd like [Bobby Lee Cook] pleading my case."

It's reported he wins at least 90 percent of his cases, so he's not accustomed to losing.

A Matter of Conscience

In his early days as a lawyer in Summerville, he defended many bootleggers and moonshiners. And he never underestimated them or their wisdom. In fact, he's smart enough to know, when talking with mountain folk, sometimes the less said, the better. In the March 2009 *American Bar Association Journal*, Curriden began his article with a tale that proves the point.

It was 1949, and in one of his first murder trials, Cook was defending a man who had killed another man for calling him a "goddamn son of a bitch."

After admitting in opening statements that it was wrong to call someone such a bad name, the prosecutor told the jury it didn't give the defendant a right to take another's life.

After the prosecutor took his seat, Cook walked to the witness box. Looking at the jurors, he said quietly, "I have a question for you. What would you have done if someone had called you a goddamn son of a bitch?"

From the back row, an older mountain man with a long gray beard, replied, loud enough for everyone to hear, "I would have killed the son of a bitch."

Smiling, Cook told Curriden, "I had an entire opening statement planned. But I just looked at the man, looked at the jurors, nodded, walked back to my chair and sat down."

The next day, the jury acquitted his client.

Today as Bobby's trial begins, Cook assesses the jury with the same keen insight he showed in 1949. Leaning forward—his gnarled hands resting lightly on the wooden rail cordoning the jury—he studies the men and women in front of him, like a preacher surveying his flock. Then he speaks in a slow Southern drawl, his words like sweet molasses dripping from his lips. His voice is easy on the ear, almost melodic, sometimes hypnotic, as he reminds the jury the events surrounding the trial occurred 31 years ago. Way back then, he says, he was just a young, country lawyer.

The message is clear—the intervening years have been long enough to transform a youthful whippersnapper into a white-haired, semi-stooped man who, outside of court, often puffs on a hand-carved, Sherlock Holmes-type pipe. He himself is proof of the ravages of time.

The Trial Begins

"The evidence will disclose in this case that many of the principal actors, that many of the witnesses, are either dead, gravely ill or their whereabouts unknown," he confides to the jury.

"In 1957—and some of us remember it very well—World War II had only ended a short while and the Korean conflict, a short time after that. In 1957 America was pretty well still in our age of innocence. We had not seen the drug problem ravage our society. We had not yet heard of the onset of AIDS, and Vietnam was not even in our vocabulary."

Every white-haired person in the room nods, transported back in time. Yes, many remember 1957. And all have been altered, even warped by time.

"In that summer Bobby Hoppe had just completed his junior year at Auburn University," Cook says, like a proud father. "He was attending that university on a scholarship—the first of his family to be able to attend college."

Cook pauses, his voice softening. "The evidence will show that my brother Mr. Evans referred to him as a hero. Bobby Hoppe has never thought of himself as a hero."

Motioning toward Bobby, Cook says, "The evidence will show in this case that then, as now, he was a shy, kind, humanistic, gentle, understanding young man and also, as he developed into manhood, has remained the same."

Beginning in low tones that rise in a crescendo, Cook says Bobby was born "to a hard-working, God-fearing, decent American family, which constitutes the backbone of this country."

Truth be told, Bobby did not have an idyllic American family. It was decent, not perfect.

Cook lays it out—a father crippled during World War II, a mother left with supporting the family, sisters who doted on Bobby as the only boy and the baby of the family. And Cook admits, for a time, one sister lost her heart, soul—and Bobby would say, her mind—to a violent bootlegger, an infatuation that triggered a lifetime of heartache for the family.

"I would be dishonest and less than candid, as I look at you in this jury box, if I told you Bobby Hoppe or his mother or his crippled father or the other daughters approved of the arrangement," Cook acknowledges.

40

"[They] looked upon it, as Mr. Evans has said, with disdain and disfavor because they, as all of us—hopefully, all of us—would hope for something better for our own blood and muscle."

Cook wants the jury to understand: The Joan-Don dalliance was one more burden on a family already laden with problems in the years following the war that altered the life, not only of the father, but also the mother, the brother, the sisters.

Cook's words take Bobby back to the times he talked with his mother and his sister Martha about Joan's infatuation with Hudson. How mortified they all were to witness Joan cavorting with a whisky runner. How embarrassing for his friends to know. With a slight shake of his head, he recalls his relief when his mother told him Joan had broken up with Hudson.

* * *

Life was hard back then, moving from one rented home to the next...never enough money.

Out of that bleak background came a boy whose status at Central and Auburn made him popular with the girls, even girls whose family trees sprouted generations of blue-blooded gentry. As a football star, Bobby was invited to their parties—but he never felt accepted by the families, most of whom he felt looked on him as they did a prize Tennessee walking horse.

So when he came home from Auburn for a weekend in July 1957, Bobby turned to Barbara Jo Campbell. He had grown up with her in North Chattanooga. With her, he could relax.

Beautiful, demure, and totally taken with Bobby, Barbara Jo was Bobby's date the night Don Hudson was killed.

By the 1988 trial, the once beautiful girl is a woman ravaged by cancer. But her mind is unaffected, Cooks tells the jury. She will say she recalls that night with complete clarity. What she remembers is that nothing about Bobby was out of the ordinary.

Methodically, Cook lays out the entire evening, leading the jury from the time Bobby takes Barbara Jo home, around midnight, before turning his car down Bell Avenue.

Cook talks about the short, tense moments—which, to Bobby, seemed an eternity—until Bobby pulls into his own driveway, less than an hour later—not knowing what happened after he watched in his rearview mirror as Don's car careened into a tree.

Still scared Don will come after him.

* * *

I sit transfixed. Surprised and perplexed. Cook is putting every detail of that night in vivid motion. Now the jurors—and the prosecution—know everything. Almost.

...two cars slowly moving side-by-side down Bell Avenue, one with its lights out...a shotgun blast rings in the night...a panicked Bobby flees, his heart in his throat...nowhere to retreat...no place to go....

I thought Bobby's confession would come from his lips, not Cook's. But Cook knows how to tune his fiddle in front of the 12 jurors. He wrote the score, and he's playing with a rhythm unknown to me.

I breathe deeply and relax a bit, glancing sideways at Evans. Everyone at the prosecution's table is leaning forward, alert, stunned. Despite his embarrassment, Bobby feels relief spill over him like a gentle spring rain, washing him clean. His secret has been laid open. Hearing Cook say he shot Hudson was sickening, but the catharsis, for the moment, is worth the shame.

Bobby knows tomorrow's headlines will be bad, but they won't be devastating. The horror for him has lasted 31 years. For the moment, the truth has set him free. Burdened so long by guilt and fear, Bobby briefly feels unshackled. Unlike Quasimodo, the hunchback of Notre Dame, he no longer has to hide that which is ugly and repulsive in him.

The self-defense plea has taken the prosecution by complete surprise. At least I knew it was coming, even if I didn't know when. The prosecutors had expected Bobby to deny killing Hudson. The State's whole case has been turned upside down.

Cook moves from the shotgun blast to Bobby's return to Auburn the following Monday.

He lays out the many variations key State witnesses will put forth in testimonies. In measured staccato, he taps out the legal travesties of the last 31 years:

...a coroner's inquest from which Bobby's attorney was excluded.

...a missing transcript of that inquest.

...a detective who carted case files to Florida when he retired.

A Matter of Conscience

...a grand jury that heard the State's key witness in 1966 but failed to return an indictment.

...a grand jury's records of those proceedings mysteriously missing.

Thirty-one years. A long time. Cook tells the jury, "This is a tragedy that needs to be put to sleep."

Chattanooga News-Free Press photo

Sherry and Bobby Hoppe being escorted into the courtroom by an
unidentified deputy at the beginning of Hoppe's 1988 trial

CHAPTER FIVE

The First Witnesses

Truth is more of a stranger than fiction.
–Mark Twain

"The State will call its first witness."

Hudson's own flesh and blood.

A somber reality hits Bobby as Roy Hudson, Don's 83-year-old father, rises with difficulty from the hard wooden bench and walks haltingly toward the witness box.

Although stooped and life weary, Hudson seems proud. Proud that after 31 years, the man he believes killed his son is being tried. Thinking he knew all those years, but never sure.

Bobby watches him closely, then lowers his gaze, letting it rest on the table in front of him. His struggle to forgive himself reaches new depths with the appearance of the elderly father still grieving for his son after all these years.

Roy Hudson's 83 years haven't been easy. He has struggled to make a decent living for his seven children. Putting food on the table and clothes on their backs didn't give him much time to keep up with what they were doing.

Like any parent, he wanted to believe the best about his kids. Still does.

Catching a collective breath as the family patriarch stumbles and then steadies himself, the Hudson family sits silently on one row, just across from where I'm wedged between my sisters. Bobby's sister Doris and several of her children sit beside us.

Two families inexorably linked by one tragedy. None of us were there that night. None of us took part in the sad event that shadows our lives more than three decades later. But here we all are, in the same room, watching the same scene unfold.

I don't blame the Hudsons. I would have been relentless in pursuing anyone who killed a member of my family.

If my own emotional bank weren't depleted from worrying about Bobby, I would feel for their loss. I might even try to believe that, had he

45

lived, their son could have turned his life around. But I can't think about that right now.

Even so, they did lose a child. A loss Bobby knows is not diminished by their son's dubious activities. Theirs has been a long bereavement made longer by unanswered questions. Such thoughts make Bobby drop his head lower.

His stoic face can't mask his pain. The shell cradling his emotions is paper-thin, ready to rupture at any provocation.

* * *

Evans starts slowly, working up to asking old man Hudson about his son's relationship with Joan Hoppe Voiles. For a time, Hudson and his wife believed Joan and Don were married.

Hudson tells Evans it was Joan who told him they were husband and wife, but later he found out they just lived together, "somewhere in the neighborhood of five years." His family disapproved. And they didn't appreciate being lied to by Joan. They knew right from wrong.

So they were glad when Joan and Don called it quits, about 30 days before he was killed, Hudson thinks, but he's not sure. Thirty-one years is a long time.

"Did your son run moonshine whisky?"

"He was accused of it, but personally I never did see him do it."

* * *

Roy Hudson doesn't say it, but running moonshine was the big thing back in the '50s.

In 1988, John Taylor, head of homicide, told a reporter, "This is kind of the Bible Belt—we got churches on every corner—but people drink liquor, too.

"To some young men [back] then, this was an exciting life, driving a whisky car. An adventure. Somebody who transported liquor and drove a hot car was a hero to some people."

Maybe that's why, in 1957, Hudson's parents weren't concerned about his activities. Why, some folks even looked up to their son. And, if he got arrested occasionally, it was no big deal.

"He had some run-ins with [the police]," his mother said in an interview after the indictment. "He'd go racing a lot. He was good at it."

A Matter of Conscience

* * *

"Now, July 19, 1957—did you see your son on that day?"

"Yes, sir, if it's the day before Don got killed—on late in the evening between 3 o'clock and 5, somewhere in the neighborhood of that time. I sat and talked to Don.

"He said, 'Daddy, I got to go down to the filling station. A guy owes me some money and I want to collect it. I'm broke.'" He repeats his son's words without emotion. It's been a long time.

Witnesses told police Don "collected some money from a bootlegger that night," before returning the car he borrowed to avoid driving his own easily recognized DeSoto.

When Evans yields Hudson for cross-examination, Leroy Phillips is respectful, mindful of his age. If he is too rough on the old man, jurors may not like it.

Gently, Phillips nudges Hudson to face his son's clashes with the law.

"Sir, you stated you never saw Don run whisky. You know he went to the penitentiary for it, don't you, sir?"

Glaring at Phillips with age-shadowed eyes, Hudson asserts, "He didn't go to the penitentiary. He went to a correction home in St. Peters, Va.—St. Petersburg."

Just a few run-ins with the law, nothing to be concerned about.

Phillips lets the old man go. No point belaboring his son's brushes with the law. No point in stoning the father for the sins of his son. Let him believe the best about Don. That's all he has.

Everyone in the room breathes a sigh of relief when Phillips lets Hudson step down.

The State calls its next witness: John D. Stargel, Jr., a retired detective from the Chattanooga Police Department.

Back in 1957, the city of Chattanooga had only two detectives in its homicide division, Stargel and Bobby Cornish. Neither had much investigative experience. Stargel had been in homicide only a year or so and Cornish, less than six months. Neither had specific training in investigating homicides.

"What training we got was on the job," Stargel remembers.

So when the dispatcher called for a detective in the wee hours of July 21, 1957, telling him to go to Erlanger Hospital because a man had been shot, that's what Stargel did, without going to the scene of the shooting. He also didn't contact the policemen who responded to Signal 13—a wreck—and he didn't order them to preserve the crime scene. When he finally got to the scene of the shooting after a wasted trip to the hospital, Stargel learned a wrecker had removed the car.

And people were milling around everywhere. Walking, unimpeded, all over the crime scene.

It was around 2 a.m. before Stargel had someone take pictures of the scene, while he began to look for witnesses. He found one—Tommy Smith, a 17-year-old who had been sitting in his car with his girlfriend, a couple of blocks away.

A few days ago at the preliminary hearing, Stargel had read notes from his interview with Agnes Rivers, a woman who swore she heard two shots that night, but he fails to mention this at the trial. Twenty years later, I will recall Rivers saying she had heard not one but two shots—the importance magnified by a recent discovery.

The morning after the accident Stargel made it to Cain's Garage, where the car had been towed.

The only evidence he found in the car was "one little shotgun pellet." Don's personal effects, anything of evidentiary value, had been removed. Removed by someone unknown. And Stargel says he never recovered a weapon in the course of his investigation.

He did hear about a gun, one that a Riverview pharmacist, William McCutcheon, traded for a pistol. Traded with Bobby Hoppe on the 20th of July.

He recalls this from McCutcheon's testimony at the coroner's inquest in 1957. He also recalls McCutcheon saying Bobby test fired the shotgun at a chert pit on the day of the trade.

But no one ever told him Hudson was seen with a gun on the day he was killed.

* * *

Evans walks back to the prosecution table and takes a seat.

A palpable silence falls over the courtroom as Bobby Lee Cook steps in front of Stargel and stares at him for several uncomfortable seconds. Then under Cook's quick fire, Stargel admits he deviated from standard practice in dealing with witnesses, failing to take signed statements from any of them.

"I never had any report about what was found at the scene," Stargel says confidently in response to another question from Cook.

Unconvinced, Cook swings again. "Who looked into the automobile at the scene and made an inventory of the effects that might have been found there, including any weapon?"

Stargel tries to dodge the blow, repeating, "I don't have any record of any weapon at all at the scene."

Cook presses, wanting to know if Stargel has any record—or has ever seen one—as to what was found in the automobile at the scene.

"No record. I don't have any record," Stargel responds, repressing his irritation.

Behind me, I hear murmurs, but I'm focusing on the squirming detective.

Leaning forward, Cook hits harder. The more he rams Stargel, the more ridiculous the detective's answers seem. Bailiff Kelley cuts his eyes toward the jurors, assessing their reaction to Stargel's answers.

"Did you ever try to find an inventory of what was found in the automobile?" Cook prods.

"Inventory would have been given to me if it had been found."

"Well, where is the inventory?" Cook presses.

Now openly belligerent, Stargel replies, "Well, there wasn't nothing found."

Matching Stargel's tone, Cook goads him. "How do you know that?"

With clenched teeth, Stargel hisses, "I would have an inventory."

Round One ends. Cook has cornered Stargel, forcing him to admit his investigation was incomplete. Cook pounces again as Round Two begins, asking Stargel if the file he described—the one entered as evidence—was the complete file.

"I'd have to go through it, but I would say this is all of my file."

The lanky attorney looms over the increasingly agitated detective. "Do you remember telling this Court under oath on the 13th of June 1988, that part of this file was missing?"

Paling, Stargel replies, "I think it was a few sheets missing. It's been 31 years."

Cook replies with a slight smile, "I understand."

The reprieve is brief. Under pressure again, Stargel divulges he has "some idea" of what's missing. Stargel clears his throat, looking beseechingly at Cook before saying he interviewed some witnesses for whom he doesn't have notes. At the preliminary hearing, Stargel testified he had even talked with Bobby Hoppe—at the county coroner's office— but he has no record of the discussion and can't remember if Bobby's attorney was present.

Stargel, halfway serious, says his memory is so bad, he couldn't even say if Cook was at Currey's office that day.

Undaunted, Cook asks Stargel if he knows of anything else important that's missing.

"I couldn't—like I said, 31 years is a long time."

Without cracking a smile, Cook repeats himself: "I understand."

Now Stargel is flustered, almost stuttering. "I'm 66 years old, and they could be other things missing but I couldn't say what they are."

"You and I are hitting along on about the same..." Cook starts.

"We [are] probably close to the same age," Stargel interrupts, eager to agree.

Flashing a disarming smile, Cook asks, "It makes a lot of difference, doesn't it?"

"It does—it seems like it does to me," Stargel responds wearily.

"Does to me, too," Cook admits, turning toward the jury to see if they get the point. It's been a long, long time.

Changing course, Cook asks what happened to the Hudson case file after Stargel retired.

"I took it with me."

Incredulity raising his voice a full octave, Cook says, "Even though it belonged to the City of Chattanooga and was an official record, you took it with you?"

Almost proudly, Stargel says, "That's correct."

"Isn't that sort of strange?"

"Not to me," Stargel replies.

A wry smile tugging at his lips, Cook prompts, "Well, I guess you took it down to Florida to work on when you retired there."

On the back row, juror Timothy Teeters grins slightly. Other jurors seem to be enjoying the show. Yet Stargel has no clue he's become the jester in a Shakespearean-like tragedy.

Even DiRisio has come to life, his head jerking up from a paper he was studying on his desk. He looks at Stargel with disbelief.

Oblivious to everyone's amazement, Stargel proudly tells Cook he took the file everywhere he went. "I was in Florida. I lived on Sand Mountain. I lived in Trenton. I lived on the lake—and it was wherever I was."

A ripple of laughter trills across the courtroom, and two jurors on the front row laugh aloud. DiRisio pounds his gavel, but the corners of his mustache twitch as he suppresses a smile.

"You took the file—the official file—with you?" Cook asks.

Turning so the jury can see his shock, Cook adds, "Did you take any more files with you?"

"A few more."

Stargel admits it didn't turn out to be 200 like he had said at the preliminary hearing.

Listening to the former police officer reverse his testimony, Cook asks in a scathing tone exactly how many files Stargel took with him.

Cornered, Stargel begins a tally. "Four murder cases, two rape cases, about 20 burglary cases, 15 armed robbery cases, two or three suicides. I guess a grand total of 50 cases. Total."

Already impeached, Stargel is determined he won't back down, so he comes out swinging. In a supercilious tone he declares, "I think [taking the files] was the right thing to do."

"Think it was the right thing to do? And you still think so?"

"Yes, sir, I sure do. I sure do," Stargel states emphatically.

Cook shakes his head, and the bell sounds on Round Two.

Round Three begins. Cook wants Stargel to admit he told Detective Richard Heck on March 25, 1988, that Former Police Chief Pete Davis might know the location of the original murder file, but Stargel doesn't recall whether he told Heck or not.

Without another word, Cook shows Stargel the transcript of his conversation with Heck.

Lifting his eyes from the transcript, Stargel says, "If that's what the statement says, I did."

"Would that have been a true statement or a false statement?" Cook prods.

"It's hard to say, you know, when you are on the telephone and your statements are put in a warehouse for you," Stargel responds, his personal pride at risk.

Cook strides back to the defense table and then turns to look at Stargel, "Is it harder to tell the truth on the telephone than it is off the telephone?"

"It's hard sometimes—sometimes it's hard to tell the truth either place," Stargel demurs.

Bluntly, Cook asks Stargel if he has difficulty telling the truth.

"I never have. Not too much. I told the truth most of the time."

"Most of the time?" Cook asks as he casts a knowing smile at the jury.

"I think so."

Close to a knockout in Round Three.

Following a bench conference in which DiRisio hears Evans' objection to the upcoming round of questions, Cook continues to attack Stargel's credibility.

Leading Stargel to acknowledge the honesty of Ed Davis, a former attorney general in Chattanooga, Cook asks if Stargel remembers telling Heck that Ed Davis and the Hoppe family were friends, and that's why the case was never brought to court.

Shaking his head, Stargel doesn't know whether he told Heck that. After a pause, he adds he's sure he had heard Davis at one time was a lawyer for the Hoppes.

Then uncertainty returns. "I said I can't remember. I can't remember it. I don't say I didn't say it, but I can't recall it."

Stargel shifts in the hard chair before adding. "When he called me on the telephone, me and him discussed this case—stuff I didn't realize was going to be brought out in court. To me—at that time, I didn't think the conversation on the telephone was very important," Stargel says.

Before he leaves the stand, Stargel reluctantly testifies he never interviewed anyone, except Tommy Smith, who went to Hudson's car before the police arrived.

With anger bubbling below the surface, Stargel admits he made no effort to find out where Don Hudson had been that night or who might have been the last person to see him.

He did not visit any of Hudson's haunts to learn if anyone saw Hudson prior to the shooting, to find out if Hudson had a gun or what kind of mood he was in that night.

Cook reminds Stargel that when he was asked at the evidentiary hearing whether anyone could have removed a gun from Hudson's car before the police arrived, Stargel had responded, "Absolutely, absolutely, because it was some 30 minutes before it changed from a wreck to a homicide. It could have been simple to do."

Behind me, the courtroom buzzes.

The fight is over. Stargel is dismissed, and DiRisio calls for a recess.

As we step into the hall, Bobby and I talk about the former detective's testimony, shaking our heads. The State can't *disprove* Hudson had a gun when he wrecked. There's no record of what was found at the scene; and, before the police arrived, the place was overrun with onlookers. Surely, the jury will see Hudson *could* have had a gun.

I nod, hoping we're reading the jurors correctly, but I'm concerned about Marjorie Simpkins. Regardless of what's said on the stand, she just sits there with that smug smile on her face.

I'm beginning to wonder if Bobby's trial ultimately "rests on contrasts of light and darkness" similar to those painted so well in "Big Two-Hearted River."

Like Hemingway's descriptions of the two stretches of river— "one, where all is bright, clear sunlight and pellucid water and the swamp into which it flows"—today's testimonies seem sometimes to point toward moments of light before descending into a dark, unfathomable bog.

CHAPTER SIX

The Indictment: Coming to Terms with Reality

When it is dark enough, you see the stars.
–Charles Beard

The media throng outside the courthouse converges on us as we make our way to Phillips' office for a lunch break. Bud Yarnell, Phillips' no-nonsense investigator, carves a path with his bulky body, blocking reporters and camera crews. Close on his heels, Leroy, Bobby Lee Cook, and Sally Weaver clip along together, heads bent in thought.

Behind the trio, Bobby and I walk silently. Words must wait until we're safely ensconced behind the massive doors of Phillips' office.

Thankfully, the building comes in sight, its sidewalk lined with flowering crabapple trees, an oasis from the relentless sun.

Seeing the bright blooms, I recall the first time Bobby and I came here—a cold, dreary day four months ago. The crushing fear we felt then hasn't diminished. It's intensified.

I cannot recollect how Bobby chose Leroy to defend him. Bobby had several Chattanooga friends who were judges, so he may have asked one of them for advice when rumors of an indictment started to swirl. Or maybe Bobby just knew of Phillips' excellent reputation.

Anyway, amid whispers the Hudson case had been reopened, we made an appointment to meet with Phillips, knowing we had to be prepared for the worst. We arrived at his second-floor office early, anxious to talk with him, yet hesitant to start a process that might shift our fears from the unbelievable into reality. Wordlessly, we waited to learn what we faced. Within moments, Phillips strode into the room, exuding the confidence we needed to see. Extending his hand, he motioned us inside.

Leroy Phillips, though not tall, is a commanding presence. We were aware he clawed his way to the top of Chattanooga's legal community—no easy climb for a boy from his blue-collar background.

The son of a mechanic, Phillips worked his way through college and law school, flipping burgers at Krystal and standing over pits of molten metal at American Lava and Siskin Steel. Steam from the grill and heat from the furnace toughened him to a flinty hardness that intimidates witnesses who dare try to shimmy around his piercing questions.

Like Bobby, Phillips grew up on the streets, convincing bullies he could defend himself. Truth be told, he can be a bully himself, never shying away from hitting hard to get at the truth.

Described in a 1988 newspaper article as "one of Chattanooga's most celebrated and successful defense attorneys," the silver-haired Phillips once won acquittal for Marshall Thrash on charges that the Ku Klux Klansman shot three black women in downtown Chattanooga.

In nearby Dunlap, Tenn., Phillips won acquittal for a client accused of killing two people. In Dayton, the site of the famous monkey trial, he obtained a verdict of voluntary manslaughter for a man accused of first-degree murder.

Leroy Phillips was experienced. He was tough. He won difficult cases. Exactly what Bobby needed if an indictment were handed down.

Phillips listened intently as Bobby told the story—first, his fear of an indictment; then, the unvarnished account of what happened in the early morning hours of July 21, 1957.

Phillips registered absolutely no surprise. After all, he was around when the shooting occurred. Along with other Chattanoogans, he probably suspected who had killed Hudson.

* * *

Immediately after our first official visit with Phillips, Bobby's new attorney telephoned the district attorney's office, confirming an investigation was ongoing. But he assured us, should an indictment be handed down, the DA had agreed to allow Bobby to turn himself in.

Even though the thought of arrest triggered anxiety for Bobby, if the worst were to happen, he was relieved he wouldn't be arrested at home or at work. But it was an agreement that would not be honored. Beginning with Bobby's arrest and continuing throughout the trial, reporters, photographers, and TV crews dogged our every step. They seemed to know what was happening before we did. While we believed the detectives and the DA's office were driven by the prospect of solving a three-decades-old killing, it was easier to understand the media coordination when we learned Heck once worked in the Chattanooga police department's public information office.

The Indictment: Coming to Terms with Reality

After confirmation of the investigation, weeks passed with excruciating slowness. By sheer will, Bobby went to work at Chattanooga State each day, despite his anxiety. Somehow he went through the regular routines, meeting with people, attending athletic events, trying to remain himself with staff members. But the possibility of an indictment never receded into his subconscious. It swam just below the surface, constantly bobbing up unbidden.

In Nashville, where I was serving as interim president of Nashville State Technical Institute, I, too, went through the motions—burying my unrest in the routine of running a state college.

Ours was a life of total pretense. Fearing the impending gale, we told no one what was coming our way.

At night, we talked at length by phone—Bobby pouring out his fears as I tried to comfort without giving false hope. The house of cards was about to fall. Then everyone would know. No more secrets. When Bobby worried about my job, I told him I would be OK.

My attempts to allay Bobby's fears didn't work. He sank lower, the shadows thickening over his head. We made it through the weeks apart, impatient for our weekends together. Usually, I drove to Chattanooga to be with him. Safe in our home, we held tight to each other, knowing a conviction would forever end the sweet press of our bodies, the wonder of waking up side by side in the morning. Sometimes, when Bobby could no longer stand being alone, he joined me in Nashville. In the complex of the Bellevue condo where I was living during my interim presidency, we walked for miles, talked for hours. Trying to prepare for the inevitable. We hoped for a miracle but felt we were on a runaway train we were helpless to stop.

And then it happened.

Bobby had left work for lunch when, more than a hundred miles away in Nashville, I got a surreptitious call from a sympathetic police captain, saying officers were on their way to arrest Bobby at Chattanooga State, where he was director of athletics.

The DA's commitment to let him turn himself in had been broken. A public arrest would make a juicier news clip than Bobby's walking into the Justice Center to hand himself over.

Despite a walnut-sized knot in my throat, I telephoned a former Chattanooga State colleague, who knew nothing about the investigation and asked for help. It was tough. To tell a friend my husband—and her colleague—was about to be arrested for murder.

But I could not have asked for a more clear-headed response. Doris Evans walked to the entrance of Chattanooga State, waylaid Bobby and told him to drive directly to me in Nashville.

Alarmed but alert, Bobby knew he needed to run home to grab some clothes. Concerned the police might be waiting there, Doris drove ahead of Bobby to East Brainerd, checked the parking area, and motioned him in. Solid as a rock, she stayed until Bobby returned to his car—then followed him to Interstate 24, making sure he was well on his way before she headed back.

Bobby drove as far as Monteagle Mountain, about an hour out of Chattanooga, before he called me from a pay phone, knowing in his gut why I sent for him, praying he was wrong.

Summoning a calm I didn't know I had, I outlined what was happening. I couldn't see him, but I knew Bobby's blue eyes were clouding over, unwilling to see the certainty of apprehension. I told Bobby I'd call Phillips so he could ensure the DA kept his promise to allow Bobby to turn himself in.

With a quick "I love you," he hung up. Then, it hit me: Bobby's indictment could be on the Nashville news that very evening.

Hurriedly, I called my senior staff together at Nashville State. Struggling to keep my composure, I broke the shocking news to them. I'd only been interim president about three months, so I didn't know what to expect. But when I finished, their eyes reflected only concern. Dean Pam Munz sniffed back tears. All offered their love and support. After the indictment hit the Associated Press wire, the Nashville State community wove a soft cocoon that buffered me in the months ahead.

After meeting with my staff, I raced across town to the offices of the Tennessee Board of Regents to notify my boss, Tom Garland, chancellor of the system. With no time for a real explanation, I swallowed my pride and warned him of the embarrassment about to descend on me—and on Nashville State and the TBR.

It was the most difficult professional discussion I'd ever had. Surprisingly, Chancellor Garland didn't ask me to resign or take a leave of absence. Although I didn't know what tomorrow would bring, I was comforted in knowing I still had a job. Bobby wouldn't have to bear the guilt of my losing my position—not now, anyway. One less worry for his overburdened conscience.

I hurried back to my condo to be there when Bobby arrived. He was still on the road, so I swung into action, calling Phillips for instructions. His words chilled me to the bone. I wondered how I would ever be able to share them with Bobby.

Then, in a strained voice, I called my sisters—neither of whom had an inkling Bobby had ever been accused of murder. Somehow I poured out the horrific news. Though shocked and heartbroken, they pledged their support.

They wanted details. Not now, I told them. I simply could not go through the whole sordid saga right then. There was so much they didn't know.

Then the hardest call of all. Kevin. I had to tell our son the man he dubbed "Padre" was to be indicted for murder.

Kevin was stationed on a submarine tender off the coast of the naval base in Kings Bay, Ga. If there were a chance he wouldn't come ashore and hear about the trial, I'd have protected him from knowing. It was a risk I couldn't afford. If Kevin had to hear, it must come from me.

When Kevin answered the phone, he almost immediately perceived something was wrong. As clearly as I could, I spelled it out for him.

He insisted he was leaving as soon as he could get permission from his commanding officer. Kevin, like his Padre, is hardheaded, but I knew it was an argument I couldn't lose. Finally, I told him it would be too difficult for Bobby to have his son witness his arrest. To have him hear the allegations. To be in the courtroom if his Padre were convicted.

Kevin understood. But he felt powerless, wanting to support his Padre and Madre. To be honest, I wanted him closer. But I knew it was best for him to be far away from the cameras and microphones. Far from the scandal and shame that would shroud us in coming months.

* * *

That dreaded call behind me, I focused on what to do next. How could I help us get through this trial? Out of my muddled mind a name surfaced: Sally Weaver.

A Matter of Conscience

Why hadn't I thought of her before? I tried to call this dear friend, now a successful Atlanta attorney, but her husband said she was at a meeting in California.

When I told him why I must talk with her, he said he'd track her down, have her call me back. While waiting for her call, Bobby arrived. We fell into each other's arms sobbing, our pent-up emotions overflowing. Fear and hurt, anger and dread.

When we'd cried until there were no more tears, we talked, my hand in his. Phillips had advised us to return to Chattanooga so Bobby could turn himself in that very night. As we prepared for what would be the longest journey of our lives, the phone rang. It was Sally.

Kindred spirits from the day we met as colleagues at Chattanooga State, her office next to mine, Sally and I were as unalike as any two people could be.

Yet, for whatever reason, we took an instant liking to one another. Perhaps it was our differences that drew us together or maybe it was because we both have "strength of mind" and pure guts. In short, we're fighters—something we immediately respected in each other. Almost from the very first, our connection was rock solid.

As a counselor-in-training several years before I met Sally, I had become mesmerized with the psychotherapist Albert Ellis. After hearing him at a conference, I adopted one of his tenets: Nothing is 100 percent bad; it could always be worse.

It became the way I faced life's problems, big and small.

Ellis' philosophy had held me in good stead during difficult times, so I was quick to share it whenever anything bad happened. If someone had a flat tire, I'd say, "It could be worse; you could have wrecked and been killed." Sally heard her share of this philosophy during the year we worked together at Chattanooga State and later, as I encouraged her throughout law school.

So, when I answered her call, the first words out of her mouth were, "Damn it, Sherry, now you tell me this isn't the worst possible thing that could happen!"

From somewhere, I reached for a bit of levity. "Well, at least when I look back on this, I'll be able to say, compared to what happened then, nothing is bad anymore."

But as Pico Iver once said, "Comedy is nothing more than tragedy deferred," and flippancy faded as I turned to the task at hand: Sally's advice on attorneys. Bobby was comfortable with Leroy, but the trial ahead demanded the best legal minds we could find.

Sally was a partner in one of the largest corporate law firms in Atlanta—Powell, Goldstein, and Frazier. She knew many first-rate attorneys and said she would ask whom they would want if *they* were accused of murder. Before saying good-bye, she told me not to forget Albert Ellis.

Bobby and I began the long drive back to Chattanooga. After an hour and a half on the road, just as we topped Monteagle Mountain, a half moon riding high in the sky, it hit us. We'd never be able to outrun the desolation nipping at our heels. It was too much; we couldn't go on.

We swung the car into a rest stop at Hales Bar Dam, got out, and walked to the edge of the lake. Looking at the wide expanse of water, we stood for a while, holding hands. Then, without even thinking, I began reciting the Lord's Prayer. Bobby, his voice just a whisper, joined in.

"For Thine is the kingdom and the power and the glory forever and ever. Amen." The floodgate was open. For the next half hour, we poured out our hearts, praying for help and mercy. Not knowing what was ahead, we asked God to take control of our future.

Then we said the 23rd Psalm. A benediction. When we left, we felt less burdened.

From that day forward, whenever we traveled to and from Nashville, we never failed to pull into the rest stop at Hales Bar Dam, walk to the edge of the water, and say a prayer.

It was a trip we made often, even though Bobby—on a leave of absence from Chattanooga State—moved to Nashville to be with me to await his trial. There, though despondent, at least we were together. During the day, I had to go to work, but Bobby remained at the condo with Pepi, his sheepdog. Pepi stayed close, aware his master was deeply disturbed.

At noon each day, I escaped from work, eager to meet Bobby at the nearby Bellemeade Cafeteria. There we talked—and tried to eat a few bites, but we just picked at our food. Over the three months between the arrest and trial, Bobby lost more than 30 pounds, and I lost 15.

Nothing in our lives was stable. We were living in an apartment in Chattanooga, having sold our home after buying a small piece of land on Chickamauga Lake. We were ready to begin construction of our dream home on this waterfront lot when I was asked to go to Nashville State.

So, when we arrived in Chattanooga the night of the arrest, it wasn't even to a familiar home. We returned to a sterile apartment. Despite having our own furniture, we felt homeless.

Even if it had been the house where we had lived the past 12 years, coming home would have been hard for Bobby. At one time, he was the city's most famous football hero, but soon everyone would know Bobby Hoppe once shot and killed a man in his hometown.

"Home is where, when you go there, they have to take you in," Mary told her husband Warren in Robert Frost's "The Death of the Hired Man." But Bobby wasn't like Silas, the hired man. He hadn't come home to die. He'd come home to be tried for murder. And he felt any goodwill he might have accrued over the years was simply used up—waste buried beneath the mire into which he thought he'd dragged us.

Earlier that evening, when I dialed the telephone to notify my family, I felt, as Warren's wife Mary did, that I "ran on tiptoe down the darkened passage to meet [them] with the news. And put [them] on guard. To tell them [Bobby] was coming home, to ask them to be kind."

When we walked into our apartment about 11 that night, my family huddled there, waiting for us, intent on surrounding us with love and support, giving it without judgment then and in the days ahead. Later, near midnight, Bobby refused to let anyone, including me, go with him to the Justice Center to turn himself in. He wanted to spare me the inevitable media circus, but it hurt not to be at his side when he and his attorney walked into the building for booking. Later, I was comforted to learn Father Jim Curtis, our rector, was there when Bobby arrived.

Although Bobby turned himself in without resistance, he was handcuffed and shoved into the back of a patrol car for the drive to the Hamilton County Jail.

The patrol car pulled to the curb and Bobby stepped out, hands behind him but head held high. He was booked and posted bail, surprised the bond was only $7,500—the first sign some people within the justice system weren't aligned with the investigators and the DA's office.

After fingerprinting and being pushed against a wall for photographing, Bobby's handcuffs were removed, and he walked out with Phillips and Curtis on each side, cameras flashing.

Returning to our apartment in the waning hours of the morning, Bobby collapsed into my arms, spent and disgraced. We wondered why he was told to report to the Justice Center instead of going directly to the jail, where the media got more dramatic footage of the hometown hero, handcuffed, in the back of a police car. Dramatic and, for Bobby, horrifically humiliating.

The night was long and sleepless. The next morning, as feared, the story made headlines—in newspaper, television, and radio—not only in Chattanooga but across the nation, from Florida to California: *FOOTBALL HERO ACCUSED OF MURDER IN 31-YEAR-OLD CASE.*

Bobby's picture was everywhere. Now the world knew what had been hidden in his heart more than three decades. It was a nightmare spinning unstoppable into reality.

While we were reading the morning papers, Sally called to report that every person she asked about the best attorney for a murder trial gave her the same name: Bobby Lee Cook.

The highest recommendation came from her neighbor, Mike Abbott, a criminal attorney, who said if he were on trial for murder, he would want Cook defending him. Mike had told her, "I would like to take the case myself, but that would be a disservice to you and your friend."

Sally also met with John Marshall, head of her firm's ethical and professional response division, who advised her to open a *pro bono* file so she could talk confidentially with Bobby. When Sally told me she planned to attend the trial, I was so grateful I didn't even protest her taking time away from her busy career. Bobby and I knew Sally could guide us through the labyrinth of legalese, explaining and interpreting what the other lawyers said and did.

And having attorney-client privilege would make it possible for Bobby to talk to her, as he would with Phillips and Cook. A three-person team—pulling together for Bobby, I liked that.

Years later, in the 1998 true-crime novel, *Secrets Never Die*, author Robin McDonald said Cook has "an international reputation as a lethal inquisitor and an ardent defender of the damned." I witnessed this 10 years earlier at Bobby's trial: Cook's skill matched his reputation.

But convincing Bobby to hire another attorney was difficult. He did not want to offend Phillips by suggesting a co-counsel. I knew Leroy Phillips was highly competent, but with Bobby's life on the line, I argued that two great minds were better than one.

I refused to settle for less than the best attorneys we could find. Bobby, on the other hand, didn't want to deplete our savings. It was difficult enough for him to spend our hard-earned money on one attorney—but I was willing to spend whatever it took to keep him out of jail.

Ultimately, I prevailed, but our negotiations required I ask Phillips if he was OK with a co-counsel. Plus, Bobby refused to meet with Cook initially, saying I could "check him out" and if I felt he could make a difference, then I could talk with Phillips. Setting his jaw, Bobby told me, "I'm not going to meet with Mr. Cook unless Mr. Phillips gives his blessing."

Sally drove from Atlanta to join us in the tiny town of Summerville, Ga. Bobby rode along, but being there didn't mean he was going to talk to Cook that day. Instead, Bobby took a seat in a nearby restaurant while Sally and I rushed down the street to keep the appointment.

From the lush gardens surrounding Cook's office to the massive front door crafted of old oak, everything said this was not the office of a hick lawyer. Crystal-clear water cascading from a marble fountain created a symphony among the floating water lilies. It was a soothing setting.

Inside the building, a large circular library echoed the serious but serene atmosphere of the office, with shelves of age-worn volumes rising 16 feet toward the rotunda ceiling, the pages of the casebooks thumbed countless times in pursuit of justice for their owner's famous and infamous clients.

Our immediate impression was one of refinement and easy elegance.

But the appearance of the man who walked through the door was a shock, although I tried not to show it. Cook was tall and gangly, and stooped-shouldered, a modern-day Ichabod Crane with a wispy white goatee. At first glance, he did not emanate poise and confidence. Even in an old-fashioned, hand-tied bow tie, he didn't "fit" these surroundings.

But when he spoke, he exuded assurance and support and, more importantly, intelligence and compassion. Suddenly, his eccentric appearance seemed courtly and grandfatherly. With a gentlemanly sweep of his hand, he offered a chair. Within moments, like a parishioner saying penance, I poured out the story of what happened the night Hudson was killed.

The Indictment: Coming to Terms with Reality

Cook sat back in his chair, head bowed, thoughtfully puffing on his bent pipe. When I finished talking, he didn't move a muscle. He didn't meet my eyes. Silence shrouded the circular library, searing me with fear. Slowly, he lifted his head, studying me with piercing eyes.

When he finally spoke, his words shocked me as much as what I had said stunned him.

"Mrs. Hoppe," he began softly, stopping to take another puff on his pipe. "When you scheduled this appointment, I fully expected you to come in here and tell me your husband did not kill Don Hudson.

"I *never* expected you to say he did it."

Sally Weaver was as taken aback as Cook, but she concealed her astonishment, not even raising an eyebrow. Later, I realized, although I had told her about the indictment, I had not told her Bobby killed Hudson. Looking back now, I'm not sure whether I just couldn't say the words or if, in distress, I simply omitted that detail.

After Cook expressed his surprise, every word he said was aimed at proving Bobby was not a murderer. I knew deep in my gut, if Bobby were to remain a free man, Cook, working hand-in-glove with Phillips, could make it happen.

Grasping the sensitivity of a local attorney accepting a "big name" attorney's help, Cook was the soul of diplomacy.

He called Phillips, assuring him that he would be the "lead" attorney and that he, Bobby Lee Cook, would play second fiddle. And Cook was cautious never to overshadow Phillips in the trial or the media; he simply ensured that Bobby had the best defense possible.

With much lighter steps, Sally and I returned to the restaurant to give Bobby the gist of our meeting. Acquiescing to my wishes for a second counsel and respecting Sally's concurring opinion, Bobby agreed to retain Cook.

So we moved forward with two attorneys. Two men who, over the next few months, worked as one on Bobby's behalf, researching and preparing a defense that would take the prosecutor totally off-guard when the trial began.

* * *

It's hard to believe, after all these months of worried waiting, we're in the middle of the trial. Difficult to even consider eating—but DiRisio has called a lunch break, so we're back in Leroy's office. Someone has ordered sandwiches, but Bobby doesn't even look at them. Choking on the first bite, I push it aside. It's tasteless. Glue on the tongue.

Unable to eat, we talk. Bobby and I ask a few questions about Evans' opening statements and Stargel's testimony, then fall silent.

With nothing more to say, we head back to the courthouse, Bud running interference again.

Today one group lining the sidewalk catches our attention, so we ask Bud to stop. Standing elbow-to-elbow along our path are dozens of Bobby's former students. They have waited in blistering sun to offer encouraging words as Coach Hoppe pauses for hugs and handshakes.

Moving away slowly, we hear the students shouting, "Hang in there, Coach," as we open the front door of the courthouse and push through the crowded hallway to our reserved seats.

Waiting for the judge's entrance, Bobby thinks of his students standing outside and his mind wanders back to his own senior year at Central High, back to the halcyon days when he basked in a different kind of spotlight, one made possible by the brilliant plays designed for him by Coach Red Etter.

CHAPTER SEVEN

All-American!

Glory is like a circle in the water
Which never ceaseth to enlarge itself
Till by broad spreading it disperses to nought
–Shakespeare 1564-1616

With Bobby's senior year approaching, expectations were high for the Purple Pounders. Nothing less than a third state championship would satisfy team members who wanted their last year to be their best.

But according to John Shearer, writing in the *Chattanooga Times* in April 2008, the 1953 season began on a down note, with mighty Memphis Central humbling Chattanooga Central, 16-7, before 12,000 fans at Chamberlain Field.

Despite the team's drudging, Hoppe did well as evidenced by the opening drive in which Central showed "Robert the Rabbit on the famed Georgia Tech belly play, an 18-yarder."

After the embarrassing loss to Memphis, Central beat Atlanta's Marist High School, 49-0, at Chamberlain Field. Hoppe carried the ball six times, scoring four touchdowns, finishing the game with 141 yards in eight carries.

The following Friday, Central traveled to Kingsport where it defeated the home team, 26-7. Hoppe had 14 carries for 95 yards against the previously unbeaten Indians. He scored two of the Pounder's four touchdowns, with James Cannon and Max Parris picking up the others.

On Oct. 3, 1953, Central buried Red Bank, 48-0. Tate scored the first TD, circling left end on a belly play fake and pitch-out by Parris. Etter kicked his first of six conversions.

In the second quarter, Red Bank somehow made it to Central's one-yard line. After four tries, Red Bank never budged from the one-yard line, so Central took over, 99 yards from pay dirt.

Gene Etter was standing beside his dad on the sidelines. After his dad sent a player in with instructions on the next play—a trap play with Hoppe carrying the ball—Coach Etter said, "Here goes a 100-yard touchdown."

Well almost. Bobby took the handoff, blew through the right tackle, and flew by two Lion defenders, breaking away and going 99 yards for the TD. Bobby took the ball again four plays later after Red Bank got nowhere and had to punt. Bobby streaked 40 yards for his second TD.

Tate, Paul Elliott, Merritt, and Charles "Indian" Cantrell tallied four TDs for the night.

* * *

Early in the 1953 football season, Miami Senior High, the historical powerhouse from south Florida, made a trek north to play Central High. Those golden boys from the Sunshine State never knew what hit them.

The next day's headlines for the *Chattanooga News-Free Press* sports section told the story: Hoppe Shines as Central Breaks Miami Jinx, 27-0.

Since final game stats were unbelievable, George Short began his article: "This story is true."

Miami wished it weren't. And it could have been worse.

Before the game, a Central alumnus saw Hoppe smoking a cigarette and told Coach Farmer just as the team was running out on the field. When the game was over, Hoppe came huffing and puffing to the sidelines.

Farmer grabbed him by his shoulder pads, slinging him against a hedgerow fence. Startled and wide-eyed, Hoppe exclaimed, "But, Coach, I just ran my fourth touchdown of the day!"

Pulling Hoppe closer, the fuming Farmer shouted, "And just look how many you could've run if you hadn't been smoking."

The writer of one article about the Miami game must not have known about the infraction. He reported, "Bobby Hoppe is in the backfield, and according to some, you would be correct if you left out the *in* as far as offense is concerned."

Sports writer Dexter Van Zant agreed: "As in all games played by the Pounders this year, Bobby (Hippity) Hoppe was the bellwether of the offense. The hard-charging halfback, equipped with rocket getaway and a passing gear, scored three of the Central six-pointers."

Although he started out in front of Hoppe, Miami's highly touted 100-yard-dash champion couldn't get close to catching Hoppe on "a 95-

yard gallop just before the final whistle, which provided the points that made it the most decisive win in the six-year history of the series."

Short noted, "Hoppe broke through quickly and outdistanced a pooped pack of pursuers in the same manner a fox leaves a pack of hounds at sun-up."

On another scoring play, Short said Tate took the ball and made another quick handoff to Hoppe, who "was hit by the line, bounced off tacklers into the secondary and sprang through the secondary's arms spinning crazily, light-footedly into the end zone sideways."

Another win for the Purple Pounders. The team careened off the field, heady with victory. After the game, in the showers and locker rooms, amid souring towels and stinky socks, a tight brotherhood grew. Men who would have each other's back forever, who offered rough hugs after a win and looked the other way before a game when a brother vomited fear into the sink.

* * *

In 1953, almost a decade after the U.S. flattened Hiroshima with an atomic bomb, Central High unleashed its own explosive device— Bobby Hoppe—who pulverized the powerful and unbeaten Isaac Litton High in Nashville.

A local paper reported, "Central High dropped its H-bomb on Isaac Litton over at Nashville last Friday, and when the blinding flashes faded away, Central had established its gridiron superiority over Litton by a score of 34-13.

"The H-bomb, Hoppe to you, scored four of his team's five touchdowns, with Cantrell scoring the fifth," on runs of 2, 18, 62, and 87 yards, gaining a total of 312 yards in 22 carries.

Chattanooga sports writer Hays Clark, saying Hoppe was "as poison with the pigskin as Hopalong Cassidy was with only one bullet left in his gun," told his readers, "If I were a pig, I would never let Hoppe pass without tipping my bonnet."

And he ended with a personal plea. "I listened to the broadcast by Lee Sheridan over WDOD. Now I am going to make a simple request of Bobby Hoppe.

"I wish he would let me know the next time he is going to put on another show like he did last Friday, and I will get a good night's sleep the day before. I ran every yard with him and the next morning, I was so tired I could hardly get out of bed."

Moving on to Baylor, a perennial challenge, Central defeated its Chattanooga neighbor, 21-7, sealing its third consecutive state championship. Playing with team captain and left halfback Bobby Hoppe on the award-winning 1953 team were several men who not only had Bobby's back during Central games but also showed their continuing loyalty 31 years later.

* * *

By season's end, Central's reputation had seeped deep into Florida, so the Pounders were invited to the Kiwanis match-up, a post-season charity game in the famed Orange Bowl.

The *Miami Herald* reported the damage: "The lightning-quick Hoppe was the difference in the game. He struck fear in the hearts of Miami High followers in the first quarter with an 80-yard scoring run to remind his foes that his All-Tennessee ranking wasn't just a gift."

In the fourth period, Hoppe outdid that amazing run with an 89-yard kickoff return for a game-winning TD. And, according to Etter, that wasn't his best play.

"His run the last play of the first half, just yards short of a touchdown, was the most sensational bit of running I've ever seen."

Describing the play, Short wrote, "With about 10 seconds left, Hoppe pulled what may well be one of his finest runs in a sterling four-year career. Parris, in close, faked a jump pass and handed back on a modified Statue of Liberty to Hoppe coming around the left side. Hoppe, like a cop directing traffic, steered blockers up the left sideline.

"Then, picking his route as a barefoot boy in a briar patch, [Hoppe] cut to midfield and, almost hemmed in there, cut back to the left. He slanted between bewildered Stings at full speed and change of pace. At the seven, he was tripped up by a diving desperation tackle. [Hoppe] skidded to a halt on his pockets as the half ended."

Back home in Tennessee with the chill of winter already settled deep in the valley, Central fans unable to attend the Rabbit's final romp made a dash to the Riverview Pharmacy for newspapers. They stood in the brightly lit store, reading each sentence written by George Short of the *Chattanooga Times*. He was their eyes and ears in Miami.

All-American!

The first go-round, they scanned the article. The second, they read it slowly, savoring it. Then, they read it aloud to each other. It was a victory they shared. Their boys went down there and whipped up on Miami again!

"Bobby Hoppe put the finishing touches on Miami's annual Christmas pageant tonight, leading Chattanooga Central to a 21-14 victory in the annual Kiwanis Charity game.

"Robert the Rabbit, playing what is called one of the greatest games any high school back has shown in this big bowl, turned into a whole team of Santa's reindeers to put Central on top of a talented Miami Senior High team to stay in the fourth quarter."

A spontaneous early-morning celebration broke out in the Riverside Pharmacy and homes throughout Chattanooga. Then came the reality that the Pounders' Miami victory marked the end of Hoppe's high school football career.

Short wrote, "He was Dancer, Prancer and Der Dasher, all rolled into one, as he capped, among other things, a brilliant four-year career."

The next day—Dec. 13, 1953—Short continued to brag in his column, "Short Shots," datelined Miami Beach.

"Last night, in his great swan song, his run on the game-winning kickoff return was from an unusual alignment. Hoppe played possum for a few moments. Just stood there, "like a bump on a log," said another sports writer. Then Tate, heading for the right sideline, deftly handed the ball to Hoppe. From almost a standing start, Hoppe hipped back to the left and fell right into a kickoff return lane formed by some seven Central players."

Too late, the startled Stingaroos changed direction. "Chattanooga chicanery" is what one writer termed Central's ruse.

"The rest is now history. How [Hoppe] followed the escort down that corridor for 79 yards after Miami had tied the score 23 seconds before is well known. But what is not well known is that the Pounders practiced the carefully planned maneuver only five times. That it worked is a tribute to the team, to Etter, and to Hoppe."

"That's the guy who routinely ran twice the number of yards he gained due to the veers and switches. Sometimes he ran 110 yards or more on a kickoff return."

An exuberant Short told his readers, "(Hoppe) is a very much sought-after young man."

A Matter of Conscience

The morning after the Miami victory, Hoppe stepped from the shade of the Cadillac Hotel's Cabana Club. With a smile, he blinked in the sudden brightness, one eye swollen from the previous night's 21-14 victory. Speaking to reporters who had dogged him for months, Hoppe confirmed his college selection.

"Yes, I'm going to sign with Auburn...it's definite," although in his column Short said Miami tried to get Hoppe to stay a few extra days to see the school "and then be flown home commercially to make up his mind."

Despite that last-minute pitch, Robert the Rabbit will "hop down the bunny trail to the Loveliest Village of the Plains—Auburn," Short wrote.

Hoppe was a special target for recruiters, Short noted, saying he weighed the Tennessee Vols' offer carefully before casting his lot with Auburn. "He must have felt—and probably with a little prompting from various sources—that his talents were more fitted to Auburn's T than Tennessee's single wing."

Alabama was believed to be Hoppe's runner-up choice, but Georgia, Tennessee, SMU, and his hometown Chattanooga were among the final contenders. In all, 19 top schools went after him. They all wanted the fleet-footed rabbit who, in his senior year alone, gained 1,453 yards rushing for an average of 9.85 per carry, scored 114 points and had, among other TDs, touchdown runs of 97, 95, 89, 87, and 80 yards to his credit, *Nashville Banner* writer Edgar Allen reported.

* * *

Though saddened that Bobby's Central High football career was over, everyone in Chattanooga and Tennessee predicted great days ahead for him. He would prove them right.

And far into the future, old men—their cane-bottomed chairs tipped back against the dirty siding of the local pool hall—would talk about the old times at Central High.

"Those were the days," one said, spitting a stream of amber tobacco juice onto the street. "They don't play football now like they did back then. Hell, they don't make players like Bobby Hoppe anymore either."

Nodding in agreement, his buddies remembered, too. "Them were the glory days, boys. We'll never see the likes again."

All-American!

Over the years, the incredible tales of Bobby Hoppe--Hippity Hoppe, Robert the Rabbit, the Northside Express, the Chattanooga Choo Choo—were hashed and rehashed, then passed along to sons and grandsons.

It was the legend of a high school All-American, a boy-become-man who never viewed himself as highly as history does.

* * *

In 1992 when Hoppe learned the Central High football field was to be named in honor of Etter, he wrote his former coach a long letter.

It was rare for Hoppe to share feelings as deep as those in his letter. After telling Etter about his dad and how the two of them never had a close relationship, Hoppe wrote, "There was no one else in my family who was qualified to offer advice and direction concerning my future.

"It was only in later life that I realized that you, Coach Newton, Coach Seaton and Coach Farmer had become my father figures. It was also later, when I began to coach, that I realized your genius as a coach.

"Coach Etter, whatever success and most of the happiness I've experienced, I owe to the old Central coaches."

* * *

The accomplishments of Bobby Hoppe at Central High were seldom exaggerated although, without doubt, they were the stuff dreams are made of, the story a daddy tells his boy at bedtime.

When the 1953 season ended, numerous laurel wreaths would be placed on the head of the fleet-footed, purple-and-gold-clad god who sprang, like a new-age Zeus, from the streets of North Chattanooga.

Hoppe not only made All-City, All-State, and All-Southern, he took national honors.

He was one of only eight halfbacks nationwide picked by Scholastic Magazines for the 77-player squad. Chattanooga's first All-American—the entire city celebrated. Corks popped again when Hoppe got his second All-American pick in a Wigwam Wiseman competition sponsored by national radio and television commentators in collaboration with athletic and game officials.

At that year's football banquet, Hoppe wore a path from his seat to the podium, scooping up honors and acknowledging accolades from coaches and standing ovations from teammates.

A Matter of Conscience

* * *

After the awards and honors had been handed out, after most of the players' families had headed home, Bobby Hoppe, feeling both excited and nostalgic, left Central High with several football friends.

As if on automatic pilot, Bobby headed up Cherokee Boulevard. Perched at the top of the steep hill on the corner of Cherokee and Bell Avenue is Nikki's Drive-In, a popular hangout for the high school crowd. The walls of this restaurant held many of Bobby's best memories.

He and his friends had spent countless hours at the small restaurant. From the hilltop, Nikki's red-and-green neon sign glows brightly—a lighthouse drawing them into a familiar, happy harbor.

After Bobby and his gang arrived, they packed tightly into their favorite booth—three or four bulky boys squeezing into each bench with others pulling up chairs. As the evening grew later and more teens arrived, the place started to rock. One 45 after another dropped onto the jukebox turntable. Its music was the background beat for the guys, laughing and joking, hashing and rehashing a ref's bad call on a great play.

Behind the long counter running the length of the left wall, steam rose as juicy red burgers sizzled on the grill, their mouth-watering aroma wafting outside when the door was opened. The stools at the counter were filled, with more people waiting just inside the door.

From the restaurant's picture windows, the twinkling lights of Chattanooga seemed distant. Looking down the hill from Nikki's was like sitting in a hidden tree house, the world far below.

Cars coming up the hill on Cherokee Boulevard can be seen long before they swing into the parking lot to the right of the one-story, flat-topped building.

On the opposite side of Nikki's, Bell Avenue intersects Cherokee Boulevard. Unlike Cherokee, which is wide and well lit, Bell Avenue is dark and narrow with no guardrails. Few streetlights or house lights illuminate the road as it twists and turns in a steep descent through trees to the left and a trailer park off the road to the right. At the foot of the hill, Bell Avenue angles left and straightens out.

In the 1940s and '50s, Nikki's was not only the hangout for older teens, it also attracted illegal liquor runners. From its windows, they could see cars approaching up Cherokee Boulevard and, if necessary, Bell Avenue provided a quick getaway into the night.

73

All-American!

***

Despite the glow from the honors he accumulated in high school, Bobby Hoppe was no angel. A typical teenage boy, his halo was always slightly tipped and usually a bit smudged.

Over the years, Bobby repeatedly told his own favorite tale.

In Florida for a game against Miami High, the team's reservations had been made at a hotel in the middle of nowhere, most likely so the coaches could keep a close eye on the boys.

The morning after the game, the coaches and Red Brown, the team's bus driver, decided to get in a little fishing in a nearby bay before the boys awakened. When the players finally awoke and found the coaches gone, they didn't know what to do. Like all teenage boys, the guys were ravenous—and there was no restaurant nearby. Finally, one player discovered Red had left the keys in the ignition of the bus and asked if anyone could drive the Greyhound.

"I think I can," Bobby declared, hopping into the driver's seat. "All aboard. This bus is heading out."

Getting the bus into reverse was more of a challenge than Bobby thought, but he finally started backing out of the driveway. "I couldn't see behind me very well, so I flattened two palm trees," he admitted, smiling sheepishly. "About a block from the motel, I realized I was in over my head, and I finally got the bus turned around."

Back at the motel, now not only hungry but also grumpy, the team got off the bus.

When the coaches returned and saw the pitifully broken palm trees, they went immediately to the hotel manager who ratted out the team. The coaches didn't even have to ask who was driving. Coach Farmer called Hoppe aside and let him have it with both barrels. "Don't you know you could have wrecked? Don't you realize Red could have been fired?"

Finally, Farmer yelled, "OK, Hoppe, if you can drive a bus, you can thumb home."

Bobby laughed and grabbed his duffle bag and hit the road.

In a few minutes, the bus passed him, all the players' heads sticking out the windows, waving bye-bye. Hot pavement sizzling under his feet, Bobby knew he was in for a long day. But the bus pulled over about a hundred or so yards ahead and backed up.

A Matter of Conscience

"I climbed aboard and was on my best behavior the rest of the trip," Bobby recalled.

* * *

Mischievous, Bobby thinks. That was me in high school. Even in college. I wasn't a bad person, but here I sit, on trial for first-degree murder.

Lost in thought Bobby doesn't see Judge DiRisio enter the courtroom until the bailiff says, "All rise."

Now, he focuses his attention on Tommy Smith as he walks forward. Bobby studies the middle-aged man in the witness box, and sadness sweeps over him as he watches Tommy, nervously fidgeting with his tie.

Tommy was just a senior in high school the night Don Hudson was shot, Bobby reflects, too young to see death close up. When you're just a boy, how do you process that?

CHAPTER EIGHT

Testimonies Blurred by Time

When I was younger, I could remember anything,
whether it happened or not.
–Mark Twain (1835-1910)

Shortly after Hudson's death, local newspapers theorized "corn liquor" traffic had something to do with it, that the person who shot Hudson was engaged in that business. But finding concrete evidence to support the theory and make an arrest was a different story.

According to an August 4, 1957, article by Alex Corliss in the *Chattanooga Times*, "The shotgun slaying of Teddy Donald (Don) Hudson, 24, whose turbulent life ended on a street corner in North Chattanooga almost two weeks ago, may become another unsolved murder."

But Hudson's father refused to let his son's murder end up collecting dust in a cold-case file. He hired an attorney to write a "properly legal" letter to County Coroner Doyle Currey, requesting a coroner's inquest into his son's death.

At the inquest a few weeks later, jurors listened to four hours of testimony. Witnesses included Robert Cornish, John Stargel, Mrs. Homer Hollums and daughter, Rita Hollums, Charles W. Neal, Barbara Jo Campbell, William McCutcheon, Buck Everett, Richard Holland, and Tommy Smith.

After the Hoppes' attorneys, Joe Wild and James Carroll, were excluded from the inquest over their strong objections, Bobby Hoppe, his mother, and his sister Joan took the Fifth Amendment at Wild's recommendation.

After 70 minutes of deliberation, the jurors submitted their findings, which were reported in local newspapers on August 9, 1957: "Don Hudson, 24, North Chattanooga whisky runner, was slain July 21 by a person or persons unknown, a coroner's jury concluded yesterday."

But Currey felt pretty sure he knew what happened that July night. He termed the shooting, "the beginning in our community of Chicago gangsterism."

Further newspaper reports cited four outcomes of the coroner's inquest:

- Police are no closer to a solution to the crime—in fact, one officer said, "[The inquest findings] will ruin our case."
- Invoking the Fifth Amendment while testifying in judicial proceedings here is becoming more prevalent.
- A precedent has been set by which future inquests may be held— Currey said he was operating without precedent.
- Legal technicalities surrounding such a hearing have created a "field day" for lawyers, who all seem to have different opinions on how various aspects might be handled.

The coroner's inquest was the first in more than 100 years, so there were no rules to follow. Currey made up his own as he went, with several attorneys sitting in on many "caucus" sessions when the legality of certain phases was discussed.

"With no precedent, as Currey pointed out, it was up to the coroner to decide what to do and how," the *Free Press* reported afterwards. One attorney commended Currey, who had no legal training, for conducting the hearing with "decorum and ability."

But some attorneys questioned whether it was legal for the coroner to exclude counsel for witnesses. After banning Carroll and Wild, Currey announced that the court reporter's record would serve them the same as if they had been there. Yet, according to the *Free Press*, after the hearing, Currey impounded the inquest record taken by court reporter G.A. Wolfe.

Following the inconclusive findings of the coroner's inquest, further action would be up to the Chattanooga police department. A grand jury was not expected to take up the matter, according to the *Free Press*.

As one attorney observed in the newspaper: "If there was enough evidence for the grand jury to act on an indictment against someone, then there would have been no need for the inquest—the matter could have been before the grand jury already. The proof presented at the inquest only pointed the finger of suspicion at one individual but was quite insufficient to sustain an indictment or conviction."

Just as before the inquest, the case appeared headed for the homicide file of never-solved murders. It would stay there nine years before being brought up again and heard by a grand jury.

Testimonies Blurred by Time

Then, after the grand jury failed to bring a true bill, another 22 years would pass before Bobby was indicted in 1988.

* * *

Tommy Smith. The State's only eyewitness at the 1988 trial also testified at the 1957 inquest when he was 17 years old.

In July 1957, Tommy, a student at Kirkman High, had little interest in anything occurring outside Chattanooga. All Tommy wanted was to graduate from Kirkman and be with Doris. Earlier that evening, when he had pulled up at the Krystal after her late night shift, around 1 a.m., she hopped in and slid close to him. As they drove toward her house, Elvis wailed "Love Me Tender" on the car radio. Perfect, Tommy thought, smiling.

Although Doris was exhausted from standing over the steam table where the little square hamburgers were cooked, she remained in the car when they pulled up in front of her home. It was late and it was hot inside the car, but the young couple didn't want to call it a night. Tommy had cranked the windows down as far as they would go, but there was no breeze from outside, just the usual July humidity pawing at them.

He slipped an arm along the back of the seat, pulling Doris to him, cradling her in the crook of his arm. He tipped her chin up, kissed her lightly, and rested his cheek against her head, then buried his nose in her hair, inhaling rose-scented shampoo mixed with perspiration. Her face was shiny with sweat, but he wanted to kiss the freckles dancing across her turned-up nose.

Suddenly, a slight movement two streets away caught his attention. In the distance he saw a car. Thirty-one years later, he would swear in Court that, even in the dark, he could tell its make and model, even the color. Good eyes and a good memory, he'll say.

On the radio, Tab Hunter crooned, "They say for every boy and girl there's just one love in this whole world, and I know I've found mine. Just one kiss from your sweet lips will tell me that your love is real...."

A second ago, the couple had been kissing; now Tommy was distracted by the distant car. Then a second car pulled up beside it. Was it trying to pass? No, just creeping alongside. Maybe they were getting ready to race, he thought, sitting up straighter so he could see the action. Then he realized it wasn't a race—in fact, they were barely moving. He stared until the cars passed out of his sight.

A Matter of Conscience

* * *

In the courtroom 31 years later, Tommy described how his car was positioned that night: "We were sitting in a car in front of [Doris'] house headed towards Bell Avenue."

At the 1957 coroner's inquest, he had not been so specific. Newspaper reports of the inquest indicated Smith just testified he was parked in front of his girlfriend's house. And Stargel's testimony at the preliminary hearing two weeks ago disputed that Smith and Doris Bennett were sitting in the car at all. In handwritten notes from his 1957 interview with Smith, Stargel had jotted, "Sunday afternoon...me and Detective Cornish talked to a boy on Pineville Road by the name Tommy Smith. He claims he and his girlfriend was standing across the street from 205 May Street and seen, looks like a black, best I can make out here, '57...."

In Court today, Assistant DA Evans asks Tommy to describe what he saw from his car.

Tommy testifies his car was facing "right straight to Bell Avenue when a black car came down...doing maybe ten miles an hour, real slow.

"And Hudson's car came up, you know, real slow to pull up alongside. He was on the outside. Then all of sudden his car accelerated a little bit before they got out of my view.

"And I heard a gunshot"—a deep sound, he says, not at all like "a pistol going off...."

The reverberation from the gunshot was still rolling over the neighborhood when Tommy and Doris heard another loud blast. Startled, they froze for a moment, looking straight ahead. Tommy says he told a frightened Doris he thought it was the sound of a car hitting the thick rock wall along the side of lower Bell Avenue.

Curious, they got out of the car and walked to the scene of the wreck, a couple of blocks away. But, Tommy notes, they weren't the first ones to arrive; several people were already there, gaping inside the car where the driver was lying motionless, face down on the passenger side.

"The impact made his eyeball come out of the socket—when they got him out of the car I seen that," Tommy tells Evans, seeming to relish his power to shock the people in the courtroom.

Two of Hudson's sisters start to sob. Dry-eyed, his frail mother leans against her husband.

Oblivious, Tommy marches on, describing the near-dead man, telling how his blood was dripping onto the sidewalk near the wall where the car came to rest.

"As much blood as there was, you couldn't hardly recognize him," Tommy tells Evans.

At Tommy's graphic description, Bobby cringes, dropping his head into his hands. Despite the guilt he's carried for so many years, he has never allowed himself to picture Hudson right after the shooting. Now he can't block the garish image, adding horror to remorse.

At Tommy's next words, Bobby lifts his head, surprise etching his face. Tommy tells Evans, even when they "drug [Hudson] out," he didn't see a gun in the car.

Bobby's vision blurs as he fights the anxiety that's suddenly putting a vise grip on his chest. What happened to the gun? Hudson had a gun, but how can he prove it?

Bobby's thoughts jerk back to the courtroom as Tommy says he saw the car well enough to know it was a black Ford Fairlane 500 convertible with a black top—and the top was up. And he doesn't forget the only detail he cited 31 years ago at the coroner's inquest—the car was a 1957.

At the recent preliminary hearing, Stargel had read from his notes that Tommy "was sure it was a black car and nearly sure it was a '57 as there was high fins on the back of the car."

In 1957, a few days after the shooting, the police talked with Tommy, he tells the prosecutor. At the coroner's inquest, he was quoted in the newspaper as testifying he "heard one shot as he watched two cars move parallel in the same direction along Bell Avenue at Snow Street." The shot came from a 1957 model, Tommy said at the inquest, but he didn't see who was driving.

Today he adds, "I had seen Joan—I reckon that's Bobby's sister—driving a car like that." But on July 21, 1957, he didn't know who was driving.

Leroy Phillips challenges Tommy's memory as he begins cross-examination, reminding him it has been a long time. Almost 31 years, Phillips says, a question mark in his voice.

"Yes, sir," Tommy responds, sitting up straighter, radiating confidence.

"Of course, about some of these matters, your memory is not as great now as it was 31 years ago, I assume. Is that a fair statement?"

Tommy disagrees. "Some people's subject to forget things, but I have a good memory."

Leroy presses, asking Tommy if he ever forgets *anything*?

"No, not anything," Tommy responds with bravado. "I may forget, you know, some little ole something that don't amount to anything."

Phillips turns toward the jury, wanting to be sure they hear his question. "You are almost two blocks from Bell Avenue that the two cars were on?"

Tommy doesn't like the insinuation, so he pauses before answering petulantly, "But they were short blocks."

And there were streetlights, Tommy insists. Phillips wants to know if streetlights back then were like the ones in the aerial shot.

Tommy, proud of his recall, says they were the old style that hung lower on the pole.

"But they lit a corner up good," he adds, sounding more like the 17-year-old of 1957 than the 48-year-old of today. Laboriously, Phillips walks Tommy through all the streets, the stop signs, curves in the roads. Finally, pointing at the photo, he puts his finger on the place Hudson's car came to rest. He asks, isn't it "just about a half a block...from North Market Street?"

When Tommy says he isn't sure, Phillips presses the point, knowing distance will become significant later, during Bobby's testimony.

Tommy finally admits he couldn't see all the way to North Market, but he claims he could see the cars emerge from behind the church, headed that way, "doing 10 mile an hour.

"I couldn't see them any further after they passed that point," he concedes.

Lloyd Lewis, a juror on the front row, cocks his head as if pondering the brief time Tommy actually saw the cars.

As Lewis considers the question, Phillips points at the photograph. "Were you behind the telephone pole or in front of it, or do you know whether the telephone pole was there?"

Cutting his eyes toward Evans, hoping for help, Tommy discloses he doesn't believe the telephone pole was there at that time.

"You don't recall?"

Begrudgingly, Tommy repeats, "I don't recall."

Anything occurring before the cars emerged from behind the church was hidden from view, Phillips says—that does matter. In fact, Tommy didn't hear the cars before he saw them.

"And the short distance you saw them was between the church and the corner of that house?" Phillips inquires calmly.

Tommy concurs, noting the first car was the convertible, and repeating that its top was up. Incredulous, Phillips starts to ask how he could tell the top was up since the top and body were both black, but Tommy cuts him off. He saw enough to know it was a convertible with the top up. And he doesn't back down when Phillips implies he saw a lot given the conditions that night.

Soon some of the details coming from Tommy's lips end up helping Bobby, so it's hard to know what to think. Tommy could see which lane the convertible was in, too—the right lane.

Nailing the point, Phillips asks if the other car came up beside the black convertible on the wrong side of the road.

"More or less like you were going to pass an automobile," Tommy responds. "[Hudson] was on the left hand side of that car as he came up alongside of it."

On the *wrong* side of the road, Phillips forces, bringing Evans to his feet.

"We object," Evans says. "He didn't pull up on the wrong side of the road. That's not what the witness testified. He said he pulled up to pass him."

Phillips, cautioned by DiRisio not to paraphrase, takes another tack, "Of course, you don't know what his intentions were, do you?"

Back on his feet, exasperated, Evans objects again. "Mr. Phillips doesn't know either. That's the problem, Your Honor, if he would just let the witness testify."

This time DiRisio cuts Phillips some slack, telling Evans, "He may cross-examine."

Then turning to Phillips, DiRisio adds, "But don't paraphrase."

Phillips pounds home his point, wanting jurors to question what the second car was trying to do. "This car that you saw was not on the right side of the road...it was on the left and wrong side of the road?"

"Yes, sir," Tommy responds and then repeats what he testified under direct examination, conceding he could not see the vehicles when he heard the shot.

Unfazed, Tommy again tells about walking up the street to the scene. He and Doris arrived in time to see Hudson's body being pulled from the car, but Tommy thinks they left before police arrived—something he failed to reveal under direct examination by Evans.

As they walked back to Doris' house, they saw several people hurrying to the wreck, he adds under Phillips' prodding.

Turning Tommy's attention back to the photographs, Phillips asks him to identify other, shorter ways Hudson could have taken home.

Without looking at the photo, Bobby thinks to himself that Hudson had already passed two other streets he could have turned on, both of which were a more direct route to his house.

But Phillips has moved back to the second car's movements. Over Phillips' objection that he's drawing a conclusion, Tommy states, "The other car was slowing down in order to let him get along aside."

Phillips challenges that assumption, but DiRisio rules Tommy can testify to what he saw. Phillips is incensed.

"Right—not the conclusions he is now drawing."

After a bench conference, Phillips attempts to pin Tommy down. "When the Hudson vehicle went around the...the black '57 Ford convertible, was it passing it?"

"No, sir. The black '57 Ford convertible appeared to be doing [about] 10 miles an hour. And Hudson wasn't doing any more—just enough to get up along aside it. If he was going to pass, he would have went on by."

Phillips scores. Several jurors' faces show they understand the significance of what was just said—Don Hudson could have passed the Ford, had that been his intent.

Evans is clearly frustrated. His own witness just shot a big hole in one of the State's theories. He wants the jury to believe Hudson was just trying to pass when Bobby fired.

Walking slowly to his seat, spirits deflated, Evans knows he must reshape his theory.

Testimonies Blurred by Time

* * *

Like Tommy Smith, Richard Holland testified at the coroner's inquest. Unlike Tommy, Holland can't recall what he said. That's a problem, as the transcript from the 1957 inquest has disappeared. And Currey is dead, so he can't help.

When Evans calls Holland to the stand, Cook knows where the prosecutor is headed and asks DiRisio for a bench conference. Cook has read a 1957 *Chattanooga Free-Press* article that quotes Holland as testifying at the inquest he "had heard a man threaten Hudson's life last year in a dispute over a girl." Because the coroner's inquest proceedings were privileged and no charge was made in connection with the shooting, no name was given in the article.

Bobby Lee Cook doesn't care. He possesses notes Detective Heck took in 1987 or 1988 while interviewing Holland. According to Heck's record, Holland can't recall that he said he heard the unnamed man threaten Hudson.

Even that doesn't matter to Cook, who simply does not want any implication in front of this jury. If Holland can't remember what he said in 1957, Evans should not remind him now.

According to the newspaper account of the inquest, Holland said the threat occurred the previous year, when the "alleged threatener stopped Hudson's Cadillac on Cherokee Boulevard and came to the car." Holland said he was in the car with Hudson.

A close friend to Hudson in 1957, Holland wanted his killer found. At the time, Holland owed his buddy a big favor. Rumor had it Hudson had hired him to steal a load of liquor from a moonshine-runner called Georgy Boy. When Georgy Boy went after Holland, Hudson saved his ass by saying Holland was with him that night, although he wasn't.

At the 1957 inquest, newspaper reports stated Holland told the jury Joan Hoppe Voiles, "got the money when Hudson would bring in the whisky." Under the coroner's questioning, Holland said, "When [Don] would make a few runs and had money, she liked him pretty well." Maybe the threat related to that girl, Holland had surmised before the inquest jury. He didn't know for sure, but it might have.

However, during the current investigation, when Heck questioned Holland, Holland declared he had no recollection of hearing anyone, including Bobby Hoppe, make any threat.

84

A Matter of Conscience

Cook's objection presupposes Evans is going to show Holland the 1957 newspaper article and ask him about it. Evans acknowledges that during his recent conversation with Holland—just last night—"he had no recollection about it."

It's clear Evans isn't going to ask Holland whether he ever heard any threat. Satisfied, Cook sits down, and Holland takes the witness stand.

* * *

Richard Holland grew up in North Chattanooga, a couple of blocks from Don Hudson's home. Back in 1957, Holland, then 17, was closed-mouthed about the whisky-running crowd. Although he was just a small-time liquor-runner himself, he knew the code. Better not be talking about whisky runners, dead or alive. Running your mouth could be dangerous.

"I never knew Don to hijack any whisky or to inform to federal authorities on whisky men," he had said at the 1957 inquest, adding that Hudson seemed worried the last week or so of his life.

Some surmised Hudson had been threatened for doing exactly what Holland denied knowing about—hijacking whisky. In fact, it was rumored that Don Hudson, using a blue light on his vehicle like a police car, often pulled over other whisky-runners and took their contraband. To eliminate competition, Hudson allegedly informed the feds about other runners.

Whisky-runners were a tough bunch. If you crossed them, they'd come after you. Hudson, afraid some of the whisky men he hijacked would be watching for his car, often traded cars with friends when he made his rounds to collect whisky money.

On the night Hudson was killed, he had traded cars with his buddy Richard Holland. Although Hudson didn't tell Holland why he wanted his car, Phillips forces Holland to admit he *assumed* Hudson was going to pick up some liquor money.

"You just made the assumption out of nowhere?" Phillips asks.

"He was a whisky man," Holland replies simply.

When Hudson returned the car later that evening, Holland doesn't recall what kind of mood he was in. But he admits Hudson had a temper. He'd seen it erupt more than once.

Asked for an example, Holland recalls seeing Hudson and Joan fussing outside a Texaco Station in North Chattanooga. "They were just arguing about something and he smacked her."

Under cross-examination, Holland admits he was not only aware of Don Hudson's reputation as a runner, he drove whisky with him "a couple of times."

The testimony on direct and cross-examination is short, adding little except to underline Hudson's reputation—and remind the jury the coroner's inquest records are missing.

* * *

Sitting motionless at the defense table, Bobby's mind lurches backward to the coroner's inquest, and he's flooded anew with the same sick mix of emotions that swamped him 31 years ago when he was on the witness stand. The heavy truth pushes air from his lungs as he struggles against his own desire to set it all free, word after word, until it fills up the room and spills out into the universe. Until the red shame he's caused drowns his family.

Then, out of the chaos, he recalls Wild's advice: "Bobby, you should not testify. You need to plead the Fifth Amendment because your attorneys can't be present to advise you." It's a brief reprieve before he's again awash in the old familiar guilt, sinking down into it, shamelessly thankful for delayed disgrace.

Never realizing until this moment that the memory of that day has forever been branded into his consciousness.

Herman Melville viewed life as man's search for truth and moral harmony, the discovery always eluding him, separating him from the world and from himself. Bobby, recalling the storyline of Melville's *Typee*, smiles ruefully. He knows better than most that the human impulse to escape responsibility for one's actions brings only anxiety and guilt.

Certainly his decision not to testify at the 1957 inquest brought no solace, but Bobby did breathe a sigh of relief when the jury returned its findings.

Shortly after the inquest, he headed to football practice at Auburn, carrying a miserable memory that masked the real Bobby for the rest of his life. Though invisible, this mask was permanent and impenetrable. Behind it, no one saw his agony.

A Matter of Conscience

As fans yelled "War Eagle," a battle cry for the Auburn Tigers, a different cry howled within Bobby—a strangled, otherworldly sound straight from the depths of hell.

CHAPTER NINE

The Cold Case Detective

Oh what a tangled web we weave
When first we practice to deceive.
–Sir Walter Scott (1771-1832)
Marmion, Canto VI, Stanza 17

In 1957 Don Hudson was 24. Bobby Hoppe was 22. And Richard Heck, just barely old enough for kindergarten, was 5.

Back then, Heck "wasn't concerned with cars or liquor or football," reporter Dan George wrote in the March 27, 1988, *Tennessean*, published daily in Nashville.

While Don Hudson was running moonshine at night, Heck, like most little boys, was nestled deep in his bed, dreaming the innocent dreams of a child.

In 1957, Heck didn't know Bobby Hoppe was a hometown hero. He didn't know Hoppe played football at all. Unlike the rest of Chattanooga in the 1950s, Heck never worshiped Bobby Hoppe; he didn't even know he existed.

But in 1987 Hoppe entered Heck's world like a meteor from the sky. In the future, Heck will be credited with solving a "whodunit," as Assistant DA Evans calls it during his opening statements at trial. But when Heck first delved into the case that had been a mystery for three decades, he discovered nothing new. As one law enforcement officer said, what the detective did was to "put the Chinese puzzle together that led to us being able to take the thing to the grand jury."

Putting that puzzle together, getting his only new witness to come up with damning testimony, took Heck 14 frustrating months.

* * *

Sitting at our breakfast table in early 1987, I was the first to read an article in the local paper about the formation of the Friends and Families of Murder Victims group. I handed it to Bobby and watched as he read. He shuttered slightly then looked up at me slowly.

I reassured Bobby it was unlikely a case as old as Hudson's would be resurrected; and, after all, a coroner's inquest in 1957 and a grand jury in 1966 hadn't found any reason to indict. But panic settled in Bobby's chest like an old friend from his past.

A few months after we read about the Friends and Families group, Richard Heck and Steve Angel were named as a two-man task force charged with investigating unsolved murders in Chattanooga.

Within weeks, the two detectives attended a meeting of the support group. Sitting quietly in the back, Heck and Angel observed the room filled with frustrated people—all saddened by the deaths of loved ones, angry that no one seemed to care, and focused on a common goal—finding out who did it.

Among the grieving members was Georgia Hudson. It had been 30 years since her son, Don, was killed, but she could not put it behind her. Three decades of thinking she knew who killed him, but not sure. Three decades since burying her boy—and his killer still walking free. It was too much for an old woman to cope with alone, so she was a regular at this support group.

Petite and gray-haired with a slight stoop to her bird-like shoulders, Georgia Hudson was neither brave nor vocal, but she was persistent. The frail woman wanted her son's death avenged. After the meeting, she eased up to Heck, apprehension shushing her words.

As she began to speak to the taciturn detective, she apologized for bothering him, for asking him to hear her story. She knew Heck and his partner had more pressing cases, but she would appreciate it if they would look into her son's killing.

Touched by a mother's dogged determination, Heck agreed to look at the case, realizing that solving a 30-year-old mystery would be like panning for gold in a dry creek bed.

Later that evening, as Heck drifted into a deep sleep, across town a recurring nightmare jolted Bobby out of his sleep, causing him to sit straight up in bed. Fully awake, the old fear filled his chest as the sluggish sun topped the horizon. It was a fear whose depths he couldn't share—no one alive, except him, knew what really happened the night Hudson was killed.

As he promised Mrs. Hudson, Heck plowed into the case. Much of his initial information came from hours of fishing through microfilmed newspapers at the public library. He was discouraged by his paltry catch—whisky warfare and gangster references by the coroner.

The Cold Case Detective

In "Trial of an American Hero," the headline article in *True Police Cases* magazine (October 1988), writer Thomas Conway said Heck's "heart sank as he wondered how to dig into the underworld feuds of 30 years previously."

For a while, old newspaper clippings were all Heck had. Police records were missing. The case file, including an autopsy report, was nowhere to be found.

Dispassionately, Heck discovered many key figures in the 1957 case—the coroner, the court reporter at the coroner's inquest, and one of the defendant's attorneys—were deceased.

Working out of a small office jammed with two desks and a bank of filing cabinets, Heck plodded along, identifying potential witnesses. He interviewed 45 people—from Chattanooga to Mars Hill, N.C., to Auburn, Ala. At Auburn he talked with Buddy Davidson in the athletic office, peppering him with questions about Bobby.

In 2008, Davidson remembered how the detective tried to put words in his mouth. But Davidson was adamant. He didn't know anything. As soon as Heck left, Davidson called Bobby about the visit.

One more ominous warning his past was slowly but surely cracking open.

Heck tracked down one of the two original investigators in Florida, before interviewing several people who testified at the coroner's inquest.

It was only after talking to one woman several times that Heck uncovered "new evidence." A potential witness who, when questioned by Stargel in 1957, didn't know anything. Who knew nothing when Heck first queried her in 1987 or initially in 1988. But after he insinuated her husband might have been involved in the killing, Odene Neal suddenly "remembered" something during the third interview.

With Odene's epiphany, Heck believed he had enough to take to the grand jury, so he met with District Attorney Gary Gerbitz, who advised Heck to talk with the suspect. If the defense later asked Heck if he ever talked with Hoppe, Gerbitz wanted him to be able to say he had.

Gerbitz was being extremely cautious. Questions about an earlier murder trial (Jeris Bragan) were surfacing—questions that later resulted in a complaint being filed against Gerbitz with the Tennessee Bar Association Board of Professional Responsibility. Facing the possibility of attorney misconduct charges, he could not have this one—which he knew in his gut would be a high-profile case—implode.

A Matter of Conscience

With support for Bobby coming from all sides, including some within his own office, Gerbitz had to be sure he had a solid case before taking on this man now considered a model citizen. The *Tennessean* called Hoppe "the son every parent dreams of—a strapping, clean-cut young man who just happened to be the best football player in a town that, like most Southern communities, worships the sport."

And Hoppe's celebrated football reputation didn't end at the city limits. By the time of Hudson's killing, the *Tennessean* said, "(Hoppe) was already a star at Auburn, breaking a 70-yard run against Mississippi State in 1956. By the end of the '57 season, he would have led the Tigers ...to a 10-0-0 record—and their only national title."

* * *

In 1988, everyone in Chattanooga has heard of the legendary Bobby Lee Cook.

And no one ever wants to miss his arrival at Court. Dressed to the nines and looking like Big Daddy straight out of central casting for "Cat on a Hot Tin Roof," Cook glides down Chattanooga's streets in a long, black Rolls-Royce, buffed to a soft shine; the chauffeur, a tall, dignified black man.

Reminiscing about the Hoppe case in 2008, Cook, then 82 and still sharp as a tack, still winning case after case, recounted the public sentiment toward his client in 1988.

"Everywhere I went, including the hotel where I was staying—from the bellman who delivered my bags, the lady at the desk, the waiter who brought me my breakfast—they would say something to the effect, I understand you represent Bobby Hoppe.

"Everybody thought they knew Bobby. They would say, 'I've known Bobby Hoppe for so many years and he's a great guy.'" Cook added, "Never heard anything but the highest accolades. It was remarkable.

"I began to laugh about it, and eventually said, 'Hell, I don't see how Bobby could have known all of these people.'"

* * *

After 14 months of digging and prodding, it's finally Heck's day to present his case. But in Court, he seems almost reticent, speaking so softly Evans has to keep telling him to speak up.

Evans begins by leading Heck through his interviews. Roy and Georgia Hudson. Richard Holland. Odene Neal. Jody Neal. John Stargel. Robert Cornish. Leroy Kington. Joseph Godwin. Joan Hoppe Voiles.

Phillips objects when Evans asks Heck how Joan seemed when he and Detective Angel visited her at her Moccasin Bend Road home in Chattanooga, but the objection is overruled.

Describing Joan as mentally and physically "fine," Heck says she refused to talk with the two detectives, saying, "I have lived with it all these years and I have nothing to say."

With that, she turned toward the window, declining to say another word.

Evans moves on to Stargel, the lead investigator in 1957, asking Heck about Stargel's notes and a tape the old detective mentioned.

Heck eventually found the tape stored in a building behind the Police Service Center. Actually, there are two tapes, he tells the jury. A five-inch reel-to-reel tape and a cassette tape.

Then, like a bomb exploding, a third tape surfaces. It seems Heck taped the conversation when he telephoned Hoppe, at Gerbitz's insistence, just days before the grand jury hearing.

Shocked, Phillips leaps up, objecting strenuously. The exchange becomes so heated DiRisio dismisses the jury while he learns more.

* * *

By this time, jurors have begun to resent being sent out of the courtroom so often. Why shouldn't they hear what's going on, they complain to each other. Sequestered in the jury room, they create their own drama. What about Joan? What role did she play in the killing? June Ledford recalls Evans said he's not sure who, if anyone, was in the car with Bobby that night. Pam Meeks speculates someone must have been with him, perhaps one of his friends. Or maybe Joan was driving—it *was* her car. Is it possible Bobby was driving while Joan pulled the trigger?

Interestingly, a similar discussion is going on in the room where the character witnesses are sequestered. Their sequestration far exceeds that of the jurors, who are dismissed only when the judge wants to talk privately with the attorneys.

In that cramped room, isolated from the daily proceedings, Bobby's character witnesses kill time reminiscing about his sports career. Although they've read excerpts from Cook's opening statement in the local paper, most still refuse to believe Bobby killed Hudson. On several occasions, they discuss what really happened the night Hudson was killed.

"I heard Billy Joe King was the wheel man," one says.

"No. Not Billy Joe," the man next to him protests. "I always believed Joan did it."

Leaning against the wall, another man shakes his head in agreement. "They found her black shoes in the car—and, after all, it was her car."

Across the table, someone adds, "Joan said she bought that convertible with her dead husband's money, but most folks believe Don gave it to her—a little love gift."

They appreciate the irony of that, recalling rumors of Don's brutal abuse, his aggressive acts of jealousy when Joan started seeing other men.

"Well, Hudson had it coming," one witness says.

"I agree," another chimes in. "He'd beaten the hell out of that girl way too long. I'd a done it myself if I'd been her and got half a chance."

* * *

With the jury out of the room, Judge DiRisio learns Heck called Hoppe at Chattanooga State, asking him to come to the police center to talk about a case. But Hoppe said he was going into a meeting and would call back later.

The prosecution is determined to let the jurors hear that Hoppe never returned the call. Fearing the jury may see this as evasion, Phillips objects, insisting that was not the case. Phillips tells the judge Hoppe notified him, and he returned the call on his client's behalf.

Hemming and hawing, DiRisio straddles the fence, questioning both the relevancy and the objection. Cook volunteers to help.

"If I might add something else..." Cook begins with a nod to the judge. "Bobby Hoppe had no obligation to talk to Mr. Heck."

But Cook's gentlemanly manners swiftly slip as he sternly cautions, "I think it's a very dangerous area. It's irrelevant, immaterial, and it poses a threat with reference to drawing an improper or a prejudicial inference upon his right to remain silent at that point in time."

DiRisio deems it *is* relevant. "Sometimes logic runs contrary to the Constitution, and what we logically infer from facts may be prohibited by the Constitution. That's really the issue."

"I don't think it's a matter of what is logical," Cook snaps, then pulls his claws back in before purring. "As Justice Holmes said, 'The life of the law is not logic; it's experience.'"

Not to be outdone, Evans jumps in, saying although he's "not well versed in the law where I can quote cases and quote justices," he recalls that a Supreme Court Justice—whose name escapes him—once said something that supports his contention, too. Without blinking, DiRisio lets the comment pass.

Grasping at straws, Evans points out that Miranda rights are in play only when someone is being taken into police custody. It has nothing to do with one's refusal to talk with police.

Then, seeping sarcasm, Evans reminds the judge the State believes the opening statement is highly relevant—how this had been in Bobby Hoppe's mind and how he had just been *waiting* to tell someone. "[Detective Heck] contacted him and attempted to give him the opportunity to unburden himself...."

DiRisio cuts him off. "You tell me what the relevance is, Mr. Evans."

Clearly irked, Evans says the relevancy is that Hoppe's failure to return the call shows an attempt to evade the truth. He points to the opening statement, mimicking Cook saying Hoppe "has just been waiting to tell somebody."

Jumping to his feet, angry as an old Banty rooster, Cook hisses at Evans. "That's not so!"

With Cook at his throat and DiRisio pressing him to produce relevancy, the assistant DA fumbles through pages of transcript but cannot find the quote.

Inhaling slowly to regain his composure, Cook again asks to address the Court. "Mr. Evans is saying if Mr. Hoppe becomes the target of an investigation, which he obviously was whenever the conversation was directed by Mr. Heck to him, and [Hoppe] doesn't call back—I say it's prejudicial, it's unfair, and it's improper."

Glaring at Evans while directing his statement to DiRisio, Cook adds, "If it does not impede his... constitutional rights [under] the Fifth Amendment, it gets so close, it's playing Russian roulette."

In a quick about-face, seemingly unhinged by Cook's sermon, DiRisio says, "I agree with counsel."

Clearing his throat, DeRisio says louder, "That's what I intended to say if I didn't say it in so many words. What I'm concerned [about] is what we refer to as the open door. If we have opened the door..."

But Cook cuts in. "I have not opened that door. My argument is on record and not to the memory of Mr. Evans. Mr. Evans and I both are hard of hearing, but if he heard what he represented to the Court, his hearing is far worse than mine."

Evans launches into a diatribe, saying if Bobby for years had wanted to tell somebody what happened, to "unburden himself," his refusal to return Heck's call is highly relevant.

Exasperated, Cook says through gritted teeth, "We haven't wanted to tell anybody. There wasn't anything to tell. It's our contention that the State, in 1966, when this matter was presented to a grand jury, had the same facts they have in 1988."

Then to the absolute astonishment of everyone in the courtroom, Evans says, "I don't know that a case was presented to the grand jury at all."

The startled look on the faces of the judge and the bailiff says it all. The courtroom's sudden hush seems to scream that Evans' being unaware Bobby's case went to a grand jury in 1966 is dubious, at best.

Apparently blind to the significance of his statement, Evans pushes on, sure of his position that Bobby's not returning Heck's call is germane.

But DiRisio defers his decision to allow both sides to find parts of the record that will shed light on the issue.

* * *

When Evans finally passes Heck to Phillips for cross-examination, the defense attorney begins with a fury, making the detective admit he withheld statements of prosecution witnesses until the Court required him to give them over to the defense.

Heck also admits that, though he had been investigating the case for 14 months, he never talked to Joan Hoppe Voiles until the day before the grand jury convened. Phillips then takes a whack at Heck's statement that Joan appeared mentally and physically healthy. Under pressure, Heck is forced to say their brief encounter was insufficient to judge her mental state. And he concedes he never tried to ascertain if she had been in a mental hospital.

As he hears this, Bobby thinks of all the times Joan checked herself into the Moccasin Bend mental hospital. Over the years, her depression periodically became so crushing she spent days, sometimes weeks, in the psychiatric ward of the hospital near her house. Bobby often wondered if Hudson's death—and not knowing who killed him—triggered Joan's worst depressive states.

While Bobby ponders the basis for Joan's illness, Phillips touches on why Heck once talked with Detective Cornish, one of the investigators in 1957, only five minutes, never to consult him again. Stains on Heck's investigation are spreading slowly but surely.

Why didn't Evans insist Heck talk more with Cornish? And why isn't Cornish testifying? Such additional omissions may blemish the whole fabric of Evans' case, Phillips surmises.

Sensing the jurors are beginning to spot the blots on both Heck and Evans, Phillips strikes. "You didn't get the so-called file Stargel produced until *after* the indictment, did you sir?"

"That is right," Heck admits without apology.

Actually, Heck hadn't even *talked* to Stargel until April 1988—after the indictment.

Hearing this, Bailiff Kelley raises his eyebrows. Then, turning to the jurors, he lifts them even higher.

Phillips notices what's occurring but proceeds. Establishing that Stargel or Cornish visited Jody and Odene Neal shortly after Hudson was shot, the tenacious attorney wants Heck to acknowledge "neither one of them had any relevant evidence to impart."

Evans objects, so Phillips rephrases: "Sir, the alleged threat Odene Neal related to you in 1988 had not been related to the investigators when they originally talked to her in 1957, had it?"

"That's right," Heck responds, frowning.

And Heck admits Odene didn't tell him when he talked with her in 1987 or on February 14, 1988. But, Heck says, the next day Odene suddenly recalled hearing Hoppe say something—it might have been a threat, she surmised—against Hudson.

Finally something Heck could sink his teeth into, so he went to Jody Neal, Odene's ex-husband, for corroboration.

However, on the stand, Heck seems to have forgotten Jody said he could not substantiate Odene's allegation. To nudge his memory, Phillips hands Heck a copy of his own notes.

Shrugging, Heck admits Jody did not remember his wife telling him anything: "It's printed here. I guess I said it."

Evans objects to Phillips' next question but not before it is on the record, a question by which Phillips establishes additional missing evidence from the coroner's 1957 inquest.

A bench conference ensues with Evans declaring Phillips' query "is totally misleading the jury." Arguing he should be able to ask Heck about Holland's testimony regarding alleged threats if Phillips can question Heck about other missing evidence, Evans says his objection is two-fold: it's not relevant and it's misleading.

Phillips uses the opening to point out that testimony from William McCutcheon about a gun swap with Hoppe the evening Hudson was killed—testimony critical to the case—would be admissible if the elderly pharmacist were not mentally incapacitated.

To the layman, it's a confusing exchange, but DiRisio concludes, "I don't see how you could say missing records would help the defendant unless you also allow the State to show some of that record might also help the State.

"If it's good for one, it has to be good for the other. If you persist, I think that's the ultimate conclusion I have to come to," DiRisio declares.

It sounds to me as if DiRisio is saying the statute of limitations protects the State as well as the accused. That doesn't seem right, so I make a note to ask Phillips or Cook about this.

Phillips would like to continue the debate, but he knows he's swimming in perilous waters. In another bench conference, he gets on the record additional statements that could form the basis for an appeal. "What I wanted to bring out was that the records of the inquest were destroyed, that counsel was excluded...."

Phillips points out again that McCutcheon's testimony about the gun swap was lost. As Phillips talks, Bobby's mind goes back to the evening he exchanged his pistol for McCutcheon's shotgun. He didn't want the damn shotgun but, for the sake of peace, he let McCutcheon talk him into trading. If only he had held firm, he wouldn't even have had the shotgun—or any gun—in his car when Hudson tried to run him off the road. Hudson might still be alive.

But had he not had a gun, he might be dead himself. Too late to think about that. What's important is that McCutcheon's testimony at the coroner's inquest could have corroborated his account of what occurred a few hours before Hudson was killed.

But all records from the inquest are long gone. And now Mr. McCutcheon has Alzheimer's. The inquest findings are moot, Bobby thinks, a silky sadness slipping over him.

Up front, an indignant Evans makes it clear he resents the defense suggesting that missing evidence is to the detriment of the defendant.

Phillips begins to point out the State raised the issue of the gun trade through its own witness [Stargel], but seeing DiRisio's obvious irritation, he halts in mid-sentence. "May it please the Court, I read loud and clear Your Honor's admonition. I will move on."

"Never to return? Never to return, Mr. Phillips?" DiRisio insists.

With a smile, Phillips replies, "Never to return with regard to this witness. Your Honor has my pledge."

DiRisio turns to Evans, expecting the debate to be over. But Evans persists. "Do I understand they are abandoning [their] contention in opening statement that somehow this worked something ill, worked evil? It's obvious [the defense is saying] ill and evil at work deprived this client of something."

Having stood silent as long as he can stand it, Cook jumps in, outrage reddening his face. "I will answer that. I don't abandon anything, and I don't take back anything I said in an opening statement. I speak for myself and myself alone."

Although he's seething, Cook's voice remains solid. "The point I was making—however inartful it may have been—is that I find it extraordinary [and] I find no precedent for excluding a man's counsel from a court of inquiry or an inquest where he has already become the target of an investigation. It's a mockery of the system to suggest it is fair."

DiRisio, riding the fence again, reminds both sides it's been so long since an inquest, even he, as judge, is perplexed.

"I am not sure that counsel is entitled to be present. I am not sure the focus of the inquiry is entitled to be present. I am not sure what the procedures are."

DiRisio may be baffled, but Cook has a rejoinder. "They said that was the first [coroner's inquest] in Hamilton County in a hundred years and apparently they haven't had one since on account of the debacle it created."

At long last, the jury is brought back in. But almost before they get seated, DiRisio decides he needs clarification on the record. Dismissed again, the jurors march out, clearly irritated.

"This is ridiculous," Bernice Frances grumbles. "We should be able to hear everything."

Marjorie Simpkins shrugs, saying she knows Bobby killed Hudson; she's ready for deliberations.

A shocked Paula Ackman turns to Simpkins, declaring no one should decide guilt or innocence until all testimony has been heard.

But Simpkins confides she and her husband drove the route Bobby and Hudson took that night, and they decided the defense theory doesn't hold water.

Unaware of Simpkins' admission of noncompliance, DiRisio has been mulling over the arguments from the opposing attorneys.

In a hushed voice, he amplifies previous remarks. "I think there is a difference between evidence lost through the ravages of time and nature and evidence that [suggests] somebody wrongly disposed of it. That was the basis of my last ruling. Evidence lost through the ravages of time and nature is lost to everybody. It's not by anybody's design."

Evans interjects, "Again, we think the clear implication, Your Honor, is somehow this works to the benefit of the defendant. I don't know what the relevance of these deaths are."

"Facts lost to the system," DiRisio repeats, his mood darkening.

With that, DiRisio ends the day's testimonies.

Bobby is ready for a break, stiff from sitting in the hard chair between his attorneys. And tomorrow will come too soon, he thinks.

With the jury dismissed for the day, Phillips asks the Court to allow him to make a statement for the record. It's a regurgitation of what's already been said—Hoppe did not return Heck's call but he, as Hoppe's attorney, called Heck on his client's behalf.

"Let that be of record," DiRisio says, pounding his gavel in adjournment, seemingly as ready as Bobby for the day to end.

The Cold Case Detective

* * *

Twenty years later, Bobby Lee Cook talked about the Hoppe case, agreeing, as the trial transcript indicates, that he and Leroy Phillips repeatedly laid the groundwork for an appeal.

"Absolutely," Cook remarked with a smile. "That's what good lawyers do. We make a record in case something goes wrong."

This is especially important when an attorney disagrees strongly with a ruling by the judge. "If it is not on the record, you don't really have anything to take to an appellate court. Of course, it's technical, but it has to be.

"Absent that, Bobby would have had ineffective counsel."

* * *

It's been a long, difficult day. Bobby, Sally and I stop by Shoney's Restaurant in the Golden Gateway before heading home. Sally is staying at a hotel near the courthouse, and with few dining options, Shoney's has become our regular eatery after Court is dismissed for the day.

Each evening, Sally and I are amazed that Bobby can pull himself out of the doldrums to recount some funny story. Laughing to keep from crying; or, paraphrasing Mel Brooks, using humor as a defense against the universe.

According to the menu, tonight's special is ham and eggs. When the waitress stands by our table, pencil poised, Bobby tells her he wants the special but "eliminate 'dem eggs."

The waitress glares at him, and Sally flashes me a "what did he just say?" look. But Bobby just grins, telling the waitress, "Oh, never mind, I'll take the eggs."

She walks away without a word, and Sally and I are obviously confused. With a laugh, Bobby shares a story he read in the *Pecuyne Press*. A Cajun man walked into a New Orleans restaurant. Seeing the breakfast special on the menu, a plate piled high with ham, eggs, fried potatoes, and crayfish, he told the waitress to give him the special, but to "eliminate 'dem eggs."

When the waitress returns with his food, the Cajun noticed the eggs on his plate. "I thought I told you to 'eliminate 'dem eggs,'" he said.

Shaking her head, she replied, "That damn cook. I told him to eliminate the eggs, but all he knows is fried and scrambled."

A Matter of Conscience

Guffawing at this story, one Sally and I found less funny, Bobby's laughter has other patrons twisting in their seats. Their stares stifle Bobby's humor. As suddenly as it had appeared, it's gone. The mood at our table has grown somber, the comic relief over, so we eat quickly and head home.

The next morning, Court reconvenes, arguments continue, and last night's levity is lost.

Like a bulldog, Evans again insists the jury be informed Hoppe did not return Heck's call. He has hold of a leg and won't let go, demanding Heck's taped talk with Hoppe be played. But Evans doesn't know whose leg he's gnawing. If Evans is a bulldog, Cook is a pit bull.

"Might I inquire at this time," Cook asks politely, "if the Court would inquire of counsel for the State if he has any [legal] authority for his proposition?"

"We believe it's relevant," Evans replies.

"Any case law?" Cook persists.

"Any case law?" Evans asks, his face a blank.

"Yes. Any case law, decisions of the United States Supreme Court?" Cook asks.

Exasperated, Evans replies, "No."

Not surprisingly, Cook has some, telling the Court he wants to articulate the defense's objection to the introduction of Heck's taped phone call with a little more specificity.

Citing the Fifth and Fourteenth Amendments, U.S. Constitution, and Article One, Section Nine of the Constitution of the State of Tennessee, Cook says hearing the tape will permit the district attorney, even the attorney general, to argue that Bobby's refusal to speak to the detective constitutes an attempt to evade the truth.

Before we can absorb that, Cook calls the Court's attention to Doyle v. the State of Ohio, 426 U.S. 610, 49 Lawyer's Edition Second and to another statement of the U.S. Supreme Court that was the predecessor of Doyle, United States v. Hale in 95 S.Ct.2133, in which the Supreme Court ruled, "In most circumstances silence is so ambiguous that it is of little probative force."

Cook is aware the case was going to the grand jury the following Monday, regardless of what Bobby said.

With a sigh, DiRisio decides he will hear the tape himself, out of the presence of the jury.

* * *

The tape begins to play, and everyone listens carefully:

HECK: Mr. Hoppe?

HOPPE: Yes.

HECK: This is Richard Heck, Chattanooga Police Department.

HOPPE: Yes.

HECK: How are you?

HOPPE: Fine. You?

HECK: If I could get rid of this cold, I'd be a lot better.

HOPPE: I hear you.

HECK: Listen, I'm involved in working a case here at the police department.

HOPPE: Uh-huh.

The panic beneath Bobby's calm voice was not detectable. Seated at the desk in his Chattanooga State office, he appeared placid as he listened to Heck. But his calm demeanor was a sham. Heart galloping wildly, Bobby looked over his shoulder to make sure his door was shut.

HECK: I've been working with the DA's office, and we would like to talk to you about an old case that happened in Chattanooga several years ago. We'd like to sit down and see if you [can] assist us in this case. Would you be available this afternoon?

HOPPE: I tell you, I have a basketball tournament this week. We have a basketball game tonight, and I have to prepare for that....

HECK: Do you think you would be available to talk with us briefly at say two o'clock today?

HOPPE: I don't know. You got a number that I could call you back. Is it Richard Hicks?

HECK: Heck, H-e-c-k.

HOPPE: H-e-c-k.

HECK: Uh-huh.

HOPPE: I have a meeting at nine o'clock. Can I call you back as soon as I get out of that meeting?

HECK: Yes. That would be fine.

Relieved, Heck can assure the DA Bobby will meet with them.

* * *

After the tape ends, Phillips notes that four days later—including Saturday and Sunday—Heck went to the grand jury. "You had already decided to take the case to the grand jury at that point in time, had you not?" Phillips asks pointedly.

"Based on what Mr. Hoppe had to say," Heck replies in a monotone.

Sarcastically, Phillips says, "Oh, he was going to make a difference?"

"Well, I was going to the grand jury, but I wanted to offer Mr. Hoppe an opportunity to talk to me," Heck answers, becoming defensive.

But why not tell Hoppe which case he was working on? "You intentionally concealed the fact that you wanted to talk to him about this particular case, didn't you?" Phillips queries.

"No sir, I didn't intentionally conceal anything."

"You were intentionally vague about it?"

"Possibly vague," Heck replies grudgingly.

"I say you were intentionally vague about it?" Phillips pushes.

"Yes," Heck admits before being dismissed. The sullen detective takes his seat.

Evans begins arguing—still out of the presence of the jury—that Cook's opening statement unlocked the door—referring to Cook's statement that, for 31 years, Bobby believed he did nothing wrong. Evans insists Cook's opening statement implied Bobby's case had been prejudiced by the delay and that the State intentionally caused the delay...and that missing notes from the coroner's inquest had penalized the defendant. "We believe all this has created an atmosphere where this is relevant...."

Cook snarls. "What you have [is] Mr. Heck calling Mr. Hoppe, [saying] he wants to talk to him about an old case, not even identifying the case—whether it's the death of Hudson or something else. Then by [Hoppe's] refusal to talk with him, you are allowing an inference of evasion when it was the officer who started the evasive act by not informing [Hoppe] what he wanted to talk to him about.

"With no identification being made of what [Hoppe] was to talk to [Heck] about, it leaves it in a Never-Neverland and takes away the strength of the argument at all and it would have no probative value."

Evans reacts vehemently, saying counsel's statement boggles the mind because, in opening statements, the defense alleged this had been preying on Bobby's mind all these years. "The jury knows, the defendant knows exactly what it was. There is nothing ambiguous," Evans concludes.

Tasting blood, Cook pauses before ripping at Evans. "I'd better not say it, but I will say it."

"To call an individual under these circumstances at the invitation of the attorney general, knowing that a case is going to be presented to the grand jury two or three days later, knowing what it's all about, knowing the investigation has focused upon Bobby Hoppe and to tell [him] they want to talk about an old case and won't he call them back—and intentionally not disclose the case they're talking about....

"And then to come in [here] and say that's an evasion of the truth, I think that's reprehensible."

Wounded, Evans takes one last swipe, declaring his office felt it only fair to offer the defendant an opportunity to talk about the case. "If Mr. Hoppe had come forward with something about it being another individual and so forth, that might have drastically changed matters."

But Cook knows the State never attempted to talk to Bobby in the early stages of the investigation. Never tried to talk to him after interviewing Godwin. Made absolutely no effort to talk to him after prodding Odene Neal until she fed them a useful nibble.

Instead, they waited until they had one foot in the door of the grand jury. They waited until Gerbitz said, "Call Bobby," so it could be declared later that they did offer him a chance to talk.

DiRisio tries to sort through arguments. Weary, he says it's possible to construe the questions and answers as constituting evasive responses. However, he notes that evasive responses take two forms—one is an evasion consistent with silence; the other is an evasion that's intentionally misleading. A defendant who is evasive and misleading, DiRisio says, may not then claim some kind of privilege.

Ending his mini-lecture, he tells the attorneys, "If it bears the earmarks of an invocation of silence or if it is more consistent with that, then it would be a Fifth Amendment matter."

It seems DiRisio has made a decision, declaring that, "the Court does not find that [the conversation] is factually misleading, but is more consistent with an invocation to remain silent."

But before you can snap your fingers, he equivocates, saying a defendant may invoke his privilege not to testify, but he may not then argue that he hasn't had a chance to tell his story.

A Matter of Conscience

DeRisio's decision is unsettling. Surely, the jury will see Bobby wasn't evasive. That having his attorney call Heck was what any reasonable person would do.

However, if DiRisio can't see it, will 12 ordinary citizens?

But I need not have worried. After vacillating, DiRisio comes down in support of Bobby.

"The issues on the matter are very close. I'm compelled to resolve them on this occasion, subject to reopening, in the defendant's favor."

Emotionally spent, I feel as if nothing is ever fully resolved.

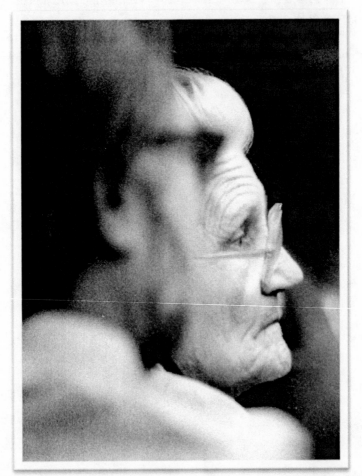

Chattanooga News-Free Press photo

Georgia Hudson in the courtroom in 1988 where Bobby Hoppe was on trial for the murder of her son, Don Hudson, on July 21, 1957

CHAPTER TEN

Stand by Your Man

"Any fool can tell the truth, but it requires a (wo)man of some sense to know how to lie well."
--Samuel Butler (1835-1902)

Born in Arkansas during the Great Depression, Ruby Odene Neal spent most of her life on Sand Mountain far up in northwest Georgia.

When Odene's family moved to the remote mountain in the early 1930s, the ramshackle building they called home housed 12 kids, seven boys and five girls. All those children cared about one another. That's why some of them show up in Chattanooga in 1988 when their sister, Odene, is the star witness in the much-touted Bobby Hoppe trial.

Some say she has the State's only piece of new evidence since 1966. This child of the Great Depression will have her 15 minutes of fame.

When Odene came down from Sand Mountain to Chattanooga to marry Charles W. (Jody) Neal in 1955, folks said she'd hit the big time. Not only was she living in the city, she landed a decent job at Dupont.

She had a nice house, too. Not big, but nice. They were doing just fine, Odene and Jody, living in North Chattanooga.

* * *

With the statute of limitations having expired on everything except first-degree murder, police had to prove premeditation if they wanted to take Bobby Hoppe to court. Finding proof of premeditation, though, was a stretch.

Odene first met Heck on February 28, 1987. Although Heck didn't tape the interview, he noted that Odene said her husband and Don Hudson were big buddies back in 1957, so she remembered when Hudson was killed. When questioned about where she was and what she was doing that night, she wasn't sure, but she thought she might have worked the midnight shift at Dupont. And Odene said she and Jody found out about Hudson's death the next morning.

The detective's next notation provided information he was able to use later with Odene. He wrote, "She could not account for Jody's whereabouts the night it happened."

Heck's notes also documented that Billy Joe King and his girlfriend, Jo Sliger, dropped by Jody and Odene's house one evening shortly after Hudson was killed. While they were visiting in the living room, County Coroner Dr. Doyle Currey arrived unannounced and began asking questions about Don's murder. He stayed a short time and left, Heck jotted in his notebook.

Neither Odene nor Jody told the coroner they knew anything about Hudson's death during that meeting.

As soon as Billy Joe and Jo left the Neal house, the phone rang, Odene recalled. She answered and handed the phone to Jody. Shortly afterward, she heard him cursing a blue streak. After he hung up, Heck logged, Jody told Odene the man on the phone threatened him, saying, "If you want to live and do well, you better not talk to that coroner again."

Odene didn't recognize the voice. Neither did Jody.

When Heck asked Odene if she knew Bobby Hoppe, she said before the murder he used to come by their house often, but she never saw him again after Hudson was killed, Heck wrote in his interview record.

His notes revealed Odene said she had heard Hoppe was furious with Hudson because he had "beat up on Bobby's sister," and Heck had underlined Odene's next comment—she heard Bobby once threatened to kill Don because of the abuse. But there was no record of Heck asking Odene where or when she heard this.

Almost a full year passed before Heck again approached Odene. On the afternoon of February 14, 1988, he called, wanting to come by and talk, but she'd just gotten home from work and said a friend was coming over. Heck persisted, so she agreed to answer some questions over the phone. This time Heck taped what Odene said.

Odene was surprised Heck hadn't given up on the old Hudson case. "Lord, you still workin' on that?

"Well, Lord. I tell you what, just like I said, I don't know a thing about it, because uh, all I knew [is] I was told the boy was killed and . . . and uh, that's just it," Odene sputtered to a stop.

Adamant, Heck said he wanted to check out some details. Odene's mind turned flip-flops as she remembered something Heck said when they talked—over a year ago.

"Well, . .but. . uh. . .Tha. . .The accusation you all made here about my ex, now, there is no way of that," she stuttered. "People gotta have proof. You know what ya'll said. Something else—uh, [it] was Jody with those guys that night, or something like that—that shocked me, I tell you."

Odene's voice dropped to a near-whisper, as if sharing something confidential. "God, he's been bad with me sometimes, but uh. . .he would never do nothing like that."

Odene wanted Heck to understand she knew what bad was, and Jody wasn't that bad. She might not live with Jody any more, but he had been her man for 28 years.

Heck repeated he must have proof. Odene, really frightened now, thought the detective was looking for proof Jody was with "them" when Don was killed. "Oh, law no, Jody wadn't with'em," she asserted, her voice rising in alarm.

"That's just a question we asked you back then," Heck explained. A question Heck failed to include in his notes from the February 1987 meeting with Odene.

Later, at the trial, when Cook hears this, his head snaps up. On the yellow legal pad in front of him, he jots a note to himself: Did Heck intentionally not record his question about Jody's possible involvement? Was he wary of documenting his insinuation? Was he trying to scare Odene?

Heck may not have recorded the question, but it stuck in Odene's mind and scared her silly for Jody. So during the interview, her heart racing, she told Heck, "Well, see, I thought...well, you reckon somebody told them that? But Lord, no, uh,..Don Hudson was like a brother to him."

Heck had her hooked and reeled in the line, saying she wouldn't believe all the rumors he's heard in the past year. But he couldn't deal in rumors, he told Odene, who jumped at the chance to agree.

"You're exactly right, and...uh, I don't know any facts, really, uh...All I know is just, you know, what, like I..."

But her agreeable words fade into nothing helpful.

Heck hoped she did know something. Stymied, fighting annoyance, he backed up and took a new approach, asking what she recalled about the night Hudson was killed.

Kicking her Achilles' heel, Heck asked if Jody was with her that night. Not initially catching the implication, Odene said she didn't remember, adding with a smile, "I reckon I's always with him, you know."

A look of understanding suddenly crossed her face and she began to back-peddle. "Oh, now...if somebody's tryin' to hang him in with it, they're all wrong. I'll never believe that."

She was petrified for her ex-husband, and Heck played her fear like a slide trombone. Panic now gripping her, Odene attempted to distract Heck by telling him Hudson used to date Bobby's sister. Seeing an opening, Heck asked if she ever saw Bobby get mad at Don.

Odene sidestepped, repeating that Bobby didn't like it because Don "beat up on" Joan.

When Heck pressed, asking if she knew whether Bobby ever *saw* Don hit Joan, Odene was forced to admit she didn't know.

But she declared she personally witnessed Don slapping Joan around, citing a time she and Jody were on a double date with Don and Joan. On the way home, "Don just smacked her up good. Lord, I didn't know what to think."

Quivering like a caged animal, Odene lapped up Heck's next words—he said it was remarkable what people remembered, even 30 years later.

"Uh-huh...Well, I *think* he told me that—now this is the day before Don Hudson was killed...I guess Jody told you what he said?" Odene asked, hesitatingly.

"Who? Who is 'he?'" Heck jumped on the word, anticipation coloring his voice. Maybe, just maybe what he had been pushing for was about to spill out of Odene's mouth.

"Bobby Hoppe," Odene replied haltingly. Heck admitted Jody never told him anything about Hoppe, but he was anxious for Odene to— and she waded right on in.

"He said...'I've got a gun out here, I gotta'—I believe he said—'a shotgun out here in my car,' and said, 'I'm gonna kill Don Hudson,'" Odene rattled on. Heck's reaction was euphoria. Unable to contain his excitement, Heck asked breathlessly, "Did he say that to you?"

"He sure did. He said, 'I'll kill him, but you better not... say nothin' about that,' he said, 'but I'll kill him,' and...well, I didn't think nothin' about it, and the next morning I came home, buddy, and Don was dead. Idn't it awful?"

Buddying up to Odene, Heck affirmed her feelings, even echoing her grammar: "Lord, that's pretty strong. Idn't it?"

A Matter of Conscience

Odene didn't recall if Jody was there when Bobby said he was going to kill Don—he might have been. But she *was* sure it was the night Don was killed.

Although she assumed she'd saved Jody, Odene now worried she'd wandered into a quagmire. She wanted to know if anyone else had told Heck.

Heck let Odene think others had corroborated her story, saying he and Detective Angel had talked to numerous people.

Heck assured Odene she had an obligation to tell him what she knew. He gallantly reminded her, if she or Jody had been killed, they would want somebody to help.

Buoyed by this smart detective's focus on her, Odene recalled something else. One night, Billy Joe King had asked her and Jody what they would do if someone tossed a stick of dynamite toward their house.

As soon as she said the words to Heck, she regretted it. "Oh, God, I oughta keep my mouth shut...I will get killed."

Heck was alarmed by Odene's next words, because it appeared she was having second thoughts. "I shouldn't be even repeatin' this, cause, golly bum—"

Knowing she'd let a big fat cat out of the bag, Odene tried to herd it back in. Backtracking with hems and haws, Odene assured Heck she and Jody certainly didn't know anything. Odene's suddenly tight nerves seemed to strangle the usual fast flow of her words.

Too late, she'd given Heck what he wanted, and he was not going to let her back down.

He hung up the phone, and as he left his office, Heck was so excited he could barely contain himself. Odene Neal was going to make it premeditation after all.

What really mattered was getting a grand jury to indict Hoppe and getting a jury to convict him. Because his interview was by phone, Heck visited Odene at her house the next morning—early—to confirm what she said. After all, her testimony would be the key to a case that had been collecting dust for more than three decades.

Sitting in her living room like an old friend, leading her through her previous comments, Heck got Odene to repeat most of what she had said on the phone the day before.

And, overnight, it seemed her memory had improved. She now recalled she worked the night before Hudson was killed.

Heck then asked why she didn't tell the police about Bobby's alleged threat in 1957. Odene leaned back in the chair, mouth shut tight, so Heck prompted, "Scared?"

"Maybe, or—they didn't really ask me. I...I don't know. I can't remember."

* * *

Unlike at the preliminary hearing just days ago, today in Court Odene appears cogent and her speech isn't slurred. She wears a neat white shirtwaist dress, reminiscent of the mid-1950s, her brown hair ringed in loose curls. In contrast to the rattled expression she wore throughout the preliminary hearing, today she looks calm.

The change in Odene is not by accident. We'll learn later the prosecutors made sure she didn't overmedicate before Court this morning. Evans can't afford for his key witness, his link to premeditation, to appear befuddled again—this time in front of the jury.

Under Evans' leading questions, Odene plays her role well. In an attempt to pre-empt the defense, Evans has her tell about the time she saw Hudson "smacking on" Joan.

Reciting what she had told Heck on the telephone, Odene describes hearing scuffling in the car's back seat. Turning around, she saw Don hitting Joan.

"I told Don, I said, 'Don't be smacking her, don't be hitting her in our car. You know, I don't like that,'" Odene says, righteous indignation in her voice.

Even when pressed by Evans, she can't say how much time elapsed between the back-seat scuffle and when Hudson was killed.

Clearly disappointed, Evans needs Odene to help him prove Joan was still dating Hudson near the time of his death. To cinch his theory that Bobby had a motivation for shooting him.

So Evans tries another approach, asking Odene about the night of the killing.

"Went to work that night," she says, her memory better than when Heck interviewed her the first two times.

It must be that Bobby came by before she left for work, since she had to be on the job at midnight. Must have been before 11:30 or 11:45 p.m.

A Matter of Conscience

On June 13, 1988, at the preliminary hearing, Odene's testimony regarding when Bobby came to her house was specific. Unequivocally, she said, "I remember the sun was shining."

At the trial when Evans asks Odene if Jody was in the house while Bobby was there, she isn't sure. After vacillating, she decides Jody was probably in the house, but he might not have been in the living room with Bobby and her.

Odene volunteers that she and Bobby just started talking about Hudson and Joan, adding that Bobby was upset because Don had mistreated his sister.

She pauses a moment, as if trying to remember something. "Seems like he started to leave and he says, 'Well, I have got a shotgun out here in my car and I will shoot him.'"

Glancing at Bobby, Odene quickly adds she didn't think he meant it at the time.

But the next morning when she came home from work and her husband told her Hudson had been killed last night, Bobby's words rushed back to her. "I said, 'Oh, my goodness.' I said, 'Oh, mercy, Jody, Bobby left here yesterday afternoon and said he had a shotgun in the car and he'd kill him.'"

Listening carefully to Odene's testimony, I note she's cited two varying times Bobby stopped by—"11:30 or 11:45 p.m." and "yesterday afternoon." When Bobby supposedly dropped by Odene's house is a critical factor, as Barbara Jo Campbell's testimony will later reveal.

Yet, inexplicably, the time discrepancy is never pursued by the defense attorneys.

* * *

Bobby dressed with care for his date with Barbara Jo Campbell. Gazing in the bathroom mirror, he once again brushed his neatly cut hair, then, with a chuckle, flexed his muscles beneath his short-sleeved shirt. Before turning from the mirror, Bobby took once last glance at his well-defined face and the crystal-clear blue eyes some say look like Paul Newman's.

And like Newman, Bobby was a natural actor—hiding his real feelings from the world. Most folks didn't know he hated being in the limelight at Auburn as much as he disliked the glory-filled newspaper articles about him when he was at Central. What he did like was the thrill of the game. Running like a rabbit, hounds on his heels.

Smiling to himself, he admitted he'd like to make some yardage tonight with Barbara Jo, but this was one time he knew he wouldn't score. Barbara Jo was a nice girl with a capital "N." Not like some girls at Central, always eager to head to the woods during lunch with a horde of guys, easy girls who notched their belts by the jocks they'd had. Tonight, he just looked forward to spending time with Barbara Jo. Ready early, he headed to the Riverview Pharmacy to hang out with friends. He hadn't been there long when the pharmacist told him Bill McCutcheon was on the phone.

The guys heard Bobby say he wasn't interested in a shotgun.

Soon, Bobby got another phone call. McCutcheon again. This conversation was longer, but friends heard Bobby repeat he had no use for a shotgun. As soon as Bobby returned, the boy-talk set in again, guys bragging about girls and what they were going to do later that night.

The third time McCutcheon called, Bobby told him he didn't have time to look at the shotgun. He didn't want to be late for his date. McCutcheon insisted, saying he knew a chert pit nearby where they could test the shotgun.

Finally, Bobby agreed to meet McCutcheon.

After they test fired the gun, McCutcheon pushed Bobby to trade for a pistol, refusing to take no for an answer. Tired of resisting, Bobby headed home to get the pistol.

After the swap, Bobby looked at his watch and saw he was late for his date. Squealing tires, he took off in his sister's black Ford Fairlane convertible. His own car was an old, beat-up Hudson, so cruising around in a new convertible was a treat when he was home from Auburn.

Even though Bobby was a bit late, Barbara Jo greeted him with a smile. She knew Bobby hid behind an invisible mask most of the time. But he was kind. And he could tell more funny stories than anyone she had ever known, sometimes making her laugh until her jaws ached.

After he greeted her parents, Bobby asked Barbara Jo if she minded if the convertible top was down. It was a beautiful June night, and she liked to feel the wind on her face. They rode around a while and then stopped at Nikki's for hamburgers and fries. They played the jukebox from their table. Johnny Mathis' "It's Not for Me to Say." Fats

Domino's "I'm Walkin." The Everly Brothers' "Wake Up Little Susie." After a while, they decided to go to a local dance hall.

Time flew, and suddenly it was time to get Barbara Jo home. She might be 21, but she still respected her parents' midnight curfew. Besides, they wouldn't mind if she and Bobby spent some time on the front porch swing.

The couple pulled into her driveway as a nearby church bell chimed 12. Sitting on the porch for 30 minutes or so, they talked about Barbara Jo visiting Auburn for a game next year. She was sure her brother, Paul Allen, would drive her down.

* * *

Knowing the defense will ask Odene why she didn't tell the police about Bobby's comments back in 1957, Evans tries to stay one step ahead.

He leads her through the visit from Currey and the "curly headed detective [Cornish]," asking what she told them, but she says they didn't ask her anything. Besides, Billy Joe and Jo were in the living room and she's not sure if they could overhear the conversation in the kitchen.

But when Jody received the threatening phone call just after Billy Joe left, she wondered if Billy Joe *might* have overheard what was said in the kitchen. So what? They didn't tell the coroner and detective anything. One thing for sure, someone didn't want Jody talking to the officials again.

But Jody wasn't afraid, Odene tells Heck. He picked up the phone and called Cornish or Currey—she's not sure which. She heard Jody say, "Now the first damn one that comes here to my house and does something, I'll shoot 'em."

At least, that's what Odene told Heck during one of the interviews.

In Court, she says Jody told Cornish, "He didn't want anybody shaking his doorknob after dark." Clearly, Jody wasn't afraid back in 1957. Had he known anything worth telling, he would have passed it on to the coroner and the detective, wouldn't he?

With anticipation brightening his face, Evans launches the tape of the February 14, 1988, telephone interview—the first time Odene told any police official that Bobby had threatened Hudson's life. Evans wants the jury to hear the initial time it came out of Odene's mouth.

"Is that the truth, ma'am?" Evans prompts after the tape concludes.

"Yes," Odene says, beaming.

Satisfied his witness has put a nail in the coffin of the case, Evans turns Odene over to the defense and walks back to the prosecution's table, taking his seat with an audible sigh of relief.

Odene came through. Thankfully, the jury didn't see her a few days ago during the preliminary hearing. Gerbitz is going to be pleased—Evans got Odene to cement premeditation in the jurors' minds.

For the defense, the gentleman from Summerville does the honors. Gold-rimmed half-moon spectacles on the tip of his nose and a wiry white goatee wrapping his chin, Bobby Lee Cook steps to the witness box. Odene doesn't know a tsunami is about to hit her. She sits straight and tall in the witness box, smiling. Cook returns her smile, briefly.

Slow and easy, he embarks on his cross-examination. He walks Odene through the dates of her three interviews with Heck and then reminds her she testified in front of Judge DiRisio in a preliminary hearing just days ago. That day, after Odene had tripped up repeatedly on her own statements, Cook had forced her to admit her memory was faulty. "Thirty-one years is a long time to remember every little detail," she had stated.

During the trial, regarding each of the times Odene was interviewed, Cook asks the same simple question: Was it the truth?

Three times Odene responds, "Yes."

"And I take it that it goes without saying that everything you said [under oath on June 13th of 1988 before DiRisio without a jury present], you knew that you had taken an oath, you had held up your hand and you had sworn to tell the truth, the whole truth and nothing but the truth so help you God?" Cook asks pointedly.

"Yes, sir."

"Every word of it?"

"Yes, sir," Odene says with a bright smile.

"To the best of your ability and to the best of your recollection?"

"That's true," she responds, nodding.

Smoothly, Cook gets her to admit she first met Bobby the summer Hudson was killed, so she had not known him long.

She insists she just doesn't know how many times she had seen Bobby that summer or how many times he had been in her home. She does know she hadn't been around Hudson much—a couple of times. But her husband knew him well—the two had known each other all their lives.

Odene adds that Jody thought the world of Don. They were like brothers, she had said in the interview with Heck. She only saw Joan Hoppe Voiles one time, the night Hudson "smacked her around." She tells Cook she has no idea how long they dated or when they broke up.

Cook pulls out the transcript of Odene's February 15, 1988, meeting with Heck—the interview in which she said Don was still dating Bobby's sister at the time Bobby allegedly threatened to kill him.

After reading her words, Cook looks at Odene over the rims of his glasses. "Is that what you said?"

Shifting uncomfortably, Odene gropes for words. "Well, that's what is here and I took it...he was...Bobby was at my house and told me—we were discussin', Bobby was telling me... "And, evidently they were dating from what he said, yes."

Cook looks Odene straight in the eyes. "Ms. Neal, didn't you tell this Court and jury no less than five minutes ago that you didn't know whether they were dating at that time or whether they had been broken up for a year or not?"

Before Odene can open her mouth, Cook turns his back on her. "That's all right. I will move on to something else."

Odene's composure cracks as Cook reminds her he asked earlier if she was telling the truth when she talked with Heck. Hesitantly, she attempts to assure Cook she did not try to mislead.

Unaffected by her assertion, Cook hammers Odene, reading every question he asked her and every response she made regarding truthfulness during the preliminary hearing.

"You recognized the importance of telling the truth [when talking with Heck]?"

Of course she did, Odene was quick to respond.

"I take it you were raised to tell the truth whether you take an oath or otherwise, right?"

"Right," Odene had responded at the earlier hearing.

So all of the answers she gave Heck during his interview were true and accurate?

Yes.

Cook has Odene where he wants her.

"Turn [the tape] on," he instructs. Methodically, he plays a portion of Heck's interview, stops to question Odene, and then repeats the pattern, revealing lie after lie.

When he gets to the part where Odene says with a laugh, "Lord, buddy, I don't know a thing about this," Cook stops the tape abruptly. "Was there anything funny about that then?"

With a subdued giggle, she replies, "No, sir...."

But Cook won't let up. Playing off her little-girl giggle, he asks if there is anything funny now. Swallowing hard, Odene says, "No, sir," with no tittering.

Well, was it the truth, Cook wants to know.

"It was not the truth," Odene confesses. "And you know why I said that to him? Because I was scared."

It has been 31 years since Hudson was killed, yet Odene says she's afraid—so she told Heck she didn't know anything. In 1957, before she had any reason to be scared, she hadn't told police officials anything either.

Pounding away, Cook reminds Odene she told him just a few days earlier that she never tried to mislead Heck. "You lied to this Court, didn't you, on June 13?"

"No, sir, I have never meant to lie to anyone," Odene stammers as she tries to dig herself out of a deepening hole.

Mimicking her voice on the tape, Cook says, "'I don't know a thing about this.' That was a lie, wasn't it, Ms. Neal?"

Pulling at a curl in her hair, Odene's face reddens. "I didn't mean it to be a lie."

His own ruddy complexion flushing even deeper, Cook lights into Odene. "What would you call it? A fib? Isn't that what you called it on June 13?"

"Maybe a little fib, yes. I didn't—I mean, I was just trying to get out—get away from answering him," Odene whines, her face going from cherry red to ghostly pale.

"Just a small fib or a big fib?" Cook starts, then curtly says, "I don't insist on an answer. Move on."

Thinking the worst is over, Odene's relief is palpable. But when the tape rolls again, she stiffens. Again, we hear her say she didn't know a thing about Hudson's death.

Again, Cook asks, "Is that another fib?"

"I was denying it, about knowing anything."

"I say is that a fib according to your characterization?" Cook leans toward Odene as she cuts her eyes to the prosecution table, silently begging for help.

Evans, watching one of his primary witnesses impeached, jumps to her rescue. "Your Honor, I think she answered the question."

"I don't," Cook says brusquely. He is in his "Were you lying then or are you lying now?" mode, and no one is going to put the brakes on him.

When Evans tries to argue, Cook announces, "I am entitled to an answer."

The judge agrees, and Odene is forced to admit one more "fib."

As the tape rolls and Odene's snickers interrupt statement after statement, Cook stops the recording repeatedly to ask if what she is saying on the tape is funny.

"No, it isn't," Odene whispers as she lowers her eyes.

The courtroom is uncharacteristically silent, seemingly shaken by the growing mound of "fibs." People are on the edge of their seats, anticipating the next one.

The tape resumes, showing Heck's subtle manipulation of Odene. The jury hears for the first time what we heard at the preliminary hearing—how Heck implied her husband was involved in Hudson's death, the panic in her voice as she realized she has to save Jody. Ultimately, they hear Odene say three times she didn't know any facts about the shooting.

But then she tells Heck, the tape reveals, that Bobby came by her house the evening of the killing, said he didn't like Hudson beating his sister, and was going to kill him with a shotgun.

Cook wants Odene to confirm in the presence of the jury that she told her husband about the threat Bobby allegedly made in 1957 since he and Hudson were such good friends.

"Yes, I certainly did. I told Jody that the next morning when I got home," Odene declares.

"Now, my question to you, having known your husband for two years—" is all Cook gets out before Evans is on his feet.

The two lawyers put on a little show for the spectators.

"This is what we object to," Evans begins.

Cook looks quizzical. "Well, he hasn't heard the question."

119

But Evans *thinks* he knows what the question will be. "It sounds like the same question."

A playful glint in his eye, Cook says, "Well, it might not be."

Evans isn't quite as congenial. "Well, we are going to object. It sounds like knowing your husband, you think he would have told someone this? *I* don't know; *she* doesn't know."

Still oozing charm, Cook says, "I don't know what she knows."

Evans continues to thrash out angrily. "It calls for a conclusion. The witness is here. He can ask the witness, Jody Bill, what he told, what he didn't tell, what he remembers. But to ask this [witness]—"

Disarmingly, Cook tries to help. "I know, Mr. Evans—"

But Evans' fuse is short. He's been through a lot this morning. He's watched his key witness admit to "fibbing" time after time. He can't afford any more damage. "If I could continue with my objection. To ask this witness--"

DiRisio has had enough and interrupts, calling the attorneys forward. The courtroom buzzes as the bench conference ensues. Lawyers leaning against the back wall whisper about Cook's decapitation of the State's witness. The Hudson family looks distressed, fearful Odene's testimony won't convince the jury of premeditation.

In the silent jury box, jurors are processing Odene's words, trying to discern any truth.

After the short bench conference, Cook continues, careful to frame his questions so Evans has no basis for objecting.

Twice, he lets Odene assure him she did indeed tell her husband about Bobby's threat—the morning after Hudson was killed.

And many times afterward? Cook asks.

"Certainly, certainly," Odene replies confidently.

And, with assurance, she says her husband knows that very well.

Cook circles back one more time, pointing out there wouldn't be any way Jody could forget something she had talked about so much.

Odene vehemently agrees. Cook pauses a moment, staring at her, then flips the tape on. The jury hears Odene telling Heck she can't remember whether she worked the night Hudson was killed. Was that true?

"It must have been false," Odene replies reluctantly, because she's now sure she worked the midnight shift that night.

An absolute falsification, Cook thunders, his head rifling back in rage.

The tape rolls again.

For the third time, the jury hears trepidation in Odene's voice as she fears the worst for her husband. "I am going to tell you, (if) somebody trying to hang him in with it, they are all wrong. I won't ever believe it."

On the tape, Heck leaves that thought in Odene's head, responding only with, "Uh-huh."

Cook moves on to the visit by Currey and Cornish. Stopping the tape, Cook asks if she heard Jody tell them about Bobby's threat.

An easy question, but Odene asks Cook to repeat it.

Cook tries to simplify. "All of you together went in, I believe you said, the kitchen?"

"Yes, all of us except [Billy Joe and Jo]. Just Jody and I went in with Dr. Currey."

"In the kitchen?"

"Yes, sir."

"How big was this kitchen?"

"Oh, not very big."

With a small smile tugging at his lips, Cook says, "My kitchen at home is a little ole tiny thing."

Charmed, Odene smiles at Cook. "Mine was, too," she says.

So they were sitting around this small kitchen, Cook repeats.

Yes, sir. "Right around that little table—yes, sir—around that little table."

With a twinkle in his eyes, Cook asks, "Around that little bitty, itsy-bitsy table, right?

With no idea she's being played, Odene responds in all seriousness, "Yes, sir." Cook is having so much fun he just can't stop. Bailiff Kelley is about to explode with laughter. Jurors are trying to contain themselves, and if I could see his face, I'm sure Bobby is struggling to suppress a smile.

"While all of you were sitting around that little bitty table—"

"That's right."

"In that little bitty room, right?"

"That is right."

Abruptly, Cook goes back to the question he asked before his kitchen table routine. He wants to know if Odene ever heard Jody tell Dr.

Currey or the detective that she had told him Bobby came by their house the night Hudson was killed, that Bobby threatened to kill Hudson.

With a shrug, Odene tells Cook Dr. Currey didn't hear anything about the threat from Jody. After a pause, she adds she never told Currey either.

Since Hudson was like a brother to Jody, Cook wants to know why not. No threatening phone call had been made before they talked with Currey. No statement about dynamite. So why didn't Jody or Odene give Currey information that would have put Hudson's killer behind bars?

Odene doesn't recall what they talked about with Currey, but she does remember Currey saying he started out by selling papers when he was just a young boy.

"I remember him telling us that," she insists.

Unable to resist, Cook says, "That's better than I did plowing with a mule."

Playing along, not knowing she's the fiddle, Odene says, "Me, too."

Serious again, Cook restarts the tape.

He lets the jury hear Odene say Jody knew the same things she did. Then the jury hears her deny it before Cook goes on the attack. "You have known from the beginning [you were the only one present when Bobby allegedly threatened to kill Hudson], haven't you? You have known all along, all along from July of 1957 to the present time that your husband didn't hear that statement, that he wasn't in that room."

Knowing she had implied otherwise on the tape and sensing she is trapped again, Odene tries to save herself, but it's too late. The jury heard her try to convince Heck that Jody had heard the threat.

Point made, Cook moves on. Playing a short section of tape, he pauses to let it sink in with the jury that Odene said, "Don *used* to date Hoppe's sister."

This time Odene wiggles out of the trap, saying she meant "used" to date her 30 years ago.

But almost immediately, she is ensnared again, forced to admit there is no basis to her statement that Don was dating Joan at the time he was killed.

"Did you just make it up?" Cook asks pointedly.

Trying the wiggle routine again, she says she just "took it they were dating" since Bobby talked about Don beating on his sister.

This time she fails. "I thought you said a minute ago you didn't know whether they had been broken up a year or not?" Cook pushes.

"Well..." is all Odene can get out. Tired to the bone, she slumps in her seat.

But Cook has no sympathy, catching her on the slide.

Odene can't recall if Bobby told her Don had been beating Joan last week, last month or last year. "No, he really didn't say," Odene admits. But Odene had testified previously that *she* told Bobby about Hudson's rough ways with Joan.

And for the upteenth time, the jury hears Odene defend Jody. Stand by your man. Even if he divorced you years ago, as Tammy Wynette sang, "keep giving all the love you can."

On the tape, the jury hears Heck tell Odene he appreciates people like her telling it straight. "When Mr. Heck said he appreciated people like you telling it straight, you hadn't told it straight, had you? You had told it crooked (and) false."

"I had begun to open up and tell him some things," she offers hesitantly.

But Cook ignores her unspoken plea for relief. "Let's let you open up then," he snorts, turning the tape on to the sound of her tittering as she tells Heck, "...and the next morning I came home, buddy, and Don was dead. Idn't it awful?" Then a giggle.

Chastising Odene again for inappropriate laughing, Cook presses her about "opening up."

Warily, she says, "I'm trying to," but Cook is unconvinced.

"Ms. Neal, I don't want to be difficult, but didn't you tell this Court and jury just a moment ago that when you said that that you had opened up, you had nothing more to hide, nothing more to conceal, and you were going to tell the truth, the whole truth and nothing but the truth?" Cook asks with thunderous contempt.

Odene gulps. "On this telephone conversation?"

"No," Cook roars. "In this courtroom."

His prey backed into a corner, Cook insists on knowing whether she told Heck the truth or a lie.

Odene can't seem to get it right. After all, she pleads, it's been 31 years ago. She's just trying to get in her mind if Jody was there.

Turning toward the jury with a sweep of his hand, Cook asks, "You tell this Court today that Jody was not there when Bobby Hoppe said this?"

Bobby is riveted. When Odene reluctantly acknowledges Jody was not there, the tense muscles in Bobby's shoulders relax a little. Odene has no one to corroborate her story.

Attempting to explain, Odene declares Heck took her by surprise, and she couldn't get it all together, she professes. "I thought about this a lot since this case came up."

"I'm sure you have," Cook says with soft cynicism as he turns the tape back on.

With a stern stare, Cook quietly adds, "But you didn't have it together, did you, and you still haven't gotten it together."

On the tape, the jury hears Heck tweak Odene's sympathy like strings on a harp, urging her to help "poor ole Mrs. Hudson. She has lived through hell, you know. Imagine something like that happening to your child. That's bad and whoever did that should be punished.

"Regardless of what kind of person anybody is, they don't deserve to die like that," Heck prompts.

Riled up with pity for Mrs. Hudson, Odene's worry about Jody has dissipated. Thankful her ex is off the hook, this is one time she agrees with Heck. Now she can turn her emotions to the poor man who was killed, telling Heck no matter how bad Hudson was, he wasn't as bad as the one who shot him. "At least Don never did kill anybody that I know of. So in my book they are worse off than Don Hudson was."

"Yes, ma'am," Heck agrees.

Clicking off the tape, Cook asks for a recess.

We all need one.

* * *

When Court reconvenes, Cook wants to talk about Odene's epiphany during which it came to her that Jody wasn't in the room when she was talking with Currey.

"Just like I say, I was talking to Mr. Heck on the phone, but I want you to know that I did not know I was being taped. I was not sworn, I was not under oath and I...I was just guessing, making a quick guess at what happened."

124

A Matter of Conscience

In his beautiful baritone, tuned to a fine Southern cadence, Cook says thoughtfully, "Oh, I see."

"That's exactly right. I did not know I was being taped, and I was just giving him a rough estimate."

Confident the jury sees through Odene's explanation, Cook moves on.

When he reads Heck's note [from the first interview in 1987] that Odene had, on occasion, heard that Bobby threatened to kill Don, she equivocates. "I don't remember that."

"You deny saying that?" Cooks asks.

"I don't remember saying that...no sir, I don't."

"You don't have any recollection of that at all as you sit here today?" Cook prods.

"I can't remember that."

"Your mind is a blank on that, am I correct?"

When she makes no audible response, Cook moves on to the last tape, but his mind is stuck on Odene's failure to recall telling Heck in February 1987 she heard Bobby had threatened to kill Hudson. As the tape plays, Cook ponders if Heck—not Odene—was the first person to suggest the alleged threat.

* * *

According to Jeris [Jerry] Bragan in his book, *Beyond Prison Walls,* before being arrested, he received a phone call from a policeman who once worked for him. The cop didn't waste time with preliminaries.

"'I probably shouldn't be talking with you. I'd get fired if they ever found out,'" he began and then abruptly told Bragan it was just a matter of time before he was charged with murder.

Bragan replied that that was ludicrous. He was innocent, so the police didn't have any evidence to connect him to the crime.

The cop friend exploded in a derisive laugh. "'Jerry, you better wake up and smell the coffee. These people don't need any *evidence.* I'm telling you, they'll make up any evidence they need, and you can be sure it will be solid enough for a jury to convict.'"

When Bragan asked his friend how the police could get the DA to go along with that, the response came back with a disgusted grunt: "'Buddy, these people work together, *together!* Do you understand what

I'm saying? Gary Gerbitz and Stan Lanzo will simply refine anything [Deputy Chief Pete] Davis offers.'"

And the officer warned, "There isn't a lawyer in town who can help you if these people decide to take you down.'"

Although Bragan's case occurred a few years before Bobby's, I didn't read about it until 2008. When I did, I was thankful once again that we had engaged Bobby Lee Cook, who knew how the system worked and revealed it masterfully to the jury.

* * *

As the second 1988 tape continues playing, the jurors hear Heck questioning Odene. This time, Heck already knows the answers, so his questions are direct. He leads her, having her confirm what she said the day before on the phone.

Cook stops the tape after she says Don was dating Joan at the time of the killing. Cook asks if she ever heard of Bobby being upset with Don before the night he was killed. At first, she says she can't remember. But then, Odene remembers *she* told Bobby while he was at her house about Don "smacking around on Joan" the night the two couples double-dated. But she doesn't remember whether it was that summer, a year before, two years before, three years before.

She just recalls what Bobby said. "If I get this right," she begins, "'I have a gun out here in my car and I will kill him.'"

What is she trying to get right? Cook demands to know.

"I was going to be as truthful as I could. I knew I was being taped and I knew then that I wanted to get it just exactly what he said."

"Nail it down?" Cook asks wryly.

"But he said shotgun," she adds.

"You said a shotgun on a previous occasion and a gun here. Which was correct? Was shotgun correct?"

Odene responds confidently, "Yes, sir."

But the tape, turned back on, contradicts her again.

On it, Heck asks, "Did he mention a gun or a shotgun?"

"I think he said a shotgun but I wouldn't—"

Cook hits again. "You didn't finish your statement. You said, 'I think he said a shotgun but I wouldn't—'"

With a demure smile, trying a different approach with Cook, Odene tells him she was just holding back.

126

But he has lost his patience, demanding to know if she was still holding back on the 15th of February.

Again, trying to charm Cook, Odene says, "I tell you the truth, Mr. Cook, I did not know what to do."

She says she was still questioning herself. She felt like she was doing the right thing but was still worried and scared.

What was she scared of in 1988?

Exasperated, Evans objects to playing more of the tape after hearing Heck lead Odene down the path he wants to go.

"I don't know where we are going with the continuation of playing the tape," Evans exclaims. "If we could get to some questions...."

"I will tell him where I'm going," Cook responds politely.

"Could we get to a specific—" Evans says before Cook can explain.

"May I finish?" the courtly lawyer interrupts. "It's my tape, at least I've got cross-examination at this point, and he wants to know where I'm going. I want to play this whole tape—under the rule of completeness—between the interview of this lady and the detective. That's where I'm going."

Stopped like a deer in the headlights, Evans stumbles. "Under the rule of—"

"Completeness—if part of the conversation is admissible, all of it is," Cook explains.

DiRisio rules the rest of the tape can be played.

Stopping the tape after Odene has said, "We were discussing this and he said, 'I have a shotgun in my car and I will kill him,'" Cook tries to get Odene to acknowledge those might not have been the exact words.

"He didn't say 'I have got a shotgun in my car and I will kill him *if he doesn't leave my sister alone?*'"

"No," Odene insists, "he did not say anything about his sister."

Without a word, Cook turns the tape back on. The jury hears Heck's voice: "You did witness Bobby Hoppe in your living room threaten to kill Don Hudson if he didn't leave his sister alone?"

And the jury hears Odene say, "Yes."

Quickly, Odene asserts, "That was Detective Heck that said sister. It wasn't me."

Like a crack of lightning, Cook snaps, "Mr. Heck had put the words in your mouth and you said, 'Yes.'"

Evans, a quick learner, asks the judge if the tape can continue "under the rule of completeness." He needs to get away from what has just been said.

Cook obliges, forcing Odene to admit another fib—a mistake, she calls it this time.

She was mistaken when she told Heck she didn't tell the coroner or the police about what Bobby had allegedly said because they didn't ask her or because she was scared. She wasn't scared because no threat had been made. She was mistaken about that.

"Please tell this Court when it was that you decided to tell the truth?" Cook hounds her.

"When I made this statement here, I told them the truth."

"Which statement?"

"When Mr. Heck called me on the phone. I was telling him the truth, the last part of it."

Odene has already forgotten Cook caught her in multiple lies in the taped telephone call.

But the jury will remember. And that's enough for Cook.

Chattanooga News-Free Press photo

Ruby Odene Neal being cross examined by defense attorney Bobby Lee
Cook during the Hoppe trial in 1988

CHAPTER ELEVEN

On the Hot Seat

Of two evils, we must always choose the least.
--Thomas a Kempis (1380-1470)

Being on the water always appealed to Bobby. He tackled a big fish with the same determination he showed as a football player bringing down an opposing team's quarterback. The soothing ripple of the waves had a hypnotic effect on him, long before 1988 when he would need their calming influence in the worst way.

But that was light years away from the hot summer days of '57 when Bobby, like an older Tom Sawyer, floated down the Tennessee River on a makeshift raft, not a care in the world.

* * *

Bobby and Jody Neal weren't buddies. As teens, they hadn't run with the same crowd. In fact, Jody tells the jury the only time he recalls spending any time with Bobby was in the summer of 1957. And it was always with a small group of former high school teammates hanging out at the lake, a crew that included Billy Joe King and his brother, Jesse.

On the stand, Jody tells the prosecutor he ran around with the Kings a good bit, much more than he did with Bobby.

In response to a question from Evans about the summer of '57, Jody responds, "Well, we was all up there together," sounding as if Bobby might have been with the King boys, implying his relationship with Bobby wouldn't have been enough to draw Bobby to the lake.

Happy-go-lucky, the young men enjoyed the good life on the water during the hot days of summer 1957. Swimming off the raft they built, doing a little fishing.

* * *

After a stint in the Army, Jody had worked at DuPont for a year or so. That's where he met his bride Odene.

It didn't take Jody long to ask the bubbly Odene for a date. He fell in love with the flirty way she pouted her lips and wanted to spend the rest of his life with her.

A Matter of Conscience

For more than 25 years, Jody and Odene's marriage endured, but once the kids were grown, Jody wanted out. Devastated, Odene fought against divorce, but in the end, Jody won.

Although rejected, Odene never stopped loving Jody. A piece of paper didn't make any difference. He would always be her man.

On the witness stand, it's obvious Jody doesn't want to dispute his ex-wife's testimony, but he won't be badgered into saying something he can't remember.

Despite prodding by Evans, he can't remember if Bobby ever came to his house. If he did, he might have come with Billy Joe.

The only time Jody *remembers* being with Bobby and Billy Joe King was up at the lake, on the raft. He is sure that was the only time he was with Bobby.

But Billy Joe was around more often back then. Over the past 30 years, Billy Joe and Jody have stayed in touch. In fact, Billy Joe was up at Jody's house in Harrison, near the lake, just last Friday—a few days before the trial began.

"Just happened by?" Evans asks, insinuating Billy Joe stopped by to talk about the case. Not so, Jody says, but he confirms he did tell Billy Joe he had a subpoena to appear in Court.

Hitting a dead end, Evans asks Jody if he recalls Bobby ever saying anything about the way his sister and Don Hudson were carrying on.

"No, sir," Jody says.

Evans persists, "You don't?"

"No." Frustration shows on Evans' face, when Jody adds he doesn't recall Bobby saying *anything* about Don Hudson and Joan.

Even worse for the prosecution, Jody doesn't recall his wife telling him Bobby said he was going to kill Hudson.

"She *said* she told me—" Jody begins, but Evans interrupts.

"I know she said she told you, sir, but you are telling the jury right now you don't recollect?"

"No, sir."

Bobby heaves a sigh of relief when Jody fails to support Odene's testimony. Looking at the aging man slightly slumped on the witness stand, Bobby thinks how hard it must be for Jody to stand up against Odene. Poor Jody will probably catch hell from his ex-wife.

And because Jody already told the Court he was never close to Bobby, his testimony cannot be attributed to friendship.

But Bobby's sigh isn't the only sound in the courtroom. Everyone is buzzing as they realize Odene's ex- is not backing her story. Jody has not corroborated the State's "new" evidence, they whisper.

Rattled by this turn of events, Evans pushes harder, leading the witness, encouraging Jody to say it isn't that Odene didn't *say* the words, it's that he just can't *recall.*

Phillips is on his feet, and DiRisio sustains the objection, meaning Evans can't go down that route again, attempting to use Jody to make his point to the jury. Walking slowly to the prosecution's table to retrieve a slim stack of papers, Evans buys time to come up with a different approach. He then asks with renewed confidence, "You said you thought you recalled something about Mr. Hoppe saying something about Mr. Hudson, is that right?"

Yes, Jody agrees. He believes he told Detective Heck he thought he heard Bobby say he might be going to whip Don or something.

Pleased with that answer, Evans is ready to move on, but Jody isn't.

"I ain't telling him I heard that—if I did tell him that, I probably didn't realize what I was talking about...I was just talking."

Soft laughter ripples across the courtroom. Like magic, Jody turns Evans' temporary score into thin air. Jody's next comments don't help Evans either. He implies Heck or the other detective "was talking all this stuff," and he just went along with what they said.

Was Jody talking truthfully, Evans wants to know.

"Well, I told him some of it—I didn't tell him some of it," Jody explains, somewhat defensively. If he did say Bobby was going to beat up Don because of Joan, he was just guessing. He doesn't recall whether he ever heard Bobby say anything about Don and Joan.

Jody's words have handed Evans a jellyfish, and he can't get a grip without being stung.

Jody does remember Mr. Hudson calling him in the wee hours of the morning after his son was shot. Jody, a longtime friend to Don and his family, hurried over to the Hudsons' house after the call. Sat out in the yard with the old man for a long time.

When Odene came home from work the next morning, Jody thinks he probably told her about Don's death.

"Well," Evans asks expectantly, "did your wife tell (you) about this thing with Hoppe and making the threat the next morning?"

Looking over at Odene, fuming in her seat, Jody tentatively responds, "She *said* she did." His statement slips out as slowly as a ship without wind in its sails.

"No, no, no," Evans exclaims.

Startled, Jody utters, "I don't remember."

Evans' irritation heats up his next question. "And you are telling the jury she did not say this?"

"No, I ain't saying Odene didn't say it. I said if she told me I probably forgot it," Jody tells the irate prosecutor, again drawing laughter from courtroom spectators.

Incredulous, Evans asks, "You could forget something like that?"

He was like a brother to Don Hudson, but Jody has no recollection that Odene ever told him Bobby threatened to kill Don. And he emphatically states he certainly never told the detective and the coroner when they came to see him back in 1957, asking about the killing.

"I told them I didn't know nothing about it," Jody states.

He recalls getting a threatening phone call after the detective and Currey left and says he immediately called Currey to say he would shoot anyone who tried any funny stuff with him. Jody wasn't scared. He didn't have anything to tell about the killing, so why be afraid?

But, Jody says, there is one thing he knows for sure.

In the sudden stillness of the courtroom, Evans wishes he had stopped his questioning before Jody says more. Too late, he hears Jody say, "I don't remember nothing about no shotgun."

At Jody's words, relief spills over Bobby like a crystal-clear waterfall. Hearing Jody's words sparks Bobby's spirit that had grown dark yesterday as he listened to Odene's testimony.

Evans has made Phillips' cross-examination easy. For the record, Phillips establishes again that Jody didn't consider Billy Joe King's 1957 comments about dynamite to be a threat. Phillips lets the jury hear again that at no time did Billy Joe make threats or even talk about the case when he visited Jody a few days ago at the lake.

Then he points out to Jody that Heck has noted: "Jody stated numerous times that he has no knowledge of who killed Don Hudson."

That's right, Jody verifies.

When Phillips tries to get Jody to fortify his statements to Heck that he knew nothing, Evans objects.

In an out-of-the-ordinary sidebar at the bench, DiRisio gigs Phillips for not objecting when Evans put Jody on the stand and then treated him as a hostile witness. Saying he would have sustained an objection, DiRisio enlightens his colleagues: "A prior consistent statement can be used to rehabilitate a witness after prior inconsistent statements have been used to show that prior to that they were consistent statements."

The convoluted mini-lecture makes no sense to lay-people, but Phillips benefits from the analysis. DiRisio allows him to question the witness in a way that confirms Jody has consistently maintained he knew nothing about Hudson's killing, he never heard Odene tell him about a threat Bobby made, and he never heard anything about a shotgun.

And then Phillips drives his point home.

"You were married to this lady from 1955 until what, four or five years ago?" he asks.

"Yes," Jody responds.

And it was only after the preliminary hearing, just a few short days ago, Phillips continues, "...after you testified and told this Court you did not remember...at any time...Odene saying to you that she had heard Bobby Hoppe threaten Don Hudson's life. It was after that hearing and after your testimony that Odene Neal called you on the phone and said, 'Don't you remember me telling you that?'"

Actually, it was Jody who called Odene's house to speak to their son. It was then she chastised Jody for making her out to be a liar.

But that's not the most important point, so Phillips continues, "Did she—hundreds of times over the years of your marriage from '57 until your divorce—tell you about this threat?"

Hesitating to embarrass his ex-wife again but remembering he's under oath, he replies softly, "No, sir."

Making sure jurors understand, Phillips presses, "You don't remember *any* time, do you?"

"No sir," Jody repeats.

Relieved, I recall Mark Twain said, "If you tell the truth, you don't have to remember anything."

Knowing Odene, his one hope to introduce new evidence and, thus, prove premeditation, has been impeached by her own testimony and that of her ex-husband, Evans tries to recover on redirect, but Jody is adamant.

A Matter of Conscience

Evans throws in the towel, and the Court adjourns for the evening. As usual, the judge warns jurors to avoid any outside newspapers, newscasts, friends or family.

"Don't discuss the case with anyone," DiRisio cautions.

That evening, all but one juror, Marjorie Simpkins, abides by his instructions. The next morning, no one steps up to tell DiRisio of the infraction.

CHAPTER TWELVE

A Sacred Confidence Betrayed

Men never do evil so completely and cheerfully as when they do it from a religious conviction.
--Blaise Pascal (1623-1662)

The Rev. Joseph Godwin and Odene Neal have something in common. Both live in towns surrounded by majestic mountains.

Godwin's home in Mars Hill, N.C., sits atop a mountain that rises to a height of more than 2,000 feet, with Clingman's Dome soaring 4,500 feet above it. Odene's home nestles in a valley deep within the Appalachian foothills in the shadow of Lookout Mountain's 2,393-foot crest. Godwin's education is loftier than Odene's, too. He claims degrees from Troy State, the University of North Carolina, and Southwestern Baptist Theological Seminary in Texas, plus he has clinical counseling certificates from Baptist Hospital and Bowman Gray School of Medicine in Winston-Salem, N.C.

When Godwin first moved to Mars Hill, the winding mountain roads, often snow-covered, tended to make trips to the big city treacherous. But it was early summer in 1957 when Godwin made his way from the hills of North Carolina to Auburn University. Icy roads weren't a concern that time of year, but he had to be vigilant about his old car's condition.

After two days on the road with—thank God Almighty—no car trouble, Godwin heaved a sigh of relief when his rattletrap rolled into campus. He was here on a mission—to further his education by studying clinical psychology. But short on money, he jumped at the chance to fill in at the First Baptist Church of Auburn while the pastor was out of town. Back home, Godwin had a wife and young son. Every penny helped.

Besides, being asked to preach in a church 20 times the size of the one in Mars Hill made him swell with pride. He couldn't wait to tell his wife.

A Matter of Conscience

* * *

Thirty-one years later, Godwin still treasures the church bulletin, printed by the Auburn First Baptist Church for the July 21, 1957, morning service. He holds it up for the jury to see—

Vol. 2, No. 29—and proudly points out his name printed on the inside.

Sometimes he thought this day might never come. But he never gave up. Back in 1966, after sending his beautifully written letter to Chattanooga's police chief, he was sure something would happen. He had spent a lot of time crafting that missive and was pleased with it.

Dear Sir:

Along about midsummer, 1957, there was a man killed within your jurisdiction by being shot in the face with a gun through the windshield of his car after which his car wrecked.

Has anybody been brought to trial for this act?

If so, would you please advise me as to who was tried, on what charge, and the verdict?

If the case is still unsolved, I will reveal the killer specifically by name under the following conditions:

1. No publicity of this disclosure shall be made unless, until and after an indictment has been made.

2. A plain clothed detective, with credentials AND THIS LETTER, comes to my home in a car owned by the City of Chattanooga to get the information.

3. The detective will bring with him a tape recorder and not mention his business to me until his recorder and mine are set up and ready to record.

Should you think this will be a confession, you are mistaken seriously. I have never been in your city except two times in my life: August 31, 1953 and May 2, 1959.

This is not a gimmick, nor do I practice fortune-telling nor witchcraft. You take it from here. I am offering to do my part for you under the conditions above.

> *Sincerely,*
> *Joseph Godwin*
> *Assistant Professor Psychology*

Godwin had composed the letter in his mind hundreds of times, so as he sat at his Royal typewriter, it was easy to put his offer on the college's letterhead stationery.

It didn't take long to get a response. Chattanooga Commissioner of Fire and Police James B. Turner called Godwin as soon as he received the letter. He was eager to talk with Dr. Godwin and would be there within the week. Leroy Kington, chief of detectives, would accompany him. Listening on his home phone, Godwin smiled, realizing his perfectly picked words had caused the desired reaction.

After the Mars Hill meeting had to be postponed for a week, Turner discovered he could not make the trip, so he sent Kington and a young detective, Billy Ray Davis.

Kington and Davis had no idea what to expect when they pulled their unmarked car into the preacher's driveway, but they never imagined the words that tumbled from Godwin's mouth.

Almost before Kington and Davis could step inside and set up their tape recorder, Godwin began ranting: "In the first place, I want to say what an ill state I'm in to have to report this because I recognize that somebody either will be in trouble or will receive justice as a result of it.

"But I not only am a minister but a professor of psychology and, as one who teaches abnormal psychology, I know the hallmarks of personality disintegration. I had begun to feel some of those hallmarks to the point I had to get in touch with you."

The two Tennessee officials glanced at each other, telegraphing their thoughts: This guy is a kook, crazy as a rabid coyote, and he admits it.

Godwin's next words confirmed their fears.

"Within the last several months—I don't know exactly how long—I thought of this every day, *every* day, and it started off—I don't know why, but—always when I'd be shaving. I'd look at myself in the mirror, and this thing would come up."

Shaving was the trigger. When he shaved, instead of seeing his own face in the mirror, he saw a man's face, half blown off. He glimpsed something else in the mirror, too.

"I could see a mother crying warm tears in her pillow while she tried to sleep at night," he added, lifting his glasses to wipe tears from his completely dry eyes. Godwin's words were so well rehearsed he would quote them again—22 years later—at the trial.

A Matter of Conscience

The images in his bathroom mirror each morning were driving him crazy. Leaning toward the two police officials, he whispered, "I was beginning to feel like what a layman like me might think of as an accessory after the fact. A co-conspirator."

Then, just to have a little peace, he began to think of doing something about it. So, smiling, he confirmed he took on a little detective work himself. In a round-about way, last summer he checked to see if the shooter had been jailed.

Learning no one had, he assumed the case never went to trial. So he waited a while longer, telling himself, "Sooner or later, something's got to be done."

Acknowledging the last few weeks have been hard on him, Godwin confided, "It reached the point it seemed to be almost an obsession; I wasn't aware of this once a day, but many, many, many times a day—almost an obsession."

The decision to write the letter wasn't easy, Godwin assured Kington and Davis, who were shifting uncomfortably on their feet as the two tape players whirred. Rolling mournful eyes toward them, Godwin declared, "I found myself on the horns of a dilemma.

"On the one hand, I could say nothing and probably experience a complete personality disintegration while trying to protect somebody else. On the other hand, I could feel terribly guilty because of what some people might think about a person who would squeal or rat on somebody."

His "psychological integrity threatened," he had to tell someone for his own state of mind, he offered, beseeching them to understand his decision.

When Godwin wrapped up his dramatic tale, Kington and Davis thanked him politely, unplugged their tape recorder, and headed back to Chattanooga.

A couple of weeks later, Kington sent Godwin a copy of the tape and a transcript. He told Godwin after "much study and consideration," no immediate action was expected, because the allegation would require corroboration before they could proceed to court.

Although Godwin was unaware at the time, a copy of the tape and the transcript were presented to a grand jury later that same year.

The grand jury found no cause for indictment.

Thorough in his follow-up, Kington also forwarded a copy of the tape to the FBI.

* * *

On the witness stand in 1988, testifying before the judge and jury, Godwin tells Evans he had never met Bobby Hoppe before July 22, 1957. But he had heard of him.

"You couldn't possibly be in Auburn, Ala., in 1957 without knowing who Bobby Hoppe was. He was an extremely large figure in Auburn football. Everybody knew him.

"The sports pages had his picture...and there had been placards in windows and on utility poles with his picture. I saw these pictures in the newspaper, and I heard of Bobby Hoppe from all sides."

At the preliminary hearing a couple of weeks ago, Godwin had also talked about Bobby's fame. "Anyone in or around Auburn who didn't know Bobby Hoppe was Rip Van Winkle, asleep for a long time. Because Bobby Hoppe was great at football at Auburn at that time."

So at the trial Godwin vows he recognized Bobby when he appeared at the door of Godwin's dorm room that Monday morning, saying he had been to the church office and was sent to Godwin since the regular minister was out of town.

On the stand, Godwin describes Bobby as "extremely, extremely agitated." He recalls him pacing back and forth in the room, wanting to say something but unable to utter the words.

"At one time, Bobby dropped to his knees and went forward on his forearms, elbows and forearms, and put his head down close to the floor. He actually crawled a short distance across the floor in that agony on his knees and elbows."

Back in 1966, when he talked with Kington and Davis, although Godwin described Bobby as "the most disturbed human being I've ever seen out free, indescribably shaken," he had not mentioned anything about crawling on the floor.

That's all new in 1988. And it's not the last time during the trial that he will add details never mentioned in 1966.

On the witness stand, though, Godwin does repeat much of what he said on the tape in 1966. He says he encouraged Bobby to talk. "I told him I was a professional counselor."

He assured Bobby he'd heard it all. Whatever he had to say could not be worse than what other people had confessed to him.

In the 1966 tape, Godwin said he could see what a turmoil Bobby was in. Sensing he was "in some kind of *awful* condition" and needed to tell someone what was upsetting him, Godwin tried another approach: "Bobby, you know I'm a minister—that's why you found out about me and it's the reason you're here. Suppose you can be still long enough for us to pray about this?"

Godwin assured him, regardless of *what* he had done, he wasn't beyond redemption.

Godwin's training is double-barreled—he's a preacher *and* a counselor. Still, in 1966, he said Bobby's having shot somebody didn't enter his mind. "I'd had people confess to bastardy and bigamy and stealing and homosexual expression, but I hadn't thought of this at all."

Sitting tall in the witness box today, Godwin adds something he didn't mention to the two detectives when they visited him at home in 1966. "I never had thought of murder. I thought of a killing rather," he says with a slight shudder, turning to make sure the jurors saw it.

A significant distinction, Phillips jots on his legal pad, wondering how the preacher discriminates between killing and murder. Since he didn't mention this 22 years ago, has he added this because the only crime the DA can charge Bobby with is first-degree murder?

I need to talk with Cook about this, Phillips thinks, circling his note.

On the stand, Godwin says Bobby finally told him what happened, describing the incident. But, in Mars Hill, he asserted on tape that Bobby did *not* tell him the circumstances. Today, he adds Bobby did mention he was having "some trouble and some disagreement with somebody, and in the process of the disagreement, he shot the man."

In another contrast, in 1966 Godwin indicated to Kington and Davis he told Bobby in 1957 he couldn't "get away with this," and Bobby responded he would not try to escape justice. During his interview with Heck, as well as at the preliminary hearing just a few days ago and finally at the trial, Godwin used varying versions of his statement and Bobby's response: saying he told Bobby they could not keep what he had told him "under wraps," that the story would have to be reported to authorities, that they couldn't keep this a secret. At different times, he has Bobby saying he knew he "couldn't get by with it," parroting almost the exact words Godwin himself says he told Bobby in 1957.

Later in 1988 at the trial, Godwin says Bobby said he recognized he "had a debt to pay to society, and I will pay my dues." Despite earlier versions, Godwin is sure of the words because they are one of the "very few absolute positive, specific quotes I remember...."

Leaning back in the witness chair, Godwin claims Bobby wanted to wait a while before turning himself in. He doesn't recall the exact words, but he knows Bobby said his mother was in extremely poor health and wasn't expected to live much longer.

He declares there's no doubt Bobby said, "If she knows this now, it will kill her."

He pauses a moment before adding, "I do remember his saying *those* words."

Exasperated, Bobby thinks, "I did say it would kill Mama if she knew I shot Don Hudson, but I never said she was in poor health and wouldn't live much longer. Rev. Godwin must have understood I was speaking figuratively."

With Godwin's next words, Bobby begins to understand why the preacher mentioned his mother's poor health.

On the stand, Godwin is asserting he's a fair man. He's willing to wait a reasonable time to let Bobby turn himself in—until his mother is dead. But eight years later, after learning Bobby isn't in prison, Godwin *has* to turn him in.

It's a matter of conscience.

But Godwin's conscience is schizophrenic. One side says it's up to him to see justice is done while the other side frets about violating a sacred confidence.

Shaking his head slightly, Bobby tries to sort through Godwin's logic. Saying Bobby had agreed to turn himself in after his mother died makes the part of Godwin's conscience—the side struggling with breaking a confidence—feel justified in turning in the man who confided in him.

Bobby listens to Godwin tell how, in the early 1960s, he first contacted the Auburn alumni office—or maybe it was the news bureau— he's not sure—to learn Bobby's whereabouts. The folks he talked to weren't sure. Perhaps playing for a pro team—Washington Senators or the Redskins.

A Matter of Conscience

So the preacher let it rest for two or three years. But it *was* bothering him more frequently, so he finally wrote a letter to the Chattanooga Police Department, asking for Bobby's address.

Oddly, he requested his letter be kept on file at the police station.

After tracking down the phone number, Godwin called, but Bobby's mother answered. Godwin tells the jury he was in a "little bit of a bind here since she was supposed to have died several years before."

When he told her it was in everyone's best interest if her son would call back, Godwin says Mrs. Hoppe persisted in wanting to know why he was calling. Turning toward the jury, a holier-than-thou look on his face, he declares, "Out of all respect and may God rest her soul, she was just a little bit curt to me in her determination to get more from me than I was willing to [give]."

In 1966, to Kington and Davis, Godwin said he fudged a bit when Bobby returned his call—the only time he admits to crocheting around the truth. "I guess maybe I lied to the extent, because the real reason was I wanted to find out if I [could] get him to say without my asking, or give me some insight as to whether or not this had come up."

In a January 1988 interview with Heck and Chief of Detectives John Taylor, Godwin changed his story, telling them he wanted to notify Bobby he was going to turn him in. Now in Court, he says he asked Bobby if he remembered their conversation in Auburn and told him, "I have carried that in my mind and...heart as long as I could.

"I had to let it out...I had to report it," he exclaimed.

Godwin says he did not "specifically and pointedly" tell Bobby he was going to call the police. He declares he just said he had to get it out of his system. According to Godwin, Bobby didn't seem to be upset, simply saying, "I understand."

He wants everyone to know he wasn't trying to get Bobby in trouble.

He wasn't trying to clear him, and he wasn't trying to convict him. "I have no interest in it except this kind of thing happened and it shouldn't go on."

Seeming to paint himself as a victim, he adds, "I just happen to know about it because of the position I was placed in by Harold Cole asking me to supply for him that Sunday."

Godwin cares how people regard him, so even in 1966, he proclaimed to the detectives, as a counselor and a minister, "I respect—

143

and it's very sacred—the confidence of a person, even to the extent of this, you see.

"This is the only violation of that confidence that I have ever made."

But Godwin had to cast aside this burden. So now he sits in the witness box, baring his soul. Under Evans' questioning, he describes what Bobby told him about the shooting. Shot him in the face, through a window or windshield.

Evans wants to know if Bobby said anything about what the man he shot was doing, to which Godwin responds, "Bobby said, 'He had been after me or he was after me.'"

Then Godwin quickly adds, "But he said that in such a way I did not get the idea this was a chase. He didn't clarify that."

Qualifying his response with, "and, all of us will remember, this has been a long time ago," Godwin adds, "I do remember in some way, without knowing specifically the words he used, there was a woman involved. He didn't name the woman. But it was something about somebody with whom he had had some kind of trouble because of a woman...."

He never mentioned a woman in the 1966 tape, so he adds, "As a matter of fact, [Bobby] may *not* have told me—but there was a woman in it somewhere."

Some people conjectured, throughout the 1988 interview and trial, Godwin amplified what Bobby allegedly told him because the preacher had read what was reported in the newspapers in 1957. He visited Chattanooga in 1959, he had said in his letter to Commissioner Turner, but he didn't say why. Cook and Phillips surmised the visit was the beginning of Godwin's detective work. While in Chattanooga, he could have read old newspapers and then later added what he'd learned to his testimony. The papers mentioned a shotgun, a woman, a shot fired through a car window—details Bobby never told Godwin. Details Godwin used to embellish his story over the years.

Having introduced a woman into the equation, Evans pauses, then asks if Bobby said anything about self-defense.

"Oh, no...he didn't tell me that," Godwin maintains, but he did say something about the person *was after me* or *had been after me*, repeating what he told Taylor a few months earlier and had said just moments ago. But Godwin wants everyone to know he's not sure if it meant Bobby was being chased when he fired the shotgun.

Next Evans wants to know if there was any discussion about forgiveness, absolution in a religious sense.

"No, sir," Godwin starts, then adds, "Let me tell you the only time anything of religious sense came up." In trying to get Bobby to a state where he was "capable of communicating," Godwin admits he suggested praying. He recalls asking if Bobby could be still enough to pray.

But strangely, he can't remember whether he prayed with Bobby that night.

"I will say praying is one of the things preachers are known for. But on this occasion, although I brought up the topic, number one, we may have prayed, number two, we may not have prayed."

Two jurors on the first row glance at each other. Disgust shadows the face of Juror Bo Nelburn. What kind of preacher lists whether he prayed like a true/false test?

Sensing the reaction in the courtroom, Godwin tries to distract with his next comment.

As for absolution, Godwin's a Baptist, and he doesn't know of any Baptist preacher ever going so far as to forgive anybody's sins.

"I never have played God to that extent," he demurs.

Evidently, Godwin is unaware priests in Episcopal and Catholic churches aren't forgiving communicants when they offer absolution for sins.

The Reverend Dr. Jim Curtis, our rector, describes it clearly: God is the one forgiving; priests are simply pronouncing what is already true. It is their role in the church, Curtis says, to declare: "You are forgiven. Your forgiveness has happened."

Godwin hasn't been schooled to think like that. He believes absolution means the priest or preacher has the power to forgive. He's not God, he repeats with virtuosity.

Godwin also wants to make sure everyone understands he is a well-trained counselor. He knows what a good counselor should and shouldn't do. He would never advise anyone on the law. Good counseling, he says, "consists of helping the person in trouble, number one, to see his troubles as they are, really as they are."

Number two, Godwin explains, a good counselor helps the person see all the possible options. And number three, a good counselor helps the person he's counseling determine the consequence of each of the possible alternatives.

And then, Godwin proclaims with a shrug of his shoulders, his job is to remind the person, "After all, it's your problem, not mine, and you will have to decide it."

Besides, Godwin insists, Bobby didn't come to him for spiritual guidance or counseling. He came for relief.

And although he wants everyone to know he has nothing to gain or lose in this case, he does hold some basic convictions that sometimes "get into opposition with each other."

He's not Solomon. He doesn't know what good could be accomplished at this late date by sending Bobby to prison. But, he proclaims, "There should be no statute of limitation on the implementation of justice. Justice isn't limited to a judge and a jury; justice in a civil society, in a democracy, is part of all of us."

After all, it is in "the gaining of justice" he was willing to travel all the way from Mars Hill to Chattanooga to help the DA.

"I don't believe there should be any sunset on justice," he concludes.

* * *

Using the preacher's words, Judge DiRisio found himself on the "horns of a dilemma" when defense attorneys argued, during a preliminary hearing, to suppress Godwin's testimony on the grounds that Bobby went to the minister seeking spiritual help. The motion to dismiss, filed on May 4, was based on confidential, privileged communication.

During the preliminary hearing on June 3, Bobby Lee Cook questioned Godwin in an animated discussion described in a local newspaper article as "rhetorical hardball."

In his article, Dick Kopper said the exchange began cordially, with Godwin citing his credentials, concluding with a bit of bragging. At 67, he had just won re-election as mayor of Mars Hill—by an 86 percent vote.

"Outstanding. I congratulate you," Cook responded.

Then, ever the Southern gentlemen, Cook asked how he would like to be addressed—as Dr. Godwin or Rev. Godwin.

"People who know me but don't know me very much refer to me as Dr. Godwin. If you know me more than a few minutes, you call me Joe."

With a slight smile, Cook said, "Well, Dr. Godwin, I might get down to the Joe level in a few minutes."

And he did, Kopper noted, calling Godwin "Joe" several times as he "relentlessly" questioned the man from Mars Hill about why critical details he told Heck and Taylor in 1988 were missing from the statement he gave police in 1966.

On the eve of the trial at the hearing, Cook and Phillips argued that Godwin's "false and fraudulent testimony was manufactured for and tailored to the sole purpose of making certain inadmissible evidence admissible under the law of the state of Tennessee."

Today, Godwin holds on to both sides of the witness box with his hands, trying to maintain solid footing under Cook's verbal assault. When he can take the pressure no longer, he beseeches DiRisio for help.

"Your honor, may I state I am not testifying here primarily what I'm remembering. I am testifying primarily what I am unable to forget."

But Phillips and Cooks asserted Godwin shouldn't be testifying at all.

Citing a 1959 Tennessee law prohibiting pastors and priests from testifying in court about information received in confidence, Phillips and Cook argued at the preliminary hearing that Bobby, not Godwin, was the only one, under the law, able to waive the clergyman/penitent communications confidentiality rule.

Section 24-1-206 of Tennessee Code Annotated states, "(a) (1) No minister of the gospel, no priest of the Catholic Church, no rector of the Episcopal Church, no ordained rabbi, and no regular minister of religion of any religious organization or denomination...shall be allowed or required in giving testimony as a witness in any litigation, to disclose any information to him in a confidential manner, properly entrusted to him in his professional capacity...."

Those who drafted this legislation felt so strongly about anyone violating a sacred communication they included a provision for penalties: Violations could result in a misdemeanor, a fine of not less than $50, and imprisonment in the county jail or workhouse not exceeding six months.

Without any legal basis in Tennessee, DiRisio ruled against the motion to suppress, saying Godwin was not Bobby's minister at the time.

Had Bobby been a member or a faithful attendee of Godwin's church, DiRisio indicated he might have been more sympathetic. Many states do include a provision that says the privileged communication must be made to the minister "in the course of discipline enjoined by the Church to which he belongs," but Tennessee has no such provision.

Moreover, the judge avowed, Bobby wasn't even a Baptist. And his Cradle Roll Certificate from Calvary Baptist Church in North Chattanooga didn't sway DiRisio.

In 2008, Bobby Lee Cook would say the judge's ruling on confidentially was the biggest surprise in the case.

"I am convinced—from a legal standpoint—Godwin's testimony was not admissible," Cook declared emphatically. According to Cook, the law in every state is settled on the matter. Communication between a person and his pastor is protected. Otherwise, why would anyone ever talk to a priest or a preacher, Cook asked rhetorically. A penitent/preacher discussion should have the same protection as that of a client seeking legal advice from his attorney.

Writing in the *Ohio State Law Journal*, Seward Reese maintained the pressure on Protestant clergymen might be greater than the sacred trust of a Catholic priest since the clergyman not only can hear but also can see the person confessing. Anonymity within the confessional booth is unavailable to a person talking to a minister. Thus, the laws of most states protect people outside, as well as inside, formal confessions in Roman Catholic churches.

"Had DiRisio ruled in our favor," Cook surmised, "that would have been the end, virtually the end of the case, because there would not have been anything left for the State."

But that did not happen. However, even back in 1988, Cook was convinced no appeals court would ever uphold a guilty verdict based on DiRisio's ruling.

* * *

In a 2008 interview about the case, Cook said with a sly smile, "Godwin is my kind of witness."

Like Sam Payne, a circuit court judge when he cornered Godwin after his 1988 testimony and exploded on him, Cook had no respect for the man from Mars Hill. The renowned attorney, who has defended hundreds of unsavory characters, said Godwin is "one of the most despicable people I have ever known. A publicity pariah—no question about that."

A Matter of Conscience

When Payne, now an Episcopal priest, encountered Godwin outside the courtroom, Payne told him one of the greatest sins a priest or preacher can commit is to break the confidentiality of one who has come to talk.

"I jumped all over Godwin," Payne recalled, telling him, "You are no man of the cloth! You are a liar."

Reese, again in the *Ohio State Law Journal*, wrote, "Among the things that are considered reprehensible and detestable by all men is the violation of a confidence by anyone. Among the most hardened criminals, as well as among the saintly and most law-abiding citizens, the feeling of revulsion is the same."

Reese added a person should know he can't confide in the town gossip, but if he cannot confide in a priest or preacher when seeking spiritual aid and comfort "this would strike at the concept of confidence in a most critical area.

"Of all people, the minister is supposed to represent the highest in ethics and morals."

In 1988, Cook declares Godwin failed that test. When Cook looked into his eyes—the windows of the soul—Cook knew Godwin was "a complete fake, a complete fraud."

Despite his high-powered credentials, Godwin didn't impress Cook. "[It was] probably the first time he was ever on the stage of life, playing his part."

As George Eliot said in *Adam Bede,* Cook believed, "He was like a cock who thought the sun had risen to hear him crow."

* * *

For Cook, Godwin crossed the line when, after testifying at the preliminary hearing, he strode over to Bobby and, with a weak smile, extended his hand.

Caught off guard, Bobby gasped as if he'd stepped on a snake but accepted Godwin's hand. Then, holding tightly to the preacher's paw so he could not pull it back, Bobby looked him in the eyes and said, "You are a liar."

A few minutes earlier, sitting soldier-straight in his chair, Bobby had listened to Godwin exaggerate what he had told him in that college dorm room so long ago. Hearing the preacher's practiced words, Bobby sat quietly, twisting his 1957 Auburn National Championship ring like he was touching a talisman.

Responding to Bobby's accusation he was a liar, Godwin replied, "Bobby, I wouldn't hit you with a toothpick."

"You are a very sick man," Bobby said quietly.

When Godwin's wife opened her mouth to defend her husband, Bobby cut her short, saying simply, "Ma'am, your husband's a liar."

Since Evans had ended his direct examination with the scene at the preliminary hearing where Godwin approached Bobby, Cook takes up there when he begins cross-examination.

He offers no cordial comments. No congratulations on his mayoral race. No buddy-buddying. The witness isn't "Joe" today. Today, he's "Reverend" Godwin.

And Cook tells Godwin he had no business approaching Bobby when his two attorneys' attention was diverted. No one invited him to talk to Bobby, did they, Cook roars in outrage.

A wide-eyed Godwin pleads ignorance of court procedure. He just knew how he felt and he wanted to shake hands with Bobby. He had a hankering to show there were no hard feelings.

Pulling a large white handkerchief from his hip pocket, Godwin wipes beads of sweat from his broad forehead, clearly relieved when Cook moves to a new line of questioning. Godwin acknowledges he keeps what his clients say in confidence, as least "insofar as saying anything that could embarrass the individual or cause him or her any trouble, I do, yes, sir."

But he's also an ordained minister, the attorney reminds him. Godwin concedes, even if he weren't preaching at his own church in 1957, "once a minister, always a minister."

So when Bobby came to Room 71 at the Auburn dormitory seeking guidance and forgiveness, he was a counselor *and* a minister.

Wriggling through to another line of inquiry, Godwin swears under oath he can be believed when he says he saw Bobby's pictures on utility poles. Perhaps the placards showed the football star in his uniform, in an action shot.

But Godwin assures Cook he is "not going to get me to say now that I know exactly what the picture looked like on a particular utility pole."

Wryly, Cook responds, "I don't suspect I would."

Were there other great football players at Auburn that summer, Cook wants to know.

"I don't know, because nobody talked of anything except Bobby Hoppe.

Turning to Bobby's visit to Godwin's room, Cook has the reverend describe the scene, down to every detail. Then Cook wants to know, despite Bobby's distressed state, did Godwin not get the idea the young man had come to him for counseling?

"No, sir, and I still don't," Godwin replies, lifting his chin defiantly. "He came because he had to get this off his chest."

Quick as a whip, Cook reads aloud a statement from the 1966 transcript: "In your professional opinion, he came to you for mental relief, aid, or assistance or guidance or counseling?" And the record shows Godwin responded, "Yes, sir."

But Godwin has had time to think about this. He's sure he can sidestep his previous words. "Those *or's* in there, look at the first one—mental relief."

"Or counseling?" Cook asks.

"This *or* this *or* this *or* this is what that statement says, and the first one is mental relief—and I'm testifying he came for mental relief."

Yet you didn't qualify your answer, sir, Cook tells him, but Godwin insists he did not say "yes" to all of the "*or's.*"

"Not when you have that many *or's* in there," he adds, oblivious to how silly it sounds.

Although the church staff told Bobby he could talk to Godwin in the absence of the regular minister, Godwin is adamant it had nothing to do with his capacity as a preacher. Why, if he had been a layman, it would have been the same thing, he contends.

If that's so, Cook wants to know why he told Bobby, "You know that I am a minister—that's why you found out about me and it's the reason you are here."

Oh, Mr. Cook, you're making "too much to do," Godwin answers with a smile.

Irritated, Cook wants Godwin to stop dancing around the question. "Isn't that what you told this man and isn't that what you meant?"

Lawyers whose clients face Cook use the word "eviscerate" to describe the way he attacks witnesses. No doubt Godwin would agree.

Shaken, Godwin admits he told Bobby he was a minister. But it wasn't what he meant. "Yes, that's what I said, but this is the only time a person is placed in a situation in which he has to get what he says right the first time, without any opportunity to explain what he meant."

After another crotchety exchange, Godwin insists on explaining: "Bobby came because he knew I was a minister. But to say that's the reason you are over here, I am not going to stick by that when I have plenty of time to think about it. Had I not been a minister and they had sent him, he wouldn't have come because I was a minister. He would have come because he had been sent—and that's my explanation, sir."

The more he elaborates, the more confused everyone becomes. When the jurors are again sent to the jury room because of another bench conference, they march out, obviously angry.

Moments later, with the jury back in the courtroom, Cook asks Godwin why he didn't correct the statement he had made back in 1966 about Bobby coming to him as a minister. After all, Godwin received a copy of the tape from Kington.

That answer is easy. The tape was broken. "I didn't have time to splice it at that time and when I had time to splice it, I didn't have the interest in hearing it and when I had the interest in hearing it, I didn't have the time to splice it...."

Hearing this convoluted logic, Chattanooga Police Captain Jack Robbs' eyes widen and, under his breath, he says, "As Shakespeare said, 'Methinks he protests too much,'"

Godwin admits he also received a copy of the transcript, but never got around to reading it.

Regardless, Godwin has said he asked Bobby to pray, telling him regardless of what he had done, he was not beyond redemption.

Godwin can't remember if they prayed, but he tells Cook he'll accept Bobby's statement that they did. He just can't recall, even though he remembers other details so vividly.

Godwin does recollect encouraging Bobby to tell him what was upsetting him. And he knows Bobby told him he had killed a man and how it happened.

Cook asks if Bobby said the man was after him, attempting to run him off the road.

"No, sir," Godwin replies.

Bobby flinches at Godwin's words. This omission from his talk with Godwin may lead jurors to question if his actions were in self-defense. But Cook is on top of his game, and his next words allow Bobby to breathe more easily.

Slowly and deliberately, Cook strides to the defense table, picks up a copy of the 1966 transcript, and reads aloud where Godwin testified, "He did say something about the person had at one time or another been after me."

It appears Godwin has been skewered with his own words.

Next, the two men tussle over Godwin's 1988 statement that a woman was involved. Cook forces him to concede no mention was made of a woman in 1966.

Cook then turns back to Godwin's role as a minister, asking how many times Godwin revealed any of the litany of sins he assured Bobby he had heard.

"Never revealed bigamy or theft..." Godwin begins.

Then he stops, deciding instead to argue semantics. "Now, when we are talking about revealing, I am talking about turning him over to the law, to a relative, to an employer or somebody. That's what we are talking about," he explains.

Cook is persistent, asking if he's ever revealed sins told him in his role as a counselor?

"You kept them in your heart, didn't you?" Cook nudges softly.

He's never revealed a confidence before, Godwin says proudly. But this time was different. Bobby did not come to him as a minister or a counselor.

"I may have told him I was a minister and a psychologist, I may have..."

"You *may* have?" Cook interrupts, his usual melodious voice crashing around the witness, a clap of thunder straight from Heaven.

"I may have, yes."

In disbelief, Cook roars, "So as you sit on the stand today...you say that you *may* have told him you were a minister and a psychologist but you don't *know* whether you did or not?"

Insulted, Godwin wails, "Sir, as I sit on this stand today, 67 years of integrity are at stake, I believe you are the first person who seems to doubt my integrity."

Cook has stripped away the preacher's credibility, leaving this mortal man with no holy cloth to cover himself.

Fully aggrieved, Godwin tells Cook he refuses to "fine hone specifically the exact words I said in order to leave an impression. I'm conveying information I cannot forget rather than trying to dig up insignificant things I can remember."

His words echo those he said to DiRisio just days earlier. He must have liked the righteous taste of them on his tongue.

Unmoved, Cook wants Godwin to tell the jury whether the answer he gave to the Court in front of DiRisio two weeks ago was truthful.

"I didn't intend to lie," Godwin says plaintively.

The truth, Cook says, is easy. All he has to do is admit he told Bobby he was a minister.

But Godwin avows just because he told Kington and Davis that in 1966 doesn't mean it was so. And even if he did tell the Court a couple of weeks ago that it was true he said that in 1966, well, now he just doesn't know whether he said those words or not.

His memory is better about whether his conversation with Bobby was in confidence. He denies he told Bobby it was. He also insists Bobby "unmistakably and unequivocally" told him his mother wasn't expected to live much longer, and he would turn himself in when she died.

And, he won't sway from his statement that a woman was involved. He just forgot to tell the detectives in 1966. But, today, he even recalls why he's so sure.

"As soon as he said that [about a woman], into my mind came the expression, *cherchez la femme*. That's the reason I remember a woman being involved."

Feigning a lack of understanding, Cook responds, "Said what?"

"*Cherchez la femme.*"

Pretending to be befuddled, Cook prods Godwin. "What are you speaking?"

French, Godwin explains, "French with a Southern accent."

"Let's put it in English...where all of us southerners who are non-French speakers can understand it," Cook says with a cragged grin.

"The words, *cherchez la femme*, mean look for the woman."

Cook's game. OK, let's look for the woman, Cook says.

In his January 1988 statement to Heck, Godwin stated, without specifics, that Bobby said something about a woman being involved.

Cook reads the preacher's own words back to him: "As a matter of fact, *he* may not have told me, but there was a woman involved in it somewhere."

Furious, Godwin spits out, "I don't have to stand here and swear that in a 26-minute tape like that—without any chance to review it or rehearse it or change it or correct it—that I get it right the first time."

Cook pounces, demanding to know what Godwin means when he says, "rehearsing" it.

"I mean you are not letting me say what it is *supposed* to say."

Cook won't let him off that easily. Godwin is on stage, probably the biggest stage he's ever performed on, but this courtroom drama isn't play-acting. What's said here doesn't need rehearsing. It just needs to be the truth.

"What do you mean by *rehearse*?" Cook insists.

Godwin explains he once wrote a newspaper column, and he never put down the first time what he intended to say. "I always had to go back, and [it had to] be written and rewritten and revised, and I'm telling you now I have not had time to do that before the tape moved on to something else."

So when writing something down or saying something on a tape recorder, "on the first occasion that's not really what you intend to say, you have to go back and revise it?" Cook queries.

In a voice saturated in virtuous umbrage, Godwin replies, "You know as well as I do that that's not what I mean."

When one speaks extemporaneously, "without any opportunity to have notes or to say what one wants to say or to organize his words such as I'm doing now, one cannot be absolutely certain of getting words just exactly right."

But back in 1966, Cook reminds Godwin he knew Kington and another detective were coming. Godwin told them to bring a tape recorder. And he also was planning to tape the interview. So he *had* thought about it, Cook goads Godwin. He had planned his revelation.

With a jab, Cook asks if Godwin can truthfully say he hadn't had time to think about it.

Not surprisingly, Godwin has an answer. He didn't write it down beforehand. He was just telling it like he saw it in the mirror while shaving. And he was telling the truth, he declares.

Cook takes a step toward the witness. Waving the 1966 transcript in Godwin's face, so close the breeze flutters the preacher's thinning hair, he reads what Godwin told the detectives.

Godwin said he had kept the confidence as long as he could to give Bobby a chance "to do something about it because as a counselor and as a minister, I respect and it's very sacred, the confidence of a person even to the extent of this. This is the only violation of that confidence I have ever made."

Exactly what did he mean by that last sentence, Cook asks—a boxer spoiling for a fight.

It's the first time he has ever turned anyone over to a policeman, Godwin vows.

Cook appears incensed. "And you said it was sacred?"

"That is right," Godwin says.

"Holy?"

"Right," Godwin affirms.

"Inviolate?"

Never squirming, Godwin says, "That is right."

"Holy inviolate?"

Yes, that, too.

Godwin's hubris is so blindingly bright, he cannot see any wrong in what he has said or done. He says it's not his fault it all started bothering him, but eventually, his "botheration, if [Mr. Cook] will let me use that word, became progressive."

Botheration. Sounds good to Cook. Go right ahead and use it, Reverend. "So when did your botheration really get next to you?" Cooks asks impishly.

"My botheration really got next to me in the early part of 1966," about nine years since he met with Bobby. That was a reasonable amount of time.

"For his mother to die?" Cook asks, cocking his head to the side.

"Yeah, die, d-i-e."

In the back of the courtroom, subdued chuckles can be heard as Cook asks how to predict someone will die within a "reasonable" amount of time.

That's why he put the word "reasonable" in there, Godwin says, "because I wasn't going to make it hidebound we are going to wait until she is dead."

And Mr. Hoppe knows that, Godwin adds.

How does he know that? Has he talked to Bobby other than the one time he went over to shake hands with the surprised defendant, the time when Bobby told him he was lying? That Godwin was sick? That Bobby pitied him and would pray for him?

His face a blank, Godwin is mystified. "He told me that? Did he?"

Well, yes he did, Cook tells the old man.

"If he did, he surely should have said it in my good ear," Godwin says seriously.

Playfully, Cook prompts, "Which is your good ear?"

Godwin points to his right ear. "This one."

With a smile, Cooks points to his left ear. "Mine is this one."

On that note of levity, the Court takes a recess.

* * *

Cook likes a good joke. And he makes no bones about liking to make good money. He's worth it, and he knows it.

Although Cook travels in a chauffeured Rolls Royce, generally collecting six-figure fees or more, he still comes across as a good ole boy. But he's more than that. He's a folk hero.

Tom Chaffin, writing in the *MVP Magazine*, told readers Cook is loyal to his mountain origins. Despite the large fees he sticks to wealthy clients, he still handles hundreds of local cases for $50—or whatever his neighbors can afford. In fact, the big fees he commands allow him the luxury of taking a case for nothing if it interests him.

John Seigenthaler, a nationally renowned journalist and long-time Cook observer, said, "With Bobby Lee, there's an innate suspicion of authority and a sense that power can be abusive."

Cook is an equal opportunity defender—he'll take on the law or the mafia, but sometimes it's hard to explain why to local folks.

Tom Chaffin told of a time a few years ago when some townsmen were giving Cook grief for defending a mobster. Cook responded by describing the majesty of the Sixth Amendment and how it guarantees all defendants a right to counsel. "They just looked at me, Cook recalled, and said, 'Well, that's a good story, but we don't think it's a very good answer.'"

About a year later, Chaffin continued, the same local breakfast group chided Cook about another unsavory client. This time, Cook took a different tack.

"I told them, 'Well, the last time you folks asked me these kinds of questions, I told you about constitutional rights and all that. But really, I was just trying to impress you. I should have been more truthful. The truth of the matter is I'm representing this feller because he paid me $250,000.'

"And they said, 'That's good, by God. We hope you *win*.'"

* * *

After the recess, Cook goes at Godwin immediately.

The two argue again over whether Godwin told Bobby he was a minister. With no sense of hypocrisy, Godwin says, "I'm telling this Court I said that—what you quoted—but I am not telling this Court I said, 'Bobby, I am a minister.' I didn't present myself as a minister. I told him he knew...from the information he got at First Baptist Church.

"I told him, 'You *know* I am a minister.'"

It's a hair-splitting, headache-inducing point, but on that, Godwin will take his stand.

Reminiscent of the last stand at the Alamo, Godwin's putting up his best defense. Even if the walls are crumbling around him, he's not going to turn and run.

Confident the jurors see through Godwin's bloviating, Cook turns back to the minister's phone conversation with Bobby's mother. Godwin denies he used the word "rude" to describe Mrs. Hoppe.

But reading from page 15 of the preliminary hearing transcript, Cook has him cold. "And with all the respect that I can give, she was a little bit unnecessarily curt or a little bit rude."

Bruised but still blustery, Godwin says, "All right. We will take that qualifier."

Still on the offensive, Cook chides Godwin for talking about a dead lady that way.

Totally serious, Godwin says, "But she wasn't dead when she was talking to me."

With that, Cook could cut Godwin off at the knees, but he lets it go. He has bigger fish to fry. He wants to know if Godwin has any interest in the case other than to tell the truth.

A Matter of Conscience

That's all, Godwin swears, but Cook knows differently. He asks Godwin if he had anything to do with an article that ran in a recent edition of *Southern Magazine*.

Godwin declares he had nothing to do with it. Someone from Arkansas called and wanted information, and he told them he had nothing to say. Further, he has made no statement to the press. He didn't know for sure anything was going to be in *Southern Magazine* until he read it.

Unless it's a magazine on Godwin's regular reading list, he must have been watching for it to come out, because he proudly tells Cook the article was on page 13.

Cook attempts to read from the page, titled "Southern Front: We heard it through the grapevine," but a quick objection by Evans is sustained by the judge.

* * *

The article, one of many appearing in publications across the southeast and beyond, asserted Bobby still has the "lean, handsome build, wolfish face, and steely eyes evident in publicity photos" from Auburn's national championship year. Hailing Bobby as a "fluid halfback and jarring tackler who was accustomed to winning," the author quickly turned to Godwin's role in the investigation. While the article didn't quote him, it did state he was a 37-year-old minister taking courses at Auburn in 1957. Moreover, the article's author knew Godwin told police Bobby had confessed to him shortly after the shooting.

Godwin maintains he didn't tell the writer anything, but Cook thinks differently.

That might not convince the jury if that is all Cook has. But it isn't.

When Cook asks if Godwin has any economic interest in the case, the preacher thinks he is talking about the "grapevine" piece, but Cook assures him he's not. Then he asks Godwin if he has been contacted by any other periodicals.

"Many," Godwin replies.

How many?

Godwin can't say.

Any offers?

Not any specific ones, Godwin claims.

Watching Godwin begin to squirm, a fish at the end of the line, Cook yanks him in.

"Have you had any offers?" The look Cook gives Godwin indicates he's tiring of the dance.

But Godwin does a little shuffle step. "I promised.... Have I had an offer? I have not had a specific offer."

What about an *unspecific* offer?

"Just a request," Godwin reluctantly responds.

Like a fisherman watching a catfish nibbling near the hook, Cook gives the line a tiny tug. "Do you remember John 8:32, 'The truth shall make you free?'"

Godwin smiles at Cook. "I'm just as free as the wind, sir."

Spectators erupt in laughter until DiRisio gives them the gavel.

Godwin is caught and he knows it. He admits he had a recent request asking, before he consults with anyone else, to get back in touch with the caller—Paul Redman.

Godwin tries to avoid telling Cook what media outlet Redman represents, so Cook laboriously pulls the information from him.

"Some book?"

"No, sir."

"T.V. station?"

"No, sir."

What, then, Cook wants to know.

Godwin has the upper hand, and he's savoring it. "Keep on guessing."

So Cook tries *National Geographic*. Wrong again.

Tired of the game, Cook asks why Godwin doesn't just tell him. But Godwin wants to keep playing. "Go ahead and guess," he says.

Cook refuses, so Godwin finally admits Redman is from *People* magazine, but discovering the amount of the offer requires another exchange.

"What was the offer?" Cook wants to know.

"No offer," Godwin says with a grin.

"Any money mentioned?"

Godwin hesitantly admits "some money" was discussed.

What kind of money, Cook demands.

"Big..g..g..g" money, Godwin says, stretching out the word.

A Matter of Conscience

Well, Cook knows what big money is in Summerville, but he doesn't know what it is in Mars Hill, N.C.

Godwin doesn't want to say, but Cook won't let up. Finally, Godwin says, "If things work out, he mentioned the possibility of two hundred thousand dollars."

Knowing looks pass among the jurors. The bailiff has a smirk on his face: the preacher has stepped in it, big time.

Cook knows it, too. He dismisses this man of the cloth.

Joseph Godwin emphasizing a point on the witness stand in 1988

CHAPTER THIRTEEN

War Eagle!

"Sweet Auburn...the loveliest village on the plains...
where crouching tigers wait their hapless prey."
–Oliver Goldsmith
"The Deserted Village," 1770

Godwin's lengthy testimony took Bobby's mind back to Auburn, back to the days when he was a carefree college student. Arriving on the Plains, anxious to hit the football field as an Auburn Tiger, Bobby was as close to heaven as anyone could get on this earth.

* * *

It was 1954—smack-dab in the middle of a decade later known as the age of America's innocence. For most people in their teens and twenties, life was better than they realized—each day, ripe with promise.

From the first scorching August day the freshman football team took the field, the Tigers lunged toward their "hapless prey" with ferocity, foreshadowing the team's undefeated season four years later when Auburn University would win its one and only national championship.

Bobby Hoppe went down in history as an integral part of that illustrious 1957 team, despite living the most traumatic year of his life.

What made Bobby cast his lot with Auburn four years earlier has been the subject of much speculation, but Bobby laid it out plainly to a *Chattanooga News-Free Press* reporter twenty years after he first walked on Auburn's campus: "I had visited a lot of schools before I went down to Auburn. I didn't care for what I found—stuffed shirts and snobbish attitudes.

"Then I went to Auburn. Here I was, a kid with no money and dressed in blue jeans. I couldn't believe it—the kids were in jeans and they were friendly."

Unlike today when $500 jeans are the "in" style for everyone from Hollywood celebs to Japanese tourists, kids in the 1950s who wore blue jeans did so because they couldn't afford anything else. The casual dress of Auburn students worked for Bobby. He felt at home.

In 1954, to the delight of Auburn fans, *Birmingham News* assistant sports editor Benny Marshall reported that Auburn scouts scored big when they recruited five Chattanoogans—Hoppe and Central teammate fullback Leroy Duchene, end Dan Wade from Baylor (a private prep school in Chattanooga), guard Jim Jeffrey and end Howard Black from Chattanooga City. All were bright prospects, but Marshall noted that folks in Chattanooga said, "The brightest of all is Bobby Hoppe, a razzle-dazzle runner whom everybody wanted."

And, Marshall was happy to tell his readers, Hoppe was not just an exceptional runner, he was also an excellent blocker and a top-notch safety.

With Bobby, Auburn reeled in a triple-threat.

When *News-Free Press* sports writer Austin White announced Bobby's decision to sign a grant-in-aid pact with Auburn, he called him "one of the most sought-after athletes in Chattanooga football history." And it didn't take long for Auburn fans to realize what a catch they had.

In the freshman game against Georgia at Auburn, a local paper reported, "Bobby Hoppe of Chattanooga lived up to his All-American reputation. He was Auburn's leading ground gainer with 76 yards in nine carries for an 8.4 average. He's fast, rugged, and elusive." Coaches loved his "pull-away runs," as well as his blocking and defensive work, *Times* sports editor Wirt Gammon reported, saying Hoppe was labeled "the most aggressive back [at Auburn], varsity or freshman."

Handing the Georgia Tech freshmen their first loss to Auburn since 1949, the Plainsmen ended a perfect rookie season. Jack Jackson, writing in the *Atlanta Journal,* noted, "The play of three characters in the annual production convinced some 10,000 fans they'll be bidding for all-star roles before graduation day."

Jimmy "Red" Phillips, a local boy from Alexander City, shone like the star he was destined to become, recovering two fumbles, catching all three pass completions by the Plainsman, and smothering "every ball carrier that sought to turn his corner."

Bobby Hoppe, the second of the three characters, was described as the "fabled Plainsman halfback from Chattanooga Central," He ran eight times, gained 98 yards for a 12.3 average, and sped 59 yards on the day's best sprint for Auburn's second touchdown, giving Auburn its game-winning points with less than two minutes remaining in the second half.

A Matter of Conscience

Atlanta Constitution sports writer Jimmy Mann wrote, "It took Hoppe 28 minutes and 35 seconds to respond to the *all the way Hoppe* chant from the partisan Auburn stands, but when he did it was a beauty."

The third character played for Georgia Tech. Stan Flowers of Memphis carried 16 times for 129 yards. Even though he had quite a day, Flowers got a bitter taste of Hoppe's speed.

According to Sentell Harper, Bobby's roommate and teammate at Auburn, Flowers' reputation for speed became a major point of discussion in Auburn's locker room prior to the game. Someone challenged Bobby to outrun him. Always up for a good wager, he accepted, heading for the field with an impish smile on his face.

"On one play, Bobby got the ball," Sentell said. "But instead of taking the clear straight path in front of him, Bobby intentionally veered toward the edge of the field where Flowers was standing. Almost brushing Flowers, Bobby veered again—this one on a dime—and headed down the field, leaving Flowers to eat his dust."

Bobby just wanted to show Flowers he could get away from him, according to Sentell.

On the sidelines, faces of Auburn coaches registered alarm as they watched Bobby's crazy run. But after the game, asked about that run, Coach Dick McGowan just shook his head, gave a big smile and replied, "Hoppe was just Hoppe today—great. He can score and you don't have to run him to death to get the scores."

As Bobby marched into his sophomore year—his first opportunity to play on the varsity squad, the *Atlanta Journal* predicted, "The wiggler from Chattanooga will step out with the big boys at Auburn."

Journal sports writer Ed Danforth said Hoppe did well in spring practice, proving he can carry his share on defense. Danforth told readers Hoppe looks like anybody else until he takes off. "Then his style is distinctive. You can't miss the fellow when he is under way unless you're trying to tackle him."

Auburn's 1955 football media guide succinctly summarized Bobby's abilities: "His past, present, and future career is so fabulous most people dare not rate him at present."

The summer after his freshman year at Auburn, Bobby got a job with the Chattanooga Street and Sewer Department, manning a mowing machine, soaking up Tennessee sunshine.

War Eagle!

Times reporter Bob Weatherly noted, "If Auburn's Bobby Hoppe cuts down his opponents next season as keenly and swiftly as he is cutting the city's grass, then the whoop of the War Eagle should be heard for miles around this fall from the Village of Tigerville."

Unfortunately, when he returned to Auburn in August, Bobby would learn that working outdoors didn't necessarily equate to staying in shape.

But that summer in Chattanooga, following an exceptional year on Auburn's freshman team, Bobby was feeling his oats. Chatting with Weatherly, he reminisced a bit about his years in Chattanooga, recalling when he was a member of Normal Park's fourth grade team.

"That's when I played my first football," he said. Little did he know a few years later he would be the first Chattanooga player to land a berth on two All-American High School teams.

But, Bobby told Weatherly with a chuckle, compared to the SEC, he didn't know what speed and hustle were.

He drew similarities between Central Coach Red Etter and Auburn Coach Shug Jordan—alike in coaching methods and the way they handled boys, each getting maximum performance from their players.

Austin White, a *Free-Press* sports writer and one of Hoppe's biggest fans, predicted he would shine when Auburn met Scrappy Moore's University of Chattanooga Moccasins. White bragged that Bobby daily outdistanced all other Tiger halfbacks in practice, saying he was "so fast he will get into the secondary more—and when he gets into the secondary, he is going to score some touchdowns."

Shug Jordan agreed, but pointed out that Hoppe was a much sounder defensive man than many people realized. As Jordan put it, "[Hoppe] is a good blocker himself and knows enough about it to be a difficult man to block. He's in your lap before you know it."

Surprisingly, Hoppe had to sit out Auburn's first game of the year— against Scrappy Moore's Chattanooga Moccasins. Reporting for practice earlier that fall, the glow of Bobby's tan paled quickly when he learned he was 10 pounds overweight.

Jordan said Bobby was paying the penalty of sore muscles for riding around all summer on a mower and not using his legs. But the coach was not worried—Hoppe would be all right.

According to Gammon, Auburn coaches said the traits Hoppe had working in his favor were "his determination, ability to keep his feet after being hit, speed with a pickup like the passing gear on an auto, great leg drive, and remarkable ability to relax between plays."

For now, Chattanooga admirers of his "unusual and electrifying ability to scat with a football tucked under his arm" would have to wait. He wouldn't be starting the season; he was simply out of shape. When he got in the Kentucky game, though, White noted, "the Wildcat defense discovered its job increased by a third."

The next week, in a clash against Tulane, Hoppe ran for the first time without his leg swaddled in a mile of Trainer Kenny Howard's adhesive tape. An early season knee injury behind him, Hoppe's flashing speed had been restored.

Against Mississippi State, he carried seven times for 52 yards in what some called his "coming out party." After Red Phillips pounced on a Mississippi State fumble on their 28, "Blazin' Bobby tucked the leather under his arm and shot toward the Maroon goal line," but he was upended on the four yard line. Joe Childress came to the rescue, exploding through for the TD on the next play, giving Auburn its final touchdown for a 27-26 win.

Against the Georgia Bulldogs, Austin White said Hoppe "electrified the capacity crowd of 28,000 as he turned on his dazzling speed to break into the clear for a 13-yard gain on a cutback, over guard."

By season's end, Hoppe had played in eight of Auburn's 10 games (missing the first two—Chattanooga and Florida—because of injuries), carrying the ball from right halfback.

At the Gator Bowl game in December, Hoppe and Red Phillips were the only sophomores in Auburn's starting lineup, and the two were rated as the fastest players on the squad.

A local Auburn paper noted that filling Fob James' spot had been a big Auburn worry for '56, "but Hoppe and Tommy Lorino made 'em forget James before the next season started." Shug Jordan said Lorino had uncanny maneuverability and Hoppe had blinding speed.

With a satisfied smile, he added, "And Auburn has them both."

The newspaper also noted, "Despite the reams of publicity they have attracted, Lorino and Hoppe still have what Arthur Godfrey would describe as humility."

And, in case anyone in Chattanooga was wondering, Austin White reported Hoppe did well on his mid-term exams.

But Bobby's mind sometimes took a rest—often to Florida. On those trips, usually with Jeffrey, Billy "Red Dog" Austin, and a couple of other football players, the jocks had no problem hooking up with bronzed beauties on the beach. When one particular weekend was over and it was time to head back to Auburn, the girl smitten by Bobby refused to part with him.

"Come on, Bobby honey, let me go back to Auburn with you," she begged, pressing her tanned body against his. Slowly, he disentangled himself and escaped.

But when he made it back to Auburn, there she was, waiting for him. Refusing to leave, she set up housekeeping in his cabin, saying she was happy to live with him and his roommates.

With his teammates razzing him for being such a Romeo, Bobby didn't know what to do. He pleaded with the girl to leave, but she wouldn't budge. Exasperated, Bobby told her he had to go see Coach [Gene] Lorendo.

Bobby knocked tentatively on the coach's door. When Lorendo yelled, "Come on in," a red-faced Hoppe stepped through the door.

"Coach, I need a little help," Hoppe said.

"What kind of help?" Lorendo asked.

"Well, Coach, it's like this," Bobby said, flushing redder under Lorendo's gaze. "There's this girl—well, she followed me home from Florida, and now she won't leave. Coach, do you think you could come over and make her go back home?"

Lorendo burst out laughing at the pained expression on Bobby's face. The broken-hearted girl was driven to the bus station and given a one-way ticket home.

* * *

Despite losing five great players at the end of the '55 season (James, Childress, M. L. Brackett, Bob Scarbrough, and Frank D'Agostino), Auburn coaches were optimistic as they prepared for the 1956 season.

Chattanooga News-Free Press stalwart Austin White reminded readers that, a year ago, Auburn coaches spoke of an overweight Hoppe who, they feared, had fallen victim to the publicity surrounding his fabulous high school career.

A Matter of Conscience

"Today, they speak of Hoppe almost reverently," White added. "He has made himself into one of the most respected young men on the campus with his determined classroom application and his exemplary demeanor on and off the athletic field."

Proud of the boy whose career he had followed since his first year at Central, White wrote, "Now firmly entrenched as Auburn's No. 1 left halfback, the spot where he made life miserable for Purple Pounder foes, Hoppe finished last year, his sophomore sojourn, with the 11th best scholastic record of 95 varsity players."

At fall's first scrimmage, with a lightning burst through the line, Hoppe streaked for an 80-yard touchdown. Before that, he had scored on a 5-yard blast, also through the left side. White said he was a constant all-the-way threat from the backfield. "Hoppe and the 5-8, 165-pound Lorino, the elusive, slippery dervish from Bessemer, give Auburn, perhaps, the finest one-two punch in the Southland at left half."

By the time Auburn was to face the University of Tennessee, Shug Jordan appeared to be struggling with where to play Hoppe. Reading Atlanta and Birmingham papers, Chattanoogans were confused. One paper said Hoppe might get shifted to right half to let Lorino operate from the left. The other reported Lorino would make the switch to right half. Still another insisted Hoppe would be the "wing man" of the backfield, alternately playing left or right half.

Jordan, caught in a "morale bugaboo," announced Hoppe and Lorino would remain at left, giving Auburn a "splendid 1-2 punch there."

That news didn't sit well with Austin White, who wrote if Jordan had such a hard time knowing what to do with Hoppe, maybe he could work up a pre-game swap with Bowden Wyatt, the University of Tennessee's legendary football coach.

"Or," White suggested, "erect yourself a bandstand and auction off Hoppe to the highest bidder. That's the quickest way we know to create a nationwide jam on the highways and in the air lanes leading to your thriving little village.

"And just think! You can pay off the mortgage on Cliff Hare Stadium in one bid and two raises. And maybe have enough left over to build three more just like it."

White didn't need to worry. After Auburn lost to Tennessee in its opening game, 35-7, Hoppe got plenty of play in every game that followed. Auburn bounced back to beat Furman and Kentucky, and by

October 20, when Auburn played Georgia Tech, Hoppe and Lorino were rated as Auburn's best two backs. Even though Auburn lost 28-7, Jordan had only praise for the two.

Later, after the season's end, Jordan would admit, "I guess trying to play Hoppe and Lorino at the same position was one of the biggest coaching mistakes I have ever been guilty of."

He added Hoppe was terrific in the stretch—averaging better than 100 yards per game in the last four, when he played right halfback, rather than sharing the left halfback position.

When the Tigers folded to Florida the next week, it was the last game they would lose until 1959. The first victory was against Mississippi State, where Hoppe ran 70 yards and Lorino, 31, for two of the four Tiger scores. Against Florida State, Hoppe and Lorino were top ground gainers in the 13-7 victory, with Hoppe picking up 90 and Lorino, 69.

In the grid finale of the regular season, Auburn "rode the strong right arm of Tubbs and the flying feet of Hoppe to a 34-7 triumph over cross-state rival Alabama." Accounting for 112 yards in eight carries, Hoppe was a "constant thorn in the Alabama side all afternoon."

Head coach Shug Jordan called Hoppe the "best all-around halfback in the conference. His blocking and defensive work rank with the best, and it's no secret that he can run. Bobby is definitely worthy of a place on the all-SEC team."

Backfield coach Buck Bradberry agreed, saying, "He's all-SEC in my book."

At season's end, Hoppe accounted for 542 yards on 83 carries for a 6.5 average. Davidson recalled Bobby had two games in which he rushed for over 100 yards—almost unheard of in the mid-1950s.

The coaches' prediction came true: Hoppe was named All-Southeastern Conference.

* * *

With a winning season behind the team, the school year seemed to drag by, but spring practice finally arrived.

At the intra-squad game on March 9, 1957, Coach Shug Jordan liked what he saw. But between the spring intra-squad game and the fall football season, Jordan faced some of his most difficult career challenges. And Bobby Hoppe was right in the middle of one of them.

A Matter of Conscience

Today in the courtroom, his mind floating free as attorneys argue a point of law before the judge, Bobby's face becomes almost luminescent, lit from within by memories of Auburn and Sentell and other buddies. Shaking his head slightly, Bobby realizes all of that occurred light years ago—back when he was young, when his days revolved around football and friends.

Cold reality jerks Bobby back from his daydreams. The light in his eyes fades, and Bobby lowers his head, realizing the battle he's waging now has more severe consequences than those faced by Coach Jordan in 1957. And it will be more challenging than the personal agony Bobby fought to give Jordan his best effort his senior year.

That championship year, he thinks to himself, my teammates dodged and sprinted past external foes, but my enemy lived within me. Smothering my soul.

CHAPTER FOURTEEN

The State Concludes
and the Defense Begins

*Justice consists not in being neutral between right and wrong, but in
finding out the right and upholding it, wherever found, against the wrong.*
--Theodore Roosevelt (1858-1919)

After days of lengthy—and often intense—testimony, the next few
witnesses pass in and out of the witness box quickly, with no major
fireworks.

As its last witness, the prosecution calls Ed Davis, district attorney
general from 1958 until 1978. Responding to Evans' questions, Davis
illuminates his only involvement in the Hudson case back in 1957 before
he was DA: Davis was hired by Roy Hudson to look at the case to see if he
could unearth evidence that might point to his son's killer.

When Davis' investigation went nowhere, Hudson asked him to
write a letter on the family's behalf requesting a coroner's inquest.
Although Davis attended the inquest, he can't recollect what happened
there.

Evans concludes his questions by asking Davis if he ever had any
legal relationship with any member of the Hoppe family.

"None," Davis responds unequivocally—wiping out Stargel's earlier
statement that he'd heard Davis was the Hoppes' legal counsel in 1957.

Phillips' cross-examination surfaces Stargel's other allegation—
that in 1966 Davis was reticent to prosecute Hoppe because Davis was
close to the Hoppe family.

Absolutely false, he says. In fact, the exact opposite was true. "My
relationship had always been with the Hudson family. I had never met
the Hoppe family or any part of them."

One of the problems in reconstructing what occurred in the 1966
grand jury when he was DA, Davis concedes, is that all records of the
proceedings were destroyed, meaning he doesn't even know which
assistant DA handled the case. With that, the State rests its case.

The jurors look at each other, puzzled. What an odd way to end the
prosecution—with a witness who not only refutes Stargel's testimony but

also supports the defense's claim that time has irreversibly ravaged critical elements of this case.

* * *

The defense opens its case with Sam "Sonny" Payne, a highly respected circuit court judge in Chattanooga for the past 13 years.

A North Chattanooga boy, Sam acknowledges he and Bobby were good friends back in the old neighborhood. However, he didn't know Hudson well, only by reputation.

"He and I didn't run with the same group of people."

Unable to resist, Phillips asks, "Good reason for that, wasn't it?"

"Yes, sir," Sam replies before Evans can leap to object.

DiRisio sustains the objection, but the point has been made.

Over Evans' objections, Payne declares that, even as a high school student, Bobby was respected, while Hudson was a pistol-packing whisky runner.

Payne tells about seeing Hudson with a gun at Nikki's Drive-In. Lots of people saw Hudson carrying a gun, he says. Jimmy Pack. Judge Doug Meyer...

Evans jumps up. "The witness should know. Reputation is confined to what he has heard."

His objection sustained, a frustrated Evans sinks back into his chair. But the damage is done. The jury realizes there are two judges— Payne and Meyer—who support Bobby. And one more, Judge William "Chink" Brown, is waiting in the wings to testify.

On cross-examination, Evans takes a new tact, asking if Payne ever talked to Bobby about the incident.

Not back then, Sam says. "I did not know [it was Bobby] to be quite frank with you."

What Payne doesn't say is he suspected it.

But in 2008, 51 years after the shooting, Payne acknowledged — perhaps for the first time—that, in 1957, he knew in his gut Bobby probably killed Hudson.

Payne also recalled hearing Hudson not only beat Joan, he hit Bobby's mother. "If he had jumped on my mother, I would have shot him, too," Payne—the priest, the former judge—said. As far as Don Hudson, Payne said, "I don't know anybody who knew and liked that boy—nobody."

The State Concludes and the Defense Begins

"Even the bootleggers at Nikki's didn't trust Don."

* * *

Father Sam Payne, now 71 and retired from his judgeship, greeted his guests in the elegantly appointed foyer of St. Paul's Episcopal Church where he serves as associate priest.

The slender, silver-haired priest led the way down a wide hall and into a spacious room with sunlight flooding through stained-glass windows. Taking the chair at the head of the table, Payne began immediately.

He recalled vividly the day Bobby and I visited him, shortly after the indictment.

"I was the first person he came to see," Payne said, tears tightening his voice a bit. "Me—a judge, but he came to see me."

Leaning forward, the former judge spoke without preamble, "Bobby had a lot of courage and a lot of guilt. A lot of guilt."

Shaking his head, he added, "One mistake that haunted him the rest of his life."

Leaning back in the chair, the priest in him back in command, Payne smiled, remembering. "I told him, Bobby, look at Moses. What a mess. What a horrible mess. And out of all that chaos, God used Moses to do wonderful things."

Payne talked about guilt, defining it as self-punishment. "God forgave Bobby—wiped his slate clean," he declared. "But Bobby couldn't forgive himself."

In 2008, the priest offered a confession: In 1957 no one wanted to arrest Bobby Hoppe. Perhaps it was due to vestiges of old common law that said if a man deserved killing and the person who killed him was the appropriate one to carry it out, then justice had been served. Or, perhaps it was simply because Bobby was such a revered hometown hero.

But neither was the case in 1988.

* * *

During his long cross-examination of Sam Payne, Evans' annoyance bubbles up.

Chastising Payne for testifying, Evans asks if he thinks it's in keeping with the office of a judge to be a character witness. After all, a judge's testimony "injects the prestige of his office into the proceeding to which he testifies and may be misunderstood to be an official testimonial."

Payne says he's sorry if he's offended Evans, but he can't help it if he's a judge. Plus, he doesn't know anything about the case, but "I do know Bobby. I grew up with the boy."

Even-tempered to that point, Payne gets a bit agitated when Evans presses him to recall what he read in the newspapers in 1957. The tone of Evans' questions grates on Payne.

"You are telling this jury that we had this inquest—headlines in the newspaper—and you never read about a Mr. Holland in 1957? You don't recall reading that [Holland] said this man, Mr. Hoppe, stopped him and Donald Hudson while they were in [Hudson's] Cadillac on Cherokee Boulevard and threatened to kill him if he didn't stay away from his sister?"

Livid, Phillips leaps from his chair. "Objection!"

Too late. Evans finally found a way to get on record that in 1957 Holland testified Bobby had threatened Hudson, despite Holland having said in 1988 he could not recall saying that, despite the judge declaring it inadmissible.

Evans disguised information as a question—and Phillips didn't see it coming fast enough.

The entire discourse is now on record.

After Phillips' objection is sustained and DiRisio reminds the jury, "The question by counsel does not itself establish any fact in the question," Judge Payne makes it clear he simply doesn't remember reading the newspaper on August 8, 1957. But Evans can't let it go, pressing him about why he can't remember; after all, the statement was about his good friend.

Seething at the insinuation, Payne says, "You may remember that—if you do, I congratulate that."

Feeling the heat of an imminent explosion, Evans steps backward. "No, sir. Sir, I wasn't even in Chattanooga then. I was not even in Chattanooga. I was thirteen years old."

DiRisio has had enough. "Let's ask questions," he instructs Evans.

But Payne doesn't know anything that will help, so Evans dismisses him.

The next witness for the defense is George "Buck" Bradbury—a familiar name to sports enthusiasts. He's the coach who helped recruit

Bobby to Auburn in 1953. Now a financial consultant and securities broker, Bradbury worked 15 years as an assistant coach at Auburn and another 19 years as executive director of the alumni association.

Phillips wastes no time, asking Bradbury about the pictures and placards of Bobby Hoppe that Godwin had testified were posted around Auburn in 1957.

Not so, Bradbury says emphatically. Bradbury tells the Court, "Coach [Shug] Jordan didn't allow our publicity office in those days to even do like they do today." Individual players were never used to advertise the upcoming season, contrary to what Godwin said about placards of Bobby being plastered all over town.

Phillips pushes on, asking about Bobby's reputation at Auburn.

Bradbury tells the Court he came to respect Bobby because he "overcame so much as a student at Auburn and just developed from the first day he walked on that campus. He was one of the most coachable people I have ever coached.

"You didn't have to worry about how hard he worked. You didn't have to worry about whether he was going to do the right thing.... He was a great team man. He was one of the most unselfish of our athletes...."

According to Bradbury, Bobby was "the best blocker on our national championship team."

Then Bradbury says something Evans will jump on with both feet during cross-examination. "Right into his senior year, you know, after this particular incident that we are talking about, by gosh, he just did what he was supposed to do."

When Phillips hands Bradbury over for cross-examination, Evans' gun is locked and loaded. He wants to go back to what Bradbury said regarding how Bobby acted after the incident in Chattanooga.

"So this killing didn't bring about any change in this man that you observed, did it?"

Bradbury hesitates, so Evans goads him. "Is that a hard question, sir?"

Bradbury acknowledges he observed no change in Bobby and starts to explain that he had been "associated with other athletes who had been through trauma and I never saw any—"

Evans cuts him off and goes into an unexpected rant. "How many athletes have you seen that killed some fellow with a shotgun and were emotionally distraught about it and believed it to be self-defense and it weighed on their mind and they were concerned about it and then went down to Auburn and had a stellar season? How many athletes have you seen like that, sir, how many, outside of Mr. Hoppe? How many? How many?"

Evans is coming at him full force, but Bradbury knows how to avoid such a knee-buckling tackle. He stands firm, both feet planted. "Are you trying to put words in my mouth?" he asks quietly, his tone in vivid contrast to Evans.

But Evans won't be distracted, taunting, "Just tell the jury how many. This is the only one, isn't it? It's the only one you know of, is that correct, sir?"

Bradbury responds, "He is the only one that has been accused of something like this."

Phillips has had it with Evans. He's not questioning Bradbury; he's just spewing out diatribes for the jury's benefit.

There's a terse interchange before Judge DiRisio, during which Evans argues it is difficult to ask questions of character witnesses before the defendant testifies. He objects to the defense calling any more character witnesses at this point.

"Why?" DiRisio wants to know.

"Because I am going to get the same response from every character witness without [Hoppe] getting up there and them being able to hear what he has to say about this killing.

"You see the State's difficulty. [Bradbury] says, 'As far as I know, he didn't kill anyone.' [Bradbury] hasn't heard it, so I guess he doesn't believe it."

Phillips tries to get Evans to be willing to use "assuming" in talking about Bobby's role in the killing, But Evans won't compromise, responding, "No, I'm not going to assume a thing."

Phillips makes another attempt, reminding Evans it has been admitted in the opening statement that Bobby killed Hudson. Why not use that?

Evans rejects that outright, pushing for a total victory in this battle. "Let's have Mr. Hoppe tell [Bradbury] right now he killed a man."

Phillips is outraged. "No. No. Come on," he pleads.

Sensing the judge's tacit agreement with him, Evans demands, "Let's call the defendant."

The State Concludes and the Defense Begins

His face flushed, Phillips turns to Evans. "No, you are not going to govern my proof!"

A recess is called to see if a resolution can be reached, but it's a debate with no middle ground. When Court reconvenes, Phillips has forfeited his position: No more character witnesses until Bobby testifies. Bradbury is dismissed subject to recall, and Phillips calls Barbara Jo Campbell Gurganass.

Now 48, the ravages of breast cancer have eroded Barbara's dewy youthfulness, but the contours of her face reveal her former beauty. Totally composed, she looks at Phillips, her eyes saying she's ready to enter this fray.

She tells him Bobby picked her up the night of July 20, 1957, between 6:30 and 7 p.m. and took her back home around midnight "or maybe even later."

* * *

Later, sequestered again in the jury room, the chosen 12 discuss the timing put forth by Odene compared to the timing outlined by Barbara Jo.

"The gun swap with McCutcheon occurred in the early evening, around 6:30 or 7," Juror Belle Rucker says. "If Bobby was at Odene's house in the afternoon, as she said at one point, that was before the gun swap, so Bobby couldn't have had a shotgun in his car."

Across the table, Juror Mitchell Thomas pipes up. "On the other hand, Bobby's being at Odene's house around 11:30 or 11:45 p.m.—the time she often cited—is also problematic. Barbara Jo said Bobby didn't leave her at her house until midnight or later."

His buddy sitting next to him jumps in. "I see where you're going with this. By that time, Odene was already at Dupont—working the midnight shift."

Juror Mary Carr thinks Barbara Jo could be lying, but others disagree, saying a woman dying from cancer is not likely to be lying under oath, before God.

By now, most of the jurors question whether Odene can be believed at all.

A Matter of Conscience

* * *

Barbara Jo testifies after Bobby picked her up on July 20, 1957, they rode around in the convertible a while. Then they drove to Nikki's. After a quick stop, they decided to go dancing.

Time flew by and, realizing it was late, Barbara Jo asked Bobby to take her home. It was about midnight when they got to her house, but they sat on the porch swing a while longer.

Did she notice anything unusual about Bobby that night?

No, she replies. "He was in a good mood and happy. He acted no different at all."

Beginning his cross-examination, Evans isn't interested in how Bobby seemed to Barbara Jo. He wants to know if she recalls certain details about the car she and Bobby were in the night Hudson was killed. What kind of front seat did it have? Was it a bench seat or did it have bucket seats? Was there an opening in the front seat's back?

Barbara Jo doesn't know for sure, but she doesn't remember any opening. She thinks it was a bench seat, and that seems to please Evans.

Satisfied, he tells Barbara Jo she can step down. Her older brother Paul Allen helps her back to her seat, before taking her place in the witness box. His testimony is short. He confirms he knew Hudson from seeing him at a community center in North Chattanooga.

What about Hudson's reputation?

"We just considered him a thug." And Hudson had a reputation for carrying a gun, for being armed, Paul Allen adds.

It's been a while since Paul Allen has seen Bobby, he says. Probably about five years ago when Bobby was inducted into the Sports Hall of Fame in Chattanooga.

For Evans, this testimony is useless. He asks a couple of innocuous questions and lets Paul Allen go.

The next defense witness is also on and off the stand quickly. Jo (Sliger) Alexander, whom Odene testified was with Billy Joe King at the Neals' house when the coroner and a detective came by, doesn't recall seeing any coroner or detective that night. Despite pressure by Evans, she won't corroborate Odene's account.

Jerry Cannon takes Jo's place in the witness box.

Cannon's volunteering to testify took great courage. A retired bank executive, he grew up in North Chattanooga, first meeting Bobby when he was in the sixth grade. About three years later, he met Hudson.

The State Concludes and the Defense Begins

Today, Cannon stands before a judge and jury to share a part of his life that's ancient history—a part for which he's deeply ashamed.

Disclosing to his family and friends that he once ran whisky with Don Hudson is not easy for a man who's now a respected member of the community. His family never knew of the short time during the 1950s when he hauled whisky for Hudson.

Going public takes guts, but Cannon discovers what Anias Nin did many years before: "Life shrinks or expands in proportion to one's courage." Years later, Cannon will say, after his testimony, family and friends, rather than shunning him, looked on him with a deeper respect.

After testifying about his brief association with Hudson in the whisky business, Cannon describes Hudson's reputation. "It was real bad. He was a violent person."

Then Cannon recounts why he severed his relationship with Hudson. "I was at a house one night with him and Joan, and he beat her up real bad with his fists. She ran out of the house, and he grabbed his gun and he emptied the gun at her feet, chasing her around the house. She begged me to call her mother or Bobby."

That was in late '54 or early '55. He never again had anything to do with Hudson. "I was afraid," he says.

Coming forward to testify was hard, wasn't it, Phillips asks.

"Yes, it's very hard."

In short order, Evans decides not to cross-examine.

* * *

A burly man settles himself into the witness chair. Johnny Roberson, now an officer at the Hamilton County Penal Farm, was once a policeman for the Chattanooga Police Department.

But, he confesses, as a 15-year-old boy, he sometimes hung with the wrong crowd.

Roberson testifies that, back when he was hanging out with a rough brunch, he saw a .38-caliber pistol in Hudson's car the night he was killed.

It was about 11 or 11:30 p.m. Roberson was at the Pig House, a restaurant on Cherokee Boulevard, a hangout for tough teens as well as whisky runners who relished the hero worship of teens who dawdled away their time there.

180

According to Roberson, on that July night in 1957, Hudson cruised up to the Pig House, stopping to talk to a couple of friends. Interested in what was happening, the young Roberson wandered over and spied the pistol on the front seat of Hudson's car.

A short time later, Roberson and other Pig House customers heard sirens and dashed out to follow them to where Hudson's car had crashed into a rock wall and utility pole.

Roberson is the first—but not the last—person to testify Hudson had a gun in his car the night he was killed, although it had disappeared by the time police arrived at the scene.

Evans makes an attempt to discredit Roberson. Why didn't he come forward in 1957? Why didn't he go to the police in 1988 when he read about the trial in the newspaper?

Irritated that the witness talked with defense attorneys rather than the State, Evans loses ground when Roberson says police never tried to interview him. For that matter, they never tried to interview anyone at the Pig House or at any of Hudson's other haunts, repeating what Stargel had admitted earlier.

Rattled, Evans again goads Roberson about why it didn't occur to him earlier that his testimony might be important.

With a slight smile, Roberson says, "A thirty-one year old case, I don't think you're going to get the truth out of it no way."

"That's a nice thing for a law enforcement officer to say, isn't it?" Evans snaps.

That brings Phillips to his feet, objecting.

"Sustained," the judge says, giving Evans a stern look.

At the defense table, Bobby reflects on Roberson and his testimony, thankful he came forward to substantiate what Bobby saw all too closely that night—Hudson had a gun.

Brick by brick, the defense is laying a foundation of corroborating evidence for self-defense. It's not over, but Bobby is beginning to feel better about his chances.

* * *

The targeted witnesses on the short list continue to take the stand, beginning with William L. McCutcheon. His testimony supports the contention that evidence is lost. He knows it first hand—he tells the

Court his father, in the last stages of Alzheimer's, is mentally incompetent.

He says his father frequently traded guns, so pushing Bobby to swap guns wasn't unusual. Asked about Hudson, McCutcheon says he "carried a gun with him wherever he went."

Evans tells the judge he has no questions, so McCutcheon steps down.

The long, trying week is over, with the Court adjourning for the weekend. The jury selection on Monday has been followed by four intense days of testimony.

Preparing the jury for the weekend, DiRisio gives his lengthiest lecture yet. Telling them they will live with the job they do as jurors for many, many years, he says they will be "shorting the system...shorting everyone involved in the case and especially yourself and your own integrity as a juror" if they violate his prohibitions by making "independent inquiries, contact with other people, discussion of the case, forming premature opinions or anything of the sort.

"Give yourself the best crack at doing the best possible job on the case," DiRisio tells the twelve. Don't discuss the case with anyone. Don't read newspapers or watch television coverage of the case. "Make your decision based on the evidence and on the law and nothing else."

Turning a deaf ear, one overzealous juror drives again with her husband to Cherokee Boulevard, turns down Bell Avenue, and confirms her own deductions about what occurred.

Discussing the case with her husband before jury deliberations begin, Marjorie Simpkins arrives at her personal conclusions about what happened on the night of July 20-21, 1957. Long before the trial is over—before Bobby testifies—her opinion is sealed in concrete.

When Court reconvenes on Monday, DiRisio asks the jury whether anyone violated his rules over the weekend. Not one juror speaks up.

* * *

The weekend is both too short and too long. Too short for the reprieve we both need and too long for Bobby's preparation for what will be the mother of cross-examinations.

I've dreaded the approach of each day since the trial began, but on this day, June 27, 1988, I'm limp with fear. Inside the courthouse, I move by sheer determination through the crowd in the hallway, greetings and good wishes floating above me, garbled and far away.

A few minutes later, settling into the row behind the defense table, I do the countdown in my head. Five days down and how many to go? Bobby could be on the witness stand two days or more, I think, hopeful the trial will end this week.

And Bobby won't even be the first to testify today—that makes it even worse. He'll have to sit through two other testimonies before he takes the stand.

As the second week of the trial begins, the defense calls M.C. Gross, who served as the grand jury foreman for a 10-year period from 1963-1973.

Gross adds little except to document the missing grand jury records, destroyed after the end of his service as grand jury foreman. Under questioning by Phillips and Evans, it's clear he has little independent recall of the Hudson case when it came to the grand jury in 1966.

The one exception—he remembers the Godwin tape.

With that, a record has been solidly established: In 1966, a grand jury heard that tape. It is not new evidence in 1988.

* * *

The courtroom crackles with tension when Phillips calls Billy Joe King as the next defense witness.

Amazingly, the first time any police officer talked to King about the Hudson case was in May 1988, when Richard Heck and John Taylor paid him a visit. But back in 1957, no official ever contacted him.

Today, King rips another hole in Odene's testimony. He not only doesn't recall being at Jody and Odene Neal's house when Dr. Currey and a detective came by in 1957, he's adamant it never happened.

"No, sir. I know Dr. Currey very well, and I would have knowed if he had been there," he tells Phillips. "It never happened."

King also doesn't recall ever saying anything to Odene or Jody— jokingly or otherwise—about someone throwing dynamite on their porch. Later, under intense cross-examination by Evans, King repeats, "I will say I didn't say it."

The State Concludes and the Defense Begins

He does remember vividly that Taylor and Heck told him he was in the car with Bobby on the night Hudson was killed. Today on the stand, with no hesitation, King says it was a lie.

Phillips hands King over to Evans for cross-examination, who begins by prodding King into admitting he likes hard liquor.

Then Evans wants to know if King knows what "inhibition" is. Without waiting for an answer, he explains, "Inhibition is where you keep something in. Do you find that when you drink that maybe it loosens your tongue a little?"

King tells the attorney he doesn't drink much anymore, but Evans finally badgers him into saying drinking a lot "loosens everyone's tongue, don't it?"

Now, back on track with the trip to Jody's lake house, Evans notes that his visit coinciding with Jody's subpoena seems strange, but King's jaw is set. He denies knowing Jody had been subpoenaed until Jody told him at the lake. And despite Evans' prodding, King doesn't budge.

King is steady on the stand, refusing to let Evans provoke him. But when Evans uses the word "murder" to describe Hudson's death, Phillips jumps full-tilt into the fray.

With Phillip's objection sustained, Evans walks back to the prosecution table to regroup. Suddenly, he feels inspired.

"Well, you sort of lost contact with (Jody) after Don Hudson had his brains blown out, is that right?"

Laughter ripples across the courtroom, but DiRisio doesn't think it's funny. Glowering at the prosecutor, he gavels the courtroom into silence.

But Evans has more ammunition in his gun. He wants to know if King ever went to a barbeque place on Hixson Pike and picked up ten thousand dollars in cash.

Trying to avoid the bullet, King says, "I sure did not."

Evans doesn't buy that answer, so he pushes on as if he hadn't heard. "[Brought] it back in a grocery sack to a card game, do you remember that?"

Before any response, Evans adds, "It is going to be hard to forget that, isn't it? Do you remember that, Mr. King?"

Looking sheepish, King says, "I don't think it was a barbeque place."

Another wave of laughter followed by another thump, thump of the gavel.

Clearly annoyed, Evans says he doesn't care if it was a barbeque place. He just wants to know if King recalls the incident.

Looking quickly at the floor behind the irate attorney, King comes clean. He recalls the ten thousand cash in a paper sack and, yes, it was at a card game. Back in 1979.

With King's credibility gaping, Evans goes for the jugular, asking if he was with Bobby Hoppe the night Hudson was killed.

At first King says he's certain he wasn't, but when Evans won't let up, he says, hesitantly, "Well, I am almost certain I wasn't with him."

"Almost certain, sir? Almost certain?" Evans presses, eagerness filling his voice.

"Well, I wasn't with him," King finally decides.

But Evans won't let go. "No, you said *almost certain*. I like that answer, sir. You are almost certain you weren't with him."

Furious, Phillips objects. The commentary is totally unacceptable. The judge agrees, instructing the jurors to disregard Evans' remarks.

Once again, the words hang in the air, then nestle down into the minds of the jurors.

Having regained his composure, King repeats he's sure he wasn't with Bobby that night.

Evans says, derisively, "Well, isn't it true, Mr. King, that years ago when you would drink and become a little loose tongued, you would talk about how you were the driver of a car when a certain individual got his brains blown out in Chattanooga?"

He never said that, King declares. He would remember it if he had. Out of nowhere, King recalls an English class in high school, his junior year—something about Ernest Hemingway saying an intelligent man is sometimes forced to be drunk to spend time with his fools.

Not being known as a scholar, thus doubly proud of himself for remembering this bit of literature, King thinks he might have had to drink to tolerate some of his friends, but if they told such a tall tale, they were drunker than he was.

Evans is convinced the witness did brag about driving the hit car. To get under King's skin, Evans goes on a verbal rip, ending his tirade by repeating the question.

Cool as a cucumber, King responds, "Never."

The State Concludes and the Defense Begins

And King adds he hasn't seen Bobby in more than 20 years.

Satisfied he's gotten as much as he can get from this witness, Evans lets King go.

Phillips calls the next witness. Bobby Hoppe.

My heart in my throat, I watch my husband rise and walk to the witness stand.

CHAPTER FIFTEEN

A Conscience Unburdened

Conscience is God present in man.
–Victor Hugo (1802-1885)

In most police and crime fiction, movies, and television shows, the defendant almost always takes the stand. The audience expects it, almost salivating to hear the accused defend himself. The defendant's testimony often creates the crescendo of the drama followed by the *denouement,* where the mystery of the story is finally "untied" for all to understand.

If the defendant does not testify, the anticipated drama in the courtroom dissipates quickly. The audience feels short-changed, irritated that, after days of debate about what the defendant did or did not do, the defendant's own words will not be heard. But on the strong advice of counsel, most defendants choose not to testify.

When Cook and Phillips originally explained this to him, Bobby questioned why anyone wouldn't want to tell his own story to jurors.

A danger arises in taking the stand, Phillips cautioned. If it doesn't go well, a defendant can become his own hangman. Under prosecutorial pressure, some defendants squirm and sweat, appearing guilty.

In other instances, defendants simply cannot articulate their own cases effectively. Trying too hard to sound credible, they often come across as less than believable. When this happens, the sound of jurors clucking their tongues becomes almost audible—which tends to make the defendant even more flustered and incoherent.

But both Cook and Phillips have assured Bobby they aren't concerned how he will present himself on the witness stand. The decision to testify is his, they have determined.

For Bobby, it's not a decision to discuss. From the day he was indicted, there was never any doubt he would testify.

Bobby knew that whatever came his way as a result of his testimony, nothing could be worse than the private hell he'd occupied for the past 31 years. Despite anticipating a no-holds-barred attack from Evans, Bobby is ready to take the stand.

A Conscience Unburdened

The time has arrived. Today, Bobby will put his hand on the Bible and take an oath before God. Then he'll step into the witness box and tell the jury what really happened that fateful night more than three decades ago. After sitting silent for eight tension-filled days of testimony, he will look at the jurors and ask them to believe him—believe him instead of the State's witnesses, some of whom have distorted the truth or, for whatever reasons, made it up from scratch.

I'm not worried about what Bobby will say—he's ready to tell his story, hopeful his public confession will bring him peace. But Evans is good, very good—and I dread his cross-examination, knowing he'll spring like a wild wolf, sinking bared fangs into Bobby's throat.

Once again, Judge DiRisio is late. Today, his tardiness doesn't irritate me. In fact, it brings a reprieve, a few additional moments before the assault begins. All around me in the courtroom there's electricity, an inaudible crackling that precedes a summer storm.

For a moment I recall how much Bobby loves watching storms brew over the ocean, wondering if sea breezes will push them inland, producing sheets of fat raindrops.

That peaceful thought disintegrates as I glance at Evans, picturing him as the Roman god Jupiter, a jagged thunderbolt held high over his head, ready to hurl with a mighty force at Bobby. I stare hard at Bobby, willing him to feel my thoughts, wanting to warn him to be ready because this storm may be fiercer than any he has ever seen. But without eye contact, I can't tell if he senses my alarm.

Sitting quietly at the defense table, his steady gaze fixed on Evans, Bobby projects a preternatural calm in the eye of the storm.

Just moments before, as we walked from Leroy Phillip's office, the overcast sky above Chattanooga seemed a bad omen. Like a gray wool blanket spread across the city, it brought no relief from the choking humidity. For the first time this week, though, the sun didn't scorch our faces as we make our way to Court. Instead, the elderly black man on the corner was our personal ray of sunshine today. As we scurried by, he lifted his hand in greeting, offering a toothy smile and a hardy "good luck."

It isn't the first time someone on the street has shown support. Each day as we hurry down the sidewalk, good wishes from complete strangers have become routine. Even in the courthouse, people we don't know step from their offices to say, "Hang in there," or "It's going to be OK."

And every day of the trial, Jack Robbs, a captain with the Chattanooga Police, positions himself at the door as we enter the courtroom, squeezing Bobby's shoulder or shaking his hand. After we pass, Robbs takes his place near the door through which the jury will enter—a silent sign of his support for Bobby. Robbs has taken vacation to be here for his former teammate at Central and at Auburn. Still watching Bobby's back. Still making a way through the line for him.

On this particular day, however, Robbs partially blocks our entrance into the courtroom. Taking Bobby by the shoulders, he whispers, "Pretend you're blocking a lineman when Evans hits you. Stop him dead in his tracks. You can outrun him, old buddy. You're Hippity Hoppe."

That brings a slight smile to Bobby's face as he walks to his place in the courtroom.

Now he sits in front of me, shoulders bent forward, head down. In his hand, he holds the laminated card I gave him months ago. I wonder which verse of scripture he's reading.

"All rise," the bailiff drones, kicking off Bobby's testimony. At least the first inquisitor, Leroy Phillips, is on our team. Bobby slips the well-worn card into his suit coat pocket, stands up straight, and walks to the witness stand. As he takes his seat, rather than looking at his own attorney, Bobby looks directly at the prosecutor with eyes as clear as a mountain stream.

Phillips starts slowly, asking Bobby to tell about his job, my job, his family. Next he leads Bobby briefly into his sports career, including his short stint in the professional leagues. In 1958, Bobby had been the third draft choice for the San Francisco Forty-Niners. But haunted by memories of the 1957 tragedy, Bobby returned home after a few weeks. Later, he was given a chance to go back but, just before his return, Bobby was traded to the Washington Redskins. For a short time before injuring his knee, he played for the Redskins. Back then, with only 10-12 professional football teams and no union representation, players weren't protected like today. So, he tells Phillips, after his knee healed, he was released and sent home.

But Shug Jordan, Auburn's head football coach, had not forgotten what Bobby Hoppe did for the Tigers, so he contacted Bobby, encouraging him to return to school one semester to complete his degree and help coach the freshman team. Bobby not only finished his degree, he fell in love with coaching and made it his career for more than 20 years.

During those two decades, he completed his master's degree and served as head football coach at two Georgia high schools. And, as Bobby tells Phillips, he had a massive heart attack.

Evans snaps to attention when Phillips asks Bobby about his heart, objecting on relevancy. Without pausing, Phillips goes back at Evans, telling the judge he wants to "put the attorney general on notice about this man's extremely bad heart condition."

In a voice sticky with sarcasm, Evans interjects, "Oh, and eliminating cross-examination?"

Phillips pivots to glare at Evans. "No, in governing your conduct."

After a short bench conference, DiRisio allows questioning to continue.

Phillips moves on to the health of Bobby's mother back in 1957. Excellent, Bobby says. Contrary to Godwin's testimony that Mrs. Hoppe was dying in 1957, she was well and working full time at Erlanger Hospital as a housemother for nursing students. She enjoyed good health until she was diagnosed with cancer and died in 1982.

What about his sister Joan? Bobby tells the jury Joan has suffered for years with severe depression, confined to a mental hospital numerous times. She also has painful, crippling arthritis that significantly limits her mobility.

Phillips asks about our son, Kevin, establishing he was adopted when he was eight and is now in the U.S. Navy.

Evans objects, not even rising from his chair. Relevancy again. He doesn't want Bobby painted as a man whose heart was open to adopting a young child who had suffered the loss of both parents.

But the objection doesn't matter. Phillips has accomplished his goal of putting Bobby at ease. Now comes the hard part. Phillips hits it straight on, asking about the gun exchange, even having Bobby describe the gun.

"...a .410 shotgun, over under. It had two barrels, one on top of the other. The top barrel fired a .410 shot, and the bottom fired a .22," Bobby says, looking directly at the jury.

And how did he obtain the gun? Under what circumstances?

A Matter of Conscience

On the way to pick up his date, Bobby says, he dropped by the Riverview Pharmacy. He was standing in the back of the store, shooting the breeze with Gene Harmon, the pharmacist, and some friends, when Bill McCutcheon telephoned, asking to talk with him.

Describing McCutcheon as kind of a "horse trader" who swapped antiques, coins, stamps, guns, even cars, Bobby says McCutcheon wanted him to come by and see the .410 shotgun because Bobby had a pistol McCutcheon wanted.

But Bobby didn't want McCutcheon's .410. He had no use for the shotgun.

"I had a .22 rifle at home. The .410 was half way to a .22 rifle and had a .410 shotgun. I don't hunt, so I didn't want the .410. I told him I didn't want to [trade]."

But McCutcheon called again and again, asking Bobby to at least look at the gun. Bobby eventually agreed to meet him to test fire the gun. He headed home to get his pistol and then drove to a chert pit on Lupton Drive to meet McCutcheon.

Bobby continued to tell McCutcheon he didn't want the gun but, finally, he made the trade. Late for his date, he didn't take time to drive home to put the gun away before he hurried to pick up Barbara Jo. They cruised around, occasionally stopping to talk with friends. About midnight, Bobby took her home, and they sat on the front porch a while.

Surprisingly, Phillips fails to point out that Bobby couldn't have been at Odene's house the evening Hudson was killed since she had to be at work at Dupont at midnight. At midnight, Bobby was still at Barbara Jo's. More importantly, at the preliminary hearing, Odene had said it was daylight when Bobby came by her house. Since Bobby did not swap guns with McCutcheon until almost 7 p.m. and then rushed to get to his girlfriend, there was no way he could have gone by Odene's *after* the trade and before she went to work. Yet, this critical time sequence is not called to the jurors' attention.

Instead, Phillips abruptly swerves away from the lead-up to the evening Hudson was killed, asking Bobby about his sister Joan. He ascertains from Bobby that Joan, who was four years older than Bobby, was not dating or living with Hudson in the summer of 1957.

Bobby tells Phillips the relationship had ended the previous fall—both his mother and his sister Martha told him the affair was over when he came home for the 1956 Christmas break. Over Evans' matter-of-fact objection, Bobby says by July 1957, Joan and Hudson had been separated nine months, contrary to Odene's assertion that they were a couple in July 1957.

Moving on, Phillips asks about Jody Neal.

Jody was one of several boys that summer who helped Bobby build a crude raft—a rickety Tom Sawyer raft made by wiring barrels to a platform of wood. A big deal to the guys.

And how many times did Bobby see Odene that summer—or anytime, Phillips asks.

"I can recall we were working on the raft one day, and she brought sandwiches and cold drinks up there. That's the only time I recall her being on the lake, because we weren't going on the lake to be with her. We were a bunch of boys wanting to fish and have a good time."

"Do you ever recall being in her home on any occasion?"

"Yes," Bobby responds. "I wasn't in her home very often, but I recall a group of people in her home one night and I was there."

Bobby says he might have been in the Neal home two or three times, but he only recalls the one time. And when it comes to Bobby getting into a real conversation with Odene, Bobby points out he would never open up to a woman who's little more than a stranger. Phillips realizes it's important for jurors to hear Bobby describe how limited his acquaintance was with Odene.

"But did you all hang around with [Jody's] wife or his wife hang around with you all?"

"No, no, no," Bobby responds emphatically. He spent time with Jody, but not with Odene.

"Sir, you heard [Odene] sit there where you are and state that you came to her home on the night Mr. Hudson was killed and made certain statements to her that you had a gun in your car and you were going to kill Mr. Hudson. Did you make statements like that at all to her, sir?"

From several feet away, I sense Bobby stiffen, repugnance darkening his demeanor.

"That is the biggest lie. No, I never made a statement like that to that woman. Listen, she and Jody were good friends of the Hudson family. Jody and she herself said [Jody] was like a brother to Don."

Shaking his head slightly, his sapphire eyes fading to gray, Bobby adds, "If I was going to confide in someone....If I had the heart—which I couldn't murder anybody, period—to plan a murder... And murder is not part of me.

"If I were going to do something like that, I would go to a friend or a minister I could trust. I wouldn't go to some woman I didn't know— absolutely not."

Sensing Bobby's emotions are running high, Phillips returns to Joan and Hudson's relationship. After establishing that, to Bobby's knowledge, Hudson had not abused Joan in the nine months preceding July 1957, Phillips asks about the period when Joan was dating Hudson.

Trying to remain calm, Bobby speaks through clenched teeth, saying he saw suspicious bruises on Joan a few times. And friends would say, "Don had whipped my sister...."

"I don't suppose you liked that, did you, sir?"

Voice steady, eyes piercing, Bobby replies, "No, I didn't."

"Did you kill anybody over it, sir?"

Solemnly Bobby says, "Don Hudson has never, as far as I know, done anything to me or any member of my family that would warrant me murdering him....

"I have never talked to Don Hudson to his face or driven a car up to him, written him a letter, called him on the phone nor gotten a third party to carry a threatening message to him. Absolutely, concretely, no, never."

And, he repeats, at the time Hudson pointed a gun at him and tried to run him off the road, it had been more than a year since Bobby had heard any rumors about Hudson abusing Joan.

Before Joan broke it off with Hudson, Bobby's family tried to talk with her. Exasperated with the situation, Bobby's sister Martha told him, "Joan is in love with Don, and only time will help her to see that he is not the type of person she should be associated with."

At that point, Bobby tells the jury, he gave up, declaring he would no longer worry about the toxic relationship. "It was a long time before they broke up that I washed my hands clean of the affair."

Phillips reminds him the prosecution said Joan was married while she was living with Hudson, but Bobby testifies Joan's husband died in 1954. Contrary to what Evans said, it was almost a year after her husband's death before she started dating Hudson.

So why was the family so opposed to the relationship? What did Bobby know about Hudson back in the mid-50s?

A Conscience Unburdened

"Well," Bobby says, turning slightly to face the jury, "general knowledge...general talk in North Chattanooga was that [Don] was known to carry a gun; he was a bootlegger; a whisky runner; an informer. He would inform on other bootleggers.

"Hoping [to] get in with the police [so they] would let him carry his liquor, he would turn other [liquor runners] in."

A volatile and violent man, Hudson wanted what he wanted when he wanted it, regardless of the consequences. Bobby tells the jury about one incident rumored around town: "This man was in a phone booth, and Don wanted the phone. Don beat the man over the head with a gun and knocked him out of the booth, so he could use the phone."

Bobby also recalls hearing about the time Hudson kidnapped a black man and had a friend hold him at gunpoint while Hudson beat him to a bloody pulp, leaving him by the side of the road to die. It was said all three were moonshine-runners. And there were stories about Hudson losing fingers in a drive-by shooting. A hit-and-run accident where Hudson left behind his car, loaded with whisky. Stories of Hudson, a spotlight on his car, chasing other bootleggers—making them think he was the police and then stealing their load of liquor. In the mid-50s, these were just a few of the tales about Hudson. He was hotheaded, ruthless.

Without conscience.

Then Bobby—almost as if watching from afar— tells the jury a few things they've never heard. On one occasion, Hudson went after a man with a tire iron because he was dating Joan. Another time, Joan and some man were sitting in a car, talking, when Hudson reached through the window and punched the startled man full in the face.

After Joan broke up with Hudson, he began acting crazy, Bobby says. Some folks said he was high on drugs.

With that, the background testimony by Bobby is over, all leading up to this—time to tell the jury what happened the night Hudson was shot. My heart gallops, then misses several beats. What Bobby is getting ready to share—these horrific recollections—have been locked inside this very private man more than 30 years.

Bobby's memories of that night have become oozing sores that never heal. They may have scabbed over briefly when he was doing something he loved—huddled on the line of scrimmage or coaching a game—but the scab never stays intact. Often, people scrape it away inadvertently.

But most of the time, it is Bobby who picks at it, inviting the pain back, refusing to believe he deserves to be whole again.

Maybe, Bobby thinks to himself, he'll be able to heal after he swings the door open on July 21, 1957. Only he knows the horrors that have taken up residence on the other side.

* * *

One December day in 1987, Bobby and I met after work, as usual, to unwind and share the day's events during an hour-long stroll inside the local mall, bright and festive with holiday decorations. On this particular day, shoppers rushed in and out of stores, shopping bags bulging with Christmas gifts.

It was blustery and cold in the parking lot. Yet, when Bobby saw the scurrying shoppers, he insisted we walk the outside perimeter of the mall, so I turned up the collar of my coat, linked my arm through his and slipped an ungloved hand into his coat pocket.

My conversation was light, laughter underlining my tale about a colleague. Suddenly, my words froze—hanging suspended in the evening air—as I realized Bobby was not hearing me. He was somewhere else. It showed in his face, the set of his jaw.

For a second, he turned hollow eyes toward me. They were flat—a gray lake, frozen over. Bobby shuddered and then uttered words so soft I wasn't sure he was talking to me.

Leaning closer, I heard my husband struggle for words, his strained voice cracking, "Sherry, I did it—I killed Don Hudson."

Seventeen years earlier, in late 1970, Bobby had also struggled with words. We had just become engaged, and he quietly said he couldn't marry me until he shared an ugly part of his past—that he had once been accused of murdering a man. But that night, he stopped short of the whole story. The full burden he had shouldered alone for almost 14 years remained secret, his words flavored by fear of my reaction.

"I want you to know I never murdered anyone," he had added emphatically that long ago night. Then he proceeded to outline a grand jury's "no true bill" decision a few years earlier. He was calm, but I sensed unspeakable emotions rippling beneath the surface. On that night in 1970, I reached across the seat, took his hand, and held it tightly, as I did almost two decades later on the cold December night, the wind howling around us.

Walking the mall's perimeter, my mind replayed that awful night in 1970, forever etched in my mind.

Now, his words flew by me like snow in a blizzard. How could this be, I thought. He told me long ago he had never murdered anyone, and now he's saying he killed Don Hudson? It's incomprehensible. I tried not to react, but my mind spun at warp speed.

To Bobby, there was no contradiction— he killed Hudson, but he did not murder him.

Sentence upon sentence poured out as Bobby told me about the night Hudson died—a torrent of words from the bowels of hell. The winter wind, pushing skeletons of leaves along the pavement, no longer chilled me. Bobby's words raced like wildfire through my veins.

A second later, I was shivering so hard I was afraid Bobby would notice, so I pulled my hand from his pocket. My thoughts plummeted and tossed like a bird shot from the sky but caught in a swirling current.

Bobby stopped walking and looked at me, gauging my reaction— and I saw pure panic shimmering in his eyes. We linked hands and moved on.

Dusk turned pitch black, hiding our fear from each other. When there were no more words, when Bobby was talked out, we realized we'd been walking more than three hours. How many circuits around the mall? Gripped by the horror of what might happen, we'd lost all sense of time or place.

Later that night, when reason returned, I recalled a recent call from George Roush, a post office supervisor in North Chattanooga. Bobby had worked for Roush during Christmas breaks, effortlessly tossing huge bags of mail onto mail trucks, and the two men had become friends.

As time went by, Bobby would occasionally stop by to visit Roush. So Bobby was not surprised when he called. But he wasn't prepared for what he had to say: Roush was having lunch in a local restaurant when he overheard two detectives talking about the old Hudson case.

At first, he only picked up bits of the conversation, but as the two became engrossed in the excitement of solving a decades-old murder, they grew animated and began talking louder. Roush heard them say they were close to taking the case to a grand jury. Their heads leaning together, the two men discussed seeking an indictment against a hometown hero.

Lowering their voices, the detectives recalled how tough it had been getting witnesses to recall information after so many years, but they finally found one who "remembered" something. They laughed about putting the fear of God in her by making her believe her ex-husband was involved in the killing. But they assured each other it was just part of the job.

Roush called Bobby as soon as he arrived home that evening.

That brief phone call foreshadowed our three-hour walk and the confession that gushed from Bobby like putrid wastewater, wiping away our safe and unsullied life.

* * *

Now, the world will know what I know—what Bobby told me on that blustery winter evening six short months ago.

This will be difficult for Bobby, so Phillips guides him gently, telling him to share what he did after leaving his date the early morning of July 21, 1957.

"I drove by Nikki's; I didn't see anyone I knew. I didn't recognize anybody's car, so I started home on this back road that runs behind Nikki's."

This was the way he usually went home from Nikki's, Bobby adds, the most direct route.

As he drove down the winding road, Bobby reached to adjust the radio to pick up a Nashville station. There was only static, so he pulled Joan's car off the road, cattycornered to a small side road sloping down to a trailer park. As he fiddled with the radio, a car came up Bell Avenue and stopped, its blinker indicating the driver wanted to turn into the trailer park, so Bobby pulled the Ford Fairlane back on the road and headed on down Bell Avenue.

Going slowly, still adjusting the car radio, Bobby sensed something to his left. "I looked and there was a car with no lights on. The hood, the grille of the car, was about even with my back tires...it scared me; it shocked me. I immediately swerved to the right to get away. The car fell in back behind me."

Bobby didn't recognize the car, but he figured it was friends playing a joke on him. So he kept driving down Bell Avenue, pausing at a stop sign where the curves end and a straight stretch leads to North Market Street.

Bobby pulled slowly away from the stop sign, allowing the darkened car to pull up beside him, expecting to see some guys laughing at him for being startled by their prank.

The car paralleled him again, this time more quickly, and it wasn't filled with friends. But he didn't know that. He was struggling to keep his own car from being hit as the other car pulled tighter to him as if trying to run him off the road.

"[The other car] swerved into me, and I swerved to the right and put my brakes on," Bobby explains, his voice shaking. "I almost came to a complete stop. I was still rolling a little bit forward. And as I rolled forward, I rolled past him."

The other driver pulled in behind the Ford Fairlane, coming within a hair of Bobby's back bumper.

"As he fell back behind me, I recognized the person in the car, and he hollered something and pointed a gun at me.

"I had the radio on and didn't hear what he said, but he pointed the gun at me." Bobby is pale, shaking, his eyes closed as he dredges up the memories.

The car behind him stayed so close Bobby thought it might be touching his bumper. Barely moving, realizing it was Hudson brandishing a gun, Bobby remembered the shotgun. Reaching behind him and grabbing it by the long barrel, Bobby yanked the gun over the seat. He reached into the open box of shells, grabbed one and, with one hand, loaded it. With a single smooth move, Bobby stuck the barrel of the shotgun out the window.

Bobby tells Phillips he was hoping, if he fired, Hudson might hear the gun or see the flash. "But that was a fleeting thought. I couldn't aim the gun and drive the car, too.

"I was afraid it might—the pellets might ricochet and hit someone or hit a house, and I decided against firing. Plus if I fired, I wouldn't have any more ammunition. And I would have to load the gun again—I didn't want to do it again. I was scared. I didn't know...I didn't know what to do really. I didn't want to fire the gun," his words taper off, low and thick.

Strained from reliving the moment he knew Hudson was going to kill him, Bobby pauses to collect himself before continuing.

"I felt like the best thing I could do was just keep going. I gained a little speed, and he gained speed and stayed on my bumper. I realized if he hit the back of my car, I would go out of control. So I immediately slowed down. I was hoping traffic would come from Cherokee Boulevard and catch up with us. I slowed down [to] about ten miles an hour."

Bobby sucks in a deep breath. "It was all I could do, really, to keep myself under control, because I knew he had a gun and I knew his reputation. I was really frightened."

Trying to get to North Market Street where there might be other cars, Bobby decided to run a stop street. "[I] would put my brake light on and make him think I was going to slow up, and then I was going to give it the gas and run the stop street. I was thinking he wouldn't expect me to run the stop sign."

The plan failed. Bobby had to speed up to get far enough ahead that Hudson wouldn't plow into him when he braked. But as Bobby hit the brakes, he heard the roar of an engine.

"I looked back, and he was coming around me." Bobby trembles as he remembers.

Bobby's mounting terror has jurors hanging on his words. There's no way to minimize the impact of what they are hearing, although later Evans will try.

As he talks, Bobby's eyes grow wide, the whites showing around the blue irises, but he isn't seeing Phillips or the jury or me. He's back on Bell Avenue.

Suddenly, he refocuses. Knowing he must stop reliving the fear he felt at the time, Bobby takes a deep breath and continues, "I looked and saw him, and I was having to drive with one hand and hold the gun with the other. I looked back to see if I was in my lane, and there were cars parked on the right side of the road. I was afraid I would run into a car. And I looked and saw him coming, and I looked back to see where I was, and I looked back again—and he was right beside me, again pointing the gun at me."

Bobby's voice breaks. His terror is tangible, thickening the air in the room.

"And I turned back to see where I was and at the same time I fired! I fired. And Mr. Phillips, when I fired, I was not trying to hit him. I was not...

"Killing him had never entered my mind. I fired out of sheer fear, out of fright. I was just desperate. I was trying to get away from him. I, you know, I felt like then and I feel like now in my heart that if I hadn't taken that action, I would be dead."

Bobby's head drops slightly, his face drained of color. After a few minutes, he regains his composure. With a weak voice, he says, "It was really an accident, and I was forced into it. I wasn't even trying to hit him. It was accidental that I did hit him."

The solemnity of what occurred, the description of death, fills the mahogany-encased room. The crowd, uncharacteristically quiet, seems as spent as Bobby. Hearing him relive the horror of that night has taken its toll on everyone. Jurors. Spectators. Even the judge looks ashen.

A car without lights on a dark night, a known bad man trying to run him off the road. A gun pointed straight at him. Frightened. Remembering the shotgun. Loading it. Firing without aiming.

It all occurred so quickly.

But the aftermath lasts a lifetime.

When he shot, Bobby says, he didn't realize he hit Hudson. He was just trying to get away. He doesn't recall hearing Hudson hit the wall. He doesn't recall looking in the rearview mirror. But he knew Hudson had wrecked.

Heart pounding, Bobby headed home. "Then," he says, "I realized Don might get his car started again. I knew he had a pistol, and I didn't know he was hurt. I was afraid to go home."

Hudson might follow and kill him. Instead of going home, Bobby drove to the house of an older, wiser friend, Harry Friedman, who lived nearby. Friedman was one of several older men who befriended the young man whose father shunned him.

On this night, desperate and drowning in despair, Bobby thought of Harry, knowing Harry would welcome him, even at this hour. He bolted up the porch steps and rang the doorbell, its chimes echoing through the still house. Harry opened the door, at first perplexed, then smiling as he ushered Bobby into the den.

Words tumbling out in a frenzy of anxiety, Bobby told Harry what happened and admitted he was afraid to go home because he didn't know if Hudson could still drive his car.

Friedman said solemnly, "Boy, you better hope Hudson died when he wrecked. If he's alive, he'll come gunning for you. You won't be able to run fast enough to get away from him."

That scared Bobby even more, but after he and Friedman talked a while, Bobby's panic receded a bit. He decided to drive toward home, stop at Five Points, and look to see if Hudson's car was at the house. If it was, he'd hightail it back to Friedman's.

Hudson's car wasn't there. Bobby swung into the driveway, and slipped into the house, not wanting to wake his mom. In the darkness of the room, his featherbed like a cocoon, he spent what was left of the night staring at a ceiling he could not see, reliving the terror, worrying that Hudson would come after him the next day—or even that night.

Before dawn, a car door slammed in the driveway. Bobby leaped out of bed, his heart racing, peeked out the window, and saw a policeman at the front door. He heard his mother say Bobby was asleep. Then, he saw Joan leave with the police officer. He watched the officer touch the tires of Joan's car, checking to see if they were still warm, before putting her in the patrol car.

Once the sun was up and he heard stirring in the kitchen, Bobby made his way downstairs where Martha was making biscuits. Unsuspecting, she told Bobby that Hudson had been killed. And, she said, rolling her eyes for emphasis, the police questioned Joan a long time last night.

It seems, after the police officer hauled Joan away, Mrs. Hoppe had called Joe Wild, and Wild called Joan at the police station to see if she needed him. Joan told him she was fine. She wasn't letting anybody give her a hard time. She could take care of herself, she insisted.

Later, however, when the police finally told her Hudson had been killed, she burst into tears. Even though she hadn't dated him in months, she still cared for him.

Decades later in 2008, as she sat in a nursing home talking about Hudson, Joan asked rhetorically, regret ringing in her voice, "You don't choose who you love, do you?"

But she confirmed she had finally wised up and had broken off the tempestuous relationship–almost a year before Don was killed. As much as she loved him, after he grew increasingly erratic and prone to jealous rages, she told him it was over.

A Conscience Unburdened

In the shaded courtyard of the nursing home, Joan—aged beyond her years—said she suspected Don was on drugs. Her friend Kitty and she had seen him at Mrs. Hollums' house, where, it was rumored, drugs flowed freely. That, combined with Don's abuse, did it for Joan.

The long affair was over, even if passion, maybe love, still smoldered inside her.

* * *

Joan had spent much of the evening of July 20, 1957, with her friends—Kitty, Buck Everitt, Billy Joe King, and others at Obo's Drive-in, another Chattanooga hangout. As they sat in a front booth talking, they saw a wrecker tow a car into Cain's Body Shop across the street.

Glancing at Joan, Billy Joe said, "That's Don car they're pulling—it looks like he's had a wreck." Curious, they walked over to see how badly the car was banged up.

When Joan opened the car door, she was shocked—blood coated the front seat, the dashboard, and the floorboard.

"I told Billy Joe," Joan remembered in 2008, "Don must be hurt bad."

"It sure looks like it," Billy Joe responded. "That's a whole lot of blood."

After standing around a few minutes, wondering about Don, Joan steeled her resolve. She was through with him, so she turned her back on the wrecked car and headed to her mother's house to pick up her son Tommy. She's been at the Hoppe home about 30 minutes when two detectives arrived and told Mrs. Hoppe they needed to take Joan in.

"You can take me in, but I haven't done anything," she told them with a defiant toss of her head.

At the police station, Stargel and Cornish offered her a cup of coffee, but Joan saw through the niceties. "I told them I didn't want their coffee—I was as smart with them as I could be. I told them to get their questions asked, because I needed to get back to my mother's. She was worried about me."

Later, after questioning Joan, Stargel and Cornish told her when they picked her up, they had enough to arrest her.

Joan smarted off again: "You didn't—and you can't hold me. You know I haven't done anything."

A Matter of Conscience

About that time, Joe Wild called the police station. Shortly afterward, Stargel offered to drive Joan home. Stepping from the police cruiser in front of her mother's house, Joan turned around and gave Stargel her best "I told you so" smile.

* * *

On the stand, Bobby is recalling what it was like the morning after the shooting. Hearing Martha say Don is dead and Joan had been hauled in for questioning, Bobby somehow managed to keep his eyes down, busying himself with buttering the hot biscuits on his plate.

He was calm on the outside but inside his stomach was roiling. He swallowed back the urge to heave, forcing down a bite of biscuit.

"It made me sick," Bobby says, tears streaking his face. "I took a man's life...."

Seeing his distress, Phillips offers him a glass of water, telling him to relax for a moment.

As we wait for Bobby to regain control, I remember the words of Mahatma Gandhi, words Bobby and I have discussed many times over the past few months: "There is a higher court than courts of justice and that is the court of conscience. It supersedes all courts."

Gandhi was right. Nothing this Court does can punish Bobby more than he has punished himself. Living with the knowledge he took another's life, even in self-defense, has torn at him for more than three decades.

And then, the questioning continues.

Bobby explains he already had plans to go back to Auburn on Monday to see friends. Now, desperate to get away from his family, none of whom suspected he was involved in Hudson's death, Bobby made the trip south. Needing time alone to think.

Today in Court, his red-rimmed eyes pleading for understanding, Bobby tells Phillips, "I felt I was justified as far as man's law was concerned, because I was forced to act the way I acted. But I realized I had to talk to a minister. I wanted to be justified in God's sight."

When he got to Auburn, he decided to go to the minister at the First Baptist Church, where he had attended in the past. The lady in the church office told him the minister was out of town, but he could talk to a preacher who had been substituting for him.

203

A Conscience Unburdened

With a hopeful heart, Bobby drove to campus, went directly to Joseph Godwin's room and introduced himself. Apologizing for intruding, he explained he needed spiritual help and said the office staff at First Baptist had sent him to Godwin.

Godwin assured Bobby he could help, invited him in and gave him a seat on the bed. Godwin sat down beside him.

Did Godwin seem to recognize him? "No." Bobby says, "He didn't know me from Adam."

But, Phillips asks, your pictures were on placards on telephone poles and in windows, weren't they? Or that's what Godwin said.

With a hint of his old smile, Bobby responds, "Mr. Phillips, I am not trying to be funny, believe me, but if my picture had been in the bathroom, I would have been happy. I would have been in high cotton.

"My picture was nowhere to be seen at Auburn nor were anyone else's pictures. That wasn't done. Even [in] our field house, there were no pictures of football [players]."

Contrary to Godwin's allegations, this echoes Coach Bradbury's earlier testimony.

But back in 1957, Bobby was young, and trusting. He thought preachers kept confidences and were always truthful. So, without hesitation, Bobby sat on the bed beside Godwin. His eyes swollen from hours of crying, Bobby warned Godwin that what he had to say was very serious, and he didn't want to tell him unless he was assured it would be held in confidence.

"He told me it would be confidential and sacred, that he would not repeat—"

Phillips breaks in. "Did he give you examples of confidences he had taken on?"

"He told me [all the sins] people had confessed to him but [I] refused to tell him. He told me nothing I could do or say would shock or embarrass him, that he had heard it all. He saw that I still hesitated. I didn't want to tell him, so he suggested he read the Bible. Then he suggested we pray. We got down on our knees and, laying across the bed with our torso, upper body—"

But Phillips interrupts, wanting to know if Bobby's description differs from Godwin's.

On his feet, Evans objects to the way Phillips poses the question, but Phillips doesn't even pause. "Did you ever get down on your hands and knees and crawl around?"

With a slight smile, Bobby responds, "He said hands and elbows."

The bailiff grins at Bobby's clarification.

"Did you ever do that, sir?"

With certainty, Bobby responds, "No, nor with hands and knees. I did not. No."

So what did the two of you do, Phillips prompts.

"We got down on our knees, and he said a prayer. When he got through, he asked would I like to say a prayer. I said a prayer, and I cried when I prayed," Bobby replies, shifting slightly to relax tight muscles in his back and legs.

Rising from their knees, he tells Phillips, he and Godwin sat back down on the bed. The preacher again asked Bobby what was bothering him.

"I told him again I wanted to be sure he would not repeat it. He told me, in so many words...'Bobby, the reason you are here, you know I'm a preacher and you know you want to talk to me and you know you can trust me,' so I proceeded to tell him what had happened."

When Bobby finished his confession, Godwin asked several specific questions, curious about the details, but there was never any mention of a woman, Bobby declares.

Bobby says Godwin asked if his family knew about his role in the incident. "I told him, no, I didn't want to upset them, that they are very proud of me. I had won a scholarship to Auburn, and I was the only one in my family, my immediate family, who was able to go to college.

"He asked me what kind of scholarship, and I told him it was a football scholarship."

Oddly, Godwin said Bobby wasn't big enough to play football. "He asked me four or five times about my size. He couldn't believe a man my size played football at Auburn."

Yet Godwin testified he recognized Bobby as soon as he saw him standing at his door.

Bobby tells Phillips Godwin never mentioned anything about keeping the confidence only for a specified period of time, despite Godwin's earlier contention that—nine years later—his "conscience" drove him to break the confidence.

A Conscience Unburdened

Hot anger toward Godwin exploding in my chest, I wonder how he would have responded to the question once posed by Eleanor Roosevelt: "When will our consciences grow so tender that we will act to prevent human misery rather than avenge it?"

Maybe the minister's conscience was just set wrong. Maybe it should have been recalibrated to go off if he broke a sacred trust.

Bobby is talking, so I turn my mind back to him. He says before he left, Godwin suggested they have a parting prayer, and Godwin prayed. Godwin "told me...God had forgiven me, that I was justified in God's sight and for me to pull the pieces together and to go on with life."

Godwin suggested that Bobby seek an attorney for legal advice when he returned to Chattanooga. He recalls Godwin's final words: "I will be following your career very closely."

Bobby shook hands with the preacher, his heart not hurting as badly as when he entered the dorm room. Not forgetting the tragedy, but more at peace than he had been since hearing Hudson was dead.

Some nine years later, as Godwin had testified, he called Bobby's home and spoke to his mother. When Bobby returned later, he testifies, he didn't want his mother to overhear the conversation with Godwin, so he went down to the drugstore to use a pay phone.

But, Phillips prods him, Godwin said you called back so quickly you must have been in the room with your mother.

Not so. Looking directly at the jurors, Bobby says, "I heard him say that and, of course, I have heard other things he said. Why he lies about small things, I don't know—I don't know. He wants to make things dramatic, I guess. I don't know."

"It was a long time before [Godwin] came to the line, 45 seconds or maybe more," Bobby says. So long Bobby thought he might have lost the connection, until he heard something slide, like a person picking up something.

"I assumed he was picking the phone up—and he still didn't say hello."

Then Bobby heard a click and Godwin said hello. That click, Bobby thought, was a tape recorder being started. Believing Godwin was recording, Bobby was cautious in his responses.

Godwin's earlier testimony indicated he was paranoid about others recording his conversations—a common thread in all of his interactions with the Chattanooga police.

A Matter of Conscience

When this taped conversation with Bobby never surfaced during Godwin's testimony, Cook and Phillips assumed it either didn't exist or it didn't support what Godwin wanted to say.

On the witness stand, Bobby outlines what Godwin said. "He asked how I was doing, what I had been doing and what I planned to do. He said, 'Well, from time to time I will be checking with you. I just wanted to know. I am glad everything is all right with you.'"

Godwin never mentioned anything about Hudson's death, and Bobby didn't either.

Turning back to 1957, Phillips queries Bobby about what he did when he returned to Chattanooga after the weekend in Auburn. Bobby replies he visited Harry Friedman again, asking if he knew a good attorney.

Friedman told him Joe Wild was his neighbor and friend. And, Bobby was aware his mother called Wild after Stargel and Cornish took Joan to the police station. So, it was logical he would turn to Wild for help.

Wild became Bobby's attorney, advising him during the coroner's inquest. At Wild's request, Bobby turned the shotgun over to him.

At this point, Phillips remembers something he forgot to ask Bobby about the gun swap. He wants more details on the pistol Bobby traded to McCutcheon.

"It was an automatic, and I think it was a foreign-made automatic, but I don't know what—I don't know."

How many bullets would it hold?

Probably 9 or 10, maybe 14 or 15, Bobby thinks, but he isn't sure. He used to take it to the river to shoot at floating logs or buoys. Always carried it in his tackle box because there were snakes in and around the river—and Bobby was terrified of snakes.

He never carried the gun just to be armed. He didn't have it with him the night McCutcheon talked him into trading. He had to go home to retrieve it from his tackle box.

From Bobby's perspective, if he had wanted to kill someone—and he never had—the automatic pistol he already owned would have been a better choice than the bulky shotgun.

Did he tell his girlfriend about the trade?

Yes, he had to explain why he was late. No reason not to tell her.

A Conscience Unburdened

Shifting back to his 1957 conversation with Godwin, Philips asks if Bobby told Godwin someone was after him on the night of the incident.

"Yes, I told him. He's well aware of that, because he asked."

Bobby is wearing down after hours on the stand, so Phillips wraps up quickly, having him confirm a few points. No, he never threatened anyone back in 1957. He had no connection to the phone call Jody Neal related. And no one was with him in the car the night Hudson was killed.

Getting it in the record one more time, Phillips has Bobby tell about hearing the outcome of the grand jury proceedings in 1966. From what Phillips knows, all evidence presented thus far in this trial, with the exception of Odene's statements, was presented to that grand jury. Bobby confirms, from what he's heard, that assessment is correct.

With that, Phillips concludes his direct examination.

Bobby, bone weary and stiff, steps down from the witness box.

The judge calls for a lunch recess, but I wonder how he thinks we can eat, knowing that soon Evans will be trying to serve up Bobby's head on a platter.

CHAPTER SIXTEEN

The Courtroom as Theater – Part I

Conscience is but a word that cowards use,
Devised at first to keep the strong in awe.
–William Shakespeare (1564-1616)

The first words from Evans' mouth send a chill down my spine. Not wasting time on cordialities, he puts Bobby on notice he's going to test his composure, try to rile him.

Standing motionless, a tiger eyeing his prey, Evans looks intensely at Bobby for a moment. His eyes steely, Bobby glares back without blinking. It's a signal to everyone: This is going to be a battle of two strong-willed men: one, fighting for his life, the other, for his career.

When Bobby doesn't drop his eyes, Evans, says with a smirk, "In the course of my questions, if I begin raising my voice to you, tell me, and I will lower my voice. Sometimes I tend to start yelling, and I don't mean to yell at you when I am asking questions."

It's a warning. Evans may begin innocuously, but it won't take him long to move into his well-documented courtroom theatrics.

Although they're the same questions Phillips asked Bobby—about his education and football career at Auburn and in the pros—Evans' questions are sharper, implying Bobby was untroubled by Hudson's death, that he moved on without any concern for the man he shot.

With this contention firmly planted, Evans begins his journey down a path to prove premeditation. To do so, he'll have to refute the parts of Bobby's testimony that show he acted in self-defense and convince the jury Bobby's version of events is implausible. He'll also attempt to establish motive. In substantiating his theory, Evans will try to demonstrate Bobby trivialized the tragedy, going on with life as if nothing happened. Even worse, he will trivialize Bobby's faith.

Asking the same questions over and over, Evans will badger Bobby, building his case on repetitive points buried within questions. The first line of attack focuses on his conjecture that Hudson's death meant nothing to Bobby, that Bobby didn't miss a beat in his football career.

Yes, Bobby replies, I played half back on Auburn's national championship team in 1957.

Evans pushes the point. "Half back—[that] was the following fall and winter following the *murder*—excuse me, the killing of Donald Hudson?"

The word "murder" brings Phillips out of his seat, but Evans corrects himself before Phillips can object. Mission accomplished—the jury heard the M word. And it lands hard on Bobby, branding him like the red A branded Hester Prynne in Hawthorne's *The Scarlet Letter*.

Ignoring the insinuation, Bobby answers the question.

"Well, you see, I played a minor part. There were 40 or 50 other kids on that ball club. I certainly was not responsible for the championship."

Scoffing, Evans tries again. "As a matter of fact, you were considered—and I think we already heard from a coach of yours—that you were one of his best players, even though you didn't make All-American. You heard him say that, correct?"

Bobby smiles, letting the blow pass, responding simply, "Yes, sir."

Sarcasm dripping with every word, Evans pushes Bobby. "I understand there is maybe 50 people on the team, but as far as getting out there and running that ball, executing those plays, making those touchdowns, making the first down, putting in that extra effort for the team, sir, that all occurred after Donald Hudson was killed out here on Bell Avenue, didn't it?"

Bobby knows what's coming, but his answer is calm. He tells Evans he was happy for an opportunity to keep his mind occupied. "Yes, I played ball, and I gave it a hundred percent."

Piercing Bobby with cold eyes, Evans won't let it go, saying he knows he played football and was glad for the opportunity. That's not the point. The point is Bobby had all that success after he killed Don Hudson. And he's pushing Bobby to agree.

Remembering not to give one-word answers, Bobby replies, "Yes, and every day, there wasn't a day—there is not a day that's gone by since then—that I have not thought about that and prayed about it."

Oh, we'll get to that, Evans assures him. We'll get to your thinking and praying about it, he adds with scorn searing his words. But that's not what he wants to discuss right now. He wants to know whether Bobby ever told anyone, including his wife, about killing Hudson.

In fact, he wants to know if Bobby ever lived in Chattanooga or any place other with anyone other than his current wife.

A Matter of Conscience

Bobby glances at me—an "I'm so sorry" in his eyes. Aware many people—including my family—don't know about his previous marriages, Bobby hesitates before saying he once was married to a young woman named Geraldine.

What he doesn't say—something Bobby told me long ago—is that Geraldine called him shortly after he graduated from college, saying she was pregnant. Quickly acknowledging Bobby was not the father since they had not dated in more than a year, she asked him to marry her to give her child a name. Bobby could have refused, could have said, 'Hell, no,' but he didn't. He felt sorry for Geraldine, so he agreed. A total sham, the marriage was annulled immediately. A few years later, Bobby signed adoption papers so Geraldine's new husband could be the child's legal father.

With a smartass smirk, Evans asks if Bobby has had any other wives. Well, Bobby says, he once was married to another Sherry, an airline stewardess.

Bobby looks over at me, and I give him a conspiratorial wink. I know the real story—one Bobby told me before we married. Back in his devil-may-care days, Bobby and the first Sherry were drinking with friends when one of the guys dared them to find a justice-of-the-peace right then and get married. Everyone had had too much to drink, and the next thing Bobby remembered, he woke up a married man. After their heads cleared, they decided to try to make a go of it, but the marriage ended in a few months.

Since Evans' research appears good, I wait anxiously for him to ask the next question. But the query never comes, so I relax, relieved the sad saga of previous marriages ends prematurely.

* * *

Evans makes a big deal out of Bobby's not telling anyone, even his wives, about killing Hudson. It's a galling denigration he will revisit, but for now he circles back to Bobby's college days, wanting to know if he remembers a player named Red Phillips, who made All-American at Auburn. Did Bobby ever room with him?

Yes, as a freshman. They lived in the same cabin a while.

As if to keep Bobby off balance, Evans switches directions again, but I'm sure he'll return to Red Phillips. There's more to that story.

"So you went back to see your friends and your girl friends after you determined that Mr. Donald Hudson had been killed by your shotgun blast?" he asks, pulling no punches.

With a hint of anger, Bobby replies, "No, I didn't say that. That's not why I went back."

Before Bobby can explain, Evans cuts him off abruptly. "You had friends, numerous friends," he says, repeating, out of context, part of Bobby's testimony on direct.

Knowing it is only going to get worse, Leroy Phillips beseeches the judge. "Let him finish. May it please the Court, he asked a question, so [Hoppe] has a right to answer."

DiRisio agrees, admonishing Evans to let Bobby answer without interruption.

Ignoring Evans, Bobby turns to the jurors, telling them he already planned to go to Auburn before the encounter with Hudson. Under great pressure at home to act normal, he welcomed the opportunity for a trip already planned so he could have time alone to think. He was sick with worry, in a bad way mentally. Getting away meant removing at least one element of pressure.

"No, I wasn't going to Auburn to see friends or to party or to date...." Bobby's words taper off, lost in his sadness.

Like a dog with a shoe, Evans pulls and twists, holding to his premise that Bobby went back to Auburn to party. Six times he reframes the same question, knowing Bobby is not going to say he went to Auburn to have fun. He's just using rhetorical skills to get under Bobby's skin.

Evans' efforts to disparage Bobby's agony after the shooting cut deeply. No one but me, Bobby thinks, will ever know I was falling apart while trying to keep Mama from noticing anything was wrong. I couldn't stay in that house a second longer.

When Evans starts hammering again, Leroy Phillips has had it. Standing, he skewers Evans with a look before addressing DiRisio. "May it please the Court, he has asked the same question four times. I object to the repetition."

"Four times" is generous. By my count, he has asked the same question seven times.

The Court sustains Phillips' objection, but it doesn't stop Evans. Doggedly, he again asks the same question, and Bobby gives the same answer, adding, "I went to Auburn and prayed with a preacher."

A Matter of Conscience

Failing to score, Evans reaches deeper into his bag of tricks and pulls out a new question, still trying to make the point that Bobby was nonchalant about killing a man.

"Did you have anything in your mind about having your team have the best year of its possible history in 1957? Was that in your mind at all at any time prior to July 20, 1957?"

Of course he thought about his team having a good year. He thought about that every year, Bobby responds.

"And you carried through with those plans, didn't you, sir?"

Hanging his head at the repeated badgering, Bobby lets his mind slip back to his return to Auburn after the inquest, recalling the dual challenge Coach Jordan had faced in the fall of 1957.

One of his star halfbacks had been implicated in the killing of a whisky runner back in his hometown. And, just as the team was gathering for fall practice, two other starters, including the quarterback, were booted from the squad for scholastic and disciplinary reasons. The two had been the hope of the offense, but they had been cutting classes, breaking rules, testing Jordan's patience. Then over the summer, they broke into a women's dorm—and got caught drinking.

Enough was enough—Jordan met with the team, advising the players of his decision and telling them, "Down through the years, we here at Auburn have learned to live with adversity. But adversity, as we know, tends to draw men together."

Jordan was speaking of the loss of his star quarterback and another starter, but to Bobby, the coach he loved was talking directly to him. Totally traumatized by killing a man in Chattanooga, Bobby had returned to campus only days after the incident.

But as Shug Jordan told his players 31 long years ago, adversity draws men together. When Bobby needed him, Shug was there, driving from Auburn to Chattanooga for the inquest, even though Bobby had not asked him.

For weeks after the inquest and after he returned to Auburn, Bobby listened for hours on end to a 45-rpm record of "The Man with the Golden Arm." According to his roommate Sentell, Bobby would sit quietly, staring off into space, as strains of the melancholy music rose around him. Occasionally, Sentell would ask Bobby if he was all right. Looking up slowly, his eyes shadowed and sad, Bobby would say, "Yes, good buddy, I'm OK."

Sentell knew his friend was not OK, but he didn't know what was at the root of Bobby's blue funk. At the time, Sentell had never heard of Don Hudson.

Bobby, struggling to maintain his sanity, suffering from overwhelming guilt, was thankful when fall football practice started. Focused on blocking and running, his mind could temporarily escape the anxiety that plagued him night and day. With his team already having lost two key players, Bobby was not going to let Coach Jordan down.

The players were "dumbstruck to learn of the dismissals, wondering now who the hell was going to play quarterback," so there was no way Bobby would add to the team's stress. Although fighting his feelings off the field, when Bobby hit the turf, he played with his old intensity. Paul Hemphill, writing in the 50th national championship anniversary edition of the *Auburn* magazine, called him the "slashing senior Hoppe—bigger, faster, meaner and a devastating blocker." What Hemphill didn't know was that Bobby was battling to block out the demons haunting him.

When the coaches announced Lloyd Nix would be the quarterback, the team was dubious. Hemphill says, "Nix was a knuckle-balling lefthander who had run the ball 30 times and thrown exactly one pass the year before as a third-string halfback."

On the practice field, Nix quickly proved to be a good choice. Auburn quarterback coach Vince Dooley saw him as the perfect man for the job—smart with a winning attitude. In the first game-like scrimmage of the season, Nix completed 10 of 11 passes for 125 yards and ran for a 69-yard touchdown. The quarterback who had been dismissed wasn't even missed.

In the pre-season rankings that fall, *Sports Illustrated* failed to pick Auburn to finish in the top 20. *Look* magazine—featuring a full-page picture of Bobby Hoppe blocking for his halfback running mate Tommy Lorino—placed the Tigers near the bottom of their ranking—18th. The Associated Press poll never mentioned Auburn. A pre-season poll of 12 sports editors from across the Southeastern Conference did rate the Tigers better, predicting a second-place finish in the SEC, behind Tennessee.

At times Shug Jordan seemed pleased with his team's prospects, declaring, "The presence of Bobby Hoppe and Tommy Lorino makes me optimistic, but time will tell."

A Matter of Conscience

Max Moseley, sports editor for the *Montgomery Advertiser*, predicted the SEC title would be decided in the opening game between Auburn and Tennessee. And famed *Atlanta Journal* sports writer Furman Bisher said the winner would be Auburn, basing his pick on "line experience, depth and excellence of backs and general balance of material." With players in 1957 going both ways—offensively and defensively—depth would prove to be critical for Shug's teams.

Lorino had proved himself to be a "triple-threater who very capably handles all of the punting and some of the passing," but Lorino was quick to share the glory. "Anyone could run with a guy like Hoppe blocking for him. Gosh, he's terrific."

Jordan agreed, saying he wished Lorino could block for Bobby the way Bobby blocked for Tommy. If Lorino could, Jordan said, "there is no telling how much yardage Hoppe would gain."

And Jordan told Austin White, "Hoppe has made himself into one of the finest defensive backs in the league. We used him—in four different games—at both sideback positions, at safety and, occasionally, at the corner linebacking slot."

Content to play wherever he was needed, Bobby told White, "I know it may sound crazy coming from me —but I get just as big a bang out of delivering a good block as I do in scoring a touchdown."

But that was in 1956, and Bobby went through a lot between seasons. The question was whether adversity would make him stronger or would sideswipe his football career.

CHAPTER SEVENTEEN

The National Championship Year
The Rolls Royce of Football in 1957 (Paul Reeder)

Do thine, sweet Auburn, thine, the sweetest train
Do thy fair tribes participate [his] pain?
–Oliver Goldsmith
"The Deserted Village," 1770

When the season-opening whistle blew on the long-awaited game between the Volunteers and the Tigers, a rain-soaked field greeted the players—better for Tennessee, who hugged the ball well, than for the visiting Tigers.

But Shug's boys didn't give a damn. After warm-up drills, instead of walking around the Tennessee players to get to the locker room, the Tigers strolled through the middle of the home team. Bad field or not, Auburn threw down the gauntlet.

"The one score of the evening was engineered by Lloyd Nix, with an infantry attack led by lieutenants Bobby Hoppe, Tommy Lorino and Billy Atkins, all three of whom danced through the rain for first downs," Paul Reeder reported.

In the end, it was Atkins who cracked the goal line for the TD on a fourth down. His extra point kick made the score 7-0.

Although Auburn came close to scoring several more times, Tennessee and the soggy weather combined to halt the drives. Auburn dominated the game, rushing for 207 yards and passing for ten with eleven first downs. Hoppe, described by Reeder as "the mercury-clad right halfback," led all rushers with 59 yards. Atkins added 56, and Lorino tallied 36.

Jordan called it "a sweet victory," but Frank LaRussa, talking with Reeder in 1990, recalled more fervor in the coaches' reactions. "After we put a whipping on Tennessee, the coaches went berserk," he exclaimed. "You could tell they knew this team could be a good one. They danced around the locker room as much as the players!"

After the game, Auburn, unranked in the pre-season AP poll, catapulted to seventh in the nation. The War Eagle had spread its mighty wings, and America took notice.

A Matter of Conscience

White recalled a comment by a disappointed Vol supporter four-and-half years previously when Hoppe passed up Tennessee and a flock of other SEC schools to cast his lot with Auburn: "Well, he's the kind of boy who is liable to pop up and beat us some day."

Hoppe, along with Lorino, Atkins, Nix, and others, did just that, making most of his yards the hard way, "on cross-bucks over guard," as well as playing his usual fine defensive game.

Gingerly rubbing his mid-section after the game, Hoppe winced as he said with a grin, "Guess I stopped Al Carter once too many."

White reports to readers, "That would have been when Bobby conceivably blocked a Tennessee touchdown by bumping Carter out of bounds in the fourth quarter at the Auburn 22. . . one of the day's most brutal collisions."

Back at Auburn in the cabin with his roommate Sentell, who had been sidelined for the season by an injury, Bobby turned on his record player and flipped off the light. The melancholy strains of "Man with the Golden Arm" filled the room. Sentell knew it wasn't a good time to talk to Bobby, whose bruised body was splayed on his bed but whose mind was floating far away.

Bobby wasn't thinking about the game, about grabbing the ball, clutching it to his side, then pushing, pushing until he ruptured the line, blasting into the end zone. In his mind, he was reliving another collision—the one on Bell Avenue.

He stared into the dark. As the tempo of the music picked up, Bobby watched the shadows of two cars, side by side, moving in slow motion across the ceiling. He squeezed his eyes closed, trying to block out the shotgun blast that was coming—but it reverberated through his memory so loudly he no longer heard the music.

His eyes flew open, his whole body trembled, remembering the roar of the car beneath him as he took off. His stomach clenching into a hard knot, he heard the other car slam into the wall.

Then there was total silence except for his heart, pounding like a jackhammer in his chest.

* * *

Compared to the Tennessee Vols, Chattanooga didn't pose much of a threat to Auburn. Among the first-stringers, Lorino and Hoppe chalked up most of the yardage in the early part of the game. But that wasn't the only game news. The lead for Neal Ellis' article in the *Birmingham News* was: "Now it can be told." He continued, "It's a story of determination and fortitude, of desire and courage that comes along maybe once a football season, maybe once a decade.

"It's the story of Bobby Hoppe, Auburn's 'Mr. Right Halfback.'"

Neal revealed that Hoppe had been keeping a significant secret. Trainer Kenny Howard made the announcement: Bobby Hoppe played the first two games of the season—against Tennessee and Chattanooga—with three dislocated ribs.

Before the UT game, Hoppe sustained the injury in an intra-squad scrimmage. He had a knack of quickly spinning to elude a tackle. In one of those twists, cartilage tore loose. It would have been better, Howard declared, if Hoppe's ribs had been broken—less painful and quicker to heal. Regardless, Neal said, "Hoppe didn't relish the idea of riding the bench while his teammates went out to battle Tennessee's Goliaths."

According to Neal, Howard's bandaging of the 175-pound senior was a work of art. Bobby's injury was so well concealed not even his own teammates knew the truth until after the Chattanooga game. Hoppe entered both games with "his same rugged, happy-go-lucky" drive he always took into battle. But if you were watching closely, you might have seen him clutch his side a time or two. Better known for blocking, Hoppe became the leading ground gainer at Tennessee to the amazement of those who didn't know the whole truth. The same held true for the Chattanooga game, where Hoppe "turned in a yeoman's job, finishing second only to Atkins as the top ball carrier in the game." Auburn won 40-7.

Ellis compared Bobby to two former greats—Georgia's Frank "Broken Jaw" Jones and Bear Bryant, who once "sparkled against Tennessee despite a broken foot." There have been others, Ellis notes, but "now they must move aside to make room for a tank-like youngster from the Plains who showed he has as much courage as any of them."

What Ellis didn't know was Bobby welcomed the physical pain—it eased his mental agony.

* * *

By the time Auburn faced the University of Kentucky, Hoppe's injuries had healed, and he was ready to run at full speed. The Tigers' second leading rusher, according to Reeder, Hoppe was considered by some to be the SEC's swiftest football player.

To prove his point, Reeder reminded folks Fob James, one of Auburn's greatest football players, had attended a private prep school in Hoppe's hometown. Once, during a 100-yard dash featuring both men, Hoppe won. "James was extremely fast, but Hoppe was just faster."

Amazingly, Auburn fell two spots in the AP poll after beating Chattanooga, so the Tigers were gunning to prove themselves at Kentucky. And they did— in a slim 6-0 victory.

Preparing to board the train for Georgia Tech the next week, the Tigers were unhappy the AP poll still ranked them No. 9, failing to move them up after the Kentucky win. Not a good time for the train conductor to mess with one of their strongest supporters—a one-legged black man, who had adored the Tigers and whom the team had dubbed both the "Dean of Freshman English" and "Dr. Hodge." The "dean" always made it to away games to cheer for his boys.

Although named for his grandfather, an educator, Hodge had no college degree; he ran a shoeshine stand. That didn't matter to the Tigers—they loved the old man. He was not only a character but also a rabid fan. At home games, the "dean" took over a small section of the stands where 25-30 African American fans sat. Dr. Hodge routinely led this group in raucous cheers—and he decided who would or wouldn't get in his section. If you didn't cheer loud enough, you lost your seat. And following the team on its travels, Dr. Hodge became almost a second mascot.

This one time, however, as the team was boarding a train for the Georgia Tech game, the conductor refused to let the Dean of Freshman English aboard. This was during the era of racial segregation, but when Bobby looked out the window and saw Dr. Hodge standing forlornly on the platform, his top hat perched askance atop his head, he lifted his window and yelled, "What's wrong, Dr. Hodge? You'd better hurry and get on, or you're going to get left behind."

"I's canst, Mr. Bobby, they won't let me on. Says there's no nigger car on this train."

Already irked by the AP ratings, this was the final straw for Bobby. He grabbed his duffle bag and jumped off the train. "If Dr. Hodge doesn't go to the game, neither will I."

He plopped his duffle bag on the concrete platform and took a seat on it.

Suddenly, the entire Auburn team scrambled off the train and sat beside Bobby, saying they would all stay home if the conductor wouldn't let the "dean" go, too. A strong-arm tactic, but it didn't take long for the coaches to convince the conductor to let Dr. Hodge on.

The "dean" boarded the train, flashing a toothy smile at the conductor, and the team jumped on behind him, all ready to head to the game.

The Dean of Freshman English never again had trouble getting on an Auburn train car.

* * *

For some reason, Auburn and Georgia Tech didn't play "home and home," so Auburn had to enter unfriendly territory every year to meet the Jackets, who were always ready to battle the Tigers. But this year the Tigers were leading nationally in total defense. In the *Auburn* magazine in 2007, Hemphill said the two teams started by "feeling each other out like heavyweights in the opening rounds of a fight."

For Auburn to do its best, Reeder noted, Atkins, Nix, Hoppe, and Lorino needed to get on track at the same time. Although they made some good plays, including a fumble recovery by Hoppe, along the way Lorino fumbled and Hoppe lost two yards. Hoppe's yardage loss had one positive effect—it set up a field goal attempt by Atkins, who had never before attempted a field goal. When he split the uprights for the only points of the game, Jordan declared he "had never seen a more beautiful sight." Atkins was the hero of the 3-0 win.

As a sidebar to the Auburn-Georgia Tech game, it was noted that Atlanta police made eight arrests for ticket scalping, with $5 tickets going for as much as $25.

* * *

After the Auburn/Georgia Tech game, when the Tigers moved to fifth place in the national rankings, they began to believe they could go undefeated on the season. Maybe win the conference championship. "These were no longer just things to talk about and think about," Jordan noted. "Here they were for the asking."

He worried about getting his team psyched up for the non-conference game with Houston, but the Tigers "poured it on in every way imaginable—on fumble recoveries and interceptions, by land and by air, by veterans and by rookies, winning in a blowout."

Entering the game, Atkins had scored all of Auburn's points against SEC opponents and led the Tigers in rushing, followed by Hoppe, second, and Lorino, third. The three, combined with Nix, Phillips and a host of other Tigers tallied a total of 375 yards. Auburn won 48-7.

* * *

Homecoming, the final game at Cliff Hare Stadium for the seniors known as the Dirty Dozen, put the players in an enviable position. They had never lost a home game. And they didn't intend to start with Florida, even if Florida was in the top 20 and had just thrashed LSU.

The Tigers, ranked No. 4 in the nation, dominated the gallant Gators. Reeder says Auburn was unbeaten, thanks to several key players: Phillips, Lorino, Hoppe, Jackie Burkett, Ben Preston and Bobby Lauder. And the sextet worked their magic against Florida, leading Auburn to a 13-0 win.

Auburn climbed to third in the national polls.

* * *

The L&N Railroad ran a special football train from Montgomery to Birmingham's Legion Field, where Auburn was taking on 17th ranked Mississippi State. Round-trip cost? $3.63.

Auburn would make significant strides toward its first SEC football title if the Tigers made it past the Maroons. Reeder said Auburn placed its offensive hopes on Lorino, "who was beginning to rock and roll," along with Hoppe, Nix and Phillips. When the teams left the field at halftime and Mississippi State led 7-0, fans began to wonder if Associated Press sportswriter Mercer Bailey had been accurate in his prediction that Auburn's 10-game winning streak would end at Legion Field. But the War Eagle cry sounded from the diehards in the stands as the team sprinted past, heading to the locker room.

Hemphill reported there were no half-time histrionics—at least, none recorded—in the locker room despite the score. Jordan calmly urged his players to "stay the course," and they did, taking home a 15-7 win to run their record to 7-0.

Hoppe racked up enough mileage to be one of the three players Jordan singled out for praise. Lorino and Atkins shared the honors. And a slew of others helped make the win possible.

221

The National Championship Year

When sophomore Burkett was named National Lineman of the Week, he was gracious. "Golly, not me! No joke? With fellows like Lorino and Hoppe in there, I can take chances and know when I'm wrong they will take care of things."

Auburn was never short on players who shared the glory. Lorino once said Hoppe's blocking was a big factor in his success. And Phillips, an All-American at Auburn, had high praise for Hoppe, telling Hemphill his former teammate, the Chattanooga Choo-Choo, "was not only a speedy and talented runner but also a ferocious blocker. When we watched game films, everyone was following Bobby's movements to see who he was going to put a crack back block on next. Bobby was a tough football player and a valuable asset to the team."

And he was. But it was sheer determination that kept him focused only on the gridiron.

* * *

Losing to Georgia would be a disgrace, but Auburn almost let it happen. Although on the decline, the Bulldogs were as good defensively as Auburn, and they had a dangerous passing game. It just wasn't good enough to save Georgia Coach Wally Butts' job, and Auburn assistant Vince Dooley would be tapped to replace him.

Before that move occurred, the Tigers didn't show much to Georgia—they certainly didn't look like the No. 3 team in the nation. But even with fumbles, penalties, and getting stopped at the goal line, Auburn finally made one score—grabbing a crucial 6-0 victory, giving the Tigers their 12th straight win. The only undefeated and untied team in the nation. But it wasn't enough for Auburn to be ranked No. 1. That honor went to Michigan State. It just wasn't Auburn's time.

It was time, however, for two Auburn backs to hit career marks. Hoppe pushed his career rushing total to 1,050, placing him fifth on the Auburn all-time list just below Charles Hathway's 1,055 yards. Lorino pushed his total to 1,044 yards.

* * *

Florida State University Coach Tom Nugent once said playing Auburn was like entering battle without guns.

A four-touchdown favorite over the Seminoles, the Tigers took nothing for granted. They wanted to join the elite group of one—the University of Tennessee was the only SEC school to have become national champions. Resting on their laurels wouldn't get Auburn where they wanted. They would have to be better than ever.

And they were. Auburn hit the Seminoles straight and hard, like arrows from a bow, winning 29-7.

* * *

The last game of the season—against Alabama in the Iron Bowl— was a night to remember.

On this particular evening, it was just too easy. Auburn posted its first TD in Birmingham within the first two minutes of the game, continuing to pour it on until clobbering Alabama 40-0. Every single dressed-out Auburn player got into the game, becoming part of the legend.

Sitting atop the AP poll—finally No. 1—Auburn was unstoppable. Before a sell-out crowd of 45,000 fans, Auburn's Atkins went over from the one-yard line and then kicked the PAT after Zeke Smith, pouncing on a fumble, moved the ball within scoring distance.

The second touchdown began with Hoppe running for four, followed by a Nix-to-Lorino toss good for 28 yards. Nix threw to Lorino for 21 additional yards, and Hoppe made a quick three. Then Atkins crashed across the line, making the score 14-0—the beginning of a rout.

And on and on it went in front of the wildly ecstatic Auburn fans and shell-shocked Alabama supporters. Just after Hoppe picked up another yard, disaster struck. His arm was injured, and supporters groaned along with him as he was led, grimacing, off the field.

Hoppe sat on the sidelines, a towel draped across his shoulders, his collegiate career over, thinking that not getting to finish the last game of his senior season hurt much more than his arm.

Hemphill described this scene, one he never forgot: "As the gritty Chattanoogan sat dejectedly on the Auburn bench, head down and probably with a tear in his eye, his coach sensed the need for saying one last word of gratitude to the one who had exemplified the Auburn spirit throughout the football season that was almost ended.

"I'll never, ever, forget the look of fatherly pride in Shug Jordan's eyes as he cupped Bobby Hoppe's chin in his hand and lifted his head to say a simple 'Thank you.'

"That was loyalty, pride and respect. And I'll remember [it forever.]"

The National Championship Year

The Dirty Dozen, along with their underclassmen teammates, were true Tigers, bringing home the school's first and only national championship. Auburn received 210 first-place votes for the honor. The second-ranked team, Ohio State, received only 71 votes.

As Reeder declared, "The Auburn Tigers were the Rolls Royce of football in 1957."

Because of a recruiting violation, Auburn was on NCAA probation and prohibited from competing in a bowl game. It didn't matter. The 1957 Tigers, from the "loveliest village on the plains," had pounced repeatedly on their hapless prey, bringing each to its knees with a ferocious defense and a worthy offense.

When the Auburn Tigers were named No. 1 in the nation, Hemphill says Auburn fans "ran amok, screaming War Eagle into the night at Toomer's Corner, until—it would please the city-slickers to know—well, until the cows came home."

* * *

The end of the season hit Bobby hard. Throwing himself wholeheartedly into football had offered an escape from the turmoil flooding him whenever he was still. Without football, he began to lose interest in his studies and, ultimately, did so poorly he didn't have enough honor points to graduate. Humiliated and disgusted with himself, he headed to Chattanooga. What should have been a hero's return was a sad homecoming. His mother was furious and embarrassed because he hadn't completed his degree.

Letting her down nearly destroyed Bobby, so after his short stint with the 49ers and the Redskins ended with a knee injury, Bobby enrolled at the University of Chattanooga (now the University of Tennessee-Chattanooga), determined to complete his degree. But restless and haunted, he dropped out to join the National Guard. After completing his military duty, he finally fulfilled a promise he made to Austin White back in Auburn on an early September day in 1954.

White remembered that day well. Auburn was a steaming cauldron as he sat with Hoppe and Leroy Duchene on the steps of the athletic association building. The boys had dragged from the football field, carrying helmets and soggy towels. After they rested on the steps, in

224

the shade of nearby trees, they talked about their first few weeks in "the hottest hamlet in the Southeast."

It seemed Hoppe and Duchene had discovered quickly they were just a couple of "would-be" players at Auburn University. Down there, everyone was good, they said—and chances were most of them outweighed you a good 30 or 40 pounds.

As they sat, discussing their tenuous situation, Bobby and Leroy made a promise to Austin White. "We know football isn't everything. Regardless of what a lot of people might think, we're down here to get an education, and we'll get one.

"We'll get that degree."

It took Bobby a few more years than Leroy, but he fulfilled that promise, earning his Auburn degree in December 1962. He fought and scrapped for that degree, White said, in the same fashion he used on the football field.

Talking with White about finally completing his degree, Bobby recalled how he had rubbed shoulders with men whose names will long be remembered for their exploits with the Tigers—Lorino, Atkins, Nix, Rawson, Harvard, Phillips, Wilson, Sansom, James, and Childress.

Telling White he never quite hit his stride as a runner at Auburn, Hoppe acknowledged his senior year was not his best showing. And White knew why: A lot of water went over the dam between Bobby's junior and senior years.

But White also knew what a lot of Chattanoogans—including Bobby's high school coach, Red Etter—thought. The Auburn offense wasn't geared to Bobby's style. Etter always believed Auburn played Hoppe at the wrong position—at wingback in a T-formation, so he seldom got to run the ball. But, White says, Bobby was determined to remain in the front line so he perfected his blocking—and became one of the best in Auburn's history.

In fact, according to White, Bobby developed into one of the most dedicated and vicious blockers the conference ever produced. Buddy Davidson once said that, pound-for-pound, on offense *and* defense, he was as good as anybody who ever put on an Auburn uniform. Shug Jordan described Bobby as an intense competitor whose blocking and receiving were instrumental in winning the national championship, noting he "ran over everything on every field he ever played on—he was murder returning kicks."

The National Championship Year

But fame wasn't all that important to "Bobby Hoppe, the restless, ambitious boy, and to Bobby Hoppe, the mature, well-adjusted man he was to become," White wrote.

What became most important, Bobby tells White, was his degree. About how Shug Jordan cared enough to bring him back to Auburn as a student coach so he could complete his degree.

In yet another among hundreds of the articles he wrote about the young Central player whom he followed throughout his career, Austin White told about a letter Bobby wrote to Jordan after his former coach announced his retirement.

"I've read and re-read it, many times," a reflective James Ralph "Shug" Jordan said, his misty eyes scanning the two-page letter from one of his "boys"— Chattanooga's Bobby Hoppe.

Shug told White during a tough final season, whenever he got low, he read the letter again, "It is absolutely the greatest I have received from a former player in all of my 43 years of coaching.

"You know, a coach needs something to fall back on every now and then. And when I think of Bobby Hoppe—and the scores and scores of boys like him—it all seems worthwhile," Jordan concluded as the legendary coach ended a disappointing season, his final.

Bobby's letter, reprinted in White's article, summed up how legions of players felt:

Dear Coach Jordan:

A few months ago when the papers announced your coming retirement, many thoughts came to my mind. The first was that old brown suit you wore to all our ball games. I guess the people in the stands thought you couldn't afford a new one—but your football boys knew why you wore it; a lot of luck sure came our way.

A great number of other thoughts raced through my mind concerning your actions toward your players. For example, we never heard you use profanity; nor did you ever blame or condemn us when Auburn lost. Instead, you always set an example that we could and did admire. In fact, years ago I heard Vince Dooley say that if he ever became a head coach he could think of no better person to copy than you.

Coach, I know of no self-made man in this world. Rather, men become what they are because of the influence of those around them.

A Matter of Conscience

I'll assure you that a great many former Auburn football players will agree with this statement—probably hundreds will.

There are some men who vividly come to mind—Frank D'Agostino, Billy Atkins, Jeff Weekley, Leroy Duchene, Jim Jeffrey, Ronnie Robbs, Jim Walsh and me—who would most certainly agree.

For you see, Coach, we remember how you cared for us as human beings instead of just football players.

We remember the discipline that helped us to mold our lives; but, we remember more the times you called us in and bragged on us when we began to grow into maturity.

The strongest thought that keeps coming to mind when I think of your retirement is not who will succeed you as coach, because Auburn football will take care of itself.

My main concern is whether or not the new coach will care about and help young men—for football players need people like you and Coach Senn around to take care of them....

While at Auburn I had many experiences, especially when we won the national football championship; but, the one I cherish most is when I graduated three years late and you were there with a graduation present....

Who would ever believe that after a boy had played out his four years of football you would still be concerned three years later whether he graduates or not....

In closing, Coach, I want to say that I know how your entire being aches when Auburn loses. But, when the record books are opened in the end, they won't tell how many football games you won or how many bowl games Auburn was in.

Rather, it will show how you helped your fellow man.

Especially, it will show you helped many an Auburn football player to have a decent chance at life.

You know, Coach, if I could just fill one of your shoes and help just half the number of young men that you have, I would not have any fear when the time comes to look my Maker in the face.

Thanks for the degree.

> *Sincerely,*
> *Bobby Hoppe*

CHAPTER EIGHTEEN

The Courtroom as Theater – Part II

You may my glories and my state depose,
But not my griefs. Still I am king of those.
–William Shakespeare

In 1988 in the hushed Chattanooga courtroom, Evans pounds away at his theory that Bobby was unaffected by killing Hudson. That, after taking another's life, Bobby simply set his sights on having his best year ever at Auburn.

"And you carried through with those plans, didn't you sir? Praying, I understand, praying, thinking about this every day. Who else did you pray with?"

In a quiet voice, Bobby acknowledges he prayed by himself. Remembering how utterly alone he felt, Bobby thinks how much he would have welcomed the prayers of others, to have someone share his burden. But he couldn't do anything to disgrace the Hoppe name.

Evans' next question—about the nature of his prayers—brings Bobby back to the present.

"I asked God to forgive my sins," Bobby responds, wiping his nose, fighting back tears.

"Excuse me, sir," Evans says, feigning politeness, "I don't want to misstate, but you said earlier, you told the jury, Dr. Godwin told you that you were forgiven religiously."

Calmly, Bobby explains Godwin didn't forgive his sins. The preacher said God had forgiven him.

Evans mocks him. "So you continued, even though Dr. Godwin exonerated you? You tell the jury he told you God forgave you, [but] you continued praying about God forgiving you."

On the surface, Bobby is amazingly composed. But inside, he's melting like late April snow. Shaking his head slightly, he recalls how long he has wanted to believe he is forgiven. Sometimes he almost gets there, but doubts rush in and crush his fragile faith. Even when he acknowledges God's forgiveness, Bobby can't forgive himself.

228

A Matter of Conscience

Again, Evans' harsh tone jerks him to attention. Almost snarling, Evans wants to know, in the long hours he spent in prayer, did he ever once think of Hudson's parents.

"I prayed for them as well. I prayed for Don, also," Bobby responds quietly.

Sitting in the courtroom, hearing Bobby say he prayed for the Hudsons is poignant. The words of St. Thomas Aquinas flow over me like a cool breeze: "The splendor of a soul in grace is so seductive that it surpasses the beauty of all created things."

Then I recall passages from Brennan Manning's The Ragamuffin Gospel. Manning describes the Good Samaritan, a model of Christian compassion, as a heretic despised because of his mixed pagan and Jewish ancestry. "He was so unclean already that, unlike the priest and Levite who passed by with their halos on tight, he could afford to express his love for the wounded man left for dead."

Bobby had highlighted this passage in Manning's book, putting three stars in the margin where Manning says we cannot achieve forgiveness or perfection on our own: "To be alive is to be broken; to be broken is to stand in the need of grace."

Although Evans doesn't know it, Bobby is in the place Manning describes. A sinner with a tilted halo whose transgressions, fears, and guilt don't make him a lesser person than someone whose halo has never tilted.

Has Evans' halo ever been tipped and tarnished, I wonder, as he trivializes how Bobby felt after killing Hudson, as he questions Bobby's spiritual misery.

Evans continues his questioning, each query more strident than the one before.

"While praying and thinking about Mr. and Mrs. Hudson, did it ever come across to you perhaps, as part of your character, you should go to them and say, 'Mr. and Mrs. Hudson, it had nothing to do with [Don's] illegal activities. Let me tell you what really happened. Your boy came after me with a gun; he was pointing a gun at me and, as God as my witness, I had to shoot him in self-defense. And it's a horrible thing. I am sorry.'"

Evans' voice rises higher and louder with each word. Jurors are staring, seemingly surprised he would question the sincerity of another's prayers.

The Courtroom as Theater – Part II

More words by Brennan Manning surface in my mind: "There are as many ways of praying as there are individual believers. Pray as you can; don't pray as you can't."

Bobby has prayed as he could—for more than three decades, he's prayed. It just doesn't match how Evans thinks he should have prayed.

After his harangue, Evans gets to the question. "In the past 31 years, have you thought about [telling the Hudsons], sir?"

Bobby blinks back tears, pauses a moment, and speaks with more animation than he has shown since the trial began. "I have thought about this every day and in my heart as I sit here, I know as I knew back when it happened, that I was forced to do what I did. If I had not taken those actions, I would have...I'm sure, I would have been killed.

"To not worry my parents, I tried not to tell them or anyone else. I was afraid. I didn't know what to do. I had contacted an attorney and was taking his advice."

At this, Evans hoots. "Oh, here we come. Mr. Wild, the deceased attorney, is that right?"

Now wound as tight as a top, Evans doesn't give Bobby time to answer. Without taking a breath, he yells, "I don't want to know about Joe Wild, your lawyer, yet. I don't want to know about these other people. Did you think about saying that to [the Hudsons]?"

"No, I didn't," Bobby replies, his soft answer in stark contrast to Evans' screech.

Emulating Bobby's tone, Evans says, "But they were in your prayers, and they were in your thoughts."

"That is correct."

Evans glances at the jurors, hoping they're with him. But a few, those whose own halos may have tilted somewhere along the way, look away, distancing themselves from his words.

Noting the disapproval, Evans calms himself and tries another tact.

He wants to know why Bobby didn't give the gun he used to kill Hudson to the police rather than his attorney. The police knew he had it. So did McCutcheon. So did his girl friend.

"And," Evans says, ranting again, "they knew poor Don Hudson died from a small bore shotgun blast—right in the eye. Correct? And the gun was not a secret?"

"That's correct," Bobby replies steadily.

A Matter of Conscience

"Did your girlfriend say, 'Hey, hey, Bobby, did you shoot him with that shotgun you had in the car?' Did she ever say that to you?" Evans demands.

Taken aback, Bobby replies, "Why, no."

In response to another question, Bobby says he doesn't know how many times he dated Barbara Jo after that because, shortly after the shooting, he returned to Auburn for fall practice.

"This killing didn't interfere with your fall practice, did it?" Evans says with a smirk.

"The preacher advised me—" Bobby begins before Evans abruptly cuts him off.

"I am not asking about the preacher, sir. Can you just answer yes or no? Can you answer yes or no?"

But Bobby knows yes and no answers can be misleading, that Evans can use them out of context. So he explains, "I was trying to pick up the pieces of my life."

Striding to the witness box, Evans puts his hands on the railing and leans close to Bobby's face. "Can you answer yes or no, sir?"

"I was trying to—"

Evans cuts him off again. "Did this interfere with your fall practice?"

Again Bobby tries to explain, but Evans bats the words back at him. However, Bobby is as stubborn as Evans, and he finally gets the sentence out, reiterating he was trying to pick up the pieces; he couldn't quit living. "I had to occupy my time."

Eyes still on Bobby, Evans steps backward, making sure the jury sees his disgust. But Bobby doesn't blink. Sarcasm and ridicule can't touch the pain he's been living with for years.

But Evans keeps taunting Bobby, "For 31 years you couldn't quit living, could you?"

And on and on it goes. Hour after hour. By now, there's a rhythm. Evans rants and raves, burying a question in his tirade. Bobby tries to stay on his toes, continually making an effort to say what needs to be said without falling into a trap.

Over and over, Evans attacks Bobby's 31-year silence.

"And that silence, you are not ashamed of your silence— you think that was good advice. And it would have been good advice because it would have caused—"

Bobby tries to interrupt, tries to answer, but Evans squashes him. "Let me finish my question, sir, and see if you agree with this, all right?"

After a moment of strained silence, Evans continues, his voice becoming a scream by the time he concludes.

"Can I finish my question, Mr. Hoppe? Can I finish my question? Would it have been good advice and resulted in Mr. and Mrs. Hudson going to the grave never knowing for sure what happened to their son? That's good advice?"

Evans' bellow bounces around the mahogany walls of the courtroom. Trapped in the vortex of this onslaught, Bobby simply stares straight ahead.

* * *

Conscience. Some say conscience separates normal people from sociopaths.

For more than 30 years, Bobby has taken up lodging with his conscience, as Origene Adamantius said, "as a chamber of justice."

De Balzac describes conscience as "a cudgel which all men pick up in order to thwack their neighbors instead of applying it to their own shoulders."

Bobby has thwacked himself harder and longer than Evans ever could.

In this courtroom, Evans inevitably preaches a long sermon before getting to his question.

This time he takes Bobby's previous testimony about Odene and twists it into an accusation that, if Bobby were planning a murder, he would go to a preacher, not to a person he hardly knew.

Exhausted, Bobby says, "That's not the way I meant it."

Shaking his notes in Bobby's face, Evans says, "That's what you said. I am just quoting you, sir. And you tell the jury if I am misquoting you."

Bobby tries to answer, but Evans tosses his words back at him. After Evans has hammered the same topic for 15 minutes, Phillips objects, saying Evans won't let Bobby respond.

Unfortunately, the objection just gives Evans a chance to go through the questions again.

Slowly and clearly, Bobby says he did not, would not plot a murder. But if he had it in his heart to do so, he would never have gone to a mere acquaintance. He would go to someone he could trust.

After an interminable exchange, Evans moves on to the moment Hudson was killed. Time to establish motive.

Of course, you "fired out of fear," he quotes from his notes, contempt thick in his voice.

Looking beyond Evans, Bobby speaks to the jurors. "I reacted; my actions were based on Don's actions. Don Hudson was the last thing in my mind that night. He wasn't dating my sister for quite a while."

"You don't know that." Evans snaps. A statement. Not a question.

Again addressing the jury, Bobby emphasizes he wasn't worried about Hudson; he wasn't even thinking about him.

Evans asks how Bobby knew his sister was no longer dating Hudson, since it was an on-again, off-again relationship.

Under fire, Bobby explains he was going to college and wasn't home much, so it was possible Joan could have gone over to see Hudson within 30 days of the killing.

Evans continues to pick at this. Finally, Bobby says he was told Joan was no longer seeing Hudson. His parents and his sister told him. And he had no reason to question their veracity.

With a jab, Evans declares it's mighty convenient that Bobby's parents and sister are dead; they can't testify and corroborate his story.

Evans pushes on. "[In] 1957 people knew, people told you Don had been beating up on your sister and they knew you didn't like that, is that right? I mean you told them, 'Hey, I know and...I just don't know what to do.' What did you tell them? 'Nothing I can do about it?'"

Bobby tries to answer the multiple questions. When Evans interrupts, Phillips comes to the rescue, telling the judge Evans not only stacks up questions, he won't let the witness respond.

The judge instructs Evans to keep quiet while Bobby answers. Irked, Evans steps back, seeming to listen.

"It's possible a friend or several friends would come tell me they saw Don beating my sister. They were my peer group, and I was a normal boy [and] brother. Of course, I would probably answer, I am going to whip his butt if he didn't leave her alone—or similar to that."

"But," Bobby continues, "I don't recall saying that. I don't deny it, but I don't remember it. But, if I did, it was a normal thing to respond to—and I must remind you: Her husband died in 1954, and during all [the] time [Joan dated him] I never laid a finger on Don Hudson nor did I ever approach him and threaten him in any way or form or fashion."

Again, Evans turns to the judge, complaining. "Your honor, I really don't think this is responsive to my question. That's my problem. That man keeps going on and on and on—and not in response to the question and not an explanation."

A lawyer in the back of the room whispers, "The pot calls the kettle black."

Oblivious, Evans presses on. "These friends of yours, you say they may have heard you physically threaten to do something about it? It would have been a natural thing to do, you say?"

"In the course of normal peer-group talk, I might have said I would whip his 'behind' or something like that," Bobby repeats.

"You would have said "behind"—seriously?" Evans chides.

"I might have said 'behind,' but it might have been 'butt,'" Bobby admits with a grin.

The grin irritates Evans, so he restates the question. "Well, surely you wouldn't have told your friends you would whip his *behind*, would you?"

Bobby, now also irritated, tells Evans he used that term back then and he still uses it.

Yielding on what seems a silly battle in semantics, Evans wants to know if all of Bobby's good character witnesses—those who spoke so highly of his "peace and quietude"—ever asked him if he killed Hudson.

No, Bobby tells him. His friends said things like, "I have faith in you, and I don't believe anything like that; I don't believe you would hurt anyone." But no one asked if he were involved.

But Evans wants to know what he would have said if they had asked.

"I would say I never murdered anyone. And I never have murdered anyone."

A simple response—yet it seemed paradoxical when Bobby told me last December as we walked the mall perimeter, that he was the one who did it—the one who killed Don Hudson.

Now, it makes perfect sense to me. There's no contradiction. Killing and murdering are not the same. Evans isn't trying Bobby for killing in self-defense. He's trying him for first-degree murder.

A Matter of Conscience

Tears fill my eyes as I realize the letter burned into Bobby's soul is a K, not an M.

* * *

Evans can't get a rise out of Bobby, so he kicks open a new door. "At the inquest, you again listened to your lawyer, didn't you? Your lawyer said, 'don't say a word,' so you didn't."

"That's right," Bobby responds.

"And when Joan went before the hearing, she didn't say a word. She took the Fifth Amendment. Now, whose advice was that?"

Phillips launches himself from his seat like a rocket. "Objection, Your Honor. I object. That is most improper."

Stunned by the outburst, the judge blinks rapidly behind his horn-rimmed glasses, calling counsel to the bench.

Glancing at the jury, I note that Bo Nelburn, the juror who had his eyes closed previously, is now sound asleep.

In an off-the-record bench conference, Phillips starts his objection. But before he gets one sentence out, Cook asks for the jury to be excused. DiRisio sends the jury out, and Cook waves Evans aside, telling him, "Now if you will move over, I've got a motion to make."

The courtroom is teeming. Something momentous is about to happen. You can hear the suppressed anger in Cook's voice.

Red-faced, almost apoplectic, Cook speaks with a fury, demanding a mistrial on the grounds of the question and the statement made by counsel for the State.

"Asking this witness as to why Joan Hoppe, if indeed she did, took the Fifth Amendment at the inquest—that is highly prejudicial. It violates the rule against fundamental fairness.

"It is highly improper and it is reprehensible to ask such a question in the presence of the jury. It is completely inadmissible in this case, and it's the first time in 25 years that I have heard of such conduct.

"We move for a mistrial in this case," Cook thunders, all the while glaring at Evans.

Startled by Cook's outburst, DiRisio says he needs to hear the question again. Barbara Bradford, the court reporter, reads back Evans' question. Before DiRisio can say thanks, Cook is in full voice.

"Making a statement in the presence of this jury that when Joan went before the inquest, she took the Fifth Amendment—he is making a categorical statement, which is a prejudicial statement and which was well known to counsel or the State that he should not have made it.

"I simply don't understand it. It goes beyond the bound of propriety. As the United States Supreme Court said in United States versus Burger, you can strike hard blows but you shouldn't strike foul blows.

"We move for a mistrial," Cook concludes, his melodious baritone now sharp and strident.

DiRisio wants to know about the Burger decision. Cook slowly explains it to him.

Cocking his head toward Evans, the judge asks for a citation to support his contention the question is allowable.

"It's relevant, Your Honor. If I might address the relevancy issue," Evans pleads.

But DiRisio will have none of that. "I don't need addressing [about] the relevancy, but I need addressing as to the legality."

He sends counsel for both the defense and the State to the law library to find citations. Fifteen minutes he gives them.

Cook says that's not reasonable so DiRisio tells the attorneys to check back with him in 15 minutes and tell him how it's going, then stands and shuffles from the courtroom.

It's a welcome break for Bobby. He steps from the witness box, and we walk down the hall from the courtroom and slip into a private room. We discuss how his testimony is going, and I tell him how proud I am of him, reminding him of one of his favorite quotes by Nietzsche: *Was mich nicht umbringt, macht mich starker."* (That which does not kill me makes me stronger.)

If Bobby can just survive this trial, he will be stronger, I think. Perhaps he can put his fears aside, even forgive himself.

Giving me a quick hug, Bobby admits all this is hard, very hard, but he's thankful to finally be able to tell the world what happened that night so long ago.

* * *

When Manning described the audience for his book, he could have been describing Bobby: "bedraggled, beat-up and burned-out."

A Matter of Conscience

According to Manning, a recovering alcoholic, he wrote the book for "the sorely burdened who are still shifting the heavy suitcase from one hand to the other.

"For the wobbly and weak-kneed who know they don't have it altogether and are too proud to accept the handout of amazing grace.

"For the inconsistent, unsteady disciples whose cheese is falling off their cracker.

"For the bent and the bruised who feel that their lives are a grave disappointment to God."

For Bobby.

* * *

During the break, Sally Weaver tells me Cook's motion has thrown her into a panic. If a mistrial is declared, Bobby will have to go through all this again. Knowing Cook is the master trial lawyer, Sally is hesitant to say anything, but while she and the other attorneys are in the law library, she expresses her concern.

With a slight grin, Cook tells her not to worry. It's all just a bluff. DiRisio is never going to approve a motion for a mistrial. Cook just wants to put one more appeal factor on the record. Relieved, Sally manages to relay this to me as the attorneys step from the law library.

As we walk down the hallway, I tell Phillips and Cook about Bo Nelburn, the juror who keeps nodding off.

"That man slept through half of the testimony this morning! Bobby is on trial for his life, and that juror can't even stay awake."

"We're going to request the judge remove him and seat an alternate juror," Phillips responds. After the break, the judge chastises Nelburn and removes him.

Isabelle (Belle) Rucker, a teacher, replaces him.

It's a decision I will later regret.

* * *

When the lawyers return to the courtroom more than an hour later, Cook presents Grunewald v. the United States, a decision by the Supreme Court reported in 353 U.S. 420 and written by Justice Harlan.

Cook also tells the Court the defense is relying on the U.S. v. Singletary, a Fifth Circuit case, 646 Federal Reporter, 2nd series, 1018.

But Evans' search wasn't so fruitful. He didn't find any case citation to support his position, so he decides to turn the argument into why *he* thinks his question was not prejudicial.

When Evans winds down, Cook raises a bushy eyebrow, admonishing Evans he "might glean some wisdom in his spare time, if indeed he has any spare time, by reading the decisions which I've cited."

DiRisio also has found another case, this one in California, People v. Carnett, 104 Pacific 2nd 794. He adds a long, legalese-filled explanation regarding instances when mentioning the invocation of the First Amendment is barred.

Abruptly, DiRisio ends with a split decision. He rules Evans' statements prejudicial, but he does not rule them so prejudicial as to require a mistrial.

To say the least, Cook is displeased. What Evans did was not a slip of the tongue, he argues. "It was an intentional infraction by the attorney general...and we do not feel it can be undone or unforgotten by simply instructing the jury to disregard it."

Since this is exactly what DiRisio proposes to do, Cook has a bit more to say on the matter.

"As Judge Wisdom, the Fifth Circuit Judge who now has senior status and wrote the Singletary decision, said, it is very difficult to unring a bell. As I have said—not being as intellectually astute as Judge Wisdom—it's like throwing a skunk in the jury box and telling them that they don't smell it.

"That's all I have to say, Judge."

Cook wants to know if Evans has any other "skunk-like" questions in his arsenal.

Evans admits he does. He wants to ask Bobby if Joan ever told authorities what she knew about the case. After all, the defense made a big show of saying Joan can't speak for herself because she is mentally unstable.

Asking Bobby what Joan may or may not have known doesn't sit well with Cook, so he asks the judge to require Evans to question Bobby outside the hearing of the jury before deciding if the jury can hear the questions and answers. Or, Cook says with a shrug, "Maybe I should just sort of lay back and wait."

DiRisio gets the message. Cook will fire his gun before Evans asks the question, or he will fire it after the question has been shot across the bow of the jury box. Firing after-the-fact will give Cook another reason to call for a mistrial.

DiRisio wants no more of that, so he sends the jury out and instructs Evans to "put his foot forward and tell us which direction he is going."

Evans turns toward Bobby and asks if he ever discussed "this" with his sister Joan.

"No," Bobby responds.

"You never told her you killed Don Hudson?"

"I never discussed it with her at all."

Given that, DiRisio rules it is impossible Joan and Bobby conspired to keep silent, meaning Evans can't ask the questions in front of the jury.

Furthermore, after the jury returns, DiRisio instructs the jurors "they should draw no inference as to the guilt or innocence of this defendant from the invocation...of the self-incrimination privilege, by any other person including his sister Joan...."

But the skunk's already been hurled, its scent suspended over Bobby's head.

Then Evans goes after Bobby again, questioning him another nine times about whether a friend ever asked him if he killed Don Hudson. Nine times Bobby tells him, "No."

Pursing his lips, Evans finally accepts defeat, but not gracefully. He starts hounding Bobby for the details of his date with Barbara Jo Campbell. When Bobby can't remember exactly where they went or what they ate, Evans hurls another zinger.

"Sir, are you telling the jury after you shot Don Hudson in the face, you didn't think, 'Well, I wonder will it ever become important as to what I was doing beforehand, before I shot Don Hudson?' You never had that thought back in 1957?" he demands.

"No, I didn't, not that I recall," Bobby answers.

Sarcastically, Evans says, "Just didn't concern you?"

"That's your word, not mine," Bobby says strongly but not confrontationally.

"Did it concern you?"

His brow drawing into a furrow, Bobby replies, "It certainly did."

Now openly scoffing, Evans revisits his contention that Bobby's praying about the incident every day didn't truly indicate concern since he went his merry way at Auburn.

Enough is enough. Phillips rises. "May it please the Court, I object to the repetition. He has asked him that 42 times."

The judge agrees, instructing Evans to avoid repetition.

Amazingly, Evans asks the same question again without using the word, "Auburn."

And on and on it goes. Finally, Evans moves to Bobby's visit to Godwin. First he wants to establish Bobby wasn't a regular church-goer in Auburn, nor in Chattanooga, for that matter.

Evans knows what Cook knows. The admission of Godwin's testimony was highly questionable and would make a guilty verdict appealable. So he's trying to lay a foundation to support the inclusion of a confession that many believe should have been protected by pastor/penitent confidentiality.

And then Evans switches gears, jumping from Godwin back to Joan's car. Bobby knew Hudson had bought her the sleek new convertible, didn't he?

"That's news to me," Bobby says.

Evans doesn't believe Bobby. How did he think she could afford such a nice car? Was she working? Didn't Bobby ask her where she got the new Ford convertible?

In fact, on a balmy fall day in September 2008, sitting outside the Collegedale Lifecare Center where Joan had lived several years, she wanted to make it clear she "bought that damned car" herself—with government money she received after her husband Clyde, an Army veteran, died.

But back in 1988, Bobby didn't know the car was bought with Clyde's money. On the stand, he can't answer the barrage of questions hurled at him before Evans lobs another one.

Like multiple sets of dice, all dropped at one time, Evans peppers Bobby with questions, jumping from one topic to another so quickly I don't know how Bobby is keeping up with him.

Then Evans scoops up the dice he's been dying to toss—right in Bobby's face. The gun.

"I'm going to show you a gun and ask if this looks at all like the gun you traded for, if it's similar."

Bobby carefully examines the gun Evans hands him and says it looks similar, but he thought the 22-gauge barrel was on the bottom, not the top like the one Evans gave him.

"Other than that, any significant difference? I mean you shot the gun."

Pausing, Bobby says he can't say how closely this gun resembles the other gun because he didn't have that gun in his possession long.

With a sneer, Evans strikes quickly. "Just long enough to kill Mr. Hudson?"

Startled, Phillips jumps up. "I object to that remark, may it please the Court."

With an audible sigh, DiRisio admonishes Evans to proceed properly.

In the jury box, several members seem shocked. Juror Paula Ackman stares at Evans, then drops her head.

This doesn't slow Evans' rapid-fire questioning. Bobby's patience totally evaporates when Evans refuses to let him answer one question before he asks another.

Phillips senses Bobby's rising irritation and objects.

Evans must be wearing on DiRisio's nerves, too, because the judge squelches the slightest possibility of debate, telling Evans to let the witness answer.

It seems as if Evans has taken the judge's warning to heart. For a few moments, his tone is almost civil, but it doesn't last long. Goading Bobby about his statement there is no new evidence except Odene's testimony, Evans asks, "Is it not new evidence that you are sitting here today, saying, 'Yes, I shot Don Hudson but it was in self-defense.' Is that not new evidence, sir?"

Cheeks burning red, Phillips objects again. "He is inferring he had an obligation to tell—"

"I'm not inferring a thing," Evans snipes back.

Infuriated, Phillips tells the Court Evans' remarks are totally improper; that Evans is trying to infer Bobby had an obligation to testify at the coroner's inquest or the grand jury.

Like spectators at a tennis match, jurors' heads are bouncing back and forth from Phillips to Evans, trying to follow the heated exchange. DiRisio tells counsel to approach the bench.

We can't hear what's said, but it must have favored the State, because Evans strikes again as soon as the conference concludes.

I'm reminded of Jeris Bragan's words in Prison Behind Walls— "when DiRisio is on the bench, it's like giving the State an extra prosecutor."

Delighted DiRisio has ruled in his favor, Evans rants on.

"It's the first time in 31 years, sir, that the State has had any idea you were going to get here and say, 'I shot him in self-defense. I have it on my heart and my mind and I prayed about it.' The first time in 31 years, sir. Right?"

Bobby tries to explain, but Evans cuts him off, turning to the judge.

"Can he answer the question, Your Honor, and then go into his little speech, please?"

A master at turning a simple question into a sermon, Evans seemingly applies different rules for the accuser and the accused.

Suddenly sympathetic to the defense, DiRisio declares Bobby can answer and then explain.

Evans uses the judge's ruling to take another jab at Bobby. "Please answer the question, and then you can go into your little explanation."

Starting to rise, Phillips objects, then sinks back into his chair. The judge's face says it all.

"Strike the editorial comment," DiRisio instructs the court reporter.

"He continues to do that, Your Honor," Phillips complains without standing.

"Proceed without it," DiRisio warns Evans.

"Well, no one but you is worthy of belief, right, Bobby?" Evans asks, then without giving Bobby a chance to respond, he adds, "Certainly, Dr. Godwin is not worthy of belief, is he?"

"Absolutely not," Bobby says. "(You'd) have to be a fool to believe him."

It continues, tit-for-tat. Evans makes a sardonic statement, ending with a question. Phillips objects. Evans does it again. Phillips objects.

DiRisio watches the exchange a while and then intervenes, telling Evans he is being argumentative and the form of his questions is objectionable.

But Evans is oblivious to the judge's growing impatience.

"Anyone would have to be a fool to believe Odene Neal, too?" he prods Bobby.

Phillips objects. DiRisio sustains, telling Evans—again—the form of his question is objectionable.

Evans thinks a minute and then shrugs before throwing his last punch. "The only person we can really believe in this case is you, right, because of all these character witnesses?"

There is a little truth here and there, Bobby responds, but the Rev. Godwin and Ms. Neal, no they were not truthful. Then Bobby adds, "I am telling the truth. You can believe that."

Walking back toward the prosecution's table, Evans seems to give up—then I see him smile. It's not over.

* * *

Pivoting toward Bobby, Evans frames his question with slow deliberation. During all the time you're riding around with your girlfriend, where is the gun?

Bobby tells Evans he had placed the gun and shells in the back seat or back floorboard of the car. "I think it was in the back seat. I'm not positive."

The equivocation irritates Evans, who wants Bobby to remember the exact location.

"This is the *only* person you've ever killed, isn't it?" Evans asks, implying surely Bobby should remember each detail of that night.

Phillips is on his feet, objecting, telling the judge the question is improper. But DiRisio allows the question, so the jury gets to hear it again.

"This is the only man you have ever killed?"

Meeting Evans' eyes, Bobby gives a faint one-word answer. "Yes."

Evans won't let it go, asking whether shooting a man is a frequent occurrence for Bobby. "This had never happened before, right? What you told this jury never happened before?"

Beaten down, Bobby replies, "I had never killed anybody before, no."

"Because of that, wasn't everything that night with respect to this shooting emblazoned onto your memory?" Evans demands.

"I can't recall...it may have been, as you say, emblazoned on my memory, but over the years things have grown dim. There's nothing wrong with my memory; it just dulls through the great number of years."

Evans spits out three more questions on the same subject. Pushing. Prodding. Goading. Then he fires with both barrels, criticizing Bobby, implying he recalls what he wants to recall. That his memory didn't fail him on the bad things he had heard about Hudson. Mockingly, he reminds Bobby he even remembered reading in the paper about these incidences and about Hudson being chased and having two fingers shot off. He ends with the accusation Bobby went through the list of Hudson's illegal activities as if he had memorized it.

Bobby tries to explain his memory had been refreshed by the testimonies of people who described Hudson's history.

"No, no, sir." Evans bellows. "This is something that was going on in your mind, sir, back when this happened. You said you remembered all these things about Don Hudson. You remembered shooting—"

No, Bobby replies patiently, "I didn't say they were *all* going through my mind at that particular time. I knew of his reputation. I knew about those things, yes. But did each one click up in my mind? No. Some of them—"

Evans interrupts. "Which ones *clicked up* in your mind?"

Bobby says he doesn't remember, so Evans attacks again. "Well, you certainly named them all just in case some clicked up and some didn't click up, is that right?"

On and on, the berating continues, reaching a crescendo as Evans scolds Bobby, wanting him to explain why he can recall in detail all the bad things about Don Hudson and yet is starting to have lapses as to exactly where he placed the gun in the car.

Bobby turns tired eyes to the jury, ignoring Evans. "You have to understand during this point in time, I was scared, I was excited. And when I grabbed for the gun, I can't tell you for certain that the gun was on the seat or laying on the floorboard."

It was probably on the seat, but he's not going to say something he doesn't know for sure.

Evans' next foray takes him to Bell Road. He starts to show a video of a car driving down the road, illustrating the trajectory of Bobby's car in 1957. But Phillips objects: The defense has not viewed the video.

A Matter of Conscience

When Cook stands, indicating he's ready to enter the fray, DiRisio sends the jury out.

* * *

Phillips argues the jury could be misled since the speed of the vehicle in the video may not be the same speed as Bobby's car was going back in 1957.

DiRisio is not convinced. He sees no material difference in photos and the videotape. It's just a different technology. If the defendant has trouble using the videotape to describe his movements, he can say so. And, DiRisio adds, Phillips can always correct misinterpretations on redirect.

Score one more for the prosecution. Pleased with winning this round, Evans tells the judge he has another demonstration he plans to use. The State has brought a 1959 Ford retractable hardtop convertible from Knoxville. The owner will testify, Evans says, that 1957, 1958, and 1959 hard-top convertibles had the same body. The only change was with exterior sheet metal.

Evans wants to have Bobby get in the vehicle in the parking lot and demonstrate to the jury how he reached around to get the gun.

"Obviously, we can't haul the car in here; we can't chop the car up. I can't reconstruct; we don't have the facilities to reconstruct the body, interior body of this car...because we feel it is vital, obviously, to the State's case that Mr. Hoppe show how he managed what we believe to be an impossible feat."

DiRisio asks Evans for some authority to back up what he is proposing. Evans argues the only alternative is to put two chairs in place—one for the front seat and one for the back seat.

DiRisio remains unconvinced. He repeats Evans must cite some authority saying it is proper for a jury to leave the courtroom and go to another location to watch a re-enactment.

As before, Evans doesn't want to go to case law to support his position. He prefers to convince the judge to go along with him, but this time it doesn't work. He's directed to go to the library when the Court recesses and bring back citations for the judge to review. In the meantime, the jury can return and he can continue his cross-examination using the videotape.

The videotape begins, with Bobby attempting to go through his movements that night—pulling off at the trailer park road to tune his radio, pulling back on Bell Avenue, seeing the car without lights behind him, thinking it was a friend trying to scare him. Realizing it was Hudson, swerving to avoid being hit, seeing the car pull up behind him again.

Suddenly, Bobby stops, saying he can't tell on the video exactly where his car was. It was dark and his speed varied, so he isn't sure.

"It was dark that night—but it sure didn't prevent you from seeing and knowing it was Don Hudson all the way across the car, sitting there, driving his car, pointing a pistol at you. It was bright enough for that, wasn't it, sir?" Evans posits.

"Yes, sir," Bobby responds, gesturing with the span of his arms. "This man sits right here—he was that close, I could see him."

Disdainfully, Evans argues with Bobby about how he could possibly see Hudson and not see where he was on the road.

"If you would like to go out and get in a car and sit next to my car and see if you recognize me at 1 o'clock in the morning, I'm sure you could. I believe I'd recognize you," Bobby replies.

"If it was pitch dark, I wouldn't be able to, would I, sir?" Evans prods, castigating Bobby because he could see Hudson a few feet away, while accepting Tommy Smith's testimony he could see a black convertible, with its black top up, from two blocks away.

Oblivious to the discrepancy, Evans continues. "There was light enough for you to see that it was Donald Hudson with his gun pointed at you, right? And can you tell the jury, can you give any estimation, sir, in your recollection of this—thinking about it day in and day out, praying about it over 31 years—can you just help the jury a little bit, sir?"

Never taking a breath, Evans plunges on. "And could you tell us along this road where it was when you first saw Don Hudson in his car sticking his pistol at you?

"Can you give us a little help in the 31 years of remembering and thinking about it and praying? Can you help the jury and tell us where it was?" Evans yells, concluding a cluster of questions.

Now completely exasperated, Bobby responds with passion. "I cannot look at that and tell you where it was on the road that happened, because it was dark and I was frightened and scared. I don't remember exactly what point it was, but it was certainly fairly soon after I turned left."

Out of the blue, Evans drops this line of questioning. Asking Bobby about the speed of his car, Evans challenges how fast Bobby says he was going while throwing in a few zingers.

"As I understand it then, sir, you saw Donald Hudson, who you knew to be a gunslinger, a whisky runner, a woman beater, and you were going about 10 miles an hour—and you saw him pointing a gun at you and you speeded up to 15 or 20 miles an hour in your '57 Ford?"

Bobby tells Evans he's twisting his words.

Putting on the pressure, Evans says, "I'm just asking you, sir, is that what happened?"

"Why don't you ask me instead of telling me," Bobby challenges. "I know what happened."

Like a broken record, Evans' questions swirl over and over, slinging Bobby's words from previous testimony back in his face.

Exhausted, Bobby finally tells him, "I'm denying anything you are saying because you are twisting my words."

Evans is just starting to get revved up, describing what he imagines happened to Bobby and Hudson on that night.

He lays it out for Bobby, as if directing a play. "You know that behind you now, he has pulled up with a gun. He has pointed at you and he pulls in back behind you. You almost, you say, stopped or pulled off. You knew you put on your brakes.

"You have got Donald Hudson behind you, and you listed off all those things, Mr. Hoppe, all those terrible things about Donald Hudson. We have heard them here in Court today and yesterday and the day before yesterday and all the days preceding this trial.

"And you knew all those terrible things about him, and this man had pointed a gun at you and he has pulled back in behind you—"

Disgusted, Phillips objects, asking the judge, "Is he going to ask a question, Your Honor?"

As if placating a child, DiRisio says, "I think it's coming now."

Evans continues. "And you are telling this jury after all the time you had to think about this that what you did in your '57 Ford was speed up to 20 miles an hour and you wanted [us] to believe that? Is that right, sir, because that is the truth?"

Bobby has a sermon of his own, and he directs it to the jury: Hudson's car was on his bumper, and he wanted to get him off it by speeding up. But he knew Hudson was an excellent driver who drove souped-up cars, so Bobby had zero chance of outrunning him.

Fear tightens Bobby's voice as he recalls that night, "He was on my bumper. I realized if he hit me, I would go out of control, so I slowed down. I slowed to about 10 miles an hour.

"I was hoping help would come from Nikki's or Cherokee Boulevard. If a car would just come down the road with its lights on, I would be safe. I was afraid to go—I couldn't outrun him, and I certainly did not want him to bump me in the rear. He had a pistol; he was a whisky man; he had been driving his cars being chased by police...

"Yes, I was frightened. Yes, I was afraid."

Evans swings again, knowing he must prove Bobby's version of events is implausible.

"He had this old DeSoto, and you slowed down because of this man you feared so much, so terribly. He was a good driver, and you figured the only way you could do anything about it—you are telling this jury—you thought about it for 31 years, you prayed about it every day, what you did was slow down to 10 miles an hour to see if you could get help. And you want the jury to believe because that's the truth?"

Drained by the endless siege, Bobby tries to explain that back then people who hauled liquor would buy old cars because they were apt to wreck them or have them impounded by police. Moonshine-runners put powerful motors in their cars—souped them up.

"Yes, that old car, with him driving, it could outrun me," Bobby concludes.

Evans waves his hand dismissively. "We have all seen *Thunder Road*, and we've heard the song."

To everyone's obvious surprise, Evans starts singing loudly, "Oh there was thunder, thunder on Thunder Road." His puts dramatic emphasis on "thunder" each time he sings it.

Suddenly, he stops and says, "And what you worried about was Donald Hudson thundering behind you in his whisky car?"

Phillips doesn't even have to object to the theatrics. As he begins, "Your Honor—" the judge looks at Evans sternly and orders him, "Leave out the testimony, Mr. Evans."

And on it goes. Evans objects to Bobby's answers, and Phillips objects to Evans' sermonizing before each question.

In one tirade, Evans says, "I remember you telling the jury you were looking around. 'Golly gee, if someone would just drive along here on Bell Avenue, maybe I would be rescued.'"

Grinning slightly, Bobby says, "I didn't say, 'Golly gee'."

Evans doesn't see the humor, so he presses on, pounding Bobby with question stacked on question about his speed and why he can't show him on the video exactly what happened where.

In exasperation, Bobby again states it was 31 years ago, it was at night, he was frightened. The strain revealing itself in his voice, in his posture, Bobby's next words are uttered softly but with gripping intensity. "It took all the nerve power I could muster to keep my speed down [with him on my bumper] because I was frightened."

Evans pounces on Bobby's words. "Just like it took you all the nerve you could muster to not say anything about this for 31 years, right, Mr. Hoppe? Is that right, did it take a lot of nerve not to say anything about this?"

Turning slate-gray eyes on Evans, Bobby says sadly, "Every day. Every day. Every day. I have thought about this. I know in my heart what happened. And I know in my heart, if I hadn't acted that way, I probably would be dead today."

Evans wants to make sure his point is clear, so he repeats his premise: Hudson wasn't afraid of Bobby. He wouldn't think twice about going after Bobby if he tried to escape. Bobby's tale is pure fiction—highly implausible. All of this presented in question after question with no allowance for answers.

Not even rising from his seat, an exasperated Phillips inquires, "How many questions is he going to ask him? I object to it."

DiRisio coaches Evans, "Ask your question, Mr. Evans."

Confident he has the judge on his side, Evans persists with endlessly repetitive questions.

Then, briefly on point, Evans asks what Bobby thought Hudson was trying to do.

Worn out with being badgered, Bobby snaps, "What do you think he was trying to do? Invite me to a birthday party?"

Laughter erupts in the courtroom, and DiRisio gavels everyone into silence.

Ignoring the laughter, Evans presses Bobby to defend his plan to fake a stop.

"Let me tell you," Bobby responds, "I think I did a very good job back then to be under the pressure I was under. I think my thinking was pretty good compared to my fear."

Mockingly, Evans says, "You did a great job. I agree with you. You did a great job—you killed the man. Go ahead, go ahead, what happened then, sir?"

Again, Bobby tries to explain he was trying to get in front of Don to give himself room to apply his brake, hoping Don would think he was going to stop at the stop sign.

And then, Evans mimics Bobby, there was a roar of the engine. "How soon was it after the roar of the engine that the shotgun went *boom?*" Evans magnifies the word, creating the rumble of a fired shotgun.

Bobby isn't sure. He only knows he acted out of fear when he fired his gun.

Evans starts back to his table, then halts. Pivoting, he ambles toward Bobby, stopping about a foot from the witness box. With a quick glance at the jury, he holds a box close to Bobby's face, offering a snide smile unseen by the jury.

"You know, we forgot something. We forgot the box, and we forgot three or four 410 shotgun shells, and we forgot to tell the jury and show the jury in our discussion how you reached around and did all these things.

"Can you show us? We just completely forgot that. We got there—"

Like a cat protecting her kitten, Phillips hisses, "Your honor, I object to his dramatics and histrionics!"

"Let's ask the question," DiRisio directs Evans.

"Exactly, and keep his comments down," Phillips demands.

Evans, confident of DiRisio's good graces, never acknowledges the reprimand. Smirking at Bobby, he announces, "We didn't tell the jury about that, did we?"

On his feet again, Phillips roars, "Keep his comments down."

Sensing he has allowed Evans to go too far, DiRisio is more forceful in telling him to restrict to questions and answers.

Subdued momentarily, Evans instructs Bobby to step from the stand and take a seat in a hard-back chair he has placed in front of the jury box.

Once Bobby is seated, Evans asks if he can picture the chair as the driver's seat.

"Can you see that, Mr. Hoppe? Can you see that in your mind's eye? You envisioned him—boy, he is right on your bumper. Think about it—you have thought about it for 31 years.

"If you have to, close your eyes and think about it. Think about it. Does it help you to close your eyes and think about it? Does it help you get a better picture, sir?"

Or, Evans chides, just think about it with your eyes open. You've thought about it so many years, it probably doesn't matter.

But, Evans adds, as if the thought just occurred to him, we need a back seat, don't we? So he pulls up another hard-back chair, placing it behind the first one, bending slowly to put the gun and box of shells on it.

Phillips has a problem with that. "This is not an adequate re-enactment of what occurred on that occasion, because there is no indication that the seating is proper. Where he reached, is the area within reason? It has got to be some kind of similarity for it to have any validity."

Evans' eyes light up like a Christmas tree. Phillips has handed him a gift. He reminds the judge he has offered that similarity.

I realize DiRisio still has not ruled on whether Evans can have Bobby demonstrate his actions in the parking lot—in a car similar to the one he was driving the night Hudson was killed.

Regardless, Evans gets his dig in.

Sweet as sugar, he asks, "Does this give you a problem, Mr. Hoppe? Is this just totally beyond your ability to show the jury how it happened?"

"[It's] certainly your problem," Bobby replies with alacrity. "I know how it happened."

Having Bobby go through the motions of retrieving the gun from the back seat, Evans tells him to pick up the shells. When he looks over his shoulder, Bobby realizes something's not right.

"You turned the gun the wrong way," he tells Evans.

"Oh, you knew which way the gun was pointed?" Evans says skeptically.

Seeing another chance to smack at Bobby, Evans goes on another tirade. "Isn't that little detail amazing, Mr. Hoppe? Let's just stop there for a minute. Let's just stop there for a minute. I turned the gun the wrong way. You are telling the jury you don't know whether it was on the seat or on the floor, you don't know where the box of shells were, but, boy, right away you knew I turned the gun the wrong way. Is that right?"

To Bobby, it's not amazing. It's just common sense to have turned the gun barrel away as he slid it into the car.

Evans' assault continues until the judge finally tells him he can't keep Bobby off the witness stand if he isn't going to ask him questions related to the chairs [car].

Point by point, Evans asks Bobby to describe every motion and every move he made as Hudson pulled up beside him, as he pointed the gun at him.

Evans notes, as if he just realized it, he doesn't have enough chairs—there is not one for Hudson's car—but he still wants Bobby to demonstrate how Hudson pointed the gun across the passenger seat. It was the passenger seat, right?

Bobby nods, adding it was then he remembered he had a gun in his car.

"I reached in the back and got the gun and brought it over the seat while I was driving," Bobby says, demonstrating as he talks.

"Let's do that again," Evans tells Bobby, but Cook calls a halt to the demonstration, saying he wants to see if the gun is loaded.

Evans tells the judge Cook's request is nothing more than a ploy to draw attention away from what his client is unable to do.

But Cook is adamant, declaring to DeRisio that before a gun is pointed at him and the jury, he has a right to see if it's loaded.

So DiRisio tells Bobby to break the gun down to check for shells.

That little safety exercise complete, Evans directs Bobby to bring the gun over the seat.

Oh, wait. We forgot something again, Evans scolds Bobby, as if he's talking to a forgetful child. "Your car had a ceiling, didn't it? Where is the ceiling in relation to your head?"

Now clearly vexed, Bobby declares he doesn't know where the ceiling was; he just knows he got the gun over the seat.

Like a director setting the stage just so, Evans points to Bobby's left hand. "Wait a minute. What are you doing with this hand here [while you are getting the gun]?"

Bobby says he is holding the steering wheel.

Then hold up that arm, Evans directs.

Bobby has trouble breaking down the gun to insert the shell, saying the gun is not well oiled. Evans doesn't listen, telling Bobby to just do it again. "Reach back around. You are driving—keep one hand on the steering wheel..."

After Evans has him go through this pantomime five times, Bobby, totally frazzled, stops. Looking up at Evans, he tells the prosecutor he has arthritis and it hurts to reach back.

Resolutely, Bobby says he will do it just one more time.

Evans disregards the challenge. "Just keep your hand on the steering wheel, Mr. Hoppe."

Seething, Bobby replies, "If you give me a steering wheel to hold onto, I will."

Bobby has played right into Evans' hands. Not missing a beat, Evans jumps on the statement, asking if Bobby wants to get in a real car and do this for the jury?

Phillips leaps from his seat, objecting loudly.

Despite the judge having delayed ruling whether a demonstration in a car outside the courtroom is permissible, he says Evans may ask the question.

Smiling, Evans repeats, "Do you want to get in a car and do this for the jury?"

Totally in the dark regarding the background for Phillips' objection, Bobby is annoyed. He glares up at Evans and says, "I can do it in a car."

Evans grabs for the gold. "You can do it in a car. Would you feel more comfortable sitting in a car and doing it?"

"It would be more realistic, wouldn't it?" Bobby asks, oblivious to the implications of his response.

Like a Cheshire cat, Evans laps up the milk. "Be more realistic—and that would be your preference?"

Phillips, red with rage, strikes an aggressive bantam pose toward Evans before turning to DiRisio. "May it please the Court, I object. That's a question of law.

"Mixed law and fact," DiRisio says.

DiRisio is a fence-straddling judge. Lawyers in the back of the room wonder if DiRisio is more concerned about being overruled by a higher court than about making any ruling at all.

The judge's apparent shift causes murmurs in the courtroom, fueling Phillips' rising fury. Now more than ready for a fight, Phillips tells the judge, "It's a question that ought to be addressed to the Court and not to this witness."

But the judge is not to be rushed. "We'll take it up in time," he says.

Oozing compassion, Evans asks Bobby if his arthritis will allow him to swing the gun around again. And this time try not to hit the dashboard.

Frustrated and exhausted, Bobby declares the demonstration is unfair. He has no dashboard and is sitting in a chair that doesn't come close to resembling a car seat.

"Mr. Hoppe, I want to be fair with you," Evans says, oh so kindly. "I want to be fair with you, Mr. Hoppe. I have got a car if—"

His face on fire, Phillips jumps up, objecting again. He tells DiRisio it is a matter for the Court to take up, yet Evans "continues to do it."

And, Phillips declares, it's not Bobby—it's his attorneys objecting to the fairness.

"All right. Let's proceed with a proper question," DiRisio tells Evans, revealing a leniency that defies reason to the gallery of attorneys grouped and growing along the back wall.

With Bobby still sitting in the chair, Evans continues to direct the play he's produced in his head. He makes Bobby repeat the scene three times, sermonizing and disparaging each response.

Evans chides Bobby for having difficulty with the box, bringing an objection from Phillips, who says this box doesn't begin to resemble a box for shotgun shells.

In the back, a young attorney whispers, "Mr. Evans knew that when he gave Bobby the box." A colleague agrees, saying the prosecutor intentionally used a box that was difficult to open. Another observer in the back of the room, a middle-aged woman, adds her two cents: "Just like he used a rusty gun. But, as they say, you do what you got to do."

Shocked by the arrogant but on-target comment, lawyers near the woman slide further down the back wall, disassociating, realizing they, too, may face Evans in court someday.

Phillips' objection results in a bench conference. When Evans returns to his place in front of Bobby, the prosecutor, seemingly chastised, tells Bobby he may go through the next scene without interruption.

Bobby narrates as he demonstrates each movement, explaining the hardback chair's seat is probably too high, and he was sitting lower in the car, a lot deeper.

He was driving about 8-12 miles an hour when Hudson's car pulled beside him, swerving toward him. Bobby tells the jury he swerved to the right to avoid being sideswiped. Then, he says, he put on his brakes, almost coming to a complete stop.

Bobby's voice begins to shake slightly, but he pushes on. "He rolled back. And when he rolled back past me, he pointed the gun at me and paused. Then he got behind my car. I realize he has a gun and then I remember I have a gun, too." Bobby says he reached back and brought the gun across. Trying to demonstrate how he reached for the shells, opened the gun, and loaded the shells, Bobby lowers his left arm slightly.

Despite his pledge not to interrupt, Evans cuts in. "No, no, show us, sir, please. Hold onto the steering wheel—"

Pausing, Bobby says he doesn't know if he pointed the gun after loading it, demonstrating how he held it across the bottom of his open window.

With the gun now pointed directly at him, DiRisio holds up a hand to stop the show, asking Evans if the shells are blank, but Evans assures the judge the shells are expended.

Quick-witted, Cook interjects, "Well, I would want to check that, too."

OK, DiRisio agrees, let Mr. Cook check them.

"Unless you point it at Mr. Evans..." Cook tells Bobby with a grin, breaking the tension.

Bobby briefly returns the smile. But he becomes plaintive as he tries to load the gun, saying Evans is making him look like an idiot. Back then, he had a whole seat to work with.

Later, Bobby will also say spent shells, such as those provided by Evans, have crimped edges, making it more difficult to load the demonstration gun than it was to load the gun he used the night Hudson was killed.

Former prisoner Jeris Bragan tells of complaining to a jail trustee about the inequities in his trial, the unfairness of his conviction. Bragan quotes the trustee as whispering, "Look, I don't want to burst your bubble, but the fix is in on you. This is Chattanooga, and the folks downstairs [in the judge and DA's office] do whatever they want."

I have to wonder if the "fix is in" on Bobby, too.

When he tries to show how he laid the gun over the window's edge, an argument ensues regarding the height of the window. After much back and forth, after grumbling from attorneys in the back of the room reaches his ears, DiRisio agrees Bobby can return to the witness box.

I breathe a sigh of relief. Maybe the worst is over.

Asked to show how he fired the gun, a frustrated Bobby says, "It's obvious I could not aim the gun. It was too heavy. It was laying on the door, and I couldn't raise the gun and aim."

"It was an accident," Bobby says, his sigh signifying resignation.

Making a show of disbelief, Evans prompts, "Resting right on the door—and you caught him in the eye?"

Bobby tells the prosecutor he doesn't know exactly how the gun was pointing, in front of him or up or down. He was too scared to take note.

Trying to bring back sanity, Bobby tells Evans, "You can see how heavy the gun is."

As he speaks, Bobby steps down from the witness box and walks straight toward Evans.

Everyone flinches at the abrupt movement. Even the judge is frozen, staring at this man who has stepped, unbidden, from the witness box with the shotgun in his hands.

Bobby strides toward the startled Assistant DA, who pales and steps backward.

"Here," Bobby says, holding out the gun, "Hold it, Mr. Evans. See how heavy it is."

After a moment, Evans takes the gun, telling Bobby to return to the witness stand. The re-enactment of the scene that occurred July 21, 1957, on Bell Avenue has finally ended.

Bobby says he speeds up, realizes Hudson wrecked, and runs the stop sign, heading home. But afraid Hudson will get his car started and come after him, Bobby goes to his friend's house.

Then Bobby tells Evans, "And I look back and I have thought about it a lot. I was under a great deal of pressure. He put me in this position. I didn't ask for this position. I didn't try to get in that position. He was not on my mind. He was the one who pointed the gun at me. He was the one who tried to run me off the road."

Bobby's explanation has irked Evans, whose invectives start again. He lectures Bobby about talking to a preacher because he wanted to be justified in God's sight. He already felt justified under man's law, right?

The litany ends with a rhetorical question. "And Godwin told you that you were forgiven. So, like, go and sin no more?"

"I don't know what you mean." Bobby says, bleary-eyed and bone-weary. "I really don't."

Despite no objection from Phillips or Cook, DiRisio gives Evans a stern look and says, "Let's move along."

I think it's almost over, but Evans revisits the coroner's inquest, asking Bobby about his lawyers being excluded.

And he was excluded, too, Bobby reminds him. County Coroner Doyle Currey ran him out of the room.

And the grand jury—you told this jury no one ever called you about that, right? What would you have told them if you had been called to testify, Evans asks.

Perplexed, Bobby replies, "I guess I would have testified if they brought me before the grand jury."

"So you were just waiting for the opportunity for someone to call you?" Evans demands.

Improper line of questioning, Phillips rises to say.

During a bench conference, Cook warns the judge Evans "is traveling on a very, very, very dangerous avenue."

Cook starts to step back, then leaning toward Evans, hisses, "You are very close to another motion."

"You make all the motions you want, Mr. Cook." Evans fumes. "You are not going to scare me back from what I feel is the proper way to present the case."

DiRisio is lost. What is the question?

The Courtroom as Theater – Part II

Evans says he is going to question Bobby about Heck's call to him at Chattanooga State.

"I have ruled that one out, haven't I?" the judge asks, looking from Evans to Cook.

Bordering on disrespect, Evans replies, "You should have ruled it in at this point."

Tired and perhaps covering his own confusion, the judge suggests a dinner break, but Phillips prefers to skip dinner and finish, so DiRisio agrees to continue. Bobby is visibly relieved; he wants to conclude his testimony before leaving tonight—regardless of the time.

Arguing with DiRisio about Heck's call, Evans loses the battle. The judge is tired, too, and wants the day to end. The question will not be permitted.

Deflated, Evans goes back to his table. After shuffling through a stack of papers, he says, "That's all we have, Your Honor."

Despite hours of endless rhetoric, Evans ends his case abruptly.

It's over. Bobby got through it. He told his story. He was calm and consistent under relentless badgering. After years of harboring his dark secret, he told the world the complete tale of what happened the night he killed Don Hudson.

In Hawthorne's book, Hester Prynne casts away her scarlet letter, only to pick it up and fasten it back on her chest. The red A has become so much a part of her she cannot leave it behind.

After 31 years, I pray that Bobby can leave his K on the courtroom floor. But as Hosea Ballou said, quoting an unknown source, "Conscience not only sits as a witness and judge within our bosoms but also forms the prison of punishment."

If Bobby escapes prison through a not-guilty verdict, only time will tell if he can free himself from the prison he's built in his own mind.

* * *

Later that evening, we are sitting in our usual seats at Shoney's, having dinner and regrouping after Court has adjourned.

Thankfully, the restaurant is almost empty. Regardless, it's a time that cries out for comic relief. Bobby, glad to be through with Evans' cross-examination, settles himself in the booth.

258

A Matter of Conscience

With a smile, he tells Sally one of his favorite books is *O Ye Jigs and Juleps,* originally written in 1904 by a little girl named Virginia who lived in an Episcopal boarding school.

Needing to relieve all the built-up tension from the trial today, Bobby's *O Ye Jigs and Juleps* tales go on and on. Finally, he says little Virginia, worn out with reading about Moses walking 40 years and never getting to his destination, declared: "I sure would have bought myself a mule."

Suddenly somber, Bobby says he felt a bit like old Moses today, wandering alone in a wilderness of endless questions.

NOTE: DiRisio delayed ruling on an out-of-the-courtroom demonstration [in a car similar to the one Bobby was driving the night Hudson was killed] until after Bobby's testimony ended. The ruling prevented Evans' desired demonstration.

Chattanooga News-Free Press photo

Judge DiRisio (L) listening to prosecutor Tom Evans, and defense attorneys Bobby Lee Cook and Leroy Phillips (R) conferring during the 1988 murder trial of Bobby Hoppe in DiRisio's Chattanooga courtroom.

CHAPTER NINETEEN

Covering Bobby's Back

The shifts of Fortune test the reliability of friends.
–Cicero (106 BC – 43 BC)
De Amicitia

His face drawn and pale, Bobby steps from the witness stand, exhausted from more than eight hours of testimony.

The courtroom is oddly quiet—the kind of quiet that sometimes sets in after a summer storm. It's as if everyone, including the judge, needs a break from the tension of the trial.

A palpable relief ricochets around the packed courtroom when the crowd realizes Bobby's character witnesses are up next, witnesses who know the real Bobby, witnesses whose lives have been intertwined with his during happier times.

Bobby flinches as Leroy Phillips prepares to call his character witnesses, aware their testimonies will dredge up old memories, memories of better times, memories sure to make his soul ache when flashed against the screen of this current nightmare.

Phillips pushes back his chair, standing behind the defense table. "Your Honor, I'd like to call William Brown, better known as 'Chink' Brown, to the stand."

Bobby watches as Brown strides to the witness box. An attorney and a circuit judge for Hamilton County, Brown is not intimidated by the courtroom setting. Over the 30 years of their friendship, he says he's never known Bobby to be violent.

After a short exchange in which Brown acknowledges his belief in Bobby, Brown is dismissed. He gives Bobby a small smile as he steps from the stand, but Bobby never sees it. His head is lowered, but he's listening.

It's just that kind words at this moment are harder for Bobby to take than cutting ones.

Sentell Harper is next. For Bobby, the sight of Sentell conjures up their years at Auburn.

Bobby hasn't been good at keeping in touch with his old buddies; he's the first to admit it. Always somewhat of a loner, after the shooting,

Bobby withdrew even more, avoiding people he feared might look differently at him. But not Sentell. Never Sentell.

Sentell, his roommate by chance and friend by choice, accepted the reclusive side of his stoic buddy. After graduation, it was Sentell who was determined to stay in touch, who called Bobby regularly, never talking long, just checking to see how he was doing.

Although Bobby never told his old roommate, he treasured those brief talks. They lifted his spirits. When Bobby said good-bye and put the receiver down, he would sit in silence a while, remembering, a new light in his eyes.

When others were whispering and holding up a finger to test the wind, Sentell called the very first day after the indictment. As always, the call was brief, but what he said was pure gold. "I'll be there, Bobby. You just tell me where and what time."

For the past week, Sentell has deserted his Auburn home to plant himself in Chattanooga, sitting for hours in the witness room, sequestered with others who have arrived from all over to speak in support of Bobby. At times, despite the solemnity in the nearby courtroom, it's been a bit raucous in the witness sequestration area as Sentell and former Auburn assistant coach Buck Bradbury recount tales about Bobby's escapades as a student on the Alabama plains.

But in Court today, the time Phillips keeps him on the stand lasts about as long as his phone calls to Bobby. Phillips establishes Sentell played football with Bobby, they roomed together off and on for four years, and most importantly, Bobby's picture was never posted on any telephone pole or window in Auburn. Bobby was important to the team, Sentell says, but he wasn't *the* star.

Ready for cross-examination, Evans foregoes pleasantries, wanting to know who *was* the star of the Auburn team,

Unperturbed, Sentell cites three Auburn players who, like Bobby, made all SEC: Tommy Lorino, Ben Preston and Red Phillips.

And then, surprisingly, Evans stops dead still and turns to Bobby Lee Cook, asking if Buck Bradbury is available. When Cook says he is, Evans tells DiRisio he's through with Sentell.

Sentell is shocked. As he steps down, everyone in the courtroom looks baffled.

* * *

A Matter of Conscience

Called next by Phillips is David Cook, wearing the dress uniform of the U.S. Army. Solid. Confident. Ready.

Immediately after hearing about the indictment in 1987, Cook wrote Bobby:

> *Coach Hoppe,*
> *A friend in need is a friend indeed. I stand waiting for your call and pledge you my full support. You've had your back against the wall before, so plant your feet and come out fighting. God be with you.*
> *David Cook*

Less than a year later, he takes the stand, eager to fulfill his promise.

Cook is 34, now a resident of Cincinnati, Ohio, where he is on active duty and teaches in the Military Science Department at the University of Cincinnati.

Focusing on the three years he knew Hoppe best—when Bobby was his coach at Chattanooga Valley High School—Phillips asks Cook about Bobby's reputation back then.

Without hesitation, Cook replies, "He has been the type of person students have asked for advice. To me, he has been a father-type image. He's given me a lot of guidance.

"I don't think I would be where I am today if it hadn't have been for the little added push and benefit of counseling I got from him. He constantly talked to me about going to college. I was raised in a family where it just wasn't a big topic. He convinced me I had the capabilities of going to college and of playing ball."

After Cook confirms Hoppe's reputation for truthfulness, Phillips takes his seat at the defense table, and Evans stands and strides toward the young man on the stand.

Evans positions himself directly in front of Cook and, for a moment Cook is perplexed by the vibe emanating from the prosecutor. Then he recalls boot camp, his sergeant saying, "Never let the enemy see you sweat," so he returns Evans' smirk with an assured smile.

Turning his back on Cook, Evans walks toward the jury, ensuring they catch the import of his question. "Obviously, what you are telling the jury is Mr. Hoppe taught you and instilled in you the values of truth, honesty and courage."

Cook, taken aback, replies, "By all means."

Evans pivots toward the witness, his tone hard and flinty. "Did he instill in you, sir, the value of the courage of coming forward when that very courage may result in drastic changes as he is viewed in society and drastic results in his career—dramatic unfavorable results?"

Members of the jury seem surprised by Evans' hostile questioning of the young soldier. All around the room, people grimace as they hear the prosecutor corner Cook, trying to get him to turn on the man he looked on as a father. Standing at his post, the bailiff's face reflects disdain.

Then, with a quick jab at Bobby, using John F. Kennedy's *Profiles in Courage*, it's over.

Abruptly dismissed, Cook shoots a buck-up look toward his former coach as he walks by.

* * *

Captain Cook is frustrated as he leaves the witness stand. What he's been able to say has been limited by the questions put to him.

Before he took the stand, he was determined to tell the jury what he had been telling Sentell and Buck Bradbury in the sequestration room—how Bobby had become so much more than a football star.

"Before Bobby became our coach," David Cook had shared with his fellow witnesses, "Chattanooga Valley had not had a winning season in a long, long time. When he arrived, we were a pretty dispirited group of guys."

One night the team was in the locker room, dressing for a game against a rival that was the strong favorite to win—and win easily. The boys were solemn, dreading the thumping they knew they'd soon get on the field as well as all the ribbing that would follow.

About that time, Cook said, Coach Hoppe walked in. Seeing his team's distress, Hoppe yelled across the locker room, "Cook, do you have insurance?"

Knowing his dad had insurance on him, a shocked Cook replied, "I guess so, Coach."

"Well, you're going to need it tonight. Those guys are so big, they're going to kill you," Bobby said loudly, before turning abruptly and walking out to the football field.

Cook said he responded exactly as Coach expected. I said, "Like hell they will!"

Cook and the other players were so pumped-up they hit the field with renewed resolve, played with wild ferocity, and trounced the other team.

* * *

David Cook's testimony takes Bobby back more than 15 years—to a time filled with as much joy as he had ever known. The days at Chattanooga Valley brought such change into his life—marriage to Sherry, the adoption of Kevin, and a career where he felt he was following in the steps of the coaches who had made such a difference in his life.

Compared to the sprawling Central High School where Bobby Hoppe reigned as king of football from 1951 to 1954, Chattanooga Valley High was a small school snuggled into the northeast corner of Georgia, five miles south of Chattanooga. Built at the base of Lookout Mountain, the rural school had fewer than 500 students in the early 1970s when Bobby accepted a position to coach and teach there.

Arriving mid-year after all classrooms had been assigned, Bobby would be a "floater," teaching in classrooms not in use during other teachers' free periods.

On the first day at school following the holidays, I returned to my classroom after grading papers in the teachers' lounge to discover Mr. Hoppe behind my desk, gathering up papers and books. What I had heard was accurate; he was handsome—sculpted cheekbones, a solid torso.

As I approached, I noticed he was not smiling. I started to welcome him, but he cut me off. "Ms. Howard, if we're going to share a classroom, I expect the student chairs to be arranged in neat rows, eight to a row, and the chalkboard should be erased thoroughly."

He turned and walked out the door, leaving me with my mouth hanging open. Maybe Mr. Hoppe had a rough first day, I thought. Coming into a new school mid-year was difficult.

The next day after my free period, he was there again. I'd be darned if I'd wait in the hall. Determined to have a civil exchange, I strode into the room, a smile plastered on my face. He was deep in concentration, head lowered.

265

"Good afternoon, Mr. Hoppe," I began. "I hope you're enjoying Chattanooga Valley..."

"I am," he said. Without raising his head, he continued, "But would you remember to have your students align their chairs before they leave? And maybe someone could erase the board."

My cheeks flamed. "Mr. Hoppe, surely..." I began. Then he looked up and I saw his eyes—the bluest blue I'd ever seen. And they were twinkling. He broke into a mischievous grin.

He was pulling my leg. I could not believe I had fallen for it.

"Mr. Hoppe, I'll leave you the straightest lines of chairs you've ever seen," I said, trying to sound serious. "Because, beyond a doubt, learning should always take a back seat—pun intended—to orderliness."

Then he laughed—a great-big, no-nonsense masculine laugh.

"We're going to get along just fine, Ms. Howard," he said, as he walked from the room, leaving me flushed, a bevy of butterflies dancing in my stomach.

A couple of weeks later, Coach Paul Chambers and his wife Pat invited me to a dinner party at their house. When I arrived, Bobby was there—standing toward the back of the room, smiling directly at me. We walked toward each other, drawn like magnet to metal. If this was a "fix-up" by the Chambers, it worked. We were married just over a year later.

The years ahead were peaceful, filled with the joy of teaching and coaching. But even during the best of times, it were as if Bobby's past— his championship days and the tragedy that colored the rest of his life— had been packed in a suitcase of sorts—one he could never put down, one that always traveled with him. Even before he arrived at Chattanooga Valley, rumors preceded him.

One football player recalled, "When it got around school that Bobby Hoppe was coming to coach, some of the kids said, 'Don't make him mad—he's been accused of killing a man.'"

Even when it seemed Bobby might be able to start a new life, he discovered he'd dragged that suitcase with him. No one ever said anything to him about the shooting, but everyone knew.

CHAPTER TWENTY

A Man of Many Faces

In prosperity our friends know us; In adversity, we know our friends.
–John Churton Collins

Leroy Phillips calls Huette Roberson to the stand, who with her husband of 29 years, lived next door to the Hoppes for eight and half years—from 1977 to 1986.

"Were you aware Hoppe's son was adopted?" Phillips asks after preliminary questions.

Behind her glasses, Huette's eyes light up. "Yes sir. I knew about him being adopted when he was eight years old. Sherry was trying to find a home for him after his parents died.

"Nobody would take the child. Bobby asked Sherry why they couldn't take him, so they adopted him."

Evans quickly objects as to the relevance.

"Sustained," says DiRisio.

With a slight smile, Phillips dismisses Huette from the stand.

A line of character witnesses follow, including former neighbor Johnny Calloway and Donald Ray Stafford, whose son Bobby coached.

Next, Dr. James Dabney Curtis, rector of Grace Episcopal Church in Chattanooga, takes the stand. Testifying to Bobby's veracity, his time in the witness box is brief. As he walks past Bobby, he touches his parishioner's right shoulder. But Bobby jumps, feeling the brush of angels' wings.

Then Buck Bradbury, abruptly dismissed when he took the stand two days ago, is recalled.

Evans has anticipated this moment. He has a question for Bradbury that should knock the glow off Bobby.

But he's waited all day, so he'll hold up a few more minutes to allow time to get in one more jab about Bobby going on with his illustrious football career after killing Hudson.

Bradbury digs in his heels, refusing to be goaded into saying something he doesn't want to say. He lets Evans know, as far as he's concerned, Bobby's record at Auburn came, not after murdering a man, but after defending his life.

Seeing he's going nowhere, Evans takes a detour, hoping to solidify his portrait of Bobby as a violent man. Evans reminds Bradbury he had described Bobby as a shy, quiet man. As if knowing what's coming, Bradbury adds that Bobby also was sometimes a jokester.

For Evans, it's time for *coup d'etat*. He wants to know if Bradbury recalls reading in the August 1958 *Sports Illustrated* that Red Phillips said Bobby once shot out the study light in Red's room and then appeared at his door, smiling brightly?

When Bradbury says he doesn't recall, Evans goes off, declaring Bradbury, an Auburn coach, surely heard about Red Phillips' story. Surely, the tale about a gun-toting Auburn football player would have made the rounds down there.

Sorry. Bradbury says, unruffled, I've never read *Sports Illustrated*. It wasn't a magazine he read regularly. And, as far as he knew, the story was never in any newspaper.

Evans tries another tactic, asking if he ever heard Bobby was prone to prowl at night.

After Bradbury avows he has never heard such stories, Evans insists he must at least know Bobby and Red roomed together. But, shaking his head, Bradbury declares after 31 years he can't even remember that. Bradbury points out that Coach Gene Lorendo was the resident counselor with the players—and, sure, they may have cut up sometimes. And sometimes they had BB guns.

Looking askance at Evans, Bradbury turns the tables, asking the prosecutor, "Have you ever been on a college campus yourself?"

Infuriated, Evans pushes harder, saying Bradbury must have heard how Bobby tacked a picture of a Communist soldier on the wall and ventilated it with his pistol. That wouldn't be a practical joke, would it?

Bradbury doesn't budge. He had heard about the boys shooting BB guns, but "I darn sure didn't hear about any pistol."

Exasperated, Evans turns him over to Phillips, who establishes that although Red Phillips was a great kid to coach, he was a bit odd and, to be honest, was sometimes the brunt of jokes.

And, Bradbury tells Phillips, he had heard some of what happened, but "not with a damn pistol, pardon my French."

A Matter of Conscience

During the 1950s, Auburn's football team lived in a village of small cottages surrounding a campus amphitheater, six guys to a cottage, three players on each side. With Coach Lorendo and his wife overseeing the cottages, there's no way playing around with a loaded pistol would have been tolerated, Bradbury insists.

Phillips feels confident he has blunted Evans' allegation of Bobby's running around campus with a pistol, but he isn't taking any chances. So, as Bradbury steps down, he asks Sentell Harper to take the stand again.

Sentell confirms what Bradbury said—Red Phillips was not the typical fun-loving jock.

As for Bobby or any player firing a gun in the cabins, Sentell says anyone who knew Gene Lorendo would confirm such antics would never have been tolerated.

And the Russian soldier? Well, Sentell reminds Evans, this was during the Cold War—America hated the Russians. And for the guys, it was like throwing darts. Lying in their beds, lined up along one wall, several players—not just Bobby—would fire BB guns at the picture.

Hell, he did it himself, Sentell says. And, no, he never saw Bobby Hoppe with a real gun on campus or anywhere else.

Evans, realizing neither Sentell nor Bradbury will ever say Bobby had a pistol, tries one more angle. He strides toward Sentell. Then, as if forgetting something, he turns and walks back to the prosecutor's table. Picking up a copy of *Sports Illustrated*, Evans reads to Sentell:

"I remember I was studying in our room one night. Hoppe was out somewhere prowling around—he was like that. You never knew where he was. I am reading and everything is quiet, and all of a sudden here is this explosion and the light goes out as glass flies all over the room. It took me a few seconds to realize someone had fired a shot through the window and hit the lamp. I don't mind telling you I was scared. Suddenly, the door flew open and someone stepped in, tripped on the overhead light. It was Hoppe—he was leaning against the doorframe with a gun in his hand, sort of smiling. I knew right then I never played with anybody like that in high school."

After he finishes the paragraph, Evans shuts the magazine and, smiling at Sentell, smacks it against the table.

Believing he's finally gotten the "real" story on the record, Evans pauses for effect as he eyes the jury. Turning to Sentell, he asks if Bobby's actions were his idea of a practical joke.

269

Never happened, Sentell says simply.

But there's more, Evans says as he opens the magazine and starts to read again.

"One night [Bobby] walks in the room with a big picture of a Russian soldier he got out of *Life Magazine*. Pinned it on the wall and said to me, 'That there is a Russian Communist soldier, Red. I hate the dirty bastards, Red. Know what I'm going to do, Red?'

"I told him I guess I didn't know, and I waited to see what he was up to. I just walked over to his bunk and sat on it staring at the picture on the wall. I kept watching him trying to figure out what he was going to do. He must have stared there at that picture for ten minutes, just sitting there, staring. All of a sudden he pulls out his gun and empties it at that picture."

When Sentell tries to respond, Evans cuts him off, bringing objections from both Cook and Phillips. Evans, seeming shocked, spins to look at the two attorneys. But what Sentell Harper is saying, Evans submits, doesn't sound like an answer.

That's because the answer is just not the one you want to hear, Phillips tells Evans curtly.

Sentell butts in, saying the first mistake Red made was saying the picture was put up at night. It was the middle of the day. And no one ever used live ammunition to shoot at the picture. No real gun. No real bullets. Just BBs—and Bobby wasn't the only one having a little fun.

Evans, turning again to the jurors, starts to make a retort but sees the smothered grins on several faces. A lost cause, he thinks, and sits down.

After chuckling, Cook grows serious, telling the judge he has an obligation to instruct the jury Evans' reading from *Sports Illustrated* "does not and would not constitute any substantive evidence...."

Before DiRisio can ask for the basis of his request, Cook spouts out that his authority is the case of Sims versus the State, a Tennessee Supreme Court decision (746 S.W.2nd 194).

DiRisio asks to see the citation; and, after a quick review, he agrees to instruct the jury using language from the case. He tells them just because *Sports Illustrated* quoted something Red Phillips allegedly said doesn't mean the incident happened that way.

Despite DiRisio's caution to the jury, Cook fears Evans may have succeeded in flinging that damned skunk again.

A Matter of Conscience

* * *

Only hours after Evans questioned Bradberry and Harper about the alleged gun incident, Red Phillips told *Chattanooga Times* reporter Larry Fleming, "'That may have sounded good back then in telling it, but you know, whether that really happened or not, I just don't remember.'"

Recalling he was naïve when he talked to "'this big-time guy [reporter] from New York,' Red added, "'whether I told him that or he picked it up from someone else, I don't know. . . I felt like he (reporter) came down here to find something dirty on Auburn. He didn't do that. He had to make his story seem good.'"

Fleming noted that "[Red] Phillips now hedges on the factual nature of the story," saying he never actually saw Bobby with a pistol.

Red also put a different twist on Heck's testimony: "'In looking back, that detective [Chattanooga police detective Richard Heck] came down here to talk to me, and, you know, I tried to remember. I told him about rumors I had heard after I left Auburn...I know that *Sports Illustrated* guy put a bunch of junk in there.'"

* * *

Heck, having watched his case unravel with testimonies that didn't withstand the scrutiny of the defense, reluctantly makes his way back to the stand. He went through a grueling cross-examination days ago, so he knows he may be in for tough questioning.

Back in 1987, Heck had advised the elderly Hudson he would need more than a gut feeling before he could "drag this man, Hoppe, into the media."

Evans' fury propels him out of his chair. How dare Phillips get the statement on the record! Heck wasn't saying he had a weak case or needed more evidence to prosecute.

Oh, but he was, Phillips counters. And that's beside the point. His point is Heck didn't say he needed more evidence before he could bring Bobby to justice. Heck's interest was publicity. And that, Phillips states, goes to Heck's bias as to how he approached the case.

His point made, Phillips moves on to the cartridges Evans gave Bobby to load during the demonstration. The shells were spent, weren't they? And spent shells swell from the heat, right?

Heck just doesn't know. He's no expert on shells, he tells Phillips. Eyebrows shoot up—from lawyers in the back of the room to the jurors in the front. Here's a police detective who doesn't know a spent shell swells. Hard to force a spent shell in the gun, one attorney whispers to another.

Before Phillips finishes with Heck, he wants to know if the detective tried to ascertain from Richard Holland where Hudson was the day and night before he was killed.

Objection, Evans jumps up to shout, provoking a heated discussion between the defense and the prosecution.

Cook declares he finds Evans' continually popping out of his chair like a damn jack-in-the box irritating and intimidating.

Evans fires back, implying it's impossible to intimidate Leroy Phillips. DiRisio, tired of the bickering, instructs Evans to stay in his chair and then sustains his objection.

Phillips moves quickly, asking if Heck ever interviewed people who lived on Manyon Street. When Heck says he didn't, Phillips tries again. Is Heck familiar with a Ms. Gladys Hollums or a Mrs. Homer Hollums? Heck knows the name, knows she lived near White Oak, but can't recall the street.

That's all Phillips needed, Heck's admission he knows the Hollums' name. He's ready for his next witness, Evelyn Diane Hollums Shirley.

CHAPTER TWENTY-ONE

The Surprise Witness

"Courage is being scared to death, but saddling up anyway."
–John Wayne (1907-1979)

After a long day on her feet at the International House of Pancakes on Brainerd Road, Diane Shirley is happy to be home.

Being a waitress is hard work. In the small front room of her house, she plops down on a well-worn, brown faux-leather recliner, slips off her shoes, and picks up today's newspaper.

Since she knew Don Hudson back in the 1950s, she's been following the Hoppe trial. As she reads about today's testimonies, especially Odene Neal's, her eyes widen in surprise and a surge of adrenalin pumps through her weary body. She lowers the paper to her lap and stares out the window—not seeing the house next door. Instead, in her mind's eye, she sees her mother's house the night Hudson was killed.

Later, in bed she tosses and turns, flipping her pillow from one side to the other, trying to forget what she read in the paper, telling herself it's none of her business. But Odene's words keep rattling around in her head.

According to the article, Odene said Bobby Hoppe threatened to kill Don Hudson the night Hudson was shot. Over and over in her mind, she replays what she heard at her mother's house that same night. To her, it's as if it were yesterday.

Finally, a bit before dawn, she must have dozed off, because now she's jolted awake by the irritating buzz of her alarm. It's 4 a.m. and, despite lack of sleep, she has to be at work by 5. Trying to dress quickly, her tired body won't cooperate. It's as if she's moving in slow motion.

Across town, Bobby is awake, staring at the bedroom ceiling. After dozing fitfully most of the night, by 4 a.m. sleep is long gone. Lying in the dark, he dreads the day ahead in Court. He tries to picture the jurors— one by one—wondering if they believed what he said happened between him and Hudson 31 years ago.

The Surprise Witness

He has no inkling a total stranger in nearby Hixson has information that could affect how jurors perceive his words about self-defense.

It's a long drive from Hixson to Brainerd, where Diane works, so she knows she must hurry to be on time. But she can't seem to focus. Even as she is steering through early-morning traffic, she thinks about what was said at the trial yesterday.

Usually Diane is good at remembering who ordered what, but today she makes one mistake after another until, finally, her boss asks if anything is wrong. But she doesn't want to talk; she wants to think. Leaning over to wipe a table with a damp cloth, she tells him she's just not feeling well. Nothing catching.

Actually, she has the newspaper article in her pocket—and she keeps slipping into the restroom to reread it. When she gets a break between breakfast and lunch, she tells a couple of co-workers about her dilemma. They both caution her "she ought not get mixed up in it."

Maybe they're right, but....

That night, bone weary from almost no sleep the night before, she pulls out the folded article again. As she scans the times Odene changed her story, Diane wonders if Odene made up the entire episode about Bobby being at her house, threatening to kill Hudson. But why?

Diane's own memory of what happened is as clear as a bell, so why did Odene have such trouble remembering whether she worked that night, whether Bobby mentioned a shotgun or a gun, whether Jody was in the room? It just doesn't make sense.

Odene's testimony plays in her head like a broken record. She's thought about it all day. But who is she to get involved? Why would anyone believe her? It doesn't matter. She knows something critical to this case. And, even though she doesn't know Bobby personally, she cannot let it go. If she said nothing, she would never be able to live with her conscience.

That night, her decision made, she falls asleep immediately. While still in a deep sleep, something wiggles to the surface of her mind and, like a bolt of lightning, she sits straight up in bed, eyes wide open in the dark.

"What if they ask me to testify?" she thinks. She feels her face grow hot, sweat trickling between her breasts. "I can't do it; I cannot stand in front of everybody and talk. No way."

274

A Matter of Conscience

She swings her legs off the bed and looks at the clock. It's a bit after 2. For the rest of the night, she paces the floor between the bedroom and bathroom and kitchen, arguing with herself.

Again, across town, Bobby's sleeplessness parallels that of Diane Shirley. While she paces in her house in Hixson, he tosses and turns in his bed in East Brainerd. In his mind, he goes over Odene's testimony. If jurors believe her story—that he stopped by her house that night and threatened to kill Hudson—he could be convicted. In the end, it's just his word against hers.

By the time the sun peeps through her kitchen window, Diane is at peace with her decision: She'll call Mr. Phillips as soon as she gets to work—before she loses her courage.

Like Diane Shirley and Bobby, Phillips has slept poorly the past few nights. After days of intense courtroom arguments, the trial is winding down. Despite the case of self-defense laid out by Bobby Lee Cook and him, Phillips shares Bobby's concern some jurors might believe Odene.

He's fairly confident Cook has unveiled her contradictions, but he can't be sure. Godwin doesn't concern him much. The holes in his testimony were gaping. But Phillips has to admit, on the witness stand, Odene did better at trial than in the preliminary hearing, so he quietly frets.

Around 5:30 a.m., sleep that has been eluding him for hours descends, wiping away his worries. Just as he settles into a deep sleep, a loud ringing jolts him awake.

"What the hell," he mutters, struggling to sit up in bed. It's the phone on his bedside table. He grabs it, answering with a gruff, "Hello?"

The illuminated face of the clock shows it is 6:30 a.m. Damn it, he's only been asleep an hour or so. Straining to hear, he wants to tell the early-bird caller—since she's awakened him at this ungodly hour—to speak up. Before he gets the words out, the timid voice says something about not believing what Odene said at the trial.

The woman at the other end of line has his attention now.

"Who is this?" Phillips asks. Her next words really startle him. He swings his legs off the side of the bed and stands up, fully awake, listening intently.

The Surprise Witness

"I read Mr. Hoppe was supposed to be threatening Don, but Don was threatening him to me," Diane says, her conviction overriding her natural shyness.

Phillips tunes out everything but her softly spoken words. When she's finished, he asks several questions, growing increasingly excited as she goes, point by point, through what she heard first hand on the night Hudson was killed.

* * *

Leroy calls early, but I'm already up, sipping coffee, so I answer the phone, hoping it didn't awaken Bobby. On the other end, I hear Leroy. He can barely contain his excitement as he tells me about Diane Shirley. I ask him to hold on a moment while I get Bobby on the line.

Although he's awake, Bobby is still curled on his side in bed, his blue eyes ringed with dark circles. I push the phone into his hand. "It's Leroy!"

I've begun crying quietly. My tears scare Bobby, but I mouth, "It's good news," and rush back to the kitchen phone. We both listen carefully, feeling the stirrings of an optimism we haven't felt since the trial began.

* * *

Arriving in Court on the day of Diane Shirley's testimony, we have a spring in our step for the first time in weeks, maybe months.

Evans, laden down with files, has arrived early and is seated at the prosecution table. Phillips, obligated to tell him about the surprise witness, walks to the assistant DA. As he listens, a shadow passes over Evans' face. His stands immediately to complain to the judge: How dare the defense spring something like this? He could care less that Phillips just learned about it.

Evans was expecting to rest his case this morning, but this new witness turns everything upside down. His closing argument practiced and ready, he doesn't want to have to deal with any new testimony.

To Evans' dismay, DiRisio rules the witness can be heard. Like a knight riding to the rescue, Evelyn Diane Hollums Shirley will be allowed to challenge Odene's story.

An unlikely heroine, Diane is a quiet-spoken woman. Although neatly dressed in a dark skirt and crisp white blouse, she's not polished, not well versed in the law, and definitely not a publicity hound.

276

Deciding to come forward, to step into the glare of the media spotlight, has not been easy. Besides her discomfort in just being within a courtroom, she's sick today, wracked by a nagging cold and a sore, scratchy throat that hurts so badly, Phillips asks her to speak up several times.

She tells the Court, when she was first married, her parents, the late Gladys and Homer Hollums, resided on Merriman Street in North Chattanooga.

"Did you know one Mr. [Richard] Holland who has testified in this case," Phillips asks.

She says she did.

"And did you know one Don Hudson who is the deceased involved in this case?"

"Yes, sir," she replies, making a conscious effort to speak loudly so she can be heard.

Phillips asks her if by chance she saw Don Hudson on the night he was killed.

"Yes, sir."

In response to the next question, she says she also saw Mr. Holland that night. In fact, Holland was dating her sister Rita back then, she adds.

"And on the evening we are talking about, where did you see Mr. Holland and Mr. Hudson?" Phillips asks.

"At my..." She clears her throat and begins again. "At my mother's house on Merriman Street."

"All right," Phillips says, before confirming she did not live with her mother at that time.

She was married and had a baby boy—about eight months old then.

Continuing, Phillips asks, "And did you have an occasion to be over at your mother's house on two occasions that evening?"

"Yes, sir."

The first occasion, she says, was when she took her baby over around 6:30 for her mother to keep while she and her husband went to a movie. Her husband was not with her when she dropped the child off.

"On that occasion, did you see Mr. Hudson?" Phillips asks.

"Yes, sir."

The Surprise Witness

Hudson was still there after the movie when she and her husband returned to retrieve their little boy, she answers in response to another question from Phillips. She says she doesn't know if he left during the intervening hours, but he was there when they picked up the baby between 12:15 and 12:30.

Phillips makes a half turn toward the jury then turns back, directing his question at the witness. "What was the relationship between Mr. Hudson and your mother? That is, how well did they know one another or how long did they know one another?"

They had known each other several years, she says. And for the last few months, Hudson had been accompanying Holland quite often when he dropped by to see her sister Rita.

Phillips turns and walks slowly toward the jury. "That evening, when you got back from the movie, did you hear Mr. Hudson make any remarks with regard to Bobby Hoppe? If so, what were they? Tell the jury."

Phillips watches their faces as they listen to Diane's answer: "Well, he said he would get him. One way or the other, he would get him."

"Who is *he* now," Phillips prods. "Who is speaking? Who is telling you?"

"Don was," she replies, a bit perplexed.

Phillips prompts, "[Hudson] would get who when he said *him*?"

"Mr. Hoppe," Diane answers, shifting slightly in the hard seat. "And he said Bobby Hoppe better be glad he could play football, because that was about all he could do, that he was a goody-two-shoes."

Upset over his split with Joan, Hudson said he would get that goody-two-shoes, she adds.

In his *News Free-Press* article, "Surprise Witness Tells of Hudson Threat on Hoppe," John Wilson quoted Diane as saying Hudson's buddy, Richard Holland, tried to tell Hudson the break-up was "not really anyone's fault."

But Hudson didn't care who was at fault.

According to Diane, during Hudson's tirade at the Hollums' home on Merriman Street, Holland told him Joan wanted to be with someone with lots of money—and Don didn't have enough money to suit her.

With a show of incredulity, Phillips asks, "Did Holland say that to Hudson?"

"Yes, sir."

"All right," Phillips says. "On that evening, ma'am, did Mr. Hudson have a gun?"

"Yes, sir." Whenever she saw Hudson, he usually was toting. She adds she specifically recalls Hudson had a gun the evening he was killed.

When she got to her mother's house with the baby, she learned her mother was out of milk. Before she could run to the grocery to get milk for the baby, Hudson stood, saying he needed beer—so he would pick up some milk, too.

"He made sure he got his gun before he left," Diane states.

When Phillips asks if the police questioned her mother right after the killing, she says she thinks so but notes they never talked to her.

Phillips pauses to let the jury focus on what's coming next. "Now, ma'am, when did you contact me as the lawyer in this case?"

"I think it was about six o'clock Tuesday morning."

Could it have been Wednesday instead of Tuesday, Phillips wants to know.

"Yes," she replies, saying she carried Phillips' phone number around all day, in a quandary about what she should do.

Looking at Phillips, she explains, "I just didn't want to get mixed up in it, you know, so I didn't call that day. I called you the morning I read the testimony in the paper that Mr. Hoppe was supposed to have threatened Don."

With resolve strengthening her voice, she adds, "And that wasn't right...Don was threatening Bobby Hoppe to me."

Stepping back from the witness stand, Phillips asks if she read in the newspaper about Odene Neal's testimony—about Odene's saying Hoppe told her he was going to kill Hudson.

Yes, that's where she learned about it, Diane replies.

"That's why I called you finally," she says. Then, blushing slightly, she adds, "I think I woke you up because you got kind of mad."

"Like 6:30 in the morning, was it not?" Phillips asks.

"Yes, sir, because I got to work at 5:30."

She confirms, during that early-morning phone call, she told Phillips all she knew about the matter. Phillips thanks her and takes his seat next to Bobby at the defense table.

Bobby looks up at Diane, sitting there quietly, waiting to be cross-examined. Bobby flinches for her, knowing Evans will be in full attack mode. She just decimated Odene's testimony—Evans' one link to premeditation.

As if summoned by Bobby's thoughts, Evans rises from his chair, straightens his cobalt-blue tie and walks slowly toward the witness, reorganizing his thoughts. He isn't prepared to deal with the scene painted by Diane Shirley. All he can do is to attack her credibility.

He goes back over part of her testimony, asking her to confirm her call to Phillips was in response to reading about Odene's testimony that Hoppe killed Hudson.

"Yes," she replies clearly.

Evans leans closer, demanding to know if she tried to call the Office of the District Attorney.

No, she did not call the DA, she tells him.

Evans asks her again if she heard Hudson's threats when she returned to her mother's home about 12:30 p.m. on July 20. But he may have opened a door he wishes he hadn't.

"Even before, when I first took my little boy over there—he was talking like that," Diane replies, adding that Hudson also was laughing about some hijacked liquor.

No more questions for this witness. Evans turns her back over to Phillips for redirect—which is short and sweet.

Phillips quickly confirms Diane read about Odene's testimony in the newspaper, searched out his telephone number in the directory, and carried it around with her for a long while before getting up the courage to call.

During Evans' re-cross-examination, Diane is more explicit, saying she read the newspaper account twice but initially didn't call Phillips because everybody told her to not get involved.

"But," she says, squaring her chin, "I just felt like I ought to tell it, because it wasn't the way Hudson told me at all."

Evans taunts her for not calling the DA or Richard Heck, the investigator.

As innocent as a babe, she looks straight at Evans. "I didn't think about calling ya'll."

The defense rests. And perhaps the tide is turning.

Former Auburn coach Buck Bradberry (L), Diane Shirley, and
Father Jim Curtis (R) outside the Chattanooga courtroom before their
testimonies in support of Bobby Hoppe in 1988

CHAPTER TWENTY-TWO

It's Not Over 'Til the Fat Lady Sings

*The character of every act depends upon the circumstances
in which it is done.*
--Oliver Wendell Holmes Jr. (1841 - 1935)

Bobby heaves a sigh of relief, thankful the trial ended with testimony that could eradicate any remaining question in jurors' minds regarding Odene.

The jury was left with Diane Shirley's testimony, given with no ulterior motive.

Just as Bobby starts to relax a bit, he learns it's not over. Evans wants to call two rebuttal witnesses. Virgil Burnette is up first, but before he takes the stand, Evans wants to make sure the defense follows the rule of the State of Tennessee in bringing up past convictions. He insists questions be limited to Burnette's previous possession of marijuana with intent to sell or deliver—a felony. Although Burnette received a two-to-five-year sentence, he served no time. The felony had been reduced to a misdemeanor, and he was placed on five years of probation.

Also assuming the trial was over except for closing statements, Cook is aggravated Evans seems unwilling to conclude his case. Cook assures the Court he is familiar with the rule, and he has no plans to impeach Burnette for a misdemeanor. Instead, he says with a wink, he'll impeach him as a drug dealer. He's already X-rayed Burnette's past and he's ready, he informs Evans.

Later, returning from lunch, Bobby, Sally and I step into a waiting elevator. Juror Marjorie Simpkins is near the back. Today, as we have done throughout the trial when we run into jurors on the elevator, we greet her with a simple, "hello." Other jurors always responded in kind but, to our surprise, Ms. Simpkins spins around and faces the wall.

We glance at each other, perplexed, hoping it doesn't mean what we think. More than 20 years later, Sally Weaver still remembers the hostility emanating from Ms. Simpkins. From the first day of *voir dire*, this was the one juror Sally and I perceived to be against Bobby.

The chance meeting in the elevator reinforces our fears. As I stand quietly, waiting for the door to slide shut, watching this woman's rigid back, a tremor runs through my body. Her mind is made up, I think, and it's not good for us.

As soon as Burnette takes the stand, Evans establishes he was once married to one of Don Hudson's sisters, Sue. But that's not what Evans wants to discuss—he wants to know about Burnette's relationship with Billy Joe King. It seems Burnette and Billy Joe had worked together twice—once at an insurance agency and later at a mobile home sales lot owned by Billy Joe.

After work at night, Burnette says, he and Billy Joe used to uncork a liquor bottle and sit around the sales lot, drinking and talking. On more than one occasion, Burnette informs the Court, Billy Joe talked about a murder, bragging he was the "wheelman...driving the car the night Don Hudson got his brains blowed out."

Cook would bet a week's wages Burnette is fabricating this story to pay off an old debt to the DA. So since Burnette talked with Heck on May 30, 1988, Cook wants to see a copy of the interview notes or transcript. Cook isn't surprised to learn Heck didn't take any notes.

Exasperated by Evans and infuriated Heck allegedly didn't record anything during that interview, Cook pounces on Burnette, asking if the State's attorney revealed all of his criminal record. That brings Evans to his feet with an objection, but the judge overrules him.

Evans breathes a sigh when Burnette says the prosecutor did indeed bring out his full criminal record. But Evans' relief withers when Cook begins rattling off a list of people, asking Burnette if he knows them.

Burnette acknowledges he knows them all. Quickly, Cook establishes, besides the one admitted felony conviction, Burnette was indicted the previous year for felonious possession of marijuana—along with the three aforementioned gentlemen. And Cook provides evidence the indictment was dismissed by the State. Cook heats up the interrogation, asking if Burnette was ever convicted of a cocaine possession. Burnette is forced to admit he pled guilty to the charge, exploding his contention of only one conviction.

Burnette was sentenced to "not less than two years nor more than five years" for possessing methaqualone (Qualudes) with intent to sell or deliver, but he served only 35 days at the Silverdale Work House. "Isn't that right?" Cook asks.

Appearing to be indignant, Burnette declares he has never been a drug dealer.

Leaning closer, Cook hisses, "What were you going to do with it? Were you going to put it on the streets, sell it to children or peddle it on Market and Broad? Look the jury in the eye and tell them what you were going to do with it, Mr. Burnette. You were going to corrupt the community, weren't you, if you could, for a profit?"

Evans objects, but even after the judge tells him to avoid comments, Cook goes off again. "What were you going to do with it? Were you going to sell it...put it at Central High or would it have made any difference as long as you could get the profit?

"And the truth of the matter is, in addition to being a drug peddler, you were a flimflam artist in flimflamming and conning other drug dealers, weren't you? You know what I'm talking about, don't you Mr. Burnette?" Cook roars at the increasingly pale witness.

When Burnette whispers, "Yes," Evans drops his head.

"And you are a thief, too, aren't you?" Cook demands. "That's the story of your life, isn't it, Mr. Burnette?"

Burnette admits Cook is right, so Cook pushes on, asserting Burnette lied because he owes the DA for past favors, and it's likely he's hoping for more in the future; probation on a two-to-five-year sentence and thirty-five days in the county workhouse after receiving a firm prison sentence of not less than five years.

In an ideal justice system, Evans would not put a witness on the stand if he felt the witness was likely to perjure himself. But, echoing the witnesses testifying against Jeris Bragan, motivation seemed to link Burnette back to the Office of the District Attorney.

Deflated, Evans moves to his next witness, whom he hopes can resuscitate Odene's credibility. Richard Holland is called back to the stand.

Almost immediately, Evans gets Holland to say he saw Don Hudson at Rita Hollums' house the night he was killed. But Holland says he didn't hear Hudson threaten Bobby. He would have remembered, because Hudson was a friend and "that is a pretty serious threat."

That's it for Evans. But Phillips isn't ready to cross-examine, complaining to the judge he just received a copy of Holland's interview with Heck and he needs time to read it. Even though the interview is lengthy, DiRisio indicates Phillips can read it while Holland answers questions.

Despite this disadvantage, Phillips gets Holland to admit he doesn't recall whether Rita Hollums Shirley was at her mother's house while he and Hudson were there.

Then Phillips throws a zinger. From a piece of paper Cook hands him, he reads from a February 1988 interview between Heck and Holland in which Holland says he wasn't even with Hudson on the night of July 20.

Today, Holland just said he was at the Hollums' house with Hudson the night he was killed. A few months ago, he said he wasn't with Hudson that night. But it gets worse. Holland declares Hudson not only didn't have a gun on him the night he was killed, he never carried one.

Flabbergasted, Phillips asks, "Oh, he never carried one?"

"Not that I saw, no, sir." Holland responds, ducking his head.

But, Phillips insists, Don had a reputation for caring a gun, didn't he?

"He might have, but he didn't because he was afraid to."

Ripples of laughter begin before the judge pounds his gavel.

As Cook would say in an interview twenty years later, "Anytime you are trying a case and are given the opportunity to discredit a State witness, it poisons the case."

And, according to Cook, Holland was a hearty dose of arsenic.

CHAPTER TWENTY-THREE

Winding Down

Fairness is what justice really is.
--Associate Justice Potter Stewart
United States Supreme Court

More than two weeks ago, the defense made a motion to dismiss the case based on pre-trial delay or pre-indictment delay. At the time, DiRisio indicated he would preserve the motion until all evidence had been presented and then decide whether delay had caused substantial damage to Bobby's ability to defend himself.

Now, with the jury out of the room, the arguments on the motion begin. Bobby holds little hope DiRisio will rule favorably, but he listens closely as Phillips lays out the reasons the judge should dismiss the case.

Deceased and incapacitated witnesses who could corroborate Bobby's story, McCutcheon, Wild, and Friedman, as well as Diane Shirley's mother and sister, who were present when Hudson said he was going to kill Bobby.

And there are those witnesses whose memories are dulled by the passage of time, including Bobby, who can't recall the precise location of the gun and shells in his car.

Many records and important government investigative files "have been scattered, lost and/or destroyed," including inquest and grand jury records.

And the list goes on and on. Thirty-one years is a long time. Seven U.S. presidents served during that time. The Vietnam War claimed more than 58,000 American lives. The Civil Rights Amendment passed. The Russians launched Sputnik, and America's Neil Armstrong walked on the moon. Life has become hectic, complicated. The world has changed dramatically.

Bobby's lawyers said, after the preliminary hearing, the evidence the State planned to produce at trial was no different from what it could have used years ago. And today, they cite a case in which a federal judge dismissed an indictment brought 20 months after the crime, citing "reckless disregard" for the defendant's ability to mount an effective defense.

While acknowledging there is no statute of limitations for first-degree murder charges, defense attorneys say the long delay clearly violated Hoppe's right to due process of law as guaranteed by the Fifth and Fourteenth amendments to the U.S. Constitution.

Moreover, Cook and Phillips add, "No case in the entire history of the United States has been found where the courts have permitted a prosecution involving a pre-indictment delay of over 30 years." Such delay is inordinate, unreasonable, and unjustified, they add.

To DiRisio, none of it matters. He says the State could not have indicted Bobby earlier because, for 30 years, they had no substantial evidence he was the killer. The first time they had such evidence, he says, was when Bobby pleaded self-defense. He makes no mention of Godwin's tape being heard by the grand jury in 1966.

In DiRisio's mind, if the issue had remained who, in fact, did the shooting, he might be able to rule in the defense's favor.

My spirits sink with DiRisio's proclamation. The judge appears to be saying if Bobby had not taken the stand—if he hadn't admitted killing Hudson in self-defense—DiRisio might find the delay prejudiced the case. The thought leaves a bitter aftertaste, like rancid wine, in my mind.

And, the judge declares, since the State was unaware Bobby would plead self-defense, the prosecutor didn't know what witnesses would be needed and what evidence should be preserved. So, in layman's terms, the State can't be blamed for not bringing Bobby to trial because he didn't tell them earlier he killed Hudson.

I bite my lip to keep from gasping. DiRisio's statements are the most convoluted logic I've ever heard.

He admits the delay was substantial, "probably the most substantial delay in criminal law history I'm aware of," but he adds the reasons for the delay "seemed to be understandable under this record."

DiRisio also cites the significance of Diane Shirley's testimony, which might not have been available had Bobby been indicted earlier. As if he suddenly realizes it's just as likely she would have come forward years ago, DiRisio quickly adds, "All these things are hypothetical."

I must be extremely naïve, I think to myself. I always believed judges made decisions on more than hypothetical conjectures. But the decision rests with DiRisio, and he dismisses the motion for pre-indictment delay.

Although Bobby had little hope the judge would approve the motion, it's still a blow. DiRisio has sided with the State. With so many witnesses gone and so many records unavailable, it's hard to believe anyone could say Bobby's case wasn't damaged by the passage of time.

But DiRisio isn't anyone. He's the judge.

The next motion is whether the judge should include definitions of lesser crimes (manslaughter, second-degree murder) in his charge since the statute of limitations has expired on everything except first-degree murder. Phillips argues the jurors should know what the options would have been if Bobby had been tried in a timely manner. It's important the jury understand the elements of homicide—what it takes for the State to prove the various levels.

Not unexpectedly, Evans argues against the motion, offering a citation to back up his position, Smith v. State. 327 S.W.2d 308.

DiRisio, who appears familiar with the citation, tells Phillips even though there is logic in his argument, he is bound by the Smith case and thus can instruct the jury only on murder one.

According to Evans, the Court erred in the Smith case by giving the jury information on lesser charges. But Phillips argues Evans has misinterpreted the case and thus the judge's decision is based on an incomplete reading of the Smith case. What actually happened in that case, Phillips notes, is the defendant was *asking* the judge to allow the lesser charges to be considered. That is not the situation with Bobby, since he has declined to waive his rights. Therefore, only first-degree murder can be considered.

More discussion ensues, but it is over the heads of everyone except the lawyers against the back wall who seem enthralled with the legal ping-pong. The ball ends up in Evans' court with the judge saying, "There are a lot of things about the law that logic and fairness doesn't rule." He concludes, "If the [Smith] case doesn't say what the State suggested, it certainly doesn't suggest what the defense suggests."

The bottom line, DiRisio declares, is the request by the defense must be denied.

The only thing I understand is that, evidently, fairness and logic don't rule. If only the jurors could hear the definitions of manslaughter and second-degree murder, they might realize Bobby's actions in no way constituted first-degree murder. Even though they could not consider lesser charges, they would be aware of other possible verdicts had Bobby been tried years ago. It would reinforce that the jury's only choice is whether the State has met the higher standard for first-degree murder—that Bobby planned to kill Hudson and did so maliciously.

My thoughts are interrupted when I hear DiRisio say the defense attorneys cannot even mention the lesser charges in closing statements.

Recessing until the next day, the judge gives the jury information on the preliminary charge, first-degree murder, and tells them this is the only charge they will be considering.

As we walk to Phillips' office, Bobby and I discuss his decision not to waive his rights to lesser charges. Bobby's more of a gambler than I, but as I squeeze his hand, I tell him this is one time he made the right call. We've rolled the dice, and soon we'll learn where they land.

CHAPTER TWENTY-FOUR

Closing Arguments

The argument is at an end.
–Saint Augustine (354-430)

When we return to Court the next morning, ready for the closing statements, the look on Evans' face is unsettling. Clearly, he has something up his sleeve.

After the judge, black robe rustling, enters, Evans quickly moves for a continuance. He wants time to travel to New York City to depose Hal Wingo, assistant managing editor of *People Magazine*, regarding the phone call the Rev. Godwin recently received, soliciting his story about the Hoppe case.

It's an offer Godwin has testified involved "big money" and one Evans declares is a "sham," perpetrated by the defense.

Phillips is quick to tell DiRisio the defense will not agree. "We respectfully submit a delay of this magnitude would delay this trial weeks on weeks. We ask the Court to proceed."

Judge DiRisio, knowing the trial is nearing its end, seems to sit taller. His dark eyes move thoughtfully between Evans and Phillips, occasionally lifting to scan the packed courtroom.

A hush falls on the courtroom as he begins to talk. "The format of a trial is not perfect. We have rules of procedure and, as desirable as it may be to have drawn out the procedures, to follow leads developed in the course of the trial, all you gentleman would be busy for the next two years following up on all manner of suggestion that was raised by the evidence.

"It would be endless...impeachment upon impeachment, collateral matter upon collateral matter. It would be never ending.

"We simply must proceed within the parameters set out for us by the law. The request for a continuance is denied."

Bobby shows no reaction to DiRisio's ruling. He sits motionless, gazing straight ahead. His spirit has been rubbed raw, leaving him numb.

He hears someone say, "The statute of limitations has run..."

Another voice intones, "Tennessee law says..."

A Matter of Conscience

Fragments of these words seem to rise and float in the room like shiny soap bubbles, each bursting above his head, the round rainbows in their bellies dissolving. Disappearing.

At the front of the courtroom, Evans and Phillips, Cook and DiRisio dip and sway through a stately dance they all know well. They move to an age-old rhythm. Point, counterpoint, decision. Point, counterpoint, decision. Point, counterpoint...

Bobby tries to focus on what's happening, but his mind, seeking refuge, drifts backward to happier days—to steamy summer afternoons shared with his buddies, floating lazily on Chickamauga Lake. Riding that rickety raft made more of dreams than wood and nails.

Then out of nowhere, Bobby feels his mouth start to water. Magically, he tastes the sweet cold of a strawberry milkshake at Nikki's. For a fleeting second, he sees the white lights of Chattanooga twinkling below like fireflies dancing with the night wind.

Suddenly, in Bobby's mind, Kevin is there. Not Kevin, all grown up in his Navy dress. Rather, the little boy who came to the Hoppe home, angry, afraid of being rejected again. Then, as if it were yesterday, Bobby feels a rush of relief when he hears Kevin whistling in the shower.

And there's Sherry Lee, a golden sunflower on a slender stalk. Resilient. His wife who loves him as he is. His own safe harbor. The coming home he never knew could be.

He forces his mind to remember his boys out there on the football field—youngsters with just the hint of a beard—who watch him like he matters, who listen to his words like they're sacred, who—just by calling him Coach—tell him he's exactly where he belongs.

Then Bobby's heart catches in his chest as, in his mind's eye, he sees his mother. Dressed in her Sunday best, sitting in the stands at Central, then at Auburn—watching his every move. Cheering as he grabs the ball and flies, carried by winged Mercury. His mother, turning to the man on her left, and pointing, "That's my son. Right there. That's my son."

Sitting in the courtroom, the long trial winding down, this rush of memories comforts Bobby, like sinking into a warm bath. Odd, he thinks, that these thoughts should come now, just as my life goes on the auction block.

Closing Arguments

DiRisio's voice, instructing the jury, penetrates his dreams: "The defendant is charged with the offense of murder in the first degree of Teddy Donald Hudson on the 20th day of July 1957.

"That charge—murder in the first degree—is the only charge which you will be considering."

The finality of the judge's words shuts down his daydreams. Darkness descends again. How did it all come down to this?

* * *

Closing arguments. So soon?

But in many ways, Bobby feels as if he's been on this stark stage, starring in a tragic drama for years. Ironic that he, who hates attention, has had to stand so long in the blinding floodlights. He wants it to be over. House lights, down.

He leans forward, his chest pressing the table, his face cradled in his hands.

Hearing a chair scrape the floor, he peeps through his fingers. Time to start. Evans is up.

"At bat," Bobby thinks. Without lifting his head, he pictures the prosecutor in his dark suit and sapphire-blue tie, stepping to the plate, a powdery dust coating the cuffs of his dress pants.

He watches as Evans pushes back from the table, stands, and fastens one button of his dark jacket before strolling toward the jury box. "Ladies and gentleman of the jury..."

Bobby takes a deep breath and holds it. Looking straight at Evans and then at DiRisio, he plants his feet, bracing for the hurtful words about to be hurled toward him.

"Words don't fly freely from my mouth," Evans begins. "I have a logical sense about me that I can point out to you, as jurors, as everyday people..."

And using this logical sense, Evans promises, he will lay out for them—beyond a reasonable doubt—that "the killing was in fact murder and murder in the first degree."

With Evans' back turned to him, Bobby's eyes sweep the jury. What are they thinking? Suddenly, he realizes one of the women on the back row is not looking at Evans. It's Ms. Simpkins—he recalls her name. Her eyes are locked on Bobby, and he can feel the cold in them—the same sensation he felt earlier today when fate placed Simpkins on the elevator with Sally, Sherry, and him.

Refocusing on what's occurring in the courtroom, Bobby hears Evans say he will not go back over the evidence. He assures the 12 he's confident they will remember all of it when they begin deliberations. Then his tone turns cautionary. "If I say anything about something that someone said or didn't say, and it conflicts with what you heard the witness say or not say—by all means—take what you heard in the way of evidence."

Evans reminds the jury, when he began presenting his case, the State's theory was constructed around a murder presumed to be a "whodunit." That is, until Bobby Hoppe took the stand and said he killed Donald Hudson in the early morning of July 21, 1957.

On top of circumstantial evidence, Evans tells the jury, they now have direct evidence. "You can conclude from the defendant's own testimony and the physical evidence that he did, in fact, murder in the first degree—maliciously and premeditatedly—Donald Hudson."

Bobby becomes aware of the deafening silence surrounding him. If Evans weren't speaking, you could hear a pin drop.

Evans pre-empts DiRisio by telling the jury, "The Court will instruct you on self-defense: In Tennessee, the defendant must have employed all means reasonably in his power consistent with his own safety to avoid danger and avert the necessity of taking another's life.

"I want you to remember that instruction on self-defense when you recall even the defendant's version of how this became self-defense."

Then Evans launches into a rehash of the State's version of Bobby's testimony, saying he will ask the jury if it jibes with the evidence. After deriding Bobby's declaration that "murder is not in me," Evans moves to what was said by Roy Hudson, the victim's father.

Evans reiterates the elderly Hudson's account of Don and Joan's relationship, reminding the jury Mr. Hudson had indicated they had been broken up "for approximately 30 days," while the defendant contends the affair had been over for months. Pointedly, Evans asks the jury, while Bobby was at Auburn, who actually lived here? Who was around to observe when the relationship ended?

The shotgun? Well, Evans says, you'll recall the State brought in Detective Stargel, the lead detective on the case in 1957. Stargel testified a weapon was never recovered.

Closing Arguments

Stepping back, appearing indignant and personally offended, Evans adds, "Suddenly, we hear for the first time in opening statement that what happened to the weapon had *never* been a secret. The defendant says he had turned it over to his attorneys."

Evans reminds the jury Tommy Smith, sitting with his girlfriend on May Street at the time of the shooting, described what he saw—"two cars, one speeding up, the other slowing down.

"Then BOOM! The shot."

Several jurors jump. As his "boom" echoes around the room, Evans takes a few steps backward to point to State Exhibit 8, telling the jury they surely can see how the sheet metal folded when the door flew open, imprinting itself against the fender.

"Now, Mr. Phillips and Mr. Cook would have you believe someone opened it up and took the gun out," Evans says. "Mr. Smith saw no one getting in and out of the car—and he was there, ladies and gentlemen. He was there until the ambulance came and drug out the body of Donald Hudson—and no gun fell out. Tommy Smith saw no gun."

Evans' goal in the first round of closing arguments is to persuade the jury to become like-minded with the State by mocking the defendant's case, casting aspersions on Bobby's character, ridiculing the character witnesses and, most importantly, demeaning Diane Shirley's testimony.

He reminds the jury Jody Neal, ex-husband of Odene, told the Court, he not only never heard Hoppe make threats against Hudson 31 years ago, he "cannot remember" if Odene ever talked to him about such threats. Not that Jody can swear Odene didn't tell him—it's just he doesn't *remember* her ever telling him, Evans mockingly parrots Jody Neal.

And what about Billy Joe King, "whose name appears in the weave of this case?" Evans reminds the jury Billy Joe, implicated during the trial as the voice on the phone talking about tossing dynamite on the Neals' porch if anyone talked to the police, surfaced again—just two days before he was to appear at trial. Billy Joe was up at the lake, near Jody Neal's cabin—and, well, Evan says with disbelief, he just ran flat out of beer. So he stops by Jody's for a couple of beers—and happens to learn Jody has been subpoenaed to testify at Bobby's trial.

Evans implies the visit from King was a reminder to Jody to keep his mouth shut.

A Matter of Conscience

Evans blows over the Ed Davis debacle—saying, sure, Davis was representing the Hudsons, not the Hoppes, as one of the State's witnesses thought. Simple mistake. What's important, Evans says, is that "Davis went around as a special investigator, as an attorney retained by the Hudson family and talked to witnesses in an effort to get information.

"Did he get any?" Evan says, turning toward the Hudson family, before answering his own question. "No. Wonder why, ladies and gentlemen. Wonder why he didn't get any information?

"Threats. And who had reason to threaten? Back then it was a whodunit. Now we know who did it. Logic, ladies and gentleman, logic. Two plus two. Very simple.

Evans pauses before saying two words, "Odene Neal."

He tries to brush off the inconsistencies in her series of testimonies, saying "any lawyer worth his salt" could trip up a witness like that. But Evans decides not to linger long on Odene.

He quickly draws the jury's attention away from Odene and onto Diane Shirley, not even trying to hide his disdain for the woman who has become his nemesis.

"When you consider Evelyn Diane Shirley, when you consider her sudden appearance—dramatic, isn't it? Wonderful that she called Leroy Phillips Wednesday morning and gave this important information," Evans says, tiny drops of sweat forming on his upper lip. "Isn't that wonderful—so it could be included ...just in time?

"My, how wonderful it is," Evans forces a smile before he begins to whine about having no time to find out about "this woman," to check on her past, no time to impeach her.

"And this wonderful witness—dramatic, bold. Boy, it's just like a movie, just like something out of *People Magazine*, isn't it?

"It sure is. It sure is," he declares with fervor.

Saying he'll return to Diane Shirley later, he jumps back to Odene, telling the jury he's so thankful they got to hear her telephone conversation with Detective Heck, "played all the way through, not stopped, not paused."

His tone increasingly sharp, Evans begins to mock Cook's interrogation of Odene, by mirroring Cook's accent: "That was a lie, wasn't it? That was a lie. That was a lie. That was a lie. Oh, you said this and it wasn't right, so that's a lie."

Closing Arguments

Evan's voice rises until he's just short of shouting. Several of the spectators glance at each other and shift nervously in their seats. Bobby listens, never moving.

As if applying the brakes, Evans rests his hands on the railing of the jury box and leans toward the 12.

"Finally, Dr. Godwin," he says, his tone much lower. Evans tells the jury he's so glad they got to hear "two uninterrupted conversations Dr. Godwin had. You decide whether, as Mr. Hoppe opinionated, you would have to be a fool to believe him. More about that later."

Pivoting to look at Bobby, Evans smirks. "Thank you, Mr. Hoppe. We've been waiting 31 years to hear the truth from you. Thank you. The jury will decide whether they heard the truth.

"There was one key to the whole thing, and he was right there—Mr. Hoppe. We showed you who did it. You heard him say how it occurred.

"The re-creation of this murder by this man right there," Evan points a long finger at Bobby, "is vitally important for you to consider. It couldn't have happened that way. It just could not have happened, physically and logically, ladies and gentlemen."

In a taunting tone, Evans continues, "Bobby Hoppe is telling you this gunslinger is coming down the road, pointing the gun at him, not once but twice."

After saying Bobby didn't know where he was on the road because he was scared and it was so dark, Evans whips around toward Bobby again. "But, boy, it was light enough for him to see Donald Hudson with that pistol pointed just like this," he says, using his finger as the pistol, looking down it as if staring down the barrel of a gun—directly at Bobby's forehead. Bobby never flinches.

"Physically, it couldn't have happened, could it, Mr. Hoppe?" Evans asks rhetorically.

Evans paints a picture of Bobby in Joan's convertible somewhere along Bell Avenue, lying in wait for Hudson, ready to give him a taste of vigilante justice. "The affair embarrasses him because he's a star, he's a hero."

And Don—what does Don see? Evans asks and then answers his own question.

"He sees Mr. Hoppe with a shotgun, and he tries to speed up and—Boom! Right in the eye. Good shot! Good shot!"

A Matter of Conscience

Evans begins to talk about Bobby's life since he shot Hudson—a good life, full of good friends willing to step up for him in Court. "A family. He has a family..."

"There comes a reckoning," Evans pronounces, reminding Bobby of Mama's old-timey preacher who loved to warn about living a life of sin. There will come a reckoning, the preacher would shout, red-faced, his voice shaking as he held a big black Bible high over his head.

Then Bobby hears Evans say something about John F. Kennedy's book, *Profiles in Courage*. He's telling the jury Bobby had to choose between courage or his best season ever at Auburn. Between courage—or being drafted by the 49ers.

"The litmus test of character is courage," Evans shouts, pounding the railing with his fist. "He failed. He failed miserably."

And, unfortunately, Bobby always believed that himself. Despite its being self-defense, he killed Don Hudson. Now the world knows. Such relief to get it off his chest, but he's destroyed the family name. For 31 years, he's struggled to make it up to God, to Mama, to the boys on his teams who looked up to him, to Sherry and Kevin.

Time for a reckoning. No need for Evans to tell him that.

* * *

Leroy Phillips, rising as Evans takes his seat, walks toward the jury, eyes behind his thick glasses, tired, thoughtful. Though Bobby can't see it, there's a glint in those weary eyes.

A reasonable doubt, that's all it takes, so Phillips begins by reminding the jurors they were selected because they promised they could be impartial as they heard the witnesses and weighed the evidence, that they would not be swayed by "sensationalism as exhibited by the press."

"Ladies and gentlemen, you indicated after we selected you that you would give the defendant the benefit of your individual judgment." That you would "render a true verdict according to the law and the evidence," not based on speculation or theories.

Like Evans, Phillips says he wants to "touch on a couple of rules of law" before getting to the evidence. Presumption of innocence—the jurors guaranteed the Court, until deliberations are over, each would presume Bobby Hoppe to be innocent.

Closing Arguments

"And on into your deliberations, I assume as you sit there now, you have not started to deliberate," Phillips says.

In the jury box, Simpkins seems to sneer at this remark. Later we will learn she and her husband had passed judgment on Bobby several days ago—finding him guilty. A jury of two, one never sworn in.

Phillips reminds the jury, "The rule of law is a man cannot be proven guilty of a crime like murder in the first degree unless it is proven beyond a reasonable doubt."

Reasonable doubt, he says, may arise from the evidence itself or from the lack of evidence. "In addition, it doesn't have to prove guilt beyond absolute certainty. There are no absolutes in life—but [Mr. Evans] has to prove beyond a reasonable doubt.

"The burden of proof is entirely on the State. Don't let Mr. Evans shift the burden of proof to the defendant. The Court will indicate to you the burden never shifts to a defendant."

Phillips tells the jury the prosecutor has put forth speculation and theories and circumstantial evidence. "Won't hold water."

What about direct evidence? "There is direct evidence my client killed the deceased. Proof of the killing of a person is not homicide; it is not murder in the first degree," Phillips insists.

Phillips scoffs at the State's contention regarding the issue of flight. "Mr. Evans places flight for 31 years. That's absurd. That's not the law.

"When [Hoppe] left the scene, did he even know the man was shot? No. No. Much less did he know he was dead." Phillips reminds the jury Hoppe, fearful Don would come after him, didn't go to his own home initially.

The next day, Hoppe went to Auburn, Phillips says. "Listen closely. He didn't hide out like some common criminal. He openly continued with his plans and went down to Auburn."

Driving to Auburn, was he bothered after learning Hudson was dead? "Of course. On the way he wanted to get spiritual guidance with reference to this thing.

"Mr. Evans shouts and screams, 'Oh, it's got to be courage to have character.' That's not the law at all. The law relates to moral character. I submit to you, ladies and gentlemen, a man who is of such character, who would plan and plot and premeditate a murder would not be...a man who would, within 48 hours, go to a minister and seek spiritual guidance. If

298

he were of the bent they want to make him out, a premeditated murderer, he would not have cared."

Phillips reminds the jury, after his time with the Rev. Godwin, Hoppe heeded his advice to talk with a lawyer. "You think he stays down at Auburn and parties? Immediately, he came back to Chattanooga, immediately consulted an individual who referred him to the lawyer next door."

To the late Joe Wild who advised Hoppe. "He sought the advice of counsel and listened to counsel—and there's supposed to be something morally wrong with it? No. That can't be."

Stepping closer to the jury, warning like a wiser older brother, Phillips says, "It is quite reasonable for one human being in this society to consult with a lawyer—and he had better listen to him—because this is an adversary system and inferences will be drawn from your conduct.

"It was reasonable for Bobby to act that way. It was not inconsistent with his innocence as has been inferred."

Phillips is indignant his client was asked repeatedly why, in 31 years, he didn't come forward, why he didn't lay to rest the Hudsons' doubts about their son's killer. "Ladies and gentlemen, that kind of question is a direct appeal to sympathy and nothing else."

Phillips turns to the Hudson family. "I sympathize, too, for Mr. and Mrs. Hudson. But, ladies and gentlemen, their son brought about his own tragic death. He lived tragically and he died tragically."

Mrs. Hudson, who has been crying quietly, sobs and leans into her husband's shoulder. Hudson, a stoic mountain man, does not react at all.

Phillips changes course, saying the State had "made fun of the fact we had character witnesses. Ladies and gentlemen, the establishment of character is important. The Court will tell you that. If you establish a good character in the evidence, it stands as a witness for you."

Pointing to Bobby, Phillips continues, "This man had good character when this event occurred and still has good character. The law says there is a reasonable inference, listen to this, that a man generally will act in accordance with his character as the law of his life—and this man did and still has superb, excellent moral character."

Tommy Smith—the State's one eyewitness. Using Exhibit 11, an aerial view of the area where Hudson was shot, Phillips points out two primary concerns: (1) Smith's window of time to view the scene was less than five seconds; and (2) had Bobby been the aggressor, it would have been easy—and logical—for Hudson to take a left onto May Street—his most direct route home. That didn't happen. Rather than turning on May Street or gunning his car to pass, Hudson pulled parallel to Bobby. Seconds later, Smith heard the sound of a shotgun, followed by a loud crash.

Using Exhibit 16, Phillips reinforces how easy it would have been for Hudson to just drive home. "All you had to do was turn right here and go to your home, if that were your intention," Phillips says, tracing the most direct route with his finger.

Then, turning back to the jury, he asks, "Who was the aggressor?"

Phillips quickly rebukes the validity of the video shown, as well as Evans' efforts to re-create the car Bobby was driving by using hard-back chairs. A ridiculous re-enactment, he declares. Saying the State has lots of money, Phillips ridicules the prosecutor for not bringing in experts to testify. "They have the burden, don't they?"

And then, he says, they dare to give his client a rusty gun and tell him to load a spent, crimped shell, and show how he was able to load a shotgun with one hand and fire it. Come on!

"Is that attempting to be fair and reasonable and re-create?" Phillips asks rhetorically. "Proof beyond a reasonable doubt? No."

Phillips, looking especially at the older jurors on the panel, says solemnly, "In 1957 Bobby Hoppe was a strapping, wiry athlete. Sitting here in this chair," he says, pointing to the straight-back chair used as the driver's seat, "was a 55-year-old man with arthritis and a heart condition.

"They want to be fair? They don't want to be fair. They want a conviction. That's their job."

Phillips disparages Godwin's testimony, noting, "The State had the same evidence in 1966 they had in 1987 when they indicted this man—with the exception of one thing. Odene Neal."

Saying her name, Phillips almost gives a "ha," wanting the jury to feel his personal derision regarding Mrs. Neal's testimony.

"With regard to Odene Neal," Phillips says, smiling. "Thirty-one years doesn't affect *Odene Neal's* testimony. You see, the passage of time with regard to memory does affect a person.

"But Odene Neal's testimony is 1988 vintage, totally manufactured. Time does not affect her. Totally manufactured."

He reminds the jury Odene repeatedly declared in 1987 she knew nothing about the shooting. Then a year later, she has an epiphany—her memory clears miraculously, but she says she didn't tell what she knew because she was afraid. Or maybe no one asked her.

"I was afraid or nobody asked me. It's multiple choice time," Phillips says. "That's absurd."

On the tape, when Mrs. Neal was heard laughing and laughing, did she sound afraid? "One of the other criteria of judging a witness is the reasonableness of their testimony. And I am going to tell you when the true character of this woman came out," Phillips vows.

It was coming back from a dance when Odene heard Don Hudson beating Joan Hoppe in the back seat of the car. "And when she told it, she laughed," Phillips says. "It was funny to her for a man to beat a woman. There is her character—little things you gather."

Speaking of being reasonable, Phillips reminds the jury Odene's various testimonies had "umpteen" contradictions. And how ridiculous would it be, were Bobby Hoppe intending to kill Hudson, to go to the home of Hudson's best friends that same night—and alert them he was gunning for Hudson. How reasonable would that be? "It is absurd."

Back to Godwin, Phillips points to the inconsistencies in the reverend's statement in 1966 and the dramatic additions in 1988. No self-defense, Godwin has said, although he admits Bobby told him a man was out to get him. No breach of pastor/penitent confidentiality according to Godwin, although he coerced Bobby into confiding in him by telling a reluctant and emotional Bobby, back in 1957, he searched him out precisely because he knew he was a minister.

"Ladies and gentlemen, in the press and elsewhere, Godwin has been depicted as some kind of hero for coming forth."

Looking from the jury to Godwin, Phillips's face darkens, "With regard to Mr. Godwin, shame on you, Mr. Godwin. Shame on you. For what? For violating a confidence that is the most sacred known to religion.

"Ladies and gentlemen, he had the audacity to look at you and say, 'I didn't violate any confidence.' Yet his own statement, when counsel read it to him said, 'This is the first time I ever violated a confidence.' That's what he said. Now unless I've lost my mind, one of those is wrong."

Phillips glares at Godwin, shaming him again—this time, for not remembering whether he had prayer with Bobby the night Bobby came to him, his soul in agony. With a harrumph, Phillips turns his back on Godwin, dismissing him and his testimony.

Turning to the jury and pointing toward Bobby, Phillips says, "To condemn this man to first-degree murder and sentence him to imprisonment would be another tragedy, because it is not justified by the evidence and the law."

Thanking the jury for their attention, Phillips returns to his seat. DiRisio glances at his watch, checks it against the clock on the wall, and calls for a recess. When the recess is over and the jury has returned to the courtroom, DiRisio asks Bobby Lee Cook if he's ready.

"Ready, Your Honor," Cook replies graciously, standing promptly.

As dapper as a Wall Street banker, Cook moves confidently across the hardwood floor until he's directly before the jury, his hands in front of him, their long fingers loosely interlaced. He looks at each juror, kindly. My friends, he seems to say without words.

A few jurors offer smiles to this long-legged stranger standing before them.

In the back of the courtroom, the wall is lined three-deep with lawyers who have hustled here for Cook's closing arguments. There's no whispering, but the courtroom crackles with electricity—like the spark that swept across the multitudes as Moses, another gray-bearded man of long ago, his staff held high, declared he would lead God's people out of the wilderness.

Displaying his Southern manners, Cook begins with a courtly acknowledgement of the judge, prosecutor and, with a smile, the jury. Then he moves fluidly into his closing statements.

"Ladies and gentlemen, I have a duty to perform in this case on behalf of Mr. Hoppe, a fellow citizen of this community. I expect to perform it with candor, and I expect to perform honorably and without any reservation or any retreat from what I believe the evidence has displayed and demonstrated in this case to be the facts and truth."

Grasping his lapels with large, liver-spotted hands, Cook declares, "It has been said that who shall put his finger on the work of justice and say it is there, it is not without us as a fact.

"Justice is like the kingdom of God. It is within us with a great yearning."

A Matter of Conscience

The words are melodious—rich and sweet as sin, yet pure as honey from the hive. Like a warm wave, they wash outward, calming the jurors, already edgy about the task ahead.

Then, unconsciously, Cook touches his wispy goatee as he begins to reminisce, taking the older jurors with him.

"I look to this jury in 1988—and I go back to the '50s or the '40s—which I remember as a young lawyer so well. I tell you, times were different.

"If I could flash back 35 or 40 years, I would not see maybe more than one woman on this jury," he says, meeting the eyes of each female before him.

"And it would be a rare occasion to see a black," Cook says, shaking his head. "There are not many benefits in getting older in my profession. But in the 40 years I have practiced law in courts throughout this country, I have seen great changes in what we call this hall of justice.

"I have seen the prayer of Lincoln answered that a nation, half slave and half free, can no longer exist or survive."

Everyone in the room is mesmerized. A black juror dabs at her eyes with a wad of tissue. "I have seen the democratic process open up, thank God, for women and minorities and those that are not privileged by wealth or high stations in life."

As he talks, Cook's voice has risen slowly, a low drumbeat growing imperceptivity. "I have seen the Constitution, which was written and struck over 200 years ago, broadened to where rights now are applied with equality and fairness in a country that has fought for fairness and freedoms [in] two world wars and in Korea and Vietnam.

"I look at this jury, as I have at many throughout this great country—and they are not different," he says, smiling at the 12. "You can travel from the east to the west and the south to the north—and they are made up of people like you."

He pauses, thinking, then lets his tired eyes caress a couple of jurors who identified themselves on *voir dire* as military veterans. He aims his next words directly at them.

"If there is any one thing that distinguished us as a great country—speaking of freedoms and liberties—it is the jury system. It is the hallmark. It is the taproot of this republic. You can't take a penny of a person's money in a civil case nor deprive him of a second of his liberty—except by a unanimous verdict of this jury. Thank God for that."

Closing Arguments

Thankfulness washes over Bobby—thankfulness that Sherry insisted they hire this gifted lawyer to represent him. Then Bobby lowers his head slightly, afraid to get his hopes up.

Calling Evans "a fine young man," Cook reminds the jury the State's theory in the case, the reason Bobby killed Hudson, revolved around Hudson's abuse of Joan. Although the State stands by that theory, Cook says, yesterday for the first time, a new component was added by the State—that allegedly Billy Joe King had said he was the "wheelman" the night of the shooting.

And how do we know that, Cook asks, his gentle tone turning sardonic. "We know that by virtue of Virgil Burnette—the State's star witness on yesterday." Cook drags out "star," not because of his Southern drawl, but to denigrate by his inflection of the word.

At one time, King and Burnette had worked together and had been drinking buddies. During the trial, the State called Burnette, who testified that, on more than one occasion when Billy Joe was drunk, he boasted about driving the get-away car the night Hudson was shot.

"My brother, Mr. Evans, talks about the dramatic appearances of witnesses. Diane Evelyn Shirley. He didn't mention Jerry Cannon or Ms. Butts or Johnny Roberson." Cook's mouth turns down as if he's swallowed something bitter. "I would be derelict in my duty as an officer of this Court and my responsibilities to Mr. Hoppe and, indeed, my responsibilities as a citizen if I did not comment further upon Mr. Burnette."

Cook's cragged face is a gathering storm, dark and furious.

"I find it shocking. I find it insulting. I find it extraordinary the State of Tennessee—in the name of its sovereignty and in the name of justice—would parade a man to the stand who is a convicted dope dealer. Who denies on the one hand he knows what cocaine is and who pushes it in this community—whether it's Broad Street or Market Street or Central High School—and places the stamp of the imprimaturs of the State upon his credibility and integrity—and then asks you to deprive a man of his liberty upon the testimony of an incredulous thug and hood."

Cook reins himself in. "You saw Virgil Burnette. You know what he is," Cook addresses the jury, before he turns, piercing Evans with his eyes. "And you know what he is, Mr. Evans."

Indignant, Cook lets his gaze rest on Burnette. "I am shocked—not simple possession of marijuana and cocaine—but large amounts with the intent to sell, to ravage this community and my community.

"The work of the devil personified—and they talk about dramatic appearances." There's a harrumph in his words.

Cook steps backward slightly. Now to a few issues about the evidence.

The lanky attorney roars with passionate oratory followed fast by facts and evidence. Up, down, up, down. It's a rollercoaster ride.

Cook asks the jury exactly what does the "un-contradicted evidence"—evidence never disputed by the State during the trial—show Bobby Hoppe knew on the night of July 20, 1957?

For one thing, Don Hudson had a proclivity for violence. "He told you—and it's the un-contradicted evidence in this case—he knew he saw Hudson with a weapon, that Hudson had kidnapped a black man and held him at pistol point while someone else beat him."

Cook pivots toward Evans, asking, if this weren't the truth, why didn't you challenge it? Cook rattles off examples of Hudson's run-ins with the law, none of which the State disputed.

Then, the defense attorney talks about a few of Bobby's character witnesses. "Ms. Butts, the lovely lady, who [like Mrs. Shirley] also made a dramatic appearance, who no one in this case even knew existed until she called Mr. Phillips and drove her automobile here from Selma, Ala., to tell you, ladies and gentlemen, 'When we saw Don coming, we got off the street.'

"Thank God there are still people in this community and in this great land that will get involved, that won't say, 'I don't want to get mixed up in this.' If we ever come to the point, ladies and gentlemen, where good, decent people don't want to get mixed up in this and won't do their part, this government and this great land and the liberties and freedoms we enjoy must disappear.

"I do not want to *inherit the wind* in that fashion."

Cook commends Jerry Cannon for coming forward to tell about the "animalistic" nature of Don Hudson—whom Cannon witnessed "beat a lady to a pulp" and, when she was fleeing, fired a pistol at her feet, laughing as she danced to the bullets bouncing off the pavement around her.

Outraged as he repeats Cannon's words, Cook declares, "Don Hudson was a thug and a gangster. I would be less than courageous if I didn't say it—and I make no apologies about it."

He reminds the Court Cannon came forward, after consulting with his brother, because he knew it was the right thing to do.

"He came here—a retired executive from a federal savings and loan association—who has led an exemplary life for 30 years. And he bares his soul and tells you he ran two or three loads of liquor for Hudson—something his children and his wife and his friends and fellow parishioners would have never known about."

Looking at Cannon, seated in the courtroom, Cook gives him a courtly nod. "Thank you, Mr. Cannon."

Then Cook turns to Johnny Roberson, "a policeman in this community for 11 years and many years in Dade County, Ga.

"He tells you on the evening tide—an hour and a half before the encounter on Bell Avenue—he saw Hudson at the Pig House and he had a weapon—a pistol—in the front seat of the car."

Cook reminds the jury, "Again, this is un-contradicted evidence, showing it was Hudson's nature to carry a gun."

"Judge Sam Payne, a distinguished, fine gentlemen, an asset to this community, a member of the judiciary, tells you Hudson was a gun carrier and he was violent and he was dangerous." And there's nothing here to refute it, Cook states.

He turns to Diane Shirley. "You heard her say it was only a few days ago she read about what Odene Neal had said in this Court, and it didn't sound right; it didn't have the ring of truth. And [Mrs. Shirley] said, 'It was the other way around—that's the way I remember it.'

"She, too, came forward. She spoke up as Johnny Roberson spoke up, as Jerry Cannon spoke up and as Ms. Butts spoke up."

Cook lowers his voice—the soft tone grabbing attention more than yelling ever could. Spectators and jurors sit forward in their seats, knowing something important is about to be said.

"After World War II, a great Protestant minister by the name of Martin Niemueller was freed from one of the prison camps in Germany, Stalag 14—placed there for seven years by Hitler. And Niemueller said this: 'When they came for the Jews, I wasn't a Jew and I didn't speak up. When they came for the Catholics, I wasn't a Catholic and I didn't speak up. And when they came for the trade unionists, I wasn't a trade unionist and I didn't speak up. And when they came for me, there wasn't anyone left to speak up.'

"I congratulate Ms. Shirley and Jerry Cannon and Ms. Butts and Johnny Roberson and all of their like. May they continue to come and refresh the blood of liberty and of justice in this society."

Wanting to defuse Evan's criticism of the "surprise witness," Diane Shirley, Cook begins by praising the prosecutor. "Mr. Evans is a fine lawyer. He is a tough lawyer—and that is what he's supposed to be. I like a good scraper, and he is good. He's a tiger.

"But he didn't lay a hand on Mrs. Shirley, because he couldn't touch her. And he knew, he knew that he couldn't get within 40 feet of anything except that which was the truth—and it flowed from her lips just as it flows from the lips of the Holy."

Cook outlines Diane Shirley's testimony about seeing Don Hudson, twice, at her mother's house the night he was killed. Don was carrying a pistol, and she recalls his threatening to go after Bobby Hoppe with it.

Then Cook returns to Virgil Burnette. "Ask yourself, would you want to buy a mobile home from him or a used automobile or a washing machine—not that he would be selling that. He would be selling dope."

He recaps for the jury his questioning Burnette, when Burnette implied, in return for testifying against Bobby, he cut a deal with the authorities, although he later denied it.

"Well," Cook says, as he gives his broad shoulders a slight shrug. "What sort of deal is it where someone is caught with 50 pounds of marijuana and a sackful of cocaine to sell—and the authorities let him serve 25 days in the work camp.

"It's insulting," Cooks tells the jury, then turns to the prosecution. "You explain it, Mr. Evans."

Evans manages to maintain eye contact with Cook, but above his shirt collar, a deep blush can be seen creeping up his neck.

Cook reiterates Stargel's story about taking 200 case files to Florida when he retired. Then when he returned to Tennessee, some files were missing. That's interesting. Furthermore, there was no inventory of any personal effects taken from Hudson's car—"which is normal police practice...even in 1957."

Then there's Barbara Jo Campbell who hasn't seen Bobby in 20 years. Cook reminds the Court Ms. Campbell testified she was dragged into the police station shortly after the killing.

And Cook reminds the jury the State did not recall Stargel to refute her testimony.

According to Barbara Jo, during her date with Bobby on July 20, 1957, he was his usual gentle self. Even more significant, her testimony establishes a timeline that refutes Odene's contention Bobby was at her house during the same time, threatening to kill Hudson.

"That is totally inconsistent and illogical with the story Odene Neal tells you," Cook declares to the jury. "It turns logic upside down.

"I submit to you that—in a spirit of reality and in a spirit of logic— the Odene Neal story is, to put it bluntly, a lie and totally unbelievable. If you can believe Odene Neal's version, we can believe you can pour water uphill—and you know you can't."

Cook lays out what Odene said, when she said it, and perhaps why. "In the February 23, 1988 statement, she said nine times...she didn't know anything about this case, she didn't have any facts whatsoever. And she said also in February of 1987—the only thing she had was rumor.

"She admitted on this stand she had lied under oath, fibbed, committed perjury under the sanctity of an oath."

Moving on, Cook reminds the Court all records of the 1966 grand jury, convened after Godwin's "revelation," were destroyed.

The tall attorney pauses, stroking his goatee. "Reverend Godwin," he says, spitting out the name as if it were gall, his disgust for the man from Mars Hill apparent.

"It's a great country, freedom of religion," Cook says. "Thank God we've got it. It's the reason many of our forefathers came to settle in this great land hundreds of years ago—to remove themselves from the yoke of the tyrant...to where they could worship as they saw fit in their own way."

Cook pauses again—then turns toward Bobby, though still speaking to the jury. "July 22, we go to Auburn—July 22, 1957."

Pointing to Bobby, whose head is lowered, Cook says, "This man, now gray-headed, not the man he once was at 21-years old. He doesn't go to the grocery story or the drugstore. He doesn't go to the pool hall. He goes across to First Baptist Church and wants to talk to the preacher. They tell him the regular minister is out of town. But they tell him, we have a Reverend Godwin here who preached this Sunday and Sunday evening, and you go see him. He is the supply minister. And Bobby goes to see Reverend Godwin."

Pausing, Cook tells the jury, as reasonable people, they can believe what they want, and it's up to them to decide the issues—it's not up to him or DiRisio or Evans or Phillips.

"The buck stops here. But I don't believe, under this evidence, you believe Bobby Hoppe would have talked with just anybody as Reverend Godwin said. Bobby Hoppe was looking for someone special for spiritual relief, for spiritual guidance."

Cook reminds the jury Godwin testified Bobby did not come to him as a minister. A growing fury can be heard in Cook's deep voice.

"I can't believe that is what lies in the heart of Godwin, because I don't believe...that is the truth. When he said, 'Bobby, you know I am a minister and that's the reason you came to me.'

"Then the preacher, after having established that blessed, sacred— and that's what the preacher said it was—sacred, holy, inviolate relationship, as one would have with their minister or priest, Godwin said Bobby poured his heart out, and Godwin told him no one is beyond redemption.

"Godwin told Bobby, 'I have heard it all—thieves, bigamists, burglars, homosexual conduct—and I never told it. I never broke that confidence because it was sacred.'

"Little things sometimes tell a lot," Cook says before proceeding to debunk Godwin's allegation he knew who Bobby was because his pictures were all over town. Then Cook refutes Godwin's assertion Bobby's mother—"God rest her soul"—was ever rude to Godwin, a man she didn't even know.

"Do you believe as reasonable people" that what occurred in Auburn happened the way Godwin described it—"if Godwin is a man of conscience and a man of God that he could have sat on what he knew for seven or eight years, when he told you it didn't bother him a bit. That doesn't make a bit of sense."

Cook continues to deride Godwin for his statement regarding the tape he made in 1966. Cook reads from Godwin's testimony: "It was broken, the tape was broken. I put it on and tried to use it. I didn't have time to splice it. And when I had time to splice it, I didn't have the interest in hearing it. And when I had the interest in hearing it, I didn't have the time to splice it."

Looking over the rims of his half-moon glasses, Cook says, "You know, the funny thing about this—there were two tapes." Cook reminds

309

the Court in 1966 when the detectives drove to Mars Hill to take a statement, Godwin made a tape and the detectives also made a tape.

Glancing down at the paper again, Cook repeats what he just read. "The tape was broken, and he didn't have time to splice it and when he had time to splice it, he didn't have any interest in hearing it. And when he had interest in hearing it, he didn't have time to splice it."

Cook smiles at the jurors. "It sounds like something Mark Twain said, 'The more you explain it, the less I understand it.'"

Then Cook reminds the jury, when Godwin flubbed his testimony, he began to sputter and make excuses that he hadn't been able to organize his thoughts on paper or practice what he planned to say. He could not "be absolutely certain of getting words just exactly right."

He was just guessing at what he recalled Bobby told him, Godwin had said. Cook says quietly, "I find that scary, scary and frightening, very, very frightening."

"Well," Cook declares derisively, "You don't *guess* somebody in the penitentiary in this country. You don't *speculate* them into the penitentiary. When you are dealing with liberty in this country, you have got to be right."

Cook speaks briefly about Dr. Curtis and Ms. Calloway and the insightful anecdotes they shared about the Hoppes. Then he moves on to David Cook.

"Captain David Cook, who is no relation to me—but I would be glad to claim him," Cook says, again targeting the veterans on the jury. "I am glad to see a little urge and fervor of patriotism has gotten back into the country.

"This proud young man tells you, Bobby Hoppe was like a father to me. He gave me a lot of guidance. I wouldn't be where I am today without him. He convinced me I had the capability of going to college and making something out of myself.

"Ms. Robinson tells you likewise—that Bobby and his wife adopted an eight-year-old child...a young man now in the service of his country. And his old classmate Sentell Harper tells you he would believe Bobby under any circumstances."

Cook pauses, stroking his goatee as he ponders what to say next. When looks up, his eyes above his glasses are as clear as a cool mountain stream. "Character—a person's life, like a piece of tapestry, is made up of many strands which, interwoven, make a pattern. To separate a single strand and look at it alone destroys the whole."

Bobby watches Cook, noting how his words surpass simple language, entering the realm of poetry. Cook steps forward, placing both of his raw-boned hands on the railing of the jury box.

"A long time ago there was a judge in the federal system by the name of Learned Hand, one of the most revered and respected jurists in this land.

"In giving a speech in New York City, he made this statement—and I think it is true today as I stand before you. He said maybe we place too much stock in the written law or in the Constitution even. He said liberty and justice, a sense of justice, lie in the heart of free people. If it is lost there, then it is lost forever."

Cook releases the railing and takes a step backward. "I ask you to do your duty, because that is what you are supposed to do. I say to you with as much fervor and candor and honesty as I can urge, under this evidence in this case, I ask you to return a verdict of not guilty, a verdict which speaks the truth of this transaction.

"You are not responsible for the consequences of your verdict," Cook tells the 12. "You are only responsible for the truth of your verdict—and may it rest there."

With a nod to the jury, Cook turns and walks back to the defense table. Before taking a seat, he lays a gentle hand on Bobby's shoulder. In the back of the room, attorneys who have stood transfixed begin to whisper about what they've witnessed. The screech of Evans' chair being pushed back from the prosecution's table interrupts the discussions along the back wall and around the courtroom.

From the beginning of Evans' response to the defense's closing arguments, it's obvious Phillips and Cook, especially Cook, have gotten under his skin. Evans, his face a bit pale, his eyes tired, begins his rebuttal, but there's little heart in what he says.

"As one might expect, ladies and gentlemen, we were not disappointed. Mr. Cook delivers a very fine address. Mr. Phillips delivered a fine address, but there were several things I believe weren't addressed in their remarks to you."

After disputing Phillip's contention the State has lots of money and, therefore, could have brought in expert witnesses to discuss the car and whether the shooting as Bobby described, was feasible, Evans takes umbrage at Phillips' saying it's the prosecutor's role to gain a conviction.

He quotes former Supreme Court Justice George Sutherland: "The prosecutor...acts as the representative not of an ordinary party to a controversy but of a sovereignty whose obligation is to govern impartially...whose interest, therefore, in a criminal prosecution is not that it shall win a case, but that justice shall be done.

"They go on to say a prosecutor may prosecute with earnestness and with vigor—and indeed he should. But while he may strike hard blows, he is not at liberty to strike foul ones."

Evans looks at each juror. "It's fair to say the average jury has confidence those obligations, which so plainly rest upon the prosecuting attorney, will be faithfully observed.

"It is not my job, ladies and gentlemen, to be not fair. It is not my job to get a conviction. It never ceases to amaze me that defense attorneys think that's the job of a prosecutor."

Evans begins to whine about being blind-sided when Bobby took the stand and admitted he killed Hudson. "I did the best I could, ladies and gentlemen, and I don't apologize for that, because I didn't know until Monday" that Bobby Hoppe was going to plead self-defense.

Having argued his personal case as a prosecutor, Evans makes a quick run at Bobby's defense, asserting again that the way he described shooting Hudson could not have happened. Again, he makes light of Bobby's character witnesses and how the prosecution painted Don Hudson as a "terrible, terrible person."

Hitting the railing, Evans says, "Ladies and gentlemen, we are not trying Mr. Hudson."

Turning quickly toward the defense table, Evans spits out, "Mr. Cook, we are not trying Mr. Hudson. We are trying the murderer of Mr. Hudson."

Evans turns back to the jury. "We are trying the murderer of Donald Hudson and not what people have said about him.

"There is no way I can attack and somehow overcome 32 years of good character. We are not trying that. We are trying, ladies and gentlemen, what happened—what happened on July the 20th of 1957. And we know it didn't happen the way Mr. Hoppe said it happened."

With a slight sigh, Evans tells the jury, "Just like Dr. Godwin said, I don't know what good can come of sending Bobby Hoppe to prison. But

Godwin went further and talked about his sense of justice, his sense of justice and responsibility in our country—the very words that are used almost for justification of the killing of Donald Hudson are the very kinds of words—the end justifies the means—that brought about Hitler and the concentration camps of which Mr. Cook speaks."

Bone-weary and realizing he's beginning to ramble, Evans focuses, declaring, "I would say to you no passage of time and no goodness in man in our society will erase this act."

The prosecutor revisits Bobby's believability in testifying how the killing occurred and whether Hudson was trying to pass him or bump him off the road.

"Hudson comes around, ladies and gentlemen, and he's wondering what the problem is here with Bobby's car. They didn't address this issue at all," he declares.

"Hudson isn't holding a gun at Mr. Hoppe. He merely turns and looks at Mr. Hoppe—and Mr. Hoppe blows his brains out. Now that's not a nice thing to say, but that's what happened."

The rest of what Bobby said is pure "nonsense," he declares. With another sigh, Evans moves on. "The character witnesses, the parade of character witnesses makes your job very, very difficult."

Then he assures the jury the State has not tried to inject sympathy into the case.

"The family, ladies and gentlemen, do not want sympathy.

"I'm not concerned with the statement of Mr. Hoppe about how, over these years and these many thousands upon thousands of days, he has prayed about it, he tells you, and he thought about it.

"But he never had the courage, the character...to face it until we brought it into this courtroom. This is a case that had to be tried because no one else who knew who the real killer was, who the real murderer was, was going to do anything about it."

Pointing at Bobby, Evans declares, "He failed in that ultimate test of character—in courage."

Turning to look at the Hudson family, sitting together, some crying quietly, all showing the wear of emotion, Evans repeats, "No, the family does not want sympathy, because the Court will say that you, under the law, have no sympathy, no prejudice in any criminal case. You look to all the facts and circumstances in the proof before you with a single eye...to truth and justice. You render a verdict as you think truth demands and justice dictates.

"If you will do that, ladies and gentlemen—and I believe you will, and I am not telling you what your verdict is going to be—but, if you will accept that responsibility and look at all the evidence and physical, irrefutable facts, that is all that Mr. and Mrs. Hudson could ask of you. It is all that I could ask of you.

"Really, ladies and gentlemen, it's all that Mr. Hoppe could ask of you. Thank you."

CHAPTER TWENTY-FIVE

The Drama Ends

"There will come a time when you believe everything is finished.
That will be the beginning.
–Louis L 'Amour

The waiting has begun.

For days, we've been anxious for closing arguments to end; now Bobby and I find ourselves wishing the trial could go on forever. As long as it continues, there's no verdict. But we can't stop time.

Now 12 citizens, sequestered behind closed doors, deliberate Bobby's guilt or innocence. Their collective conclusion determining whether he remains free or will spend the rest of his life in prison.

When closing arguments concluded and the judge finished his charge, the jurors filed out slowly at 3:12 p.m., seeming to dread their task as much as we shrink from leaving Bobby's fate in their hands. As we watched them leave, I recall the words of Algeron Charles Swinburne, "Jury duty [is] a bog of quicksand on the path to justice."

Do the jurors believe Bobby's case rests on solid ground or has it become to them a sucking mass of bottomless sand—story piled on story, testimony following testimony—all to be slogged through before the 12 can step free of the mire?

For Bobby and me, escape will be impossible if the jurors decide Bobby killed Hudson with malice aforethought on that long-ago night on Bell Avenue. Today, walking closely beside Bobby—so quiet and reflective—the possibility of prison is palpable, thick, dank. I can almost see Bobby's hope evaporating, leaving him with no will to struggle free.

After an eerily silent walk, we arrive back at Leroy's office, once again hidden from the camera's unblinking eye. This office has been our refuge during Court recesses for the past ten days, but now the atmosphere seems foreign. On other days, we talked about the most recent testimony and the jurors' reactions, the bailiff's antics, and our own concerns.

Today, unlike our typical open discussions, silence steals our words. Each of us is lost in private thoughts.

The Drama Ends

I wish Sally were here. As soon as closing arguments wrapped up, apologizing, she dashed to the airport to catch her scheduled flight to Europe, confident of a "not guilty" verdict. I promised to call as soon as she lands to relay the news.

Finally, after more than an hour of introspection, Leroy breaks the heavy hush, insisting we get something to eat because it may be a long night. Bobby Lee Cook disagrees; he thinks the jury will return a quick verdict. That brings on a brief debate about whether swift jury decisions more often mean a verdict of guilty or innocent. There's no consensus—and no real will to debate the unknown, so we fade back into our quiet fog.

Another hour slides by with the speed of a snail. Finally, Bobby leans over and tells me he wants to escape the oppressive mood in the room, so we tell Leroy we're going to take a walk. I slide my hand into Bobby's as soon as we're in the hallway. To avoid the media horde, we slip out a back door and hurry down a narrow side street. It's hot as Hades outside, but it's better than trying to breathe through the stifling stillness of Leroy's office.

And, although it goes unsaid, we both are acutely aware it may be the last sunlight Bobby sees for a long time. My heart sinks at the thought as our shadows stretch into silhouettes, but I try to reassure Bobby the jury will find him innocent. Diane Shirley's testimony made it clear Hudson was after him, not the other way around. He doesn't respond. Just walks with his head down, thinking. It's as if he's already accepted what's coming.

Not wanting to wander too far, we walk less than two blocks. As we turn to go back to Leroy's office, we see Sherry, his secretary, hurrying toward us. "The jury has sent word they are ready to come back in," she says breathlessly.

Bobby's hand tightens around mine, and we quicken our pace, following close on Sherry's heels. Back in Leroy's office, he tells us he thinks the jury's quick return is a good sign.

Bobby Lee Cook says nothing—and his tight-mouthed silence frightens me more than words ever could.

Within moments, we're back in the courtroom, Bobby taking his place between Leroy and Bobby Lee. It's 6:39 p.m. when the door at the front of the courtroom swings open and the jury files in, heads down. Not one juror makes eye contact, even those who previously looked at me.

A Matter of Conscience

Not a good sign, I think, my heart starting to pound.

"All rise," the bailiff intones as DiRisio sweeps into the room, his black robe fluttering behind him, still unzipped—perhaps indicating he had to rush back to Court, too. Not wasting any time, he asks Samuel Russell, the foreman, if the jury has reached a verdict.

Russell rises slowly, looking at Bobby, then back at the judge, before speaking. The room crackles with tension as everyone waits for his words. Taking a deep breath, Russell spells it out: The jury's deliberation "has been inconclusive as to guilt or innocence. We really feel we cannot come to a conclusion concerning that."

Seeing the scowl on DiRisio's face, Russell reiterates, regret wrapping his words, "We cannot come to a clear verdict."

Stunned, the judge looks from Russell to other members of the jury. After a moment, he says, "Of course, we would not have expected one this soon after you undertook deliberations, and you are entitled to continue deliberating as long as you think there are reasonable prospects of reaching a verdict.

With a hint of vexation, DiRisio asks, "Are you saying to the Court there are no reasonable prospects for reaching a unanimous verdict?"

Before Russell can respond, the judge hastily warns him, "Both of us must couch what we say at this point very carefully."

Assuring DiRisio he understands, Russell says the jury has "gone down all the points...but we don't seem to get any agreement. We feel there's no prospect of getting any agreement one way or the other."

Expecting a verdict, praying for "not guilty," Bobby's whole body sinks. DiRisio appears as perplexed as Bobby. Behind his large glasses, the judge squints at the jury. His voice tight, he asks the foreman if more time, perhaps a recess for dinner or overnight, would help.

Overnight. How can Bobby live through the night, knowing some jurors think he is guilty of murder? Knowing the next day, he could go directly to prison.

But the foreman explains time is not a problem.

"It's a situation that the evidence as presented is viewed different ways by different members of the jury, and we can't seem to rectify that."

DiRisio straightens his robe slightly and folds his hands on the table before him. He leans forward as he speaks, his tone almost harsh. Without room for debate, he instructs the jurors to go back to the jury room and decide one issue: whether, as a body, they are convinced they disagree—permanently and irrevocably and irretrievably.

After the jurors and DiRisio depart at 6:43 p.m., the courtroom erupts with chatter. I somehow stand, walk to the defense table and place my hands on Bobby's shoulders. As if by rote, his right hand flutters across his chest and touches the cold fingers of my left hand where they curve across his clavicle. He's much too still, too calm. Words won't help, so I keep my hands on him, willing positive thoughts to pass though my fingertips.

Bobby Lee and Leroy slowly rise to their feet, asking if we want to go back to Leroy's office, but Bobby staunchly says no. He senses the end will come quickly.

And it does. At 7:15 p.m. the jurors return.

DiRisio asks if the jury has reached a verdict. The foreman, shaking his head, says it's hopeless. Further deliberation is futile—it would not result in a decision, he adds.

From my seat a few feet behind Bobby, I watch him closely. He sits impassively, whether resigned or stunned into stillness, I'm not sure.

DiRisio asks again if the foreman thinks it would be helpful for the jurors to adjourn and deliberate longer. Russell replies somberly, "No sir. We are hopelessly deadlocked."

The foreman is clearly distressed. We will learn later he wanted to bring back a not-guilty verdict, but it was beyond his control. The division among the jurors, Russell says, is permanent.

Seemingly resigned, DiRisio wants to be sure all jurors agree, asking them to signify by raising their hands if they feel further deliberation would serve any purpose. Marjorie Simpkins' hand shoots into the air, as she declares, "We were still talking."

I suck in my breath, my eyes zooming in on her face. From the time this woman was selected for the jury, she worried Sally and me. Intuition told us she was trouble. Now I recall this is the juror who rudely rebuffed us in the elevator. Later, we will learn that Simpkins, with her know-it-all attitude, decided Bobby was guilty long before the trial was over.

Despite her contention the jury was still deliberating, the foreman tells the judge he is convinced the disagreement is not rectifiable. Those of one opinion aren't going to change, and those of the other opinion have dug in their heels.

Taken aback at the unexpected outcome, DiRisio calls counsel to the bench. Covering the microphone, he asks if they think he should accept that the jury's division is irreconcilable. Cook and Phillips believe he has no alternative but to call a mistrial. Even Evans says, "The jurors have reached that point they can't even agree on they can't agree."

Nodding his head slowly, telling the attorneys he just wanted "to be sure I wasn't misinterpreting," DiRisio ends the bench conference and turns to address the jury.

"Members of the jury, all of us conclude the position of the jury is that the difference or division among you is irreconcilable and that you will not reach a verdict—and that will be the decision here today, that the jury is irretrievable or irrevocably, irreconcilably split and divided.

"A hung jury is declared with a mistrial as a consequence."

Bobby never moves a muscle. I can't see his face, but I know his expression is stoic, revealing nothing. He's become good at that over the last 31 years.

Though the jurors deliberated less than four hours, with a quick thunk of the gavel, it's over. The lawyers who recently rushed back to the courtroom to hear the outcome express shock that DiRisio didn't order the jury to deliberate longer.

His decision, unbelievable as it may be, is unequivocal. Thanking the jurors for their service, DiRisio dismisses them before exiting the room. But spectators, frozen in their seats, look at each other, buzzing about the jury's inability to reach a verdict. Finally, subdued and bewildered, they file out of the courtroom.

After the courtroom clears, Bobby Lee Cook turns to Bobby and nudges him to his feet. I take Bobby's hand, pulling it through the crook of my arm; Sylvia takes his other arm. Our hopes deflated, we move through the teeming throng outside the courtroom. Bud Yarnell, still staving off the media, cuts a path for us.

The Rev. Dr. James Curtis, Capt. David Cook, and Bobby's other character witnesses form a protective phalanx behind us, their faces daring anyone to break the line. Covering our backs.

Before we leave the courthouse, Bobby Lee Cook whispers to us, "Get your chin up."

The Drama Ends

The picture on the front of the next morning's newspapers proves we couldn't heed his advice. After months of waiting for the trial to begin, then sitting through 10 days of gut-wrenching testimony, the photo shows us, heads tilted downward, dismay carved into our faces.

"Dejected." That's the word used in the cutline for the picture. Even worse, the cutline continues: "The former football hero will apparently be back at the Justice Building for a retrial."

When Bobby reads those words the next morning, his face ages 10 years. Searching for words of hope, I come up blank. All I can do is repeat what Bobby Lee Cook told us before we headed home the night before: "I'm with you until this is done," he had said, a gnarled hand on Bobby's shoulder. "Don't worry about additional fees. There won't be any."

Bobby Lee also told us, despite the DA putting on his best case, he had been able to convince only two of twelve jurors. "The next time," he assured us, "there won't even be two."

Then, Cook said if Bobby *were* convicted, he was confident the verdict would be overturned.

I don't want to hear "if Bobby were convicted," although I know I'm being irrational. In truth, I'm thankful Cook and Leroy laid extensive groundwork for appeal throughout the trial.

A hung jury. A reported deadlock: ten for acquittal, two for conviction. Worn and weary, we learn the lawyers will get together July 25, less than a month away, to set a new trial date—probably in September. A mountain could be moved faster than the coming weeks will pass.

In the car, Bobby's strained visage doesn't invite words, so I concentrate on driving. As we start up Missionary Ridge, Bobby reaches for my hand and squeezes it. Each of us is comforted by the other's touch, so we hold hands as we instinctively recite the Lord's Prayer, followed by the second part of our ritual, the 23rd Psalm.

As soon as we arrive home, I phone Sally in England, telling her the verdict was 10 to 2—a hung jury. For a moment, stark silence hums on the line. Completely confounded, Sally can't believe the jury did not unanimously find Bobby innocent.

"I just don't understand how the jurors could have trusted any of the State's witnesses," she says from too far away. I press my fist against my mouth, trying not to cry.

"I was absolutely convinced they believed Bobby and would find him innocent," she says, and I hear the righteous anger in her voice. "I'm so sorry, Sherry."

I thank Sally, hang up, and let the tears flow.

Before going into the living room where Bobby is holding Pepi on his lap, I wipe away the tears and blow my nose. It's a hilarious scene—a 90-pound Old English Sheepdog held like a baby. I smile, knowing Pepi's presence soothes Bobby, calming his turbulent thoughts.

* * *

Both the State and the defense have told DiRisio they have little or no hope of negotiating any kind of plea bargain.

Prosecutor Tom Evans reported in the *Chattanooga News-Free Press* that the Hudson family was "certainly not opposing another trial in the case." The paper noted several of the Hudsons indicated they were relieved to finally know who the triggerman was in Don's death.

In the same article, Bobby Lee Cook told reporter John Wilson the defense team had no regrets about its strategy, including an all-or-nothing gamble on first-degree murder. Considering the hung jury, Bobby and I are thankful the jury had no alternative to consider as a compromise.

Evans told the reporter the State would pick up steam in a second trial. Asked about retrials, he added, "If you get a hung jury after several times, then you begin to think you have a problem." Saying he had huddled with the Hudsons, he indicated they are "not out for blood, but they certainly didn't say they couldn't go through another trial."

Georgia Hudson's remarks weren't as temperate. The 83-year-old woman, who had asked the police to resurrect the case after more than 30 years, declared with a ferocity that belied her age: "We're going all the way. I don't have any use for Hoppe. I don't like killers."

Evans declared he "believed the long delay in the case and the attendant loss of evidence worked to the detriment of the State about 95 percent." He also fretted the State hadn't had time to prepare against Diane Shirley. But, he assured the reporter, the State will "X-ray" Mrs. Shirley's background prior to the next trial. Strangely, though, he adds he's not optimistic.

"The biggest problem we had was 31 years of silence by Mr. Hoppe. Why didn't he come forward—this man of character?" he lamented to reporters. "If you want to talk about character, talk about Mr. Burnette. Don't talk about Mr. Hoppe," he said, adding Burnette was willing to take the stand even though he knew he would undergo a grueling cross-examination because of his past record of selling drugs.

We're back to the waiting game—almost a month before the hearing to schedule a new trial—so Bobby and I pack and head back to Nashville. When we pull into the rest area on Hales Bar Lake, our usual meditation break, I tell Bobby, despite our disappointment, it could be worse. With much to be grateful for, we clasp hands and bow our heads. After reciting the Lord's Prayer and the Twenty-third Psalm, we offer thanks we are together—that Bobby isn't sitting in jail hoping to get out on bond while awaiting an appeal.

The next morning on the way from our condo to Nashville State, despite my heavy heart, I'm no longer without words to pray. And when I pull in my parking space, the brawny security guard who always opens my door gives me a reassuring hug. Inside, my staff has gathered to welcome me back, lifting my spirits with their support.

Amazingly, time passes quickly. Bobby and I make a fast trip to St. Augustine, soaking up the Florida sun, which brings color back to Bobby's gaunt face, while the ocean breezes clear our heads. Once again, gazing across an expanse of water soothes our souls. The uncertainty of our future looms heavy, so we treasure this respite, aware we may never share such moments again.

Back in Nashville, I get a call from Chancellor Tom Garland, asking me to come to the Tennessee Board of Regents office to meet with him. Fearing the worse, I don't even tell Bobby.

Winding through traffic along Murfreesboro Road, it dawns on me, if Garland tells me to hit the road, as Albert Ellis averred, it is not the worst thing that could happen.

When I arrive, the Chancellor ushers me into his office and offers coffee. After we take our seats, he leans forward, concern in his pale eyes, and asks how I'm doing. Lowering my head, I sip my steaming coffee, wondering if his solicitude is a prelude for the gut-punch to come.

When Garland speaks, I sit stupefied. Did I hear what I thought I did? Did he ask if I would like to go to Roane State Community College as interim president for a year after Nashville State's new president arrives? I cannot believe I'm being offered another presidency when Bobby's fate lies in limbo.

A Matter of Conscience

My first day at Roane State will be the day after the hearing date in late July.

Shaking off my disbelief, I thank Garland profusely. Still stunned, I make my way to my car and start back to Nashville State. But I can't wait to talk to Bobby, so I stop at the first phone booth and call our condo in West Nashville. Pepi is barking as Bobby picks up the phone, and I'm almost incoherent as I struggle to share the good news. Between the barking dog and my stumbling words, Bobby can't understand me, so I force myself to repeat everything slowly.

Later that evening when I arrive home from work, Bobby greets me with a wide smile and a glass of wine, ecstatic his trial has not derailed my career. After a brief celebration, we talk about what this opportunity means. A new beginning for us and a refuge after the storm.

For Bobby, if he's not convicted, it means he won't have to return to Chattanooga to live. Chattanooga—a city he once loved and one that loved him back. Now it's just a reservoir of bad memories. The dread of everyone learning he shot Hudson is over, but he's honest with himself—he knows whenever anyone in Chattanooga sees him, that person will recall the killing first and foremost.

Now with the anticipation of a new beginning, hours and days drag as we wait for the hearing to learn when the second trial will begin. We vacillate between excitement and foreboding, eager to put the past behind us, restless because the future is less than clear.

* * *

Just when we think the door is closing on our darkest days, an astounding phone call kicks it wide open again.

I'm sitting on the patio when I hear the phone ring inside. Dashing through the door, I grab the receiver, expecting it to be Leroy Phillips or Bobby Lee Cook. Instead, it's Sylvia.

Breathless with excitement, Sylvia tells me her husband just received a telephone call.

"The man on the other end said he knew who killed Don Hudson—and it wasn't Bobby."

I'm trying to take in her words, but my head is spinning with these words.

Her voice now thick with tears, Sylvia whispers, "Sherry, he left the phone number of someone he swears can provide more information."

Jotting down the number on a post-in note, I thank Sylvia and hang up, My heart in my throat, I sit down on the nearest chair and stare at the number—my shaking hand causing the digits to dance on the page. Taking a calming breath, I pick up the phone again and dial the operator to check the area code.

"Los Angeles?"

"Los Angeles," she repeats, with conviction.

Stunned, I sit another moment before walking into the kitchen where Bobby is shaking dry dog food into Pepi's bowl. Seeing my expression, he rises slowly, a question lighting his eyes. Not knowing the best way to begin, I simply repeat what Sylvia just told me.

Rather than being excited as I expected, Bobby stoops down for Pepi's water bowl, fills it from the faucet, and places it gently on the floor. He's buying time. When he finally looks at me, he has slipped back into the somberness I know so well from the trial.

I reach out to take his hand, but he steps backward, drawing away from me. Hot tears blur my vision. How dare he not be happy about this?

Seeing my distress, Bobby pulls me against his shoulder and holds me a moment. Then, his voice husky with emotion, he says, "Sherry, I shot Don Hudson. I told you, it was me.

"I don't know why someone would make up such a story, but I want you to forget it. Forget you ever heard it."

"No, Bobby..." I begin, but he cuts me off.

"Sherry, it's what I want." His eyes are pleading, so I nod in silent agreement.

And in the following days, as he requested, I try not to think about that phone call, but it keeps niggling its way back into my mind. I simply can't sit on this. So, contrary to Bobby's wishes, I call Leroy Phillips at his office, telling his secretary it's an emergency.

Leroy picks up in seconds. "Sherry, what is it?"

I tell him about the call Sylvia's husband received, and I excitedly pass on the Los Angeles phone number. Then I hold my breath, waiting for his whoop of joy.

Instead, Leroy is quiet—surprisingly quiet. Then he shifts into attorney mode.

"Let it go, Sherry," he says quietly. "I do not think it's wise to pursue such an out-of-the-blue lead. I agree with Bobby: Let sleeping dogs lie."

Exasperated, I start to debate but stop as I feel the tension vibrate along the line. I want to slam the phone in his ear; I want to shout at him for being so blasé, but I check myself. As I hang up, I'm already sure I can't "let sleeping dogs lie."

If there is a remote possibility Bobby did not kill Hudson, I have to know. My aching head says Bobby would never have told me he killed Hudson if it weren't true, but my heart wants to prove him wrong, to grab his guilt and let it fly into the sky like a balloon.

I sit quietly by the telephone, thinking. After a while I dial Leroy again and tell him I simply cannot dismiss this confession, as bizarre as it may seem.

Realizing it's hopeless to turn me around, Leroy agrees to have his investigator contact the informant in Los Angeles. Although relieved, I sleep little that night, anxious to hear from Leroy, dreading to tell Bobby what I've done.

The next day Leroy calls and asks Bobby and me to come to his office to go over what Bud Yarnell learned from the man—a man by the last name of King, Leroy says.

Now I have to tell Bobby I went against his wishes. Perplexed and aggravated, he stares at me, his blue eyes going gray.

"Sherry, I cannot believe you called Leroy. Why?"

I open my mouth, but nothing comes out, so Bobby turns on his heels and heads out the door to the car—his tacit agreement to accompany me to Leroy's office. The drive downtown is strained. But seeing Bobby's clinched jaw slowly relax, I just hope that it is because he is becoming intrigued.

It's late in the afternoon, so we find a parking spot on the street adjacent to Leroy's office. Within minutes, we take our seats around the conference table where we've spent so many anxious hours the past few months. But today is different. As always, suspense hangs in the air, but today it's not fear-filled.

Leroy nods at Bud, who starts to speak.

"Well, I called that number in Los Angeles about 1 a.m. today and reached a Mr. King," Bud says, before pausing. He looks from Bobby to me, knowing what he's getting ready to say is going to shock us—and he's right. We're stunned.

Across the table, Bud tilts his bald head and burly shoulders toward us. "Bobby, Mr. King told me, all these years, you thought you killed Don Hudson—but you didn't. He said you did fire your shotgun. And that caused Hudson to swerve and wreck his car, but you were not the one who killed Don Hudson."

My mind spins. Bobby's shot didn't hit Hudson. It just caused his wreck. Is that correct?

Afternoon shadows stretch across the conference table, creating odd designs on our pale faces. A long pause thickens the air, each of us lost in thought. Outside, the shrill siren of a fire engine jerks us back to reality. Simultaneously, we refocus on Bud, our eyes asking for more.

Realizing the impact of his words, he continues, "That's about all I know right now, except Mr. King said—let me check my notes to be precise. He said: 'I did it. I was *hired* to do it.'"

Suddenly, in my mind's eye, I can clearly see the headlines in the paper the morning following Don's death: Young Reputed Liquor Runner Slain Gangland Style in N. Chattanooga.

Is that possible? Was it a hit? By whom? A competing liquor runner?

Bud is still talking, so I silence my mind. He's saying Mr. King assured him he can provide details about the inside of Hudson's car that will match police records.

Although Bobby isn't facing me, I feel a furrow deepening between his eyes.

"How could that be true?" he whispers. Then he repeats it louder, directing the question first at Bud, then at Leroy. Under the table, Bobby takes my hand, holding on, afraid of giving in to empty hopes.

Bud sees our blank stares, so he continues. "As I reviewed my notes from the telephone call, I realized this King guy gave me two first names—Jack and Edward. I don't know which, if either, is really his name. Or maybe it's Jack Edward King."

The mounting tension in the room swamps Bud, so he takes a deep breath and continues. "Here's what he described as happening that night in 1957: Mr. King and a policeman—local, I guess—were parked on a side street. They planned to ambush Hudson as he came down Bell

Avenue. Why they wanted to kill him, he never said. Guess we'll leave that to police detectives.

"Anyway, as he and the policeman were sitting there, they heard gunfire and then the sound of a car crashing. King leaped out and ran to the scene while the policeman waited in the car.

"King said he leaned into Don's car and realized he was unconscious—slumped over the steering wheel. The right side of Don's head was bloody, but he was breathing. After glancing around, King shot him pointblank in the eye.

"Mr. King swears he can provide never-published details, details only the police could know. How does he know what the police know, and how does it link back to the policeman? At this point, we simply don't know.

"Mr. King ran back to the car and the two men took off before anyone else arrived."

Bud pauses to pour a glass of water from the pitcher on a tray in the center of the table.

After taking a long drink, Bud looks directly at Bobby. "Bobby, there *was* a gun in Don's car. When he hit the wall, the gun flew on to the front floorboard. Mr. King said, after he shot Don, he grabbed the gun from the floorboard and ran. It all happened in mere seconds."

Suddenly I recall what Agnes Rivers told police back in 1957—she heard two gunshots.

I look at Bobby, gauging his reaction. For a moment, his blue eyes are as bright as they were the day we married. I can tell he wants to believe, but he's pragmatic.

"Why did he come forward now?" Bobby asks softly. "Why would he say he killed Hudson?"

Bud shrugs slightly. "He said he thought you would be acquitted. When that didn't happen, he said he couldn't let you go through another trial when he was the one who killed Hudson."

Bobby drinks up Bud's words, letting them sink in, saying nothing.

I'm not as calm. I swivel toward Leroy with a smile, wanting to know the next step.

But Leroy is frowning. He wants to talk to Bobby Lee Cook before we go down that road.

Although I try to ask more questions, Leroy refuses to speculate—so Bobby and I leave, surprisingly jumpy and unsure what to feel.

The Drama Ends

Cook is out of the state on business, so we don't hear from Leroy right away. And before he gets back to us, it's time to return to Chattanooga for the hearing, slated for Monday morning. We arrive Sunday afternoon.

More anxious waiting. The evening hours drag by, but a call from Kevin cheers us.

Bobby is walking Pepi when the phone rings about 10 p.m. I pick up hesitantly. It's Leroy, and he's talking so fast, I ask him to slow down. Leroy is steaming. Absolutely furious. Gerbitz just called him to say he will notify the judge tomorrow he plans to drop the State's prosecution.

That's wonderful news—why is Leroy so angry?

"That son-of-a-bitch waited until the last minute to call me—waited until the evening before the hearing. I'll bet a million dollars he's known for days—maybe weeks—he was going to drop the case, but the bastard wanted us to sweat it out," Leroy sputters.

I'm so elated I could care less about the timing. I just want to get off the phone and tell Bobby. With a quick thanks, I dash to meet Bobby as he comes through the front door.

"It's over, Bobby; it's over!" I shout, grabbing him in a bear hug.

"What are you talking about?" he asks, backing away, blinking rapidly.

"Gerbitz is dismissing your case," I repeat. Then I tell him about Leroy's phone call.

Hesitant to believe, Bobby refuses to be jubilant, but I see hope flicker in his eyes. That night, I toss and turn until Bobby says he's going to sleep on the couch if I don't settle down. As soon as the newspaper hits the front doorstep, I throw off the covers and rush outside to grab it.

"Attorney general expected to drop Hoppe prosecution," declares the front-page headline. I run back to the bedroom and read the article aloud to Bobby. Sitting side by side on the bed, we hold each other, say a quick prayer of thanksgiving, and read the article again.

The article says Gerbitz has called a news conference for 9:30 this morning. Over and over again, I savor the words: "The prosecution is expected to serve formal notice on the record in the Hoppe case today that it will not prosecute the case further, according to an informed source. Though such a notice would not prevent the State from reopening the case against Hoppe in the future, it was understood that the prosecution has no plans to do so."

A Matter of Conscience

Suddenly, it sinks in. The DA could open the case again someday. A cloud passes over Bobby's face.

* * *

Bobby and I elect not to attend the Court proceedings that day.

Phillips says it's not necessary and we should avoid the media frenzy. Later we learn the process moved quickly, with Evans telling the Court, "The State is announcing we will enter a *nol pros* in the case.

"Since the trial, we have talked to other witnesses, we have done additional investigation—there's nothing of any evidentiary significance where we feel it would change the weight of the evidence that was already presented to a jury. At the best we would see another jury unable to resolve the matter. Therefore, we can see no purpose at this point in continuing the prosecution. We would enter a *nol pros*."

DiRisio quickly says, "All right. That will be entered."

That's it. It's over. It's finally over.

Although relieved we can move on with our lives, Bobby regrets the threat of a re-trial hanging over him forever. Despite that, our jubilation cannot be contained.

Across town, in North Chattanooga in the house where Don Hudson lived with his parents, Mrs. Hudson tells reporter Dick Kopper she's not only disappointed in Gerbitz's decision, she's flat mad.

"Gerbitz is no good. If he is going to turn murderers loose, we don't need him. That will get him out of office, I'll bet. I worked to get him in. I'll work to get him out."

And, she added, God will do the job if the prosecutors don't.

She tells Kopper her boy did not carry a gun or knife. He was afraid for his life the week before he died. "He knew he was going. He knew that something was happening. He said, 'If I don't come back, God is forgiving.'"

Suppressing her anger, she said, "I give my son up. But I'd like to see justice tomorrow."

When Kopper reached him, Heck refused to answer questions, although admitting he and the attorney general had worked closely together on the case. "I think we proved what we set out to prove—to show who actually killed Don Hudson. Like Tom Evans said, it was a whodunit from 1957 all the way until Hoppe took the stand and told who done it."

The Drama Ends

Back in Mars Hill, N.C., the Rev. Godwin tells *Free-Press reporter* John Wilson, "I have nothing in the world except respect for Hoppe. I just wish him the best. I think he's trying to live a good life. He's had a hard time outliving the incident that happened a long time ago.

"I don't think he could have a thing against me," Godwin asserted. Then, almost as an afterthought, he added, "But he may have."

That evening in the *Chattanooga News-Free Press*, Gerbitz's press conference is the headline. In one-inch bold type, the banner read "HOPPE WON'T BE TRIED 2ND TIME. Charge of Murder Now Laid to Rest."

Steven Epley and Michael Finn, *News-Free Press* staff writers, reported Gerbitz said he and his staff made a professional decision not to retry Bobby Hoppe for the 1957 slaying of Teddy Donald Hudson, and there were no plans to resurrect the case even if new evidence is presented. The decision was not made lightly, Gerbitz said, but it was final.

For the first time, he admitted how taken aback he was by Bobby's plea of self-defense. "You could have knocked me over with a feather." The prosecution had expected a not guilty plea.

The Hudson family remains adamant they will not give up. Sue Burnette, Hudson's sister, spoke passionately, telling the reporter, "We know Bobby did it. I think the saddest part is that first-degree murder will never be proved." Her elderly mother, she added, literally vomited when she learned Friday the DA would not attempt to take the case to trial a second time.

Now it is clear. Gerbitz told the Hudsons about his decision last Friday but waited until Sunday night to notify the defense.

After the Monday morning press conference, Leroy Phillips' temper flares again when he talks to reporters. "I appreciate the great professional courtesy of the district attorney's office," he said with undisguised sarcasm. "Now I know how Jesse Jackson felt," he adds, referring to presidential nominee Michael Dukakis' failure to inform Jackson he had selected Texas Sen. Lloyd Bentsen as his running mate.

As far as Gerbitz's promise that Bobby would not be tried again, Phillips said, "I'm extremely pleased for Bobby Hoppe. He can now go on with his life."

Phillips also told the reporter another trial would have been a waste of taxpayers' money, predicting a second trial would have resulted in a not-guilty verdict.

Gerbitz evidently agreed, saying his office could find nothing different from what they presented during trial. That left him with little choice, since "the defendant's constitutional right to a speedy trial, coupled with the fact that the prosecution already had a crack at convicting Mr. Hoppe, pretty much eliminates any chance of convincing a court to retry the matter."

Evans agreed. "With the lack of new evidence, it appears if we retried the case, we would end up with the same verdict."

Bragging on the efforts of the police department, Evans noted several positives came from the trial, including the solving of a decades-old "whodunit." He admitted the decision to try Bobby "stirred criticism from the public, and the decision not to re-try him, even though the right decision, will probably not be a popular one."

Despite Gerbitz's maintaining "the prosecution spent an embarrassing amount of time on the case," he later said the cost of a second trial was not a factor in his decision.

Although Bobby and I chose not to attend the press conference, Bobby provided a written statement to the media. He began by saying how thankful he was the case had been dismissed.

"For thirty-one years I have lived with a black cloud over my life. I have lived with rumors and insinuations I was a murderer. After the hell on earth I have been through the past few months and after watching my family's name be dragged through the mud, I know more than ever why I never tried to clear my name during all those years.

"I realize now, though, if I were ever to be vindicated and free to live life without the fear of this ugly thing rearing its head, it had to be aired in open court—even if the indictment and trial were based for the most part on false testimony."

The editorial in the following Tuesday's edition of the *Chattanooga News-Free Press* addressed the trial's uncertain end. The first two sentences set the stage, "It began with a shocking flash of gunfire that took a young man's life. Then came 31 years of no real answers." Noting it was surprising the case came to trial after so many years, the editorial asserted the whole matter had been a "highly troubling, nagging, frustrating case."

The Drama Ends

After running through the highlights of the trial, the editorial concluded, "What a tragedy that one man's life was lost, that another has lived under a dark shadow for so many years, and that anguish has been suffered by the families of both."

* * *

In our excitement following the abrupt conclusion of Bobby's case, we temporarily set aside the out-of-the-blue confession by Mr. King. Leroy never mentions it as we go through the motions of dismissal. But the hung jury, the *nol pros* and even Gerbitz's comments could not make me forget the possibility Bobby was not Hudson's killer.

After the chaos settles at bit, I call Leroy to ask if he ever talked with Bobby Lee Cook.

There's silence on the other end of the line, then a sigh. "Yes, I talked with Bobby Lee," Phillips says. "At this junction, Bobby Lee and I are concerned about reopening the case.

"Sherry, Bobby's case was dismissed 'with prejudice.' That means Gerbitz can reopen the case if new evidence surfaced."

I'm listening carefully, but I still do not understand. I want Mr. King subpoenaed and brought to Chattanooga. I want the DA to hear what he told Bud. I want the world to know Bobby is innocent. Most importantly, I want Bobby himself to hear the words.

In a controlled voice, Leroy reasons with me. "Sherry, if we give the DA the King information and it doesn't stand up under scrutiny, it's possible during another investigation the DA might unearth something we don't know about. He could decide to try Bobby again."

I start to argue, but he cuts me off. "Two details King cited are inaccurate, Sherry, and that makes me extremely uncomfortable.

"I'm afraid he might just be a kook," Leroy says, trying to calm me.

Despite his warnings, I'm not sure I'm ready to yield the possibility the guilt Bobby has carried so long could be lifted forever.

That night, Bobby and I talk about what Bud told us. Then we discuss Leroy's opinion. Finally, we turn off the light on another sleepless night.

The next morning, Bobby tells me to let it go. "Please listen to me: On Bobby Lee Cook's advice, we gambled—going for first-degree or nothing. Thankfully, we won.

"But, Sherry, I'm not a young man. A battle like we've been through takes its toll, regardless of the outcome. I'm sorry, but I'm simply not willing to risk everything again."

I look more closely at my husband. I see smudges of no sleep under his eyes again. He has wrestled with this all night. It's not a decision he's come to lightly, so I take his hand in both of mine. Pulling his hand away, Bobby draws me down into his arms, and I rest my head on his shoulder, forcing my thoughts to be still.

With regret but with total understanding, I accept Bobby's decision.

It's a decision that will come back to haunt me—20 years later.

* * *

That evening Bobby and I pack as much as we can. I must head back to Nashville State the next morning for a farewell party with faculty and staff. Bobby will stay in Chattanooga to supervise the loading of the moving van that will carry our furniture to Roane County, where I have accepted a position as interim president of Roane State Community College.

While Bobby and I work that evening, we receive two phone calls.

The first is from Leroy Phillips, who had been approached that day in the grocery story by one of the jurors who told Phillips Marjorie Simpkins was a "bitch." She said Simpkins decided Bobby was guilty long before the trial was over. In fact, Simpkins admitted she and her husband had driven the route Bobby and Hudson had taken the night Hudson was shot.

The lady told Phillips the 10 jurors who believed Bobby was innocent had no doubt Odene was lying. That woman didn't convince anyone, she declared. And they thought the preacher ought to be hung for betraying a confidence. She also said Isabelle Rucker, the other juror who held out against acquittal, was about to change her mind when Simpkins declared the jury could stay there 'til Hell froze over, but she wasn't going to change *her* mind. At that point, Ms. Rucker said there was no need to change her mind even if she now thought it likely Bobby was innocent.

The second call of the evening came from a good friend who held a high level position in Hamilton County government. She wanted to offer best wishes and also to pass along a message from Gary Gerbitz. The day the indictment was first made public, this friend saw Gerbitz at a reception at the Read House. She pulled him aside and asked what was going to happen to Bobby, explaining I was her friend. According to her, Gerbitz said, "I want you to know we are not out for blood—we are doing what we have to do. We try to do what's right."

Gerbitz told my friend that Central graduate Steve Bevil, one of his assistant DAs, was so upset he couldn't talk about the case; Bobby was his idol.

Although this good friend sent several cards during the trial, I had no idea until her phone call that she had talked with Gerbitz. Touched deeply, I tell her how much I appreciate what she did.

But she's not through. She tells me Gerbitz said he had pondered his decision to dismiss the case a long time. He told her, "I'm going to be barbequed. I don't care what they say—I did what was right."

And, she adds, "Gary wants you to know this case will never be brought up again. It's over."

With a hitch in my voice, I share this message with Bobby. A wave of relief washes over his face, and for the first time, I see real hope in his eyes.

When I learn Gerbitz told members of Friends and Families of Murdered Victims he would "retry former football star Bobby Hoppe...if adequate proof emerged," I was thankful for the message my friend shared with me months earlier.

Then, to my amazement, I read that Gerbitz also told the group he was surprised the jury failed to find Bobby Hoppe *not guilty* because of the inadequacy of the State's proof. He said a retrial would have resulted in an acquittal.

Those words brought tears to my eyes, and it seemed Bobby stood a little straighter, knowing Gerbitz told the world the State didn't have the evidence to convict him of murder.

Gerbitz was also quoted as saying he is convinced "with all of my heart that Hoppe could have walked out of that courtroom and said to every single one of you and every single member of his family, 'I told you I wasn't guilty, and now a jury has proved it.'"

When Sue Burnette, Hudson's sister, asked him if he would take the case back to court if she gave him the proof, Gerbitz responded, "Absolutely."

334

Burnette alleged she has information Hoppe was not the only one involved in the killing.

"If you all had dug a little further you would have found out a lot of things,'" she said. "There was more involved in that case. You've just got to dig. If you are just going to do it halfway, don't even bother."

After the meeting, Burnette said she is still, "developing the other information about the case and is not yet ready to disclose it."

Reading those words, my minds flashes back to Bud's revelation about Mr. King, the man from Los Angeles who said he killed her brother.

But one section of an article Dick Kopper wrote for the *Chattanooga Times* about the Friends meeting jumped off the page. Both Gerbitz and Evans told Kopper they did not believe Hoppe's self-defense account initially. But, Evans said, "When investigators later obtained vehicles like the 1948 DeSoto Hudson was driving and Hoppe's auto, it developed that Hoppe's story was not a physical impossibility."

For Bobby, that statement negated the hung jury. Gerbitz and Evans said Bobby's description of what happened that night was not only plausible; it was physically possible.

* * *

Some of Bobby's closest friends never accepted his confession. Many thought Joan shot her ex-lover and Bobby covered for her. But Bobby believed he killed Hudson, and his sureness silenced my doubts.

I buried the call from King so deeply in my subconscious it never surfaced again until July 2008 when I forced myself to travel to the oceanfront home Bobby loved. I dreaded the trip there—my first since he died. To distract myself on the flight down, I focused on my mission: I planned to read materials I had boxed and saved from the trial, pour through more than 1000 pages of trial transcripts I had brought with me, and then decide if I could continue the story Bobby conditionally agreed to let me write before he died.

My arrival at the condo was as difficult as I had expected. I walked through the rooms, gently running my hands over Bobby's books and personal collections, struggling to feel his spirit. But it eluded me, and my heart ached for what I had lost and could not find. Overwhelmed by emptiness, I turned to the task at hand and headed for the closet where the boxes were stored.

The Drama Ends

Sitting on the floor, boxes encircling me, I was reluctant to reopen the floodgate of memories. But as I resolutely began to pour through the first box, I was relieved to find it had nothing to do with the trial. It was filled with yellowed newspaper clippings from Bobby's days at Central High and Auburn. I paused to read a few, wishing I had made him tell me more about his football career.

Pulled irresistibly to the second and third boxes, I found hundreds of clippings from all over the nation—reporters' synopses of the 1966 grand jury hearing, Bobby's indictment, the investigation, and the preliminary hearing in 1988. Endless articles from the trial. Photos of Bobby and me leaving the courthouse after the mistrial—heads down, dejected, pictures of the Hudsons, a stock photo of Judge DiRisio, and a picture of Gary Gerbitz holding forth at a press conference. There were candid shots of Bobby, his face drawn, his head tilted toward Leroy Phillips and Bobby Lee Cook, listening intently. And, finally, the shot of Bobby twisting his Auburn national championship ring like a talisman.

The scrapbook of a nightmare.

Heart-wrenching memories mixed with thankfulness as I remembered the good, salt-of-the-earth people who risked their own reputation to stand by Bobby during his darkest days.

And then, at the bottom of the last box, with a jolt I picked up a piece of faded notebook paper with five yellow post-it notes long ago stuck haphazardly in a column down the page. My heart sinking, I scanned them quickly. Although the writing had grown faint, I could read it clearly—words and numbers written in my own handwriting. Los Angeles. Edward King. Jack King. A phone number. Memories hidden in the recesses of my mind emerged with a force that knocked me backward.

Stunned, I made myself read the scribbles again. The letters stretched and pulled before my eyes, growing larger and bolder as their significance magnified in my swirling mind. With the steady sound of the ocean in my ears and the Florida sun warming my back through the glass patio doors, I felt as if I'd been sucker-punched. When I could breathe again, I read through my notes once more, more slowly this time. Like a dream, hazy bits and pieces tumbled from the buried niche in my mind where they'd been stored for 20 years.

I ran for the nearest bathroom, suddenly sick to my stomach.

A Matter of Conscience

Why did I not pursue this? Why did I let Bobby go to his grave thinking he killed Hudson if there were a remote possibility it was someone else?

Then with cutting clarity, I remembered Leroy's argument: The risk was too great.

But sitting alone in the condo Bobby and I bought for our retirement, logic didn't lessen my profound regret. I lowered my head into my newsprint-stained hands and sobbed again, the maelstrom in my mind threatening to engulf me. Over and over the words played through my head.

Bobby went to his death with an indelible K on his soul: Forgiven yet burdened by guilt.

I was angry—angry with Leroy for putting me off. Angry with Bobby for not wanting to continue to fight—and, most of all, angry with myself for floating along merrily, denying us what might have been a different ending.

Light-headed from shock and dismay, I leaned my head onto my knees to keep from fainting, whispering my remorse through broken sobs.

What if it wasn't you, Bobby? What if it wasn't you, after all?

The words echoed in the silent room, bouncing to the ocean waves before being thrown back at me.

But it's too late...too late.

I cried until I was limp, 'til the red sky outside the window had turned to deep darkness.

Making myself rise from the floor, I stumbled onto the balcony where a starless night hid my tear-streaked face. Standing there, listening to the ocean waves crash on the shoreline, I recalled thinking I had cried myself out in the months after Bobby died. My heart had ached each moment since then, but this pain was different. Regret raced through my veins like broken glass. Before today, I had begun to accept the constant heartache, my numbness growing daily.

Devastating though it was, Bobby's death was beyond my control.

But this. Oh, God, this perhaps, I could have changed.

Dear Bobby, if I had pushed harder, if I had not let my relief at your sudden freedom and our unbridled happiness wash away the confession on these notes, perhaps you could have died easier.

Forgive me, Bobby...forgive me.

Looking Back

Pray you now, forget and forgive.
–Shakespeare (1564-1616)
King Lear, Act 4, Scene 7

Between the radiant white of a clear conscience and the coal black of a conscience sullied by sin lie many shades of gray—where most of us live our lives. Not perfect yet not beyond redemption.

After the life-changing event of July 21, 1957, Bobby was submerged in an inky sea. For 31 years, he existed beneath the black, putrid backwash of guilt. Believing he killed a man, even in self-defense, left Bobby with a tortured conscience, a soul filled with irreversible regret.

Bobby clutched his secret deep inside, sharing it with no one except Harry Friedman, his attorneys, and the Reverend Godwin—who had his own definition of conscience. Bobby's guilt, magnified by suspicion he perceived in others' eyes, along with the abiding fear his actions would be made public, left him just a half-step this side of Hell.

As horrible as the indictment and trial were, they released Bobby from his worst fear: After 31 years, he confessed—and survived the indignity.

And, in Court, having to relive those moments when he knew Hudson was trying to kill him seemed to assuage Bobby's guilt. As he testified about his fear, he realized he had no alternative to his split-second decision to pull the trigger. But it would take more than that knowledge for him to feel forgiven. It would take grace.

Although the jury's decision in 1988 was not unequivocal, Bobby learned God's grace is. Through grace, he was able to live almost twenty more years after his trial.

I would not say Bobby's conscience never troubled him again. But he was able to see the gray of life, rather than always feeling engulfed in total blackness. In that grace-filled gray area, Bobby lived a good and productive life.

A Matter of Conscience

Like Colin Cross, who authored *Who Was Jesus?*—a book my husband read, underlined and highlighted—when Bobby visited the Galilee region, he found it singularly beautiful.

As Cross wrote, "It seems to be the perfect setting for the teaching of eternal truths, a place for clarity and for opening the soul." It was that sense of peace Bobby found as he gazed at the Sea of Galilee, calling it the most beautiful and calmest expanse of blue he had ever seen.

Looking back, I believe it was in Israel that Bobby finally forgave himself. For him, it was a time of extraordinary grace.

But Bobby could never totally put away the stigma of having killed a man. For months, he might go without mentioning it. Then he would suddenly remember and slip back into sadness. When Auburn's National Championship Team celebrated its 50th reunion the year before Bobby died, he refused to attend, fearful his former teammates would talk behind his back—that they would glimpse the K he could not put down.

A few might have, but Bobby's true friends never saw that K when they looked at him. They saw a kind man whose long-ago action haunted him the rest of his life. They saw behind the mask, straight to his heart.

As for me, I never once doubted Bobby's love. Even when he was being a rascal—and he could be—I knew his love for me was deep and firm. He believed in me, and that belief always made such a difference.

In contrast, he frequently doubted himself. Scarred by one life event, I don't think he ever realized what a profoundly good man he was.

THE TWELFTH OF NEVER

You ask how much I need you, must I explain?
I need you, oh my darling, like roses need rain.
You ask how long I'll love you, I'll tell you true.
Until the Twelfth of Never, I'll still be loving you.
Hold me close; never let me go.
Hold me close; melt my heart like April snow.
I'll love you 'til the bluebells forget to bloom.
I'll love you 'til the clover has lost its perfume.
I'll love you 'til the poets run out of rhyme.
Until the Twelfth of Never, and that's a long, long time.
Until the Twelfth of Never, and that's a long, long time.

Music and lyrics by Paul Francis Webster and Jerry Livingston. With permission of Webster Music Co. and Spirit Two Music.

Attorney Bobby Lee Cook reviewing his notes while waiting with Bobby and Sherry Hoppe outside the courtroom during a break in one of the few moments of levity during the 1988 trial

Acknowledgements

During closing arguments at Bobby Hoppe's trial, famed criminal attorney Bobby Lee Cook used a tapestry as a metaphor for one's life. For having helped us piece together the tapestry of Bobby's life, the authors gratefully acknowledge the many people who provided information and inspiration.

For their belief in our manuscript and their endless support and guidance, we express our heartfelt appreciation to our publishers, Carol and Frank Daniels III, Wakestone Press, Nashville. Thank you for believing. Our sincere thanks also go to our publicist, Nanette Noffsinger Crowell who, with Carol and Frank, made an enthusiastic and supportive triad.

Deepest gratitude to Bobby Lee Cook for reviewing and blessing our manuscript. We appreciate the information supplied by Hamilton County Criminal Court Clerk Edna Camp, Barbara Bradford, former court reporter, Chaddra Moore, State Archive Library of Tennessee, and Jim Reese, Hamilton County Bicentennial Library.

Credit is given for legal perspective and personal remembrances provided by Sam Payne, Doug Meyer and Sally Weaver. We want to recognize Robert Baker, Peter Macdonald, and Karen Utusco for their legal insight.

We acknowledge members of the Central Connection who shared memories of Bobby's years at Central High: Bill Runion, Larry Clingan, Jim Woods, Eddie Lance, Bill (Goat) Watson, and Paul Allen Campbell. Special thanks to Gene Etter who not only provided stories but also reviewed the Central High chapters. Thanks to Katherine Farmer, Coach Stan Farmer's widow, for her remembrances.

We appreciate the many tales recounted by some of the football players Bobby coached—David Cook, Tim Miller, Billy Bruning, Eddie Upshaw, Tony Frank, and Lynn Daniel, as well as coaches Jesse Lee (Sonny) Day and Paul Chambers. We regret we could not include all of their tales.

The same can be said for Bobby's Auburn teammates, especially Bobby's roommate and lifelong friend Sentell Harper, as well as Jim Jeffrey, Lloyd Nix, Ted Foret, Tommy Lorino, and Billy Austin's widow Ginger. We offer thanks to former Auburn football staff—assistant coach

A Matter of Conscience

Buck Bradberry, manager Buddy Davidson and trainer Kenny Howard—for their contributions to the book.

Credit also goes to Linda Rudolph, Becky Glass and Bruce Speck for their critique of the draft manuscript, and we are indebted to Scot Danforth of the University of Tennessee Press for his editorial guidance.

Lastly, we offer our deepest appreciation to our family and friends. Dennie wants to thank her husband Sam and their daughters, Barrett and Lucia, for their love, support, and patience. She thanks Paula Wall for her wisdom and for keeping the faith. And she thanks Jerry and Barbara Hart and Jim and Phyllis Parrott for their endless friendship and encouragement.

Sherry expresses love and gratitude to her son Kevin, daughter-in-law Michelle, her sisters Sylvia Yates and Flavia Fleming, her niece Kacie, and her brother-in-law Ronnie Fleming for their support and contributions to Bobby's story.

Most of all, Sherry is deeply thankful for her years with Bobby Hoppe—her inspiration, her muse and the love of her life. She will be forever grateful that their love was sustained and strengthened through the trial they endured.

ADDITIONAL MATERIAL
AND SOURCES

Photos are reprinted with permission from the Chattanooga Bicentennial Library local history collection of the Chattanooga News-Free Press and from Auburn University Sports Information Office.

Summaries of the preliminary hearing transcripts, stories from Bobby's life, and photos can be seen and reviewed at:

http://www.wakestonepress.com/amatterofconscience/

CHAPTER ONE
"Bootlegging Roots," All About Racin': The Community for NASCAR Fans, April 2007.
Chattanooga News-Free Press, July 21, 1957.
Chattanooga News-Free Press, July 21, 1957 and June 1988
Redman, Bob. "The Battle for Chattanooga: 23, 24 and 25 November 1963," American Civil War.com.
The Sunday Tennessean, March 27, 1988, B-6.

CHAPTER TWO
Meyer, Doug (Judge). Interview, July 2008

CHAPTER THREE
Allen, Don. E-mail, August 14, 2008
Baker, Eddie. *Chattanooga News-Free Press*, 1961
Campbell, Paul Allen. Interview, August 2008
Chattanooga News-Free Press, September 9, 1953; Editorial, September 18, 1996
Chattanooga Times, September 12, 1952
Etter, Gene. Telephone interview, August 22, 2008
Farmer, Katherine. Interview, August 5, 2008
Gammon, Wirt. *Chattanooga Times*, 1952
Short, George. *Chattanooga Times*, November 22, 1952; various other articles, dates unknown
Van Hoose, Cecil. *Chattanooga News-Free Press*, November 28, 1952
Walker, Russ. Sports writer. Date and newspaper unknown
White, Austin. *Chattanooga News-Free Press*. Various articles, dates unknown

CHAPTER FOUR
Bedford, Sybille. "Dr. John Bodkin Adams." *The Mammoth Book of Famous Trials*. New York: Carroll & Graf Publishers, 2006
Bragan, Jeris. *Beyond Prison Walls*. Hagerstown, Md.: Review and Herald Publishing, 1993
Chaffin, Tom. "The Best Defense Is a Good Ole boy." *MVP Magazine*, June 1991
Chattanooga News-Free Press, June 22, 1988
Cook, Bobby Lee. Trial transcript

Curriden, Mark. "Lions of the Trial Bar." *American Bar Association Journal*, March 2009

DiRisio, Joseph (Judge). Trial transcript

Evans, Tom. Trial transcript

McDonald, R. Robin. *Secrets Never Die*. New York: Avon Books, 1998

Meyer, Doug (Judge). Interview, July 2008

O'Connor, Flannery. "Revelation," *The Complete Stories*. New York: Farrar, Straus & Giroux, 1971

Sandburg, Carl. "Fog." http://carl-sandburg.com/fog.htm

Schmalleger, Frank. *Criminal Law Today*. Upper Saddle River, NJ: Prentice Hall, 2005

Trial transcript

CHAPTER FIVE

Chattanooga Times, June 22. 1988

Cook, Bobby Lee. Trial transcript

DiRisio, Joseph (Judge). Trial transcript

Evans, Tom. Trial transcript

Hudson, Roy. Trial transcript

Perry, Miller et al., editors. "Introduction to 'Big Two-Hearted River' by Ernest Hemingway." *Major Writers in America*, Vol II. New York: Harcourt Brace & World,1962

Phillips, Leroy. Trial transcript

Stargel, John. Trial transcript

CHAPTER SIX

Chattanooga News-Free Press, June 22, 1988

Frost, Robert. "The Death of the Hired Man." In *United States Literature*. Glenview, Ill.: Scott, Foresman and Company, 1963

McDonald, R. Robin. *Secrets Never Die*. New York: Avon Books, 1998

Weaver, Sally. Interview, October, 2008

CHAPTER SEVEN

Allen, Edgar. *Nashville Banner*, November 7, 1953; December 18, 1953

Baker, Eddie. *Chattanooga News-Free Press*, 1953

Bratager, Pete. *Miami Herald*, 1953

Campbell, Paul Allen. Interview, August 2008

Champion. 1954 Central Annual

Chattanooga Times, September 11, 1953; December 20, 1953; February 12, 1954

Chattanooga News-Free Press, September 9, 1953; Editorial, September 18, 1996

Crawley, Stan. *The Chattanoogan.com*, "Gene Etter Recalls His Admiration for Bobby Hoppe." April 17, 2008

Etter, Gene. Telephone interview, August 22, 2008

Farmer, Katherine. Interview, August 5, 2008

Gorham, Bob. Associated Press, 1953

Hays, Clark. *Chattanooga Times,* date unknown

Hoppe, Bobby. Letter to Coach Gene Etter, 1992

Sources

Shearer, John. *The Chattanoogan.com*, "Bobby Hoppe Had Quite a Football Career." April 11, 2008

Short, George. *Chattanooga Times*, November 21, 1953; December 12, 1953 and various other articles, dates unknown

Van Zant, Dexter. *Chattanooga Times*, September 18, 1953; October 1953; November 7, 1953; November 21, 1953; and other dates in 1953 and 1961

White, Austin. *Chattanooga News-Free Press,* various articles, dates unknown

CHAPTER EIGHT

Chase, Richard, ed. "Herman Melville." In *Major Writers of America.* New York: Harcourt, Brace & World, Inc. 1962

Chattanooga News-Free Press, July 21, 1957; August 9, 1957; others, dates unknown

Cook, Bobby Lee. Trial transcript

Corliss, Alex. *Chattanooga Times*, August 4, 1957

DiRisio, Joseph (Judge). Trial transcript

Evans, Tom. Trial transcript

Holland, Richard. Trial transcript

Phillips, Leroy. Trial transcript

Smith, Tommy. Trial transcript

Stargel, John. Preliminary hearing transcript

CHAPTER NINE

Chattanooga News-Free Press, dates unknown

Chattanooga Times. March 3, 1988 and other articles, dates unknown

Conway, Thomas. "Trial of an All-American Hero." *True Police Cases*, October 1988

Cook, Bobby Lee. Trial transcript; interview, August 7, 2008

Davidson, Buddy. Telephone interview, December 2008

DiRisio, Joseph (Judge). Trial transcript

Evans, Tom. Trial transcript

George, Dan. *Tennessean*, March 27, 1988

Heck, Richard. Trial transcript; telephone interview tape, 1988

Phillips, Leroy. Trial transcript

Tennessean, March 27, 1988

Weaver, Sally. Interview, October, 2008

CHAPTER TEN

Bragan, Jeris. *Beyond Prison Walls*. Hagerstown, Md.: Review and Herald Publishing, 1993

Chaffin, Tom. "The Best Defense Is a Good Ole Boy," *MVP*. June 1991.

Chattanooga News-Free Press, June 24, 1988

Cook, Bobby Lee. Trial transcript

DiRisio, Joseph (Judge). Trial transcript

Evans, Tom. Trial transcript

Heck, Richard. Trial transcript

Neal, Odene. Preliminary hearing transcript

Neal, Odene. Trial transcript

Notes from Detective Heck's February 28, 1987 meeting with Odene Neal

A Matter of Conscience

Transcript of Detective Heck's February 14, 1988 phone conversation with Odene Neal

Transcript of Detective Heck's February 15, 1988 interview meeting with Odene Neal

CHAPTER ELEVEN

Chattanooga News-Free Press, June 23, 1988; June 24, 1988
Chattanooga Times,June 21, 1988
DiRisio, Joseph (Judge). Trial transcript
Evans, Tom. Trial transcript
Neal, Jody. Trial transcript
Phillips, Leroy. Trial transcript

CHAPTER TWELVE

"The Unsolved Case of Teddy Hudson." *Southern Magazine*. date unknown, p. 13
Chaffin, Tom. "The Best Defense Is a Good Ole Boy." *MVP Magazine*. June 1991, pp. 19-21
Chief of Detectives' letter to Godwin. March 28, 1966
Chattanooga News-Free Press, dates unknown
Chattanooga Times, dates unknown
Chief of Internal Security's letter to FBI. June 5, 1966
Chief of Police's letter to Joseph Godwin. March 17, 1966
Cook, Bobby Lee. Trial transcript; interview, August 7, 2008
Curtis, Jim. "Sin, Guilt, and Forgiveness." Unpublished sermons, August 14 and August 21, 1988
DiRisio, Joseph (Judge). Trial transcript
Eliot, George. *Adam Bede.* Edinburg and London: William Blackwood & Sons, 1859.
Evans, Tom. Trial transcript
Godwin's letter to Chattanooga Chief of Police. March 11, 1966
Godwin, Joseph. Trial transcript
Kington, Leroy. Preliminary hearing transcript, June 1988
Kopper, Dick. *Chattanooga Times*, 1988
Payne, Sam (Judge). Interview, August 1988
Phillips, Leroy. Trial transcript
Preliminary hearing transcript. June 3 and 13, 1988
Reese, Seward. "Confidential Communications to the Clergy." *Ohio State Law Journal.* Vol. 24: 1963, pp. 55-88
Transcript of interview of Joseph Godwin by Richard Heck and John Taylor, January 26, 1988
Transcript of interview of Joseph Godwin by Leroy Kington and James Turner, March 24, 1966

CHAPTER THIRTEEN

"Auburn's Hoppe, Reeves 'Most Underrated' Men." Auburn, Ala. November 29, 1956
Auburn vs. Alabama, 1956. Auburn University Digital Library

Sources

Auburn vs. Florida State, 1956. Auburn University Digital Library.

Auburn vs. Florida, 1956. Auburn University Digital Library.

Auburn vs. Houston, 1956. Auburn University Digital Library.

Chattanooga News-Free Press, August 17, 1955; other articles, dates unknown

Chattanooga Times, January 20, 1954; November 9, 1954

Danforth, Ed. *Atlanta Journal*, September 11, 1955

Davidson, Buddy. Telephone interview, December 30, 2008 and e-mail, January 22, 2009

Gammon, Wirt. *Chattanooga Times*, October 5, 1954; September 10, 1955; October 7, 1954; other articles, dates unknown

Gossett, Ward. *Chattanooga News-Free Press*, November 10, 1974

Harper. Sentell. Interview, November 12, 2008

Hemphill, Paul. "Our First Time." *Auburn*, Fall 2007

Hogan, Paul. *Enquirer*, date unknown

"Hoppe Adds to Offensive Punch As Tiger Backfield Blossoms." Newspaper, writer and date unknown

"Hoppe and Flowers." Newspaper, writer and date unknown

"Hoppe Doing Fine." Newspaper, writer and date unknown

"Hoppe Shares Auburn Honor." Newspaper, writer and date unknown

"Hoppe Will Team with James, Tubbs and Childress in Starting Backfield." Newspaper, writer and date unknown

Jackson, Jack. *Atlanta Journal*, November 9, 1954

Jeffrey, Jim. Telephone interview, November 19, 2008

Little, Tom. *Soaring Eagles: Great Moments in the Football History of Auburn University in Words and Pictures*. Montgomery, Alabama: L. & M. Corporation, 1965

Mann, Jimmy. *Atlanta Constitution*, date unknown

Marshall, Benny. *Birmingham News*, November 9, 1954; December 13, 1953

Prather, Bert. *Atlanta Constitution*, date unknown

Reeder, Paul. *The Auburn Tigers of 1957: National Champions*. Montgomery, Alabama: The Brown Printing Company, 1990

Rice, Grantland Jr. *Jacksonville Journal*, December 30, 1955

Short, George. *Chattanooga Times*, December 13, 1953

"Steck, Hoppe Rivals First Time in Gator." Newspaper, writer, and date unknown

"They Came to Run." Auburn, Ala. Newspaper, writer and date unknown

Weatherly, Bob. *Atlanta Constitution*, date unknown

White, Austin. *Chattanooga News-Free Press*, December 14, 1953; September 7, 1955; September 15, 1955; October 10, 1955; December 30, 1955; September 7, 1956; September 26, 1956; 1981

CHAPTER FOURTEEN

Bradberry, Buck. Trial transcript

Campbell, Barbara Jo. Trial transcript

Campbell, Paul Allen. Trial transcript

Cannon, Jerry. Trial transcript

Chattanooga News-Free Press, June 25, 1988

Davis, Ed. Trial transcript

DiRisio, Joseph (Judge). Trial transcript

Evans, Tom. Trial transcript

Gross, M.C. Trial transcript
King, Billy Joe. Trial transcript
McCutcheon, William. Trial transcript
Payne, Sam (Judge). Trial transcript; interview, August 1988
Phillips, Leroy. Trial transcript
Roberson, Johnny. Trial transcript
Scarbinsky, Kevin and James H. Kennedy. *Chattanooga Times*, 1988
Sliger, Jo. Trial transcript

CHAPTER FIFTEEN
Cook, Bobby Lee. Trial transcript; interview, August 7, 2008
DiRisio, Joseph (Judge). Trial transcript
Evans, Tom. Trial transcript
Hoppe, Bobby. Trial transcript
Phillips, Leroy. Trial transcript

CHAPTER SIXTEEN
Bisher, Furman. *Atlanta Journal*, date unknown
DiRisio, Joseph (Judge). Trial transcript
Evans, Tom. Trial transcript
Harper, Sentell. Interview, November 12, 2008
Hawthorne, Nathaniel. *The Scarlet Letter.* Boston: The Riverside Press, 1960
(first published in 1850)
Hemphill, Paul. "From the Notebook," *Plainsman,* date unknown
Hemphill, Paul. "Our First Time." *Auburn.* Fall 2007
Hoppe, Bobby. Trial transcript
Look Magazine. September 17, 1957
Mosely, Max. *Montgomery Advertiser*, date unknown
Nix, Lloyd. Telephone interview, December 2008
Phillips, Leroy. Trial transcript
Reeder, Paul. *The Auburn Tigers of 1957: National Champions.* Montgomery,
Alabama: The Brown Printing Company, 1990
White, Austin. *Chattanooga Free-Press*, September 7, 1956; other dates
unknown

CHAPTER SEVENTEEN
Chattanooga News-Free Press, September 6, 1957
Chattanooga Times, October 8, 1957
Davidson, Buddy. Telephone interview, December 30, 2008 and e-mail, January
22, 2009
Ellis, Neal. *Birmingham News*, October 8, 1957
Gammon, Wirt. *Chattanooga Times*, dates unknown
Harper, Sentell. Interview, November 12, 2008
Harris, Ronnie. *Plainsman*, date unknown
Hemphill, Paul. "From the Notebook," *Plainsman,* date unknown
Hemphill, Paul. "Our First Time." Auburn. Fall 2007
Hoppe, Bobby. Letter to Shug Jordan
Howard, Kenny. Telephone interview, January 22, 2009
Jeffrey, Jim. Telephone interview, November 19, 2008

Sources

Little, Tom. *Soaring Eagles: Great Moments in the Football History of Auburn University in Words and Pictures.* Montgomery, Alabama: L. & M. Corporation, 1965

Look Magazine. September 17, 1957

Reeder, Paul. *The Auburn Tigers of 1957: National Champions.* Montgomery, Alabama: The Brown Printing Company, 1990

Wendell, George. "Presenting Auburn's '57 Tigers." Newspaper, writer and date unknown

White, Austin. *Chattanooga News-Free Press*, September 30, 1957; December 14, 1975; 1981; other articles, dates unknown

CHAPTER EIGHTEEN

Bragan, Jeris. *Beyond Prison Walls.* Hagerstown, MD: Review and Herald Publishing Association. 1993

Cook, Bobby Lee. Trial transcript

DiRisio, Joseph (Judge). Trial transcript

Evans, Tom. Trial transcript

Hawthorne, Nathaniel. *The Scarlet Letter.* Boston: The Riverside Press, 1960 (first published in 1850)

Hoppe, Bobby. Trial transcript

Hudson, Virginia Cary. *O Ye Jigs & Juleps!* New York: Macmillan, 1962

Manning, Brennan. *The Ragamuffin Gospel.* Sisters, Oregon: Multnomah Publishers, 1990

Phillips, Leroy. Trial transcript

Weaver, Sally. Interview, October, 2008

CHAPTER NINETEEN

Brown, William [Chink] (Judge). Trial transcript

Cook, Bobby Lee. Trial transcript

Cook, David. Interview, November 8, 2008 and Trial transcript

DiRisio, Joseph (Judge). Trial transcript

Evans, Tom. Trial transcript

Harper, Sentell. Trial transcript

Miller, Tim. Interview, November 8, 2008

Phillips, Leroy. Trial transcript

CHAPTER TWENTY

Bradberry, Buck. Trial transcript

Calloway, Johnny. Trial transcript

Cook, Bobby Lee. Trial transcript

Curtis, Jim (Rev. Dr.). Trial transcript

DiRisio, Joseph (Judge). Trial transcript

Evans, Tom. Trial transcript

Harper, Sentell. Trial transcript

Heck, Richard. Trial transcript

Phillips, Leroy. Trial transcript

Roberson, Huette. Trial transcript

Stafford, Don. Trial transcript

CHAPTER TWENTY-ONE

DiRisio, Joseph (Judge). Trial transcript
Evans, Tom. Trial transcript
Phillips, Leroy. Trial transcript
Shirley, Diane Hollums. Trial transcript.
Wilson, John. *Chattanooga News-Free Press*, June 1988

CHAPTER TWENTY-TWO

Burnette, Virgil. Trial transcript
Cook, Bobby Lee. Trial transcript
DiRisio, Joseph (Judge). Trial transcript
Evans, Tom. Trial transcript
Holland, Richard. Trial transcript
Phillips, Leroy. Trial transcript

CHAPTER TWENTY-THREE

Cook, Bobby Lee. Trial transcript
DiRisio, Joseph (Judge). Trial transcript
Evans, Tom. Trial transcript
Phillips, Leroy. Trial transcript
Transcript, jury out hearing

CHAPTER TWENTY-FOUR

Cook, Bobby Lee. Trial transcript
DiRisio, Joseph (Judge). Trial transcript
Evans, Tom. Trial transcript
Phillips, Leroy. Trial transcript

CHAPTER TWENTY-FIVE

Chattanooga News-Free Press, June 30, 1988; July 25, 1988; July 26, 1988;
July 27, 1988; September 13, 1988
Chattanooga Times, June 21, 1988; July 25, 1988; September 13, 1988
Cook, Bobby Lee. Trial transcript
DiRisio, Joseph (Judge). Trial transcript
Editorial. *Chattanooga News-Free Press*, June 1988
Epley, Stephen and Michael Finn. *Chattanooga News-Free Press*, June 1988
Evans, Tom. Trial transcript
Livingston, Jerry and Paul Francis Webster, *The Twelfth of Never*
Kopper, Dick. *Chattanooga Times*, June 1988
Notes from telephone call from Sylvia Yates. July, 1988
Notes from meeting with Leroy Phillips and Bud Yarnell. July, 1988
Phillips, Leroy. Trial transcript
Transcript of *nol pros*, July 25, 1988
Transcript of verdict, June 29, 1988
Wilson, John. *Chattanooga News-Free Press*, June 1988

Epilogue

Cross, Colin. *Who Was Jesus?* New York: Barnes and Noble, Inc., 1970

LaVergne, TN USA
11 October 2010
200387LV00001B/2/P